INSIDE
THE
LEADING
MAIL ORDER
HOUSES

INSIDE THE LEADING MAIL ORDER HOUSES

MAXWELL SROGE

with

Bradley Highum

Maxwell Sroge Publishing, Inc.
Colorado Springs, Colorado

Publisher and Editor-In-Chief: Maxwell Sroge

Maxwell Sroge is recognized internationally as a leading analyst and spokesman for the mail order industry.

His mail order consulting and advertising firm, Maxwell Sroge Company, founded in 1966 has been responsible for the creation, development and guidance of some of today's leading companies.

Maxwell Sroge Publishing pioneered the first statistical analysis of the mail order industry. They are publishers of:

> The Mail Order Industry Annual Report
> Non-Store Marketing Report (newsletter)
> The Catalog Marketer (newsletter)
> The Catalog Marketer Suppliers Guide
> The Catalog Marketer — Best in Catalogs
> In-Depth Industry Segment Studies

Chief of Research:	Bradley Highum
Production and Marketing:	Marc F. Sroge
Designer:	Gregory Cress

ISBN Number: 0-942674-00-6

First Printing

Dedication

To America, the American marketing
system and to the people and companies
of the U.S. mail order industry.

M.S.

Acknowledgments

This book would not be possible without the assistance of the many people and clients who contributed to the building of Maxwell Sroge Company and Maxwell Sroge Publishing over the years.

Special thanks go to the people of Maxwell Sroge Publishing, especially Nance Deshazo for keeping us all moving in the right direction, and to Paul Turner and Becky Gleason for their steady hands on the operations tiller.

The mail order industry in the U.S. is not a new business. It readily traces back over one hundred years to the days of Sears and Ward. Some claim it goes back even further to Ben Franklin. Despite the fact that it has been around for awhile, it is probably one of the least understood and most maligned forms of distribution. I dare say that even in the inner circles of companies like General Mills and Johnson's Wax, which have made major acquisitions in the mail order business, it is still thought of as a strange cat.

Why is that true? Probably because the majority of senior executives in business today are in the 45-60 age group; a group which grew up in a time when mail order was in its awkward adolescence. If one were to draw a curve representing the respectability of mail order in the eyes of the populace, it would start at a high point in the 1890's and early 1900's then zoom downward through the World War II period and then march upward to a point today exceeding the starting point and moving only one way — UP!

When I started in the mail order business in the late '50's, one of my great concerns was the stature of the business. Early on I made a presentation to the Board of the Direct Mail Marketing Association requesting the establishment of a Standards of Practice Committee. I'm pleased to say they acceded to that request and today that activity continues.

Ten years ago, aware that much of mail order was still a mystery, I initiated the first statistical report on the industry. That effort has grown substantially over the years and now each new edition is eagerly awaited by the business community, governmental agencies and the press.

Quite frankly, my feeling from the earliest days has been that if I, and others, worked to raise the stature and the understanding of the industry, all of us would benefit. We would benefit, as we have, through the entrance of major corporations; we would benefit, as we have, through increased public acceptance of the products and services we offer.

This book is another step in the direction of opening up this great growing business. I regret to say that we have met with some resistance from privately-held companies in supplying us with data for this book. Nevertheless, we persevered and have gathered figures and made estimates never before available. To those who did share data with us, our deep appreciation.

How much easier it would have been for us if all the private companies acted like L.L. Bean and their fine President, Leon Gorman. I've never talked to Leon about it, but I think he shares my feeling . . . that the more that is known about mail order, the better the business will be for all. Though closely-held, L.L. Bean's figures, growth and practically every bit of important information is openly-stated. They are doing a lot right and obviously benefiting.

We do not want to hurt any company or individual through the publication of this information. We believe that when viewed in calm reflection, all those who objected to their inclusion will have reason to say, "This is a good thing for us and our business."

Mail order today is growing at almost twice the rate of retailing. Every prediction is that this growth will accelerate in the future. Toward the end of making this business a healthy growing one in which talented people can develop and prosper, and of which they can be proud, this book is dedicated.

Maxwell Sroge
June 1982
Colorado Springs

Methodology and Estimates

During the two-plus years this material has been under development, every one of the companies represented has been contacted at least five times, by mail or phone, by our researchers.

In addition to direct contacts with the companies, a wide variety of independent and governmental files and data bases were consulted.

*** Asterisks are used in the body of the Company Profiles contained in this volume to denote *estimates* developed by Maxwell Sroge Publishing analysts.**

Where figures are shown as *estimates,* we were not provided with actual data by the company. In these cases, based on our own experience and analysis of available facts, we have developed our best *estimate.*

All facts and figures presented in this study represent our sincere effort to achieve the highest degree of accuracy.

We do not guarantee any of this data and specifically deny any responsibility for any uses made of this information.

We welcome suggestions as to how this data can be made more accurate or more useful in future editions.

ABBEY PRESS

ADDRESS, PHONE
Abbey Press, Highway 460 and 62, Saint Meinrad, IN, 47577. Telephone: (812) 357-8011.

OWNERSHIP
Privately owned and operated by the Order of St. Benedict under auspices of the Roman Catholic Church.

MANAGEMENT
Timothy Sweeny, President and Archabbot; Columbia Kelly, Vice President; Ephrem Carr, Secretary; Luke Hodde, Treasurer and Business Manager.

TYPE OF MARKETER
Mail order, retail.

BUSINESS
Operations are non-profit and exist for the purpose of supporting the seminary. Business consists of : The Abbey Press, a Christian family gift catalog; The Scholar Shop, a retail outlet at the college; Abbey publications, and St. Meinrad College. The Archabbey is supported through the printing press operations and book stores. Abbey Press markets religious cards and gift items as well as other types of gift and home accessories. Company employs 170 persons, increasing to 240 during peak seasons.

COMPANY HISTORY
In 1857 the St. Meinrad Seminary was founded. The seminary, high school, college and School of Theology were incorporated in the State of Indiana on February 25, 1890. Operation is non-profit. The high school was phased out in 1967 after 100 years in the seminary. The School of Theology became affiliated with the Catholic University of America in 1943, and was granted associate membership in the American Association of Theological Schools in 1967. College has student enrollment of 150 students.

MARKETS
Customers are 35-40 years old; 75% female, 25% male; above average income.

FACILITIES
Headquarters, mail order operations, gift shop, and 350-acre campus, St. Meinrad, IN.

PRODUCTS, BRAND NAMES, PRICE RANGE
Products are: cards, plaques, posters, books, Christmas decorations, unique china, kitchen accessories, stained glass, children's gifts, religious items, etc. House brands as well as Schmid, Gorham, The Family Circus. Price range mid to low.

FINANCIAL INFORMATION

	SALES	NET INCOME	PROFIT MARGIN
1981	$12,000,000*	N.A.	--

TYPE OF ADVERTISING, PROMOTION
One hundred percent direct mail. Emphasis on quality and uniqueness. Promotional items are: surprise boxes of first-line merchandise at lower prices; free Abbey Country Fare Catalog; "free gift" when orders over certain amount.

LIST INFORMATION
QUANTITY MAILED:	9,000,000*
AVERAGE ORDER:	$21
ACTIVE BUYERS:	550,000
TOTAL LIST:	1,485,000
LIST SOURCE:	Direct mail.

COMMENTS
Abbey Press customers represent a unique, quality oriented market. They are primarily between 30-45 years; mostly female; 80% earn average or above average income. Customers are buyers of gifts and decorative accessories for the home; hardcover and paperback books, toys, greeting cards, games, stationery, plaques, posters and children's gifts. Peak sales are between Sept. and June. Year-round retail sales to local residents and tourist trade. Catalog has heavy religious orientation. Publications also offered through catalog--i.e., Marriage & Family Living. Heavy emphasis on specialty products for holidays: Christmas decorations, St. Valentine's Day items, and four pages for the Irish. Country Fare catalog is the main marketing operation of wholly-owned subsidiary Abbey Gifts, Inc.

ALDENS

ADDRESS, PHONE
Aldens, Inc. 5000 W. Roosevelt Road, Chicago, IL 60607. Telephone: (312) 854-4141.

OWNERSHIP
Wholly-owned subsidiary of Wickes Companies, Inc. of San Diego, CA.

MANAGEMENT
Robert H. Quayle, Pres.; VPs: Peter Haake, Finance; Anthony Bozich, Operations; Charles Albright, Credit; Anne Gifford, Market Development; Jack Baker, Merchandise.

TYPE OF MARKETER
Mail order.

BUSINESS
Company is fifth largest mail order catalog merchandiser of hard and soft goods in the U.S. Sells to customers between 25 and 54 years (over 50% under age 45); 42% of women work outside the home; average household income is lower than national average. Aldens direct mail subsidiary America Direct, started in 1970, creates syndicated direct mail promotions for major U.S. oil companies. Also has John Alden Life Insurance Co. and Gamble Alden Agency, Inc., wholly owned subsidiaries of Wickes. Employs about 3,000.

COMPANY HISTORY
Started in 1889 by Samuel and Benjamin Rosenthal as Chicago Millinery Co. with pocket size catalog, selling huge veiled, feathered and flowered hats ranging from $1.69 to $8.00. Added new lines and changed name to Chicago Mail Order Co. in 1905. Catalog was 118 pages by 1906; first big catalog came out with 261 pages in 1909. Name changed to Aldens in '46; merged into Gamble-Skogmo in '65; merged into Wickes Companies in '80.

MARKETS
Throughout U.S.; estimated 4,000,000 active and inactive customers.

FACILITIES

Company headquarters, other facilities in Chicago.

PRODUCTS, BRAND NAMES, PRICE RANGE

Fashion apparel, accessories, household items, consumer electronics--potentially big volume items. House and name brands. Prices competitive. Figures below include catalog and direct mail merchandising operations.

FINANCIAL INFORMATION

	SALES	NET INCOME	PROFIT MARGIN
1981	$319,000,000	N.A.	--

TYPE OF ADVERTISING, PROMOTION

Aldens mails 19 general and specialty catalogs a year to approximately 3 million customers. Some 16,000,000 showcase introductory catalogs go to selected outside lists as part of customer acquisition activities. The company also uses broadcast and space ads.

LIST INFORMATION

QUANTITY MAILED: 59,000,000
AVERAGE ORDER: Range $5 to $600
ACTIVE BUYERS: 2,800,000
TOTAL LIST: 4,000,000
LIST SOURCE: Direct mail.

COMMENTS

Aldens has been profitable since its acquisition by Wickes in 1980. Company continues to build on fashion approach which it began three years ago. In '79 installed an on-line computer system that allows daily monitoring of consumer purchasing patterns. New emphasis has been put on fashion in softlines and domestics and there has been a strong shift to brand names. Aldens has discontinued the former practices of reverse syndication, and general list sales. In 1981 Aldens achieved 40% sales increase over the previous year. Aldens is also continuing its 20-year-old practice of using a special price-cut catalog to lure new charge customers. Wickes, Inc., in its 1981 Annual Report, spoke optimistically about important contributions the newly-acquired subsidiary will make "to Wickes' future as a broad-based retailer." As of this writing, Wickes had filed Chapter XI bankruptcy.

ALLIED ELECTRONICS

ADDRESS, PHONE

Allied Electronics, Inc. 401 E. 8th Street, Fort Worth, TX 76101. Telephone: (817) 336-5401.

OWNERSHIP

Wholly-owned subsidiary of Spartan Manufacturing Corporation, of St. Louis, Missouri.

MANAGEMENT

Dave Yaniko, President; Joe E. Line, Comptroller; Donald Royer, Director of Marketing; Carl Hammabeck, Advertising Manager.

TYPE OF MARKETER

Mail order, wholesale.

BUSINESS

Allied Electronics is one of the leading U.S. mail order wholesale distributors of electronic parts and equipment. The company sells primarily to industrial and institutional concerns such as manufacturers, retailers, schools and repair shops, and reports a considerable amount of overseas distribution. Allied has 42 sales centers across the U.S. for in-store and mail order sales. They reported 300 employees in 1981.

COMPANY HISTORY

The business was founded in 1923 in Chicago, Illinois as the Columbia Radio Corporation. The company began marketing through catalogs in 1928. After WWII the name was changed to Allied Radio and later to Allied Electronics. The first Allied Electronics catalog was published in 1964. The company was purchased by Tandy Corporation, moved to Texas, and reincorporated in 1970. In 1978 Allied was spun off by Tandy and purchased by Spartan Manufacturing.

MARKETS

Industrial accounts, retailers and repair shops, schools, other institutions; limited consumer sales.

FACILITIES

Allied has 42 sales centers, four warehouses, and an 80,000 square foot central headquarters facility.

PRODUCTS, BRAND NAMES, PRICE RANGE

Microcomputers and accessories, motors, power supplies, test equipment, transformers, timers and counters, calculators, audio equipment, and technical books. Brands include: Allied, Admiral, Hammond, Mallory, Panasonic, RCA.

FINANCIAL INFORMATION

	SALES	NET INCOME	PROFIT MARGIN
1981	$40,000,000*	N.A.	--

TYPE OF ADVERTISING, PROMOTION

Approximately 85% of Allied's advertising is through their annual catalogs and direct mail flyers. The company reportedly mails between 800,000 and 1,000,000 pieces per year to new inquiries and past-buyer accounts. Remaining 15% is space.

LIST INFORMATION

QUANTITY MAILED:	1,000,000
AVERAGE ORDER:	$100
ACTIVE BUYERS:	227,000
TOTAL LIST:	750,000*
LIST SOURCE:	Direct mail, space.

COMMENTS

The sales figure above is an estimate of Allied's total mail order sales for 1981 and does not include in-store sales from the company's sales centers. In an effort to improve mail order fulfillment and increase distribution the company opened 21 new sales centers in 1981, doubling the 1980 total. Management predicts that this rapid growth will continue. They also reported plans to increase the size of their catalogs, and the total number mailed by 125,000 annually. At present Allied's catalog -- Engineering Manual & Purchasing Guide --is b&w, 9 x 11, and 260 pages. In addition to their catalogs, Allied mails 16-page brochures quarterly offering sale merchandise as well as special items from their regular merchandise lines. Allied does no manufacturing. Early in 1982 the company opened up its first foreign-based operation in Willowdale, Ontario.

ALLSTATE INSURANCE

ADDRESS, PHONE
Allstate Insurance Co., Allstate Plaza, Northbrook, IL 60062. Telephone: (313) 291-5000.

OWNERSHIP
A wholly owned subsidiary of Sears, Roebuck.

MANAGEMENT
Donald F. Cralb, Jr., Chairman and Chief Executive Officer; Richard J. Jaayen, President; H. Galen Allen, Senior Vice President of Administration; John K. O. Loughlin, Senior Executive Vice President.

TYPE OF MARKETER
Mail order, retail, direct sales.

BUSINESS
Allstate directly and through its subsidiaries writes automobile insurance (62%), homeowners and renters (18%), liability and life insurance, and nearly all other lines including surety and health insurance. The company employs 40,500 people, including 11,400 licensed agents. Some 3,000 are employed at Northbrook, IL headquarters.

COMPANY HISTORY
Sears started the business in Illinois on February 9, 1931. The first product sold was low-cost automobile insurance. In the beginning, Allstate operated only by mail. By 1933 management discovered that most sales were being made in smaller towns where the catalog business was big, while the larger metropolitan markets were not responding. As a result, Allstate pioneered the marketing concept of installing sales locations in Sears stores. In 1980 the insurance premiums and financial services rendered totaled $6.197 billion.

MARKETS
Markets multi-line insurance for individuals, businesses, and organizations; U.S. & Canada.

FACILITIES
Offices, mail order operations, sales and claim service locations throughout U.S. and abroad.

PRODUCTS, BRAND NAMES, PRICE RANGE
Allstate writes automobile insurance, liability insurance, life insurance, property insurance, surety
insurance, health insurance, plus other lines.
Prices vary based on the amount of coverage a
person desires.

FINANCIAL INFORMATION

	SALES	NET INCOME	PROFIT MARGIN
1980	$6,197,200,000	$450,400,000	7.3%

TYPE OF ADVERTISING, PROMOTION
All of Allstate's direct promotion is done through
direct mail and an extensive package insert program.
Advertising also appears in Sears catalogs. Referrals
generate significant portion of direct sales.

LIST INFORMATION
QUANTITY MAILED:	121,000,000
AVERAGE ORDER:	N.A.
ACTIVE BUYERS:	20,000,000
TOTAL LIST:	N.A.
LIST SOURCE:	Direct mail.

COMMENTS
Sears owns 100% of Allstate's capital stock. Agents
and claim centers are located throughout the U.S.
and are also located in most Sears Department
Stores. Allstate has numerous domestic and foreign
direct and indirect subsidiaries, mainly in the insurance field. The Allstate group of companies reached
a new high in sales volume in 1980. Insurance premiums written and financial services rendered totaled
$6.197 billion. Net profits between 1978 and 1979
dropped 1%, and between 1979 and 1980 increased
6.8%. Total assets for 1980 were $10,533,400,000.
Allstate has more than 20 million policies in force
and one of the largest employee claims staffs in the
world.

AMACOM

ADDRESS, PHONE
AMACOM, 135 W. 50th Street, New York, NY 10020. Telephone: (212) 586-8100.

OWNERSHIP
AMACOM is the publishing division of American Management Associations, Inc.

MANAGEMENT
Paul H. Erlicker, Chairman; James L. Hayes, President; Robert J. Butler, Vice President, Secretary; James D. Murray, Vice President.

TYPE OF MARKETER
Mail order, retail.

BUSINESS
This organization is a not-for-profit, non-commercial education organization and publisher of periodicals. The company's purpose is the advancement, understanding and application of the principles, policies and practices of management. A wide variety of management training and specialized educational programs are offered in company's catalogs. Sales are non-seasonal. Employs 1050 (500 in NY).

COMPANY HISTORY
AMACOM was originally established in 1922 and authorized by the New York State Board of Regents. The association was formed to succeed five related units which merged into the new entity, effective April 27, 1973. These five now operate as individual departments. Business has steadily progressed over the years. Sept. 28, 1972, company was incorporated as a non-profit organization. AMACOM Division has grown steadily as the chief advertiser of AMA's activities and services.

MARKETS
Company markets publications and programs throughout U.S. and abroad. Customers 70% male.

FACILITIES

Rents 50,000 sq. ft. of operating space in building known as American Management Association Building.

PRODUCTS, BRAND NAMES, PRICE RANGE

Publishes books, magazines and periodicals. Publications include over 400 titles. Cassette/workbook programs which cover many concepts and problems involved in practice of management are marketed for individual home study. Wide price range.

FINANCIAL INFORMATION

	SALES	NET INCOME	PROFIT MARGIN
1980	$15,000,000*	N.A.	--

TYPE OF ADVERTISING, PROMOTION

Approximately four to six catalogs are published annually, and distributed throughout the year. Catalogs are 8" x 11", partial color. Number of pages varies from twenty to fifty.

LIST INFORMATION

QUANTITY MAILED:	5,500,000*
AVERAGE ORDER:	$25 - $500
ACTIVE BUYERS:	N.A.
TOTAL LIST:	263,000
LIST SOURCE:	100% direct mail.

COMMENTS

Through its extensive catalog operations, AMACOM offers a variety of cassette/workbook programs for self-study. Topics include motivation, time control, interviewing, effective speaking, employee relations, etc. Special programs tackle specific managerial problems such as effective business communications, transactional analysis, and EEO compliance. The program packages include audio cassettes, information booklets and self-tests. AMACOM also offers self-test analysis through correspondence. Direct mail is used to promote A.M.A., Inc.'s conferences, seminars, four monthly publications, and Management Centers located in major U.S. cities and abroad. Company reports that AMACOM's catalog operations contribute a "very significant portion" of total A.M.A., Inc. annual revenues. Cassette/workbook programs range in price between $25.00 and $200.00. We estimate AMACOM's gross revenues to be approximately $15 million--roughly 18% of A.M.A., Inc.'s total $80,382,000.

AMBASSADOR INTERNATIONAL

ADDRESS, PHONE

Ambassador International, 711 West Broadway, Tempe, AZ 85282. Telephone: (602) 968-4411.

OWNERSHIP

Subsidiary of Amba Marketing Systems, Inc. of Tempe, AZ, which is privately held by MacDonald Companies, Inc.

MANAGEMENT

William MacDonald, President & Treasurer; Bruce Vogel, Vice President, Secretary; Howard Rabinowitz, Merchandise Director; Kris Snyder, Director of List Management.

TYPE OF MARKETER

Mail order.

BUSINESS

Ambassador is a mail order marketer of handbags, clutch purses, wallets, jewelry, luggage, and related accessory and gift items. Their catalogs contain over 500 items including personalized handbags. In addition Ambassador provides a variety of services to other mail order companies including promotion, fulfillment, lettershop and list maintenance operations. The company has retail stores in Phoenix, Scottsdale and Tempe, AZ, and Las Vegas, NV.

COMPANY HISTORY

Ambassador was founded in Canada and moved to Niagara Falls in 1961 by Joy and Murray Hollif. Originally the company sold men's and women's wallets by mail under the Joy Hall tradestyle. In 1972 the business was sold to Amba Marketing and merged with the parent company in 1974. The headquarters was moved to the Tempe location in 1970, and William MacDonald purchased the company in October of 1980. Ambassador currently employs 600 people.

MARKETS

Ambassador sells throughout the U.S.; no international marketing. Customers are 80% female.

FACILITIES

Headquarters, mail order operations and 172,000 sq. ft. warehouse at Tempe, AZ location.

PRODUCTS, BRAND NAMES, PRICE RANGE

Products are handbags, clutch purses, wallets, jewelry, luggage, and related gift items. Ambassador's major house brands are Joy Hall and Murray Hall.

FINANCIAL INFORMATION

	SALES	**NET INCOME**	**PROFIT MARGIN**
1981	$50,000,000*	N.A.	--

TYPE OF ADVERTISING, PROMOTION

The company places most of its promotional emphasis on catalog mailings and co-op and direct mail package mailings. In addition they use limited space and broadcast ads. Solo mailings usually include offer of a "bonus gift free" for ordering promptly.

LIST INFORMATION

QUANTITY MAILED: 36,000,000
AVERAGE ORDER: $30 (catalog); $18 (DM package)
ACTIVE BUYERS: 1,860,000
TOTAL LIST: 4,256,000
LIST SOURCE: Direct mail, space, co-ops.

COMMENTS

Company officials report consistent sales growth through fiscal 1978, which they attributed to expanding product lines and active building of their mailing lists. In 1979 Ambassador phased out their mail order operations in Canada and West Germany and sold the assets of these subsidiaries. Management reported that as a result 1979 sales held even with 1978, and the company suffered an overall loss in earnings for the year. Company operations were consolidated in 1980 and sales pulled back to the $50 million level. Ambassador claims to be one of the first mail order companies to do personalizing of merchandise on a large scale. They offer monograms and a variety of creative designs as an added promotional incentive. Ambassador is also one of the few companies that makes heavy use of solo mailings to rented lists.

AMERICAN EXPRESS DIRECT RESPONSE

ADDRESS, PHONE
American Express Direct Response, 175 Community Drive, Great Neck, NY 11025. (516) 487-1040.

OWNERSHIP
Part of Communications Division of publicly-held American Express Company of New York City.

MANAGEMENT
Communication Division: Sandra W. Myer, President; American Express Direct Response: Murray Miller, Chairman; Michael Adams, President; Merchandise Sales: Robert L. Meyers, Senior VP.

TYPE OF MARKETER
Mail order.

BUSINESS
American Express Direct Response is the mail order arm of the Communications Division. Communications along with Travel, Charge Card and Traveler Cheque Divisions make up the Amex Travel Related Services Group. The Direct Response division offers a wide variety of merchandise by mail to Amex cardholders and selected non-cardholder lists. The division also operates a large computer complex for direct mail operations and fulfillment, used by Amex's divisions and other commercial clients.

COMPANY HISTORY
American Express was founded in 1850 as a consolidation of Livingston, Fargo & Co., Wells and Co., and Butterfield & Wasson. The original service was shipping gold, silver, and currency. The Communications Division was formed in 1980 to consolidate publishing, mail order marketing and direct response computer service operations. While the Travel Related Services Group has turned in a 67.3% increase in revenues since 1978, Direct Response merchandise sales increased 70% in the past year.

MARKETS
U.S.A.; upscale, upper income; customer base cardholders and selected lists.

FACILITIES

Executive offices, NY; mail order division--order processing and fulfillment--Great Neck, NY.

PRODUCTS, BRAND NAMES, PRICE RANGE

Products: museum reproductions, jewelry, furs, designer apparel and loungewear, paintings and sculptures, household appliances and accessories, candies, etc. Brands: Halston, Dior, Gucci, Kyushu National Museum of Art, Panasonic, Sony, Cuisinart.

FINANCIAL INFORMATION

	SALES	NET INCOME	PROFIT MARGIN
1980	$140,000,000*	N.A.	--

TYPE OF ADVERTISING, PROMOTION

Advertising directed at cardholders and selected non-card consumers. Promotional packets are travel, education, entertainment, and insurance related. Full-color, glossy, 11 x 9, 50-page catalog.

LIST INFORMATION

QUANTITY MAILED:	25,000,000*
AVERAGE ORDER:	$80
ACTIVE BUYERS:	1,000,000*
TOTAL LIST:	5,600,000 (U.S Amex cardholders)
LIST SOURCE:	Direct mail, space.

COMMENTS

Estimates for mail order sales are $140 million or appoximately 8% of Travel Service revenue. Company reported that Merchandise Sales revenues increased by 70% in 1980. American Express mail order targets "sophisticated upscale customers who increasingly demand services and products tailored to their needs and interest." Company's mail order consumers desire elegance and personalization--high-quality national brand merchandise. Consumers also demand items that are fun, unique, and interesting--original sculptures and paintings, museum reproductions, high quality electronic products, etc. Catalogs are mailed to charge card users, as well as customers on selected lists. Charge card users are segmented by factors that identify them as green or gold card memberships--i.e., economic factors, demographics, etc. Direct mail systems are computerized--company markets these services to commercial clients.

ANNIE'S ATTIC

ADDRESS, PHONE
Annie's Attic, Rt. 2, Box 212B, Big Sandy, Texas, 75755. Telephone: (214) 636-4412.

OWNERSHIP
Privately held by Jerry Gentry Associates, Inc.

MANAGEMENT
Jerry Gentry, President; Anita Gentry, Design Vice President; Steve Kraft, Business Manager; Klaus Rothe, Marketing Manager; David McKee, Advertising Manager.

TYPE OF MARKETER
Mail order (99%), retail (1%).

BUSINESS
Company designs, manufactures, and markets needlecraft kits and patterns. In June, 1980, opened Annie's Tea Room, a restaurant which seats about 80 customers and serves lunch and dinner as well as observing an afternoon tea time. An offshoot of this is the newly developed mail order food business. Company also publishes a bi-monthly newsletter with a circulation of about 200,000. Full-time and part-time employees total approximately 130.

COMPANY HISTORY
Jerry and Anita Gentry started their business out of their home in June, 1975, with only two designs. Now they have over 300 designs, and have purchased additional homes that have been converted into office facilities. Also purchased an old high school, which they converted into a warehouse. Most recent acquisition is an old church which is presently being used for seminars and film showings. Sales have increased significantly over the past five years.

MARKETS
Primarily women whose hobby is sewing, crocheting, and other needlecrafts.

FACILITIES

All operations are out of Big Sandy, Texas (approximately 100 miles northeast of Dallas).

PRODUCTS, BRAND NAMES, PRICE RANGE

Kits and patterns for making crochet and sewing items, pillows, quilts, cloth dolls, applique patches, handbags, decorative potholders, etc. Prices range from $5.00-$17.00.

FINANCIAL INFORMATION

	SALES	NET INCOME	PROFIT MARGIN
1981	$8,000,000	N.A.	--

TYPE OF ADVERTISING, PROMOTION

Space ads for needlecraft items in women's magazines. Space ads for food items in shelter magazines. Direct mail promotions 8-10 times a year to house list and rented lists; pattern club newsletter has self-mailer; needlecraft catalog is full-color, 32 pages.

LIST INFORMATION

QUANTITY MAILED:	9,500,000*
AVERAGE ORDER:	$14
ACTIVE BUYERS:	400,000
TOTAL LIST:	600,000
LIST SOURCE:	Space, direct mail, list rental

COMMENTS

Annie's Attic began with heavy emphasis on sewing; now promotes crocheting more heavily. Also has enjoyed success with its needlecraft publications: its small newsletter and its recently inaugurated single-title books. Adding a publishing operation is not only boosting sales but also is providing a vehicle for free space advertising. Diversification into food products also looks promising, with good response to a self-mailer in the form of a mini-catalog of 8 panels. The intent is to reach a different market from needlecraft buyers. All catalogs are prepared in-house, with only the printing done outside. To keep repeat customers, Annie designs 4 to 7 new products/patterns throughout the year. Company also markets material from outside contributors, bringing the total new designs to 10-12 a year.

APARACOR, INC.

ADDRESS, PHONE

Aparacor Inc., 2500 Crawford Ave., Evanston, IL 60201. Telephone: (312) 492-1400.

OWNERSHIP

Privately held by L.A. Westerberg, M.N. Westerberg, Gloria J. Davis, James G. Davis, and others.

MANAGEMENT

L. A. Westerberg, Chmn; Gloria J. Davis. V. Chmn; James G. Davis, Pres/CEO; Senior VPs: M.N. Westerberg, Secty; Richard Wallace, Mdsng; VPs: Ronald Hubrich, Kenneth Krejcik, John Ridenour.

TYPE OF MARKETER

Mail order, party plan.

BUSINESS

Party plan Queen's-Way to Fashion recruits and trains "counselors" who conduct parties in homes and send a single party-order. Queen's Way fills and ships order C.O.D. to hostess. Counselors get commission; hostesses get fashion gifts or chance to buy at a discount. Career Guild sells coordinated fashions for working women via direct mail. A membership plan provides price leverage and wardrobe assistance. Fashion Finds sells Aparacor closeout merchandise via catalog at 40%-80% discounts.

COMPANY HISTORY

The business was started with $5,000 investment in 1952 by Larry and Mabel Westerberg in basement of their Skokie, IL home. In 1960, business was succeeded by an Illinois corporation, Queen's Way, Inc. In May, 1972 this company was merged into a Delaware corporation, Q-W Fashions Inc., changing name to Queen's-Way to Fashion. Fashion Finds was added after 1971; in 1976 Career Guild mail order and Fashion Coalition were added. Name changed to Aparacor, Inc. in 1976.

MARKETS

U.S.; middle income women who buy by mail, and via party plan.

FACILITIES
Headquarters in Evanston, IL; warehousing and fulfillment in Niles, IL; manufacturing in Miami, FL.

PRODUCTS, BRAND NAMES, PRICE RANGE
Women's apparel including dresses, suits, pantsuits, vests, sweaters, blouses, jumpers, slacks, coordinated outfits, coats, sporting apparel, nightwear, hats, jewelry and other accessories. House brands. Prices, moderate to low.

FINANCIAL INFORMATION

	SALES	NET INCOME	PROFIT MARGIN
1981	$50,000,000*	N.A.	--

TYPE OF ADVERTISING, PROMOTION
Aparacor makes heavy use of direct mail and some classified advertising to recruit the field sales force. Fashion Coalition, Fashion Finds and Career Guild mail separate catalogs throughout the year to rented lists and party plan buyers.

LIST INFORMATION

QUANTITY MAILED:	(Aparacor markets list of over
AVERAGE ORDER:	200,000 party-plan hostesses, as
ACTIVE BUYERS:	well as 5,500 counselors. No av-
TOTAL LIST:	erage unit sale, total list or to-
LIST SOURCE:	tal mailing figures are available.)

COMMENTS
Sales in Aparacor's first year of operation were $44,000, and net worth was $21,000. In 28 years, sales reportedly went over $50,000,000 and net-worth was up to $8,000,000. Direct mail programs were started "to offset the effect that would be felt should the independent sales agent status be threatened." Aparacor does not make product line distribution sales figures available, but industry experts estimate revenues break-down as follows: Queen's - Way, 70%; Fashion Coalition, 13%; Fashion Finds, 12%; Career Guild, 5%. Company manufactures about 30% of the merchandise it sells. While Queen's-Way uses classified ads to recruit salespeople, the longest sales-life expectancy is from those who are recruited at a party.

THE AUSTAD COMPANY

ADDRESS, PHONE
The Austad Company, 4500 E. 10th Street, P.O. Box 1428, Sioux Falls, SD 57101. Phone: (605) 336-3135.

OWNERSHIP
Private, family-owned corporation.

MANAGEMENT
Oscar M. Austad, President & CEO; Sharon Stahl, Treasurer & Director of Finance; Randy Austad, Vice President, Operations; Dean Thill, Director of Marketing.

TYPE OF MARKETER
Mail order; retail.

BUSINESS
The Austad Company does no manufacturing. They buy from 120-140 suppliers and sell by direct mail and through one retail store located in Sioux Falls. Golfing equipment and supplies account for 60% of products sold. Austad claims to be the largest non-manufacturing mail order distributor of golf equipment in the U.S. All catalogs and other promotional materials are designed in-house. The company employs about 160 people.

COMPANY HISTORY
Started in 1963 by Oscar Austad, then in insurance claims. Began selling golf tubes out of his basement and trunk of his car; first year's sales $80,000 with $2,000 profit. First catalog: one sheet mimeographed and sent to sports stores within 200 miles. Yearly expansion, 20-30%; Austad, with 1 employee, moved into rented warehouse and built first list from the Yellow Pages. Purchased property and warehouse in '69; additions in '72, '75, '78. Incorporated in January, 1974.

MARKETS
Sells to all 50 states and 30 foreign countries.

FACILITIES

Headquarters, warehouse and packaging plant, and one retail store in Sioux Falls, South Dakota.

PRODUCTS, BRAND NAMES, PRICE RANGE

National brands including Spalding, Wilson, Rawlings, Ram, Endicott Johnson, Nike, A&M Sports, Cushnet, AMF Voit, Ambassador, Champion, MacGreggor, Edsbyn, Igloo, Blue Ribbon Sports, Jason Empire, Leisure Imports, etc.

FINANCIAL INFORMATION

	SALES	NET INCOME	PROFIT MARGIN
1981	$16,000,000*	$480,000*	3%*

TYPE OF ADVERTISING, PROMOTION

One annual catalog of about 100 pages, full color; quarterly supplements of a 16-page, 2-color flyer; package inserts included with every order filled. Catalog is promoted through space ads in national sports and travel magazines.

LIST INFORMATION

QUANTITY MAILED:	8,000,000
AVERAGE ORDER:	$85
ACTIVE BUYERS:	250,000
TOTAL LIST:	1,000,000
LIST SOURCE:	Direct mail, space ads.

COMMENTS

Between 1977 and 1981, company's annual sales growth was about 12%. Has gone to a new catalog format for 1982: will now promote two catalogs a year--Fall/Winter and Spring/Summer--each full color, about 85 pages. Heavy mailing will be Spring/Summer with lighter mailing for Fall/Winter catalog featuring winter sports. Gift idea package inserts are now being used to test products for possible inclusion in future catalogs. Austad's success illustrates the importance of specialty marketing to carefully chosen customers, selling quality products at reasonable prices. His first house list was made up primarily of names of professionals chosen from telephone directories. Has also carefully monitored advertising and promotion: knew immediately that space ads tested in Sunday newspaper supplements were much less successful for this business than ads in national, leisure-oriented magazines. A 1981 study by the National Sporting Goods Association shows that Austad sells 87% of golf clubs bought by mail and has 3.7% of total golf club sales.

AVON FASHIONS

ADDRESS, PHONE
Avon Fashions, Inc., 5000 City Line Rd., Hampton, VA, 23661. Telephone: (804) 827-7010.

OWNERSHIP
Subsidiary of publicly-held Avon Products, Inc.

MANAGEMENT
Robert Fry, President; Wells Walker, VP Marketing; Steve Marks, VP Merchandising; Dwight Totten, VP Operations.

TYPE OF MARKETER
Mail order.

BUSINESS
The company sells women's ready-to-wear apparel through mail order catalogs. Distribution center in Hampton, Virginia. Marketing, merchandising and sales promotion headquarters are 9 W. 57th Street, New York, NY, the offices of Avon Products, Inc. Avon Fashions employs 325 people.

COMPANY HISTORY
Company was started in 1973 under the name Family Fashions by Avon. In the beginning it had problems identifying its products with the right market. The name was misleading, and customers would call or write asking for children's apparel. The name was changed to Avon Fashions in 1978, which was the company's first profitable year.

MARKETS
Mostly women buyers in all 48 contiguous states; 18 to 35 years old.

FACILITIES

Distribution center in Hampton, VA. Marketing, merchandising, and sales promotion at NY headquarters.

PRODUCTS, BRAND NAMES, PRICE RANGE

Women's sportswear, dresses, separates, footwear,
outer wear, sleepwear, intimate apparel, swimwear,
etc. Avon Fashions label. Prices are low to
medium.

FINANCIAL INFORMATION

	SALES	NET INCOME	PROFIT MARGIN
1981	$80,000,000*	N.A.	--

TYPE OF ADVERTISING, PROMOTION

Avon uses full-color catalogs; they publish two per
season making eight separate catalog editions per
year.

LIST INFORMATION

QUANTITY MAILED:	75,000,000*
AVERAGE ORDER:	$35
ACTIVE BUYERS:	1,500,000
TOTAL LIST:	2,750,000
LIST SOURCE:	Direct mail.

COMMENTS

Avon Fashions made strong gains in sales for 1980,
according to parent company Avon Products, Inc.,
and this means the catalog operation probably topped
the $80 million level. But although it has been
growing at a faster pace than the company's direct
selling activity, Avon Fashions sales still represent
only 2% of total company income. The marketing
concept that seems to be working well for this cataloger is a strategy featuring a high-fashion merchandise look at low prices. After the name change from
Family Fashions to Avon Fashions, the company
started altering the merchandise mix to concentrate
on the "18 to 35-year-old contemporary woman."
According to management, future growth lies in the
"key market" of 25 to 44-year-old women with their
higher disposable income and stronger repeat buying
characteristics. The company's tenacity and confidence in mail order marketing is commendable--
sticking with a losing operation for five years; 1978
was the company's first profitable year.

BACHRACH CLOTHING

ADDRESS, PHONE

Bachrach Clothing, 2354 Hubbard Avenue, Decatur, IL 62526. Telephone: (217) 875-1020.

OWNERSHIP

Privately held; 100% of capital stock owned by the Bachrach family.

MANAGEMENT

Henry Bachrach, Chairman; Edgar Bachrach, President and Treasurer; Stanley Tuggle, Executive Vice President; Elizabeth Bachrach, Secretary.

TYPE OF MARKETER

Mail order, retail.

BUSINESS

Bachrach sells men's clothing, accessories, and specialty gift items through direct mail catalogs and a chain of eight retail stores in the Midwest. In addition a limited line of women's apparel is marketed by the company. At present mail order accounts for an estimated 30% of the company's annual revenues. Bachrach's growth is attributed to the addition of new retail stores and expansion of mail order marketing operations.

COMPANY HISTORY

Bachrach was started in 1880 by Henry Bachrach. Upon his death in 1917, his son Edgar succeeded to control. Edgar's son Henry became a partner in 1944 and the partnership continued until 1951 when Edgar died and Henry assumed the controlling interest. The company was incorporated in Illinois on May 31, 1946. The original intention in branching into mail order marketing in 1977 was to generate store traffic. Since then, the company has found a solid market for their apparel by mail.

MARKETS

Primarily men, 19-45 years, women 19-50 years. Mail order throughout U.S.; retail IL, IN, MO.

FACILITIES
Headquarters and mail order operations in Decatur, Illinois; eight retail outlets in Midwest.

PRODUCTS, BRAND NAMES, PRICE RANGE
Products are: coordinates, suits, sweaters, sleep-wear, robes, and gifts. Celebrity lines include Johnny Carson, Ralph Lauren, Nino Cirruti. Brands include: Hickey Freeman, Grief, Gant, and more.

FINANCIAL INFORMATION

	SALES	NET INCOME	PROFIT MARGIN
1981	$10,000,000*	N.A.	--

TYPE OF ADVERTISING, PROMOTION
Catalog mailings primarily to retail customers. Emphasis on familiarizing customers with products offered by retail outlets. List based on 30-90 day charge accounts. Recent expansion to outside lists. Peak seasons are spring and fall.

LIST INFORMATION
QUANTITY MAILED: 200,000*
AVERAGE ORDER: $80
ACTIVE BUYERS: 25,000
TOTAL LIST: 100,000*
LIST SOURCE: Store charge accounts; rentals.

COMMENTS
Bachrach began using direct mail several years ago as a form of advertising for the merchandise carried in their retail stores. Currently, mail order sales account for an estimated 30% of sales or $3,000,000. But company has greatly expanded their potential customer base by marketing to customers outside the coverage of their retail operations. Bachrach's is expected to continue to increase their emphasis on mail order sales. Based on a projected total sales figure of $24 million by 1984, Bachrach's expects roughly 50% or $12 million to be generated by mail order marketing operations. Currently the company mails a Spring/ Summer and Fall/Winter catalog each year to the house list of past mail order buyers, lists of retail charge account holders, and select rented lists. The merchandising emphasis is on unique, quality fashions--upscale brands. Bachrach reported 250 employees in 1981.

BALDWIN COOKE

ADDRESS, PHONE
Baldwin Cooke Company Inc., 2401 Waukegan Road, Deerfield, IL 60015. Telephone: (312) 948-7600.

OWNERSHIP
Privately owned by the officers.

MANAGEMENT
Thomas B. Nickel, Chairman & CEO; William Baker, Vice President; Norman Seligman, President; Robert Sternberg, Vice President; Marvin Burack, Treasurer & Secretary; Roger Tillman, Vice Pres.

TYPE OF MARKETER
Mail order, wholesale.

BUSINESS
Business is a 100% mail order operation, marketing business gifts and advertising specialties, Executive Planners and pocket diaries. Company does not manufacture any of its products. Advertising is primarily conducted through promotional sale letters. Company sells its products to commercial concerns and individuals. Sales are heaviest in September, November, and the Christmas season. Company employs 120 persons.

COMPANY HISTORY
Company was started in 1956 in Chicago, Illinois by Thomas B. Nickel, Robert Sternberg and Marvin Burack. On July 29, 1957, the company was incorporated. The first product sold was the Rand McNally pocket road atlas. Shortly thereafter the Executive Planner and pocket planner were included. Mail order was an original part of the business. In January of 1980 business moved from Morton Grove, Illinois, to present location.

MARKETS
Products are sold throughout U.S. and Canada; customers are 95% male, executive types.

FACILITIES
Leases 47,000 sq. ft. in one-story building. All operations at Deerfield location.

PRODUCTS, BRAND NAMES, PRICE RANGE
Primary products sold are the Executive Planners, pocket calendars, the Rand McNally Road Atlas, business gifts and advertising specialties. Popular brands include J. W. Murdock, U.S. Diary, I.P.C., and Industrial Products Guide.

FINANCIAL INFORMATION

	SALES	NET INCOME	PROFIT MARGIN
1981	$10,000,000*	N.A.	--

TYPE OF ADVERTISING, PROMOTION
The majority of advertising is through promotional sales letters. The remainder is 32-page catalogs published once a year and mailed at three different times. Catalogs are full color, 8 x 11.

LIST INFORMATION
QUANTITY MAILED: 5,000,000*
AVERAGE ORDER: $75
ACTIVE BUYERS: 108,864
TOTAL LIST: 400,000
LIST SOURCE: Direct mail (100%).

COMMENTS
Baldwin Cooke places main emphasis on selling products, in quantity, to businesses and professionals for use as gifts, sales builders, etc. Calendars and business planners may be personalized or embossed with company name. There is a "minimum order" restriction on many of these items, and price reductions for quantity purchases. Promotional emphasis is on guaranteed high quality--"the gift that will be appreciated all year long." Advertising specialties include mini-tool sets, key chains, pens, pen lights, business card files, and the Rand McNally Atlas, with company name, address, and phone imprinted. Catalog operation is supported with heavy use of promotional letters to inquiries and past buyers. Company maintains approximately 50,000 standing accounts. Management reported no anticipated changes in catalog strategy or operations, and that annual sales were about $10 million.

JOS. BANK CLOTHIERS

ADDRESS, PHONE
Jos. A. Bank Clothiers, Inc., 123 Market Place, Baltimore, MD 21202. Telephone: (301) 837-1700.

OWNERSHIP
Wholly-owned subsidiary of publicly-held Quaker Oats Co., Chicago, IL.

MANAGEMENT
Leonard A. Ginsberg, President; Stephen A. Bank, Executive Vice President; Robert B. Bank, Executive Vice President; Thomas H. Collins, Jr., Vice President and Treasurer.

TYPE OF MARKETER
Mail order, retail.

BUSINESS
Jos. A. Bank manufactures and sells better-quality traditionally-styled men's and women's apparel at discounted prices through mail order catalogs and retail outlets. Tailored suits, sports jackets, slacks and skirts are manufactured in the company's factories in the Baltimore area. Shoes and accessories are purchased from outside manufacturers. Bank has 13 retail stores along the East Coast and in Chicago and does some limited wholesaling of its products.

COMPANY HISTORY
The business was started some 75 years ago by Joseph Bank, who began his career as a salesman for a clothing manufacturer. Bank started in the mail order business when past customers, having moved from the Baltimore area, sent requests for clothing to be delivered by mail. The company was incorporated in Maryland in 1968. Major retail expansion has occurred in the past five years, and women's fashions were added four years ago. Bank was acquired by Quaker Oats in July of 1981.

MARKETS
Company sells nationally; about 80 percent of its customers are men, middle-to-high income.

FACILITIES

Executive offices, catalog division and manufacturing facilities at Baltimore headquarters.

PRODUCTS, BRAND NAMES, PRICE RANGE

Quality, traditionally-styled men's and women's clothing sold under the Bank label. Shoes and accessories are also sold under the Bank label. Prices range anywhere from $2 for items like hosiery to as much as $300 for coats.

FINANCIAL INFORMATION

	SALES	NET INCOME	PROFIT MARGIN
1981	$40,000,000	N.A.	--

TYPE OF ADVERTISING, PROMOTION

Bank mails two different catalogs per year and supports direct mail with newspaper ads and radio broadcast. Management reports 6% of annual sales (roughly $2.4 million) is spent on advertising.

LIST INFORMATION

QUANTITY MAILED:	7,500,000*
AVERAGE ORDER:	$100
ACTIVE BUYERS:	185,000
TOTAL LIST:	305,000
LIST SOURCE:	Direct mail, space, broadcast.

COMMENTS

The acquisition of Bank by Quaker Oats represents the parent's operating strategy of "expanding direct-to-consumer business." As Bank was acquired after the close of Quaker's '81 fiscal year, its sales were not consolidated. Bank's $40,000,000 in annual sales should boost Quaker's Direct-Mail Marketing Division (comprised of Bank, Herrschners, and Brookstone) sales over $100 million for 1982. In addition, Bank's mail order sales have been growing at roughly 15% per year. Continued retail expansion and broadening lines of women's apparel over the past few years have boosted Bank's sales, and Quaker management believes that the company "has a significant amount of room to grow" in mail order marketing. Currently Bank mails two catalogs per year: one fall and one spring. Catalogs are 80 to 90 pages, full color. In its mail order, retail and manufacturing operations, Bank employs approximately 1,200 people.

BANKERS LIFE & CASUALTY

ADDRESS, PHONE

Bankers Life & Casualty, 4444 W. Lawrence Ave., Chicago, IL 60630. Telephone: (312) 777-7000.

OWNERSHIP

Private with one stockholder: MacArthur Foundation. Authorized capital: 10,000,000 shares common stock, $1 par value.

MANAGEMENT

Robert P. Ewing, Chairman, President, CEO; Edward J. Kelly, Vice Chairman; Executive Vice Presidents: W. Carroll, P. Higdon, W. Hurley, B. Murphy; Floyd A. Caldini, Vice President.

TYPE OF MARKETER

Mail order, direct sales.

BUSINESS

Bankers' main business operation is the sale of individual health and accident policies. Company has also acquired extensive real estate, its most valuable holdings being 16 office buildings and various apartments in New York City--many in midtown Manhattan. Bankers sells its insurance policies via direct mail, a full-time force of 2,800 field representatives, and 2,100 independent agents. Total employees: 5,700.

COMPANY HISTORY

Present company was formed as a result of the consolidation of three businesses: Hotel Men's Mutual Benefit Association of the United States and Canada, incorporated 1880; Bankers Life and Casualty Company, established in 1932 and purchased in 1935 by John D. MacArthur for $2,500; and John MacArthur of Illinois Standard Life Insurance Company, formed in 1942. Bankers is given the incorporation date of April 6, 1880.

MARKETS

Throughout the U.S.

FACILITIES
Headquarters in Chicago; 280 branch sales and administrative offices nationwide.

PRODUCTS, BRAND NAMES, PRICE RANGE
Personal insurance protection policies include group life, group accident and illness, group hospital, medical and surgical, and life insurance. Company offers insurance policies to the general public on a group basis.

FINANCIAL INFORMATION

	SALES	**NET INCOME**	**PROFIT MARGIN**
1981	$644,000,000*	$30,000,000*	4.7%*

TYPE OF ADVERTISING, PROMOTION
Company relies primarily on direct mail promotion, and on direct mail follow-up to direct sales contacts. Uses some space advertising.

LIST INFORMATION
QUANTITY MAILED: N.A.
AVERAGE ORDER: N.A.
ACTIVE BUYERS: 544,000 (180,000 multi-buyers)
TOTAL LIST: 1,241,000
LIST SOURCE: Direct mail.

COMMENTS
The above figures are premium income and operating profits estimates for 1981. A major accident, health, and life insurance company, Bankers has been a leader in the sale of individual accident and health policies. Federal tax law requires that the MacArthur Foundation, which currently owns Bankers, divest itself of the corporation by Dec. 1, 1983, and newspaper advertisements in anticipation of the sale began August 20, 1981. Larry Michel of Warburg Paribas Becker thinks the transaction could be close to $2 billion: Bankers' book value is nearly $500 million and the real estate holdings--acquired at low costs and considered greatly undervalued--should be worth more than $1 billion. Management reports that direct mail contributes a very significant portion of their annual revenues. Not only are policies sold completely by mail, but direct mail also plays an important role in identifying prospects for, and following up direct sales calls.

R. G. BARRY

ADDRESS, PHONE
R. G. Barry Corporation, 13405 Yarmouth Rd. N.W., Pickerington, OH 43147. Telephone: (614) 864-6400.

OWNERSHIP
Publicly held; stock listed AMSE; 3,797,000 common shares outstanding; cash dividend: $0.64 per share; market prices: high, $10.63; low, $5.25.

MANAGEMENT
Gordon Zacks, President and Chairman; Richard Burrell, VP Finance, Treasurer, Secretary; Matt Barouh, President-Bernardo Division; Lewis Goldberg, President-Quoddy Division.

TYPE OF MARKETER
Mail order, retail, wholesale.

BUSINESS
Barry designs, manufactures, and markets specialized comfort footwear for men, women and children. Company operates 10 manufacturing plants. Footwear products are sold under nationally advertised brands to department, specialty, discount, drug and variety chains, leased shoe departments and supermarkets. Quoddy and Bernardo lines are marketed through family shoe stores, western-wear stores, gift and tourist shops, specialty outlets, and outdoor oriented mail order catalogs.

COMPANY HISTORY
R. G. Barry was started by Florence Melton Zacks in 1940. Zacks began by manufacturing snap-in shoulder pads for women's fashions which she sold store-to-store to retail outlets. In 1946 the company began manufacturing "Angel Treads" foam-soled, washable slippers. The company was incorporated in Ohio in 1947. In the early 1970's Barry acquired Bernardo sandals and shoes. Quoddys was added several years later. Most recent line, Mushroom, was developed in 1978.

MARKETS
Mail order sales of shoes for men, women and children throughout U.S., Europe and Japan.

FACILITIES

Manufacturing facilities in AR, ME, NC, TN, OH, TX, and Mexico; headquarters, Pickerington, Ohio.

PRODUCTS, BRAND NAMES, PRICE RANGE

Washable, foam-soled slippers, warm-up boots, pumps, sandals, and others. Quoddy line--flats, high heels, wedge sandals, thongs, moccasins-- traditional leather-laced, rustic and "camp" styles; broad selection of pile-lines, all-leather slippers.

FINANCIAL INFORMATION

	SALES	NET INCOME	PROFIT MARGIN
1980	$126,825,000	$1,770,000	1%

TYPE OF ADVERTISING, PROMOTION

The majority of R. G. Barry's mail order promotion is through their catalog operations. Catalogs are mailed seasonally, and Barry is a heavy user of rented lists. The catalogs are full color, 8-$\frac{1}{2}$ x 5-$\frac{1}{2}$, roughly 32 pages.

LIST INFORMATION

QUANTITY MAILED:	5,000,000*
AVERAGE ORDER:	$30*
ACTIVE BUYERS:	200,000*
TOTAL LIST:	600,000*
LIST SOURCE:	Rentals.

COMMENTS

Barry sells its Quoddy and Bernardo lines through some retail outlets and through the Barry Collection Mail Order division catalogs. Both lines are upscale, quality, fashion footwear, mostly for women. Management reports that the general condition of the economy has had a negative impact on overall U.S. shoe sales. Sales in Europe and Japan reportedly continue to improve. The mail order division is planning an extensive marketing effort to expand sales overseas. In addition the fall 1981 edition of the catalog featured a variety of new designs from the Bernardo factory in Italy. Current mail order volume is estimated to be in the area of $10 million.

BARTH-SPENCER

ADDRESS, PHONE
Barth-Spencer Corporation, 270 W. Merrick Road, Valley Stream, NY 11580. Telephone: (516) 561-8800.

OWNERSHIP
Barth-Spencer is a wholly-owned subsidiary of Darby Drug, Inc., of Rockville Centre, New York.

MANAGEMENT
Murray A. Spitzer, President; Morris Matises, Vice President-Administration; Milton Kanner, Vice President-Finance; Arthur J. Manno, Vice President-Management Information Systems.

TYPE OF MARKETER
Mail order, wholesale.

BUSINESS
Barth-Spencer and its nine subsidiaries are involved in mail-order marketing to consumers and wholesale accounts. Mail order subsidiary operations include: Barth Vitamin (catalog marketer); Barth Food (wholesale vitamins and food), Barth Nutritional Supplements (wholesale food supplements); Nutra-foods (dietetic products); Pro-Nutra (wholesale food supplements); Spencer-Mead (drugs and vitamins to medical professionals); Colonial Garden Kitchen (kitchen accessories and utensils).

COMPANY HISTORY
The business was founded in 1950 by Solomon and Eleanor Levitt. It was first incorporated as Barth-Levitt Products on September 28, 1953. The name was changed to Barth Vitamin Corp. in December of 1961, and on February 16, 1966 to Barth Spencer Corp. Darby Drug began acquiring shares in the company in October and December of 1980. In January of 1981 the company purchased 96,000 additional shares increasing its holdings from 47% to a majority of outstanding stock.

MARKETS
Mail order sales to retail customers, 60% female; mail order wholesale trade to medical offices, laboratories.

FACILITIES
HQ in 50,000 sq. ft. leased from subsidiary CLJ Realty; also a 50,000 sq. ft. warehouse.

PRODUCTS, BRAND NAMES, PRICE RANGE
Products sold under the Bedford, Barth, Spencer-Mead, Pro-Nutra, and Nutrafoods tradestyles, plus a variety of brands from outside manufacturers. Wide price range; midscale price positions for consumer vitamin, supplement and generic drug operations.

FINANCIAL INFORMATION

	SALES	NET INCOME	PROFIT MARGIN
1981	$25,000,000*	N.A.	--

TYPE OF ADVERTISING, PROMOTION
All of Barth-Spencer advertising is handled by subsidiary Bradley Advertising, Inc. The consumer sales companies use a variety of catalogs and flyers for marketing. Wholesale operations mail direct mail packages and brochures to their accounts.

LIST INFORMATION
QUANTITY MAILED:	N.A.
AVERAGE ORDER:	$19
ACTIVE BUYERS:	250,000
TOTAL LIST:	750,000*
LIST SOURCE:	Direct mail.

COMMENTS
The sales figure above is an estimate of total revenues for Barth-Spencer and subsidiaries for 1981. Based on performance over the past three years, operations were believed to be at a loss. The corporation's total revenues for its last three years reporting as a public company were steady: $23.9 million in 1980; $24.0 million in 1979; $24.0 million in 1978. Management refused to comment on earnings which were $503,165 in 1978, ($52,270) in 1979, and ($150,000) in 1980. However sales for the first quarter of 1981 (last publicly reported) were up 7% over the same period in 1980 and the company had decreased its losses from ($80,000) in 1st quarter, 1980 to ($30,000) in 1st quarter, 1981. The list information above is a partial representation of Barth-Spencer's Vitamin & Health Buyers (not including Health Savings Center). The company and its subsidiaries market a wide variety of lists, both consumer mail order buyers, and commercial, institutional, and professional wholesale buyers.

BASS ANGLERS SOCIETY

ADDRESS, PHONE
Bass Anglers Sportsman Society of America, One Bell Road, Montgomery, AL 36117. (205) 272-9530.

OWNERSHIP
Privately held; 100% of capital stock owned by Ray W. Scott, Jr.

MANAGEMENT
Ray W. Scott, Jr., President; Helen Sevier, Executive Vice President; Robert B. Cobb, Vice President; Barbara Bazzell, Marketing Manager.

TYPE OF MARKETER
Mail order.

BUSINESS
Bass Anglers publishes BassMaster magazine, the society's membership organ, plus Southern Outdoors, a regional magazine with audited circulation of over 175,000. In late 1979, the company acquired College and University Press, a major publisher of alumni directories, freshman yearbooks, etc. The Bass Federation is a lobbying group established by the Society, with some 1,800 chapters and 30,000 members, in the interest of wildlife preservation.

COMPANY HISTORY
B.A.S.S. was founded by Ray Scott, who wanted to have an annual fishing tournament without having to start from scratch every year. After a 1967 tournament, he set up the Society with the 106 participating fishermen as a base. He started a small magazine as a vehicle for communicating with membership. It officially became BassMaster in 1969 and today is advertising-based, publishing 8 issues per year. Membership has grown from 6,500 in 1969 to over 400,000 members.

MARKETS
U.S. market of fishermen interested basically in bass fishing and conservation.

FACILITIES

Headquarters for all operations located in Montgomery, Alabama.

PRODUCTS, BRAND NAMES, PRICE RANGE

Membership in B.A.S.S., including free subscription to BassMaster, is regularly $15.00. Subscription to Southern Outdoors is $9.95. Periodic special introductory membership offer of $12.00.

FINANCIAL INFORMATION

	SALES	NET INCOME	PROFIT MARGIN
1981	$22,000,000*	N.A.	--

TYPE OF ADVERTISING, PROMOTION

Direct mail is one-third of B.A.S.S. promotion; space advertising in Outdoor Life, Sports Afield, and Field & Stream is another third; other contacts and referrals, from publicity and word-of-mouth, make up one-third.

LIST INFORMATION

QUANTITY MAILED:	5,000,000
AVERAGE ORDER:	$15
ACTIVE BUYERS:	N.A.
TOTAL LIST:	400,000
LIST SOURCE:	Direct mail, space, referral.

COMMENTS

B.A.S.S.' company profits originally came from membership dues. But revenues from advertising and mail order sales prompted management to look at these operations as potential high income producers, and at the burgeoning membership rolls as an excellent buyer base. Since then the "company" has grown rapidly. The Southern Outdoors publishing operation has been improved with the addition of regional hunting and fishing guide offerings. BassMaster operation has been expanded with a fishing guide and bass fishing annual report. The 1979 acquisition of College & University Press represents a significant diversification of publishing operations into collegiate and alumni publications market. Mail order sales of fishing tackle and apparel is estimated to be about 25% of total revenues. Most recent expansion came with the Fishing Tackle Retail catalog, the premier edition mailed in August of 1980. B.A.S.S. presently reports over 200 employees, and over 400,000 active members.

EDDIE BAUER

ADDRESS, PHONE

Eddie Bauer, Inc., 15010 N.E. 36th Street, Redmond, WA 98052. Telephone: (206) 882-6100.

OWNERSHIP

Wholly-owned subsidiary of publicly-held General Mills, Inc. of Minneapolis, MN.

MANAGEMENT

James Casey, President; John Quinlin, VP-Administration and Operations; Ken Wherry, VP-Retail; David Rudd, VP-Marketing; Kenneth Foster, VP-Finance and Controller.

TYPE OF MARKETER

Mail order, retail.

BUSINESS

Eddie Bauer manufactures and sells a variety of outdoor apparel and equipment. They are perhaps best known for their private label lines of goosedown sleeping bags, jackets, parkas, and vests. Merchandise is marketed through chain of retail stores and mail order catalog operation; sales are 50% retail, 50% mail order. Stores are located in major metropolitan areas, and catalogs are mailed throughout the U.S. and Canada. Company employs 1,300.

COMPANY HISTORY

The company was founded by Eddie Bauer in 1920 as a sporting goods shop. Bauer later developed the down jacket, which he initially sold to sportsmen and bush pilots. This design was also used to produce down sleeping bags and various other items. The company then started a mail order operation with one retail store carrying discontinued items. In '68 the Neimi family purchased the Bauer's interest in the company, and in '71 General Mills bought the company from the Neimis.

MARKETS

Customers are upscale outdoor enthusiasts and sportsmen; 85% male; throughout U.S. and Canada.

FACILITIES
Offices and mail order fulfillment in Redmond, WA; 71,000 sq. ft. warehouse in Seattle, WA.

PRODUCTS, BRAND NAMES, PRICE RANGE
Outdoor apparel such as goosedown outerwear, sportswear, footwear, camping and hiking equipment. House and national brands--Eureka, Wilderness, Experience, Danner, Coleman, Eveready, Thommin. Price range is $40 to $125.

FINANCIAL INFORMATION

	SALES	NET INCOME	PROFIT MARGIN
1980	$60,000,000*	N.A.	--

TYPE OF ADVERTISING, PROMOTION
Space ads in magazines and newspapers offer 64+-page color catalogs: Christmas catalog late in August, gift pre-Christmas book in late September, gift book in October, spring book in February, and summer book in early April.

LIST INFORMATION
QUANTITY MAILED:	13,000,000*
AVERAGE ORDER:	$50
ACTIVE BUYERS:	387,000
TOTAL LIST:	1,450,000*
LIST SOURCE:	Direct mail.

COMMENTS
Direct mail catalog sales generated approximately $29 million in 1980, or about 50% of estimated total revenues. The other 50% of sales came from Bauer's retail outlets, which have grown from a single outlet for discontinued mail order items, to a successful chain of stores which combine mail order and retail strategies. With the acquisition of Bauer, General Mills' Specialty Retailing division sales rose some 30%; operating profits in 1980 declined slightly due to "higher catalog costs, and liquidation of over-bought inventories at Eddie Bauer". EB has successfully implemented a telephone ordering system, and a new computer system to constantly update information on out-of-stock items, and to handle order processing. Management has proposed increasing the number of retail outlets to 34 by 1984. EB's peak sales period is July to December; approximately 70% of revenues are generated during this time.

BEACON PHOTO SERVICE

ADDRESS, PHONE

Beacon Photo Service, Inc., 482 Sunrise Highway, Rockville Centre, NY 11570. (516) 536-6360.

OWNERSHIP

Publicly held; stock traded OTC; 1,354,800 common shares outstanding; 1980 bids: high, 1-1/2; low, 3/4; no 1980 dividend was paid.

MANAGEMENT

Martin Savarick, Chairman & CEO; Alan Savarick, President & Treasurer; Maurice Weingold, Secretary & Legal Counsel; Howard Ehrlich, VP, Production; Sheldon Minkon, VP Mktg.

TYPE OF MARKETER

Mail order.

BUSINESS

The company's principal business is mail order film processing and developing. Beacon also has a mail order imprint segment which sells imprinted products and other items through the mail. They buy pens, pencils, name and address labels, etc. from suppliers and personalize them for sale to customers. Parent company also sells photofinishing and photographic products by mail, and other mail order gift merchandise under the Giftware Corner name.

COMPANY HISTORY

Beacon Photo Service was started by Michael Savarick in Brooklyn, NY in 1933. Savarick began selling film developing services, delivering film and prints to and from drugstore developing outlets. The business grew with the logical expansion into mail order marketing and later, into retail kiosks. During 1977, Beacon acquired the assets and operations of Simpson Photo, Photo Quik, The Foto Express, and Photo Store, Inc. Major disposal of 267 unprofitable retail outlets in 1979 and '80.

MARKETS

Mail order sales throughout the continental U.S.; principally to families in the Midwest.

FACILITIES

Headquarters and all mail order operations at Rockville Centre, New York location.

PRODUCTS, BRAND NAMES, PRICE RANGE

Photofinishing services plus inexpensive general merchandise from a mini-catalog included with photos returned to customers. Non-photofinishing items include name-and-address labels, personalized memo pads, pens, pencils and similar products.

FINANCIAL INFORMATION

	SALES	NET INCOME	PROFIT MARGIN
1981	$20,000,000	$500,000	2.5%

TYPE OF ADVERTISING, PROMOTION

Beacon uses co-ops, package inserts, F.S.I., and premiums. Mini-catalog of sixteen pages contains non-photofinishing items.

LIST INFORMATION

QUANTITY MAILED:	5,000,000*
AVERAGE ORDER:	$8
ACTIVE BUYERS:	1,000,000
TOTAL LIST:	3,000,000
LIST SOURCE:	Direct mail, space.

COMMENTS

The Beacon Direct Response division contributes approximately 40% of Beacon Photo's revenues annually. In recent years, Beacon Photo has not been able to keep its photofinishing and imprint products operations simultaneously profitable. In 1978, mail order photofinishing sales and profits declined while sales and profits for the imprint operation increased. In 1979, sales were up for both segments, but imprint segment operating profits declined. In 1980, the imprint segment suffered both sales and operating profit losses while photofinishing sales remained flat. In 1981, both photofinishing and imprint products sales and profits were up. Mail order buyers increased from 750,000 in 1980 to 1,000,000 in 1981--a result of increased advertising and expansion of major mailing programs.

L.L. BEAN

ADDRESS, PHONE

L.L. Bean, Inc., 35 Casco Street, Freeport, ME 04033. Telephone: (207) 865-4761.

OWNERSHIP

Privately held; 100% of capital stock owned by the Bean family.

MANAGEMENT

Leon A. Gorman, President; John Findlay, VP-Operations; William End, Exec. VP-Marketing; William Henry, Director-Direct Mail Advertising; Mac McCabe, Director-Retail Sales.

TYPE OF MARKETER

Mail order, retail.

BUSINESS

L.L Bean is a mail order marketer of outdoor and sporting apparel and footwear. Company's manufacturing operation produces hunting boots, moccasins, sailing footwear, and tote bags. Bean operates one retail outlet in Freeport which accounts for 20% of its total sales; 80% comes from catalog marketing. Men's wear accounts for 50% of the merchandise sold; women's apparel, 30%; general sporting goods and footwear, 20%. L.L. Bean reported 900 employees for 1981.

COMPANY HISTORY

The business was started in 1912 as a sporting goods manufacturer by retailer Leon Leonwood Bean, inventor of the rubber-soled Maine Hunting Shoe--a line of footwear which has become a status symbol among sportsmen. The company was incorporated in Maine in 1964, and began a period of major growth in 1967. In 1980 L.L. Bean expanded its distribution site near the company headquarters and opened a new manufacturing facility. Bean has enjoyed a steady increase over the past several years.

MARKETS

Customers are outdoor enthusiasts and sportsmen; 65% male. Mail order sales throughout U.S.

FACILITIES
Headquarters, distribution, and manufacturing are centered in one area of Freeport.

PRODUCTS, BRAND NAMES, PRICE RANGE
Clothing and footwear brand names include L.L. Bean, West Branch, Casco Bay, Country Walkers, Northwoods, Baxter State, and Timberline. Catalogs oriented to specific types of sport feature hunting gear, fishing equipment, camping gear, etc.

FINANCIAL INFORMATION

	SALES	NET INCOME	PROFIT MARGIN
1981	$121,545,000	$6,077,000	5.0%

TYPE OF ADVERTISING, PROMOTION
Majority of customer solicitation is done through catalogs. Additional promotion is carried out through space advertising in consumer magazines and a sizeable package insert program.

LIST INFORMATION

QUANTITY MAILED:	26,000,000
AVERAGE ORDER:	$48
ACTIVE BUYERS:	1,130,256
TOTAL LIST:	4,000,000
LIST SOURCE:	Direct mail, rentals, space.

COMMENTS
Spring and summer months are very active for L.L. Bean, with the retail operation enjoying particularly heavy business. Fiscal 1981 sales increased to $121,545,000, continuing a pattern of steady growth in recent years. The basic Maine Hunting Boot retains its popularity, while notable growth in 1980 occurred in sales of women's apparel. Both distribution and production facilities expanded in 1980 to keep pace with company growth. The firm generally maintains a low advertising profile, concentrating heavily on customer service. Mailings continue to grow, and the firm maintains a master list of some 4 million. Mini-catalogs tested throughout 1978-79 are now in full force as supplements to major books mailed five times a year. Through the third quarter of the 1981 calendar year, management reported that sales had increased 35%, with improved earnings.

BELSAW MACHINERY CO.

ADDRESS, PHONE
Belsaw Machinery Co., Box 593, 315 Westport Road, Kansas City, MO 64141. Telephone: (816) 483-4200.

OWNERSHIP
Privately held by the Ringer family.

MANAGEMENT
Walter M. Ringer, Jr., Chairman; Stan Field, President and General Manager; Robert Holper, Treasurer; John W. Miller, 2nd Vice President; Joe Ringer, 3rd Vice President.

TYPE OF MARKETER
Mail order, wholesale.

BUSINESS
Belsaw markets shop machinery and tools such as portable lumber sawmills and planes, table saws, power sharpeners and grinders, etc. Products are sold through catalog operations to individual consumers, and wholesale to mail order houses under their respective labels. They place heavy emphasis on providing training as well as equipment to start home businesses; customers are referred to as the "Belsaw Family of Independent Businessmen." Minimal portion of business is offering correspondence training courses.

COMPANY HISTORY
The company was started by a Mr. Bell in Kansas City, MO, in 1926. Originally Bell developed a one-man sawmill which he sold through the mail. A unique "bulletin" type of catalog was used from the outset. Correspondence courses were introduced in 1968. Business was incorporated in July, 1977, and transferred to present control when Walter M. Ringer, Jr. purchased company and 100% of capital stock. Company presently reports 90 employees.

MARKETS
98% male, do-it-yourselfers; active in home shop crafts and/or business; U.S. and international markets.

FACILITIES

Warehousing, order processing, headquarters, Kansas City, MO. Additional warehouse, Pleasant Hill, MO.

PRODUCTS, BRAND NAMES, PRICE RANGE

Products are: power tools and attachments; dust blowers and exhaust systems; one-man portable saw-mills; saw chain tools and supplies; sharpeners for home, garden, and shop tools; hand tools. House brands. Prices average $250.

FINANCIAL INFORMATION

	SALES	NET INCOME	PROFIT MARGIN
1981	$37,000,000*	N.A.	--

TYPE OF ADVERTISING, PROMOTION

Approximately 85% of advertising is through direct mail; the other 15% through space in magazines such as Popular Science, Field & Stream, Argosy, etc. Main direct mail piece is "Belsaw Bulletin" catalog, supported by direct mail packages.

LIST INFORMATION

QUANTITY MAILED: 5,500,000
AVERAGE ORDER: $250*
ACTIVE BUYERS: 110,000
TOTAL LIST: 550,000
LIST SOURCE: Direct mail, space ads.

COMMENTS

Mail order sales to consumers account for an estimated 90% of total sales; approximately $33 million. Remaining 10% of business is wholesaling of merchandise via direct mail to business accounts. Belsaw does no manufacturing. Sales growth rate is an estimated 15% annually. Main direct mail piece, the Belsaw Bulletin, is a unique catalog design. It uses a newsletter motif, the merchandise offerings interspersed with personal testimonials and small business success stories from members of the "Belsaw family." Editorial includes shop tips, and creative ideas on earning extra income. Bulletin is about 48 pages, 10-7/8" by 8-1/4", multi-colored. Catalog is mailed 4 times per year: Jan/Mar, Apr/May, Sept., and Oct/Dec. Catalogs supported with direct mail packages on specific larger products such as the one-man sawmill, the rip saw and edger. Belsaw mails about 5.5 million pieces of direct mail per year. Space in newspaper inserts (40%) and magazines (60%) is used to advertise Bulletin.

WALTER J. BLACK

ADDRESS, PHONE
Walter J. Black, Inc., 1075 Northern Blvd., Roslyn, NY 11576. Telephone: (516) 627-4920.

OWNERSHIP
Privately held; 100% of capital stock owned by the Black family.

MANAGEMENT
Theodore Black, President and Chief Executive; Walter Black, II, Treasurer; Francis Pavlak, Vice President; Genevieve M. Carter, Executive Vice President; Betty Jones, Senior Vice President.

TYPE OF MARKETER
Mail order.

BUSINESS
Black is a publisher and marketer of special reprints of classics and various other types of books, including fiction and non-fiction. The company sells its editions to retail book stores and through mail order book clubs including Classics Club, Detective Book Club and Black's Reader Service. Black has become more a marketer than publisher/printer and handles books published by a variety of outside firms. Black employs approximately 65 people.

COMPANY HISTORY
The business was started in New York in 1923 by Walter and Elsie Black. The first book they marketed was a single-volume, leather-bound edition of Shakespeare. The company was originally called Plymouth Publication Corp. and was located in Manhattan. The name was changed to Walter J. Black and the business was incorporated in July of 1927. Control passed to family members when Walter Black passed away in April of 1958. Company has been at present location since January, 1954.

MARKETS
Products are sold to retail stores, and by mail to middle-income customers in U.S. and Canada.

FACILITIES
Warehousing, offices, and ordering and fulfillment operations at Roslyn location.

PRODUCTS, BRAND NAMES, PRICE RANGE
Black markets a wide variety of fiction, non-fiction and classic books through its continuity clubs. Brand name collections include Giants of Literature, the Zane Grey Library, the Gardner Mystery Library, and Ellery Queen's Mystery Club.

FINANCIAL INFORMATION

	SALES	NET INCOME	PROFIT MARGIN
1981	$12,000,000*	N.A.	--

TYPE OF ADVERTISING, PROMOTION
Advertising appears in many of the monthly national publications, including a large number of women's magazines and The New York Times Book Review. Advertising is significantly increased in the fall and winter months.

LIST INFORMATION

QUANTITY MAILED:	N.A.
AVERAGE ORDER:	$50*
ACTIVE BUYERS:	240,000*
TOTAL LIST:	1,000,000*
LIST SOURCE:	Direct mail, space.

COMMENTS
Black's estimated $12 million in revenues comes from mail order sales. Primary marketing is through the company's various book clubs. The clubs function as continuity sales programs, and the books are sold mostly in three-volume sets. The Detective Book Club is an open-end negative option plan and new editions are constantly being added to their selection. Management reports that they will continue to improve their position as a major marketer of books (rather than publisher or printer), and that they will continue to emphasize the multi-volume sets of classical books as their primary merchandise line.

BLOOMINGDALE'S

ADDRESS, PHONE

Bloomingdale's, P.O. Box 2052, FDR Station, New York, NY 10022. Telephone: (212) 223-7111.

OWNERSHIP

Division of Federated Department Stores, 7 West Seventh Street, Cincinnati, Ohio, 45202.

MANAGEMENT

Melvin Jacobs, V. Chmn. of Fed. Dept. Stores; Bloomingdale's: Marvin S. Traub, Chmn.; James S. Schoff, Jr., Pres.; Doreen McCurley, Dir., Mail Order Operations.

TYPE OF MARKETER

Retail, mail order.

BUSINESS

Company produces some of the best traffic-generating retailer catalogs in the business and continues to enjoy status as a trendy, innovative force in U.S. upper crust retailing. Its stores feature fashionable merchandise carrying designer labels, as well as premium priced items under Bloomingdale's brand. Company retails through 11 general merchandise stores and 5 home furnishings specialty stores. Its mail order catalogs promote essentially the same merchandise to different buyers than those who purchase from the retail outlets.

COMPANY HISTORY

Business was established in 1872 in Manhattan. In the 1940's, New York's Bloomingdale's was a drab bargain store where the maids of wealthy New Yorkers shopped. Company's transformation to current chic image is the result of aggressive merchandising and show business: pioneered the "boutique" concept--clustering small specialty stores inside one large department store; often sponsors live musicians entertaining Saturday shoppers. Flagship Manhattan store began mail order catalog operations in August 1978.

MARKETS

Mail order customers throughout the U.S.; generally upper income families.

FACILITIES
Mail order planning office at New York Store; processing & fulfillment center in NY; 16 retail stores.

PRODUCTS, BRAND NAMES, PRICE RANGE
Ready-to-wear, home furnishings & accessories, giftware, sporting goods, toys and games, food gift packages, etc. Doreen McCurley says it's not the brand that sells; it's the look of the item: fashion and style. Prices are middle to upper scale.

FINANCIAL INFORMATION

	SALES	NET INCOME	PROFIT MARGIN
1981	$566,800,000	N.A.	--

TYPE OF ADVERTISING, PROMOTION
Mail order concentrates promotional efforts on full-color catalogs. Christmas catalog is the largest, with about 104 pages; other catalogs, featuring special merchandise classifications, average 32-36 pages each. Minimal space in Harpers, Vogue, for Christmas.

LIST INFORMATION
QUANTITY MAILED:	8,900,000
AVERAGE ORDER:	Varies by product: apparel, $115
ACTIVE BUYERS:	250,000
TOTAL LIST:	1,000,000
LIST SOURCE:	Primarily list rental; space ads.

COMMENTS
Bloomingdale's was the second highest performer in sales among Federated Department Stores' 20 divisions. Started its mail order business in 1978 with a list of 11,000 buyers who had purchased Bloomingdale's merchandise by mail order on their own initiative, and built to a list of 250,000 active buyers in 1981. They began with test mailings to specific mail order merchandise buyers lists to keep down the number of catalogs they needed to print. Additional funds from reduced catalog costs and discontinued newspaper insert advertising were used to purchase outside select-product buyers lists. Emphasis from the outset has been on small quantities of more, different catalogs, mailed to buyer lists segmented by specific product categories. This has been the major contributing factor in high average order and overall profitability of on-target catalog operations. Company is planning 12 separate catalogs for '82; sees potential in future for separate mail order product development and possibly wholesaling by mail.

BOOK-OF-THE-MONTH CLUB

ADDRESS, PHONE

Book-Of-The-Month Club, Inc., 485 Lexington Ave., New York, NY 10017. Telephone: (212) 867-4300.

OWNERSHIP

B.O.M.C. is a subsidiary of publicly-held Time, Inc., of New York.

MANAGEMENT

Edward Fitzgerald, Chrmn, CEO; Joan Manley, Vice Chrmn; Al Silverman, President, COO; Gloria Norris, Sr. VP, Editor-in-Chief; Lewis Smith, Sr. VP, Dir. of Marketing.

TYPE OF MARKETER

Mail order.

BUSINESS

Book-Of-The-Month Club is part of the Time Books Group which accounts for approximately 17% of Time, Inc.'s total revenues annually. The Club offers current, best-selling books, both fiction and non-fiction, on a membership basis, through Book-Of-The-Month Club, Quality Paper Backs, Fortune and a variety of other specialty book clubs. In addition the company markets gifts, apparel, and specialties through its B.O.M.C. catalog operations.

COMPANY HISTORY

Time, Inc. acquired Book-Of-The-Month Club in 1977. The acquisition was actively investigated by the F.T.C. in their media anti-trust initiatives to prevent large or vertically integrated publishers from unreasonably blocking competition by smaller firms. F.T.C.'s investigations concluded that media industry was "both diverse and workably competitive." Time, Inc.'s acquisition of the Club was judged to be clearly not in violation of anti-trust laws.

MARKETS

B.O.M.C. sells merchandise throughout the U.S. and Canada, and internationally in the U.K. and Japan.

FACILITIES

Headquarters, NY; warehousing and order fulfillment, Camp Hill, PA.

PRODUCTS, BRAND NAMES, PRICE RANGE

Best-selling books: $12 to $26; prints, sculptures, figurines: $75 to $125; gifts, household items, apparel, kitchen and bath accessories, collectibles: $5 to $100; record and tape sets of opera, classical, jazz and popular music: $20-$25.

FINANCIAL INFORMATION

	SALES	NET INCOME	PROFIT MARGIN
1981	$80,000,000*	N.A.	--

TYPE OF ADVERTISING, PROMOTION

Club advertises through space, broadcast, and direct mail. Mailings include letter, order form and 6-1/2 by 8-1/2 full-color reproductions of art items. B.O.M.C. Collection mails full-color catalog seasonally to buyer lists.

LIST INFORMATION

QUANTITY MAILED: (B.O.M.C. releases information
AVERAGE ORDER: on a compiled list of club expir-
ACTIVE BUYERS: ations to qualified inquiries only
TOTAL LIST: on a restricted basis.)
LIST SOURCE:

COMMENTS

In 1980 The Books Group, a division of Time, Inc., had half a billion dollars in revenues making it the largest of mail order book companies. Book-Of-The-Month Club accounted for approximately 16% of these revenues. Books Division annually mails 60 million direct mail pieces to a list of over 20 million households. BOMC members might be described as particular and discerning - even collectors. Cooking and Crafts and Dolphin (for boating enthusiasts) Clubs have recently been strong performers in the specialty club area. Quality Paperback Book Club (only general interest soft cover club in U.S.) is reporting strong sales. Most recent venture, in conjunction with the Smithsonian, 12-volume Smithsonian Illustrated Library of Antiques, has contributed to growth.

BRADFORD EXCHANGE

ADDRESS, PHONE
The Bradford Exchange, Ltd., 9333 North Milwaukee Ave., Niles, IL 60648. Telephone: (312) 966-2770.

OWNERSHIP
Privately held; J. Roderick MacArthur owns 100% of capital stock.

MANAGEMENT
J. Roderick MacArthur, President and Chairman; Kevin P. McEneely, Executive Vice President; Steven K. Lauer, Senior Vice President.

TYPE OF MARKETER
Mail order.

BUSINESS
Bradford claims to be the world's largest trading center for collector's plates. Marketing is through mail and Bradex Service which acts as a clearinghouse for collectors with older plates to trade. Individuals who wish to sell a plate or buy one out of production may list request with Bradford which will check its files for an appropriate buyer or seller. Charges for this service range from 20% for the seller to 3% for the buyer.

COMPANY HISTORY
Bradford Exchange was established in 1973 by Roderick MacArthur (son of John MacArthur of Bankers Life fame). As the firm grew, it expanded operations into the European market with units in Germany and England. Services are also marketed in Canada. Plans for further expansion include moving into the Scandinavian market, as well as Italy and Japan. Company reported 350 employees for 1980.

MARKETS
Bradford sells products throughout U.S., Canada, U.K., Switzerland, Germany. Customers 60% female.

FACILITIES

H.Q., Niles, IL; mail order operations in Morton Grove, IL, Germany and England.

PRODUCTS, BRAND NAMES, PRICE RANGE

Products consist of limited plate editions and newly issued collectors plates. Norman Rockwell's "Lighthouse Keeper's Daughter" plate was offered at $19.50. Prices range from $15.00 to $400.00.

FINANCIAL INFORMATION

	SALES	NET INCOME	PROFIT MARGIN
1981	$80,000,000	N.A.	--

TYPE OF ADVERTISING, PROMOTION

Primarily direct response advertising, with some space advertising. Peak mailing season is Sept. through May. Newspapers are preferred over magazines for the investment oriented ads. Has over 500 dailies on its media list.

LIST INFORMATION

QUANTITY MAILED:	51,000,000
AVERAGE ORDER:	$25
ACTIVE BUYERS:	750,000
TOTAL LIST:	2,200,000
LIST SOURCE:	Direct mail (90%), space (10%).

COMMENTS

Promotion for the product is investment oriented. The increase in value of plates is reported in editorial-style small space ads. Clauses such as "limit two plates per person to discourage speculation and profiteering" are used for promotion. The plates are also advertised on the value of their materials, construction, and well-known artists. Bradford Exchange Quotations gives the number of issues rising in value, decreasing in value, or unchanged, and the overall Bradex number, to report the value of its plates. The company says this technique is used to reinforce the customer's decision to purchase plates as well as encourage repeat purchases. Bradex subscriptions are free upon request. Advertising takes a serious no-nonsense approach that conveys an investment attitude.

BROOKS BROTHERS

ADDRESS, PHONE
Brooks Brothers, 346 Madison Ave., New York, NY 10017. Telephone: (212) 682-8800.

OWNERSHIP
Privately-held by Garfinckel, Brooks Bros., Miller & Rhoads, Inc., Washington, D.C.

MANAGEMENT
Frank T. Reilly, President; Stanley Jaffe, Senior VP; James T. Pussilana, Senior VP and Treasurer; Senior VPs: Richard A. Jiracek, Joseph E. Maloney, Robert C. Dawson, A. Marc Zoila, Peter G. Newman.

TYPE OF MARKETER
Mail order, retail.

BUSINESS
Brooks Bros. is one of seven operating divisions of the parent company. In its 164 years of business, company has been known as the clothier of American aristocracy, presidents, actors and writers. The company markets high-quality apparel, home furnishings and shoes by mail and through its chain of retail outlets. Although Brooks has historically been known as a men's specialty store, they are presently developing women's apparel lines. Brooks reports 2,200 employees.

COMPANY HISTORY
Henry Sands Brooks, son of a Connecticut doctor, founded the company in 1818 with an initial investment of $17,000. In 1915 Brooks' four grandsons took control of business and renamed it "Brooks Brothers." The company's entrenched reputation with the elite crowd enabled it to flourish during the depression. However, during WWII, ailing due to disrupted British trade, Brooks merged with Washington-based Garfinckel's department store.

MARKETS
U.S.A.; international--Japan, Canada, South America and others; upscale males and females.

FACILITIES

Headquarters, New York, NY; order-taking and fulfillment, New York and New Jersey.

PRODUCTS, BRAND NAMES, PRICE RANGE

Men's and women's clothing, furnishings and shoes. Classical three piece suits; coordinated accessories-- shirts, ties, socks, etc. Women's business suits, coordinates and accessories. Price range up to $400; median $50.

FINANCIAL INFORMATION

	SALES	**NET INCOME**	**PROFIT MARGIN**
1981	$140,000,000*	N.A.	--

TYPE OF ADVERTISING, PROMOTION

Mail order advertising 100% catalogs. Emphasis on quality, specialty lines, complete wardrobe and accessories, etc. Company offers four catalogs-- Brooksgate, Brooks Brothers, new women's line, and shoes.

LIST INFORMATION

QUANTITY MAILED:	1,000,000
AVERAGE ORDER:	$90
ACTIVE BUYERS:	207,412
TOTAL LIST:	600,000*
LIST SOURCE:	Charge list, outside rental.

COMMENTS

The above estimates are for Brooks Brothers total sales. Brooks contributes an estimated 24% of parent's total revenues. Mail order operations accounted for approximately 20% or $28 million of Brooks' total sales. The remaining 80% come from retail stores. Industry sources claim that Brooks Bros. has one of the highest profit margins in the apparel industry. Management reports sales have been stimulated by company's strong expansion drive--new retail outlets in Japan, Canada, and South America; improved catalog operations. Mail order emphasis is on better presentation of select merchandise and expansion into women's apparel market. Intention is to increase women's apparel to 15% of total sales. Several recent additions to catalog operations: Brooksgate catalog collection specializing in apparel for the young male executive; separate catalog offering men's and women's shoes; presently considering an upscale gift catalog.

BROOKSTONE

ADDRESS, PHONE

Brookstone Company, Vose Farm Road, Peterborough, NH 03458. Telephone: (603) 924-7181.

OWNERSHIP

Subsidiary of publicly-held Quaker Oats, Merchandise Mart Plaza, Chicago, IL 60654.

MANAGEMENT

Richard Chollet, President; David A. Taylor, Vice President of Direct Marketing.

TYPE OF MARKETER

Mail order, retail.

BUSINESS

Brookstone specializes in selling hard-to-find tools and fine gifts. Products consist of precision and high quality hand tools, small electric tools for metal and woodworking, and high quality garden tools. Consumers are mostly professional or advanced craftsmen, technicians and hobbyists. Most sales are generated by mail order through catalogs. Tools and some other items are also sold at the company's retail outlets in the Northeast and Atlanta areas. Total employees number 300.

COMPANY HISTORY

Pierre de Beaumont, hobbyist, machinist and craftsman, started Brookstone Company in 1965. While consulting for the Navy Bureau of Aeronautics, he noticed that specialized tools in one industry were virtually unknown to other industries. Months of research by Pierre and his wife Deland on specialized products for scores of professions resulted in the first catalog, containing 42 items. In 1980 the company was purchased by Quaker Oats.

MARKETS

Craftsmen/hobbyist market, 95% male; fine gifts market, 65% female; mail order market, U.S.A.

FACILITIES
Stores in metropolitan areas; mail order operation and warehouse in Peterborough, NH.

PRODUCTS, BRAND NAMES, PRICE RANGE
Products include: Hard-To-Find Tools Catalog--hand tools, auto accessories, garden tools, gourmet kitchenware, and unusual gifts; Fine Gifts Catalog: tableware, jewelry, fashion and personal care items, useful and unusual household necessities.

FINANCIAL INFORMATION

	SALES	NET INCOME	PROFIT MARGIN
1981	$31,000,000*	N.A.	--

TYPE OF ADVERTISING, PROMOTION
Advertising consists of small space ads in newspapers and magazines--The Wall Street Journal, The New Yorker, etc. Both catalogs and merchandise are offered through ads. Three major catalog mailings per year. Considerable list rental and exchange.

LIST INFORMATION
QUANTITY MAILED:	20,000,000*
AVERAGE ORDER:	$34
ACTIVE BUYERS:	500,000*
TOTAL LIST:	3,000,000
LIST SOURCE:	Direct mail, space advertising

COMMENTS
Mail order accounts for an estimated 75% of Brookstone Co.'s total sales: some $23.25 million. The remaining 25% from eight retail outlets. Parent Quaker Oats reported that Brookstone recorded good sales gains in all lines of its business last year, resulting in an operating income increase of 44%. Hard-To-Find Tool catalog is 50% color, 8-1/4 x 10-1/2, approximately 68 pages. The fall '81 edition introduced 68 new products. Tools can be purchased separately or in functional packages at reduced rates. Approximately 3 editions of the tool catalog and gift catalog are published per year. Space ads, special promotional packages and package inserts are used to support catalog operations. In all company mails some 20,000,000 pieces annually, to both house list and considerable rentals and exchanged lists. In addition management reports that word-of-mouth referrals are responsible for high percentage of inquiries.

BROWNSTONE STUDIO

ADDRESS, PHONE

Jean Grayson's Brownstone Studio, Inc., 1 East 43rd St., New York, NY 10175. Phone: (212) 883-1990.

OWNERSHIP

Privately held; 100% of capital stock is owned by the officers.

MANAGEMENT

Jean Paaswell, President; Roberta Nasta, Vice President; Robert Bernstein, Controller.

TYPE OF MARKETER

Mail order, retail.

BUSINESS

Brownstone offers fashionable, high-quality women's apparel and accessories by mail and through its two retail outlets in New York and Washington, D.C. Mail order operations contribute an estimated 70% of the company's total annual revenues. This percentage is expected to change slightly due to the recent opening of the Upstairs Boutique Washington retail outlet. Management reports that peak sales are in the November-January period.

COMPANY HISTORY

After working in several major New York advertising firms, Jean Paaswell started Brownstone in 1973. The company was incorporated in New York the same year. Brownstone started as an exclusively mail order marketer and later added retail boutiques. Expanding operations prompted a move in late 1981 from Madison Ave. to larger facilities at the present location. Retail boutique was opened in Washington, D.C. at roughly the same time. Brownstone presently employs 125 people.

MARKETS

Mail order sales are domestic. Market is close to 100% female, generally upper-middle to upscale.

FACILITIES
Offices and all mail order operations at NY address.
Retail stores, NY and Washington, D.C.

PRODUCTS, BRAND NAMES, PRICE RANGE
Distinctive, high-fashion women's apparel and accessories, ranging from dresses, skirts, sweaters and swimwear to shoes, earrings, pocketbooks, etc. Labels include names of top designers. Prices range $5 to $200.

FINANCIAL INFORMATION

	SALES	NET INCOME	PROFIT MARGIN
1981	$16,500,000*	N.A.	--

TYPE OF ADVERTISING, PROMOTION
Brownstone's promotional emphasis is on their catalogs mailed seasonally, supported with several sale mini-catalogs throughout the year. In addition the company uses space advertising in leading women's magazines.

LIST INFORMATION

QUANTITY MAILED:	3,000,000*
AVERAGE ORDER:	$100
ACTIVE BUYERS:	169,000
TOTAL LIST:	500,000*
LIST SOURCE:	Direct mail, space, list exchanges.

COMMENTS
The sales figure above represents an estimate of Brownstone studio's mail order and retail revenues. Retail sales are estimated to be $2.5 million. The company mails three editions of its catalog annually. The main book is full-color, 8-½ x 11, about 36 pages. The catalogs use classic locations as themes for presenting lines of merchandise. For example, presentations of the lighter-weight fashion apparel in the Spring 1982 edition are all shot on location in Greece. The fashion lines are all the "best of New York haute couture," and the location shooting according to the company adds to the quality, upscale image.

BUREAU OF NATIONAL AFFAIRS

ADDRESS, PHONE

Bureau of National Affairs, Inc., 1231 35th St. NW, Washington, D.C. 20037. Telephone: (202) 452-4200.

OWNERSHIP

Privately held by officers and employees of company and its subsidiaries; 730 stockholders.

MANAGEMENT

John D. Stewart, Chairman of the Board; William Beltz, President/Editor-In-Chief; Stanley Degler, Vice President/ Executive Editor; Ralph J. Wall, Vice Pres/Chief Financial Officer.

TYPE OF MARKETER

Mail order, direct sales.

BUSINESS

The Bureau of National Affairs and subsidiaries publish and market periodicals on specialized areas of business and government operations. Parent company itself publishes journals on labor law, environment, safety, business and economics. Tax Management, Inc. publishes tax-related information and offers computer modules for tax calculations. BNA Communications produces films and multi-media training packages. The Bureau publishes some books. In all, six subsidiaries, 1,400 employees.

COMPANY HISTORY

David Lawrence, a journalist, started the business as U.S. News Publishing Co. in 1929. First publication, U.S. Patents Quarterly, offered businessmen and attorneys detailed information unavailable through the general press. In 1933 Lawrence added U.S. Law Week, and later, U. S. News and World Report. In 1947 he sold Bureau of National Affairs to his employees; it was incorporated in Delaware at that time. The various subsidiaries were added in 1950s and thereafter.

MARKETS

Sells domestically and overseas. Market is specialized white-collar.

FACILITIES

H.Q. in Washington, D.C.; warehouse in Rockville, MD; sales offices in major U.S. cities and London.

PRODUCTS, BRAND NAMES, PRICE RANGE

Offers more than 70 publications through parent and subsidiaries. Books on various business and related subjects range from $2.50 to $95.00. Company also offers films in areas of management development, supervisory training, and employee communications.

FINANCIAL INFORMATION

	SALES	NET INCOME	PROFIT MARGIN
1981	$76,000,000*	N.A.	--

TYPE OF ADVERTISING, PROMOTION

Company makes heavy use of brochures to advertise one or more publications, with mailings ongoing. Also uses some catalogs to promote products on irregular basis. Some space in specialized magazines, legal journals, and newspapers.

LIST INFORMATION

QUANTITY MAILED:	5,000,000*
AVERAGE ORDER:	$180 to $1,000; books: $25
ACTIVE BUYERS:	210,000 subs., 57,000 book buyers
TOTAL LIST:	N.A.
LIST SOURCE:	Direct mail, space.

COMMENTS

The Bureau of National Affairs (parent) and all subsidiaries use direct mail to some degree to promote merchandise, and to fulfill orders. About 30% of parent's advertising and promotion is direct mail. Some 95% of book sales are responses to direct mail; 5% of sales contributed by field force. Other publishing divisions and film/multi-media production division are heavy mailers of direct mail packages and some small catalogs. Fisher-Stevens subsidiary provides direct mail marketing and computer services for outside firms, also mailing of sample products to medical professionals. The Bureau is positioned to provide detailed, current information to business, legal, and government officials. Management reported that even their peak fall sales were affected by the recession. However, new economic provisions and laws are expected to increase demand for their informed publications.

W. ATLEE BURPEE

ADDRESS, PHONE
W. Atlee Burpee Co., Inc., 300 Park Ave., Warminster, PA 18924. Telephone: (215) 674-4900.

OWNERSHIP
Subsidiary of ITT; parent owns 100% of capital stock.

MANAGEMENT
Tadd C. Seitz, President; Marilyn Black, V.P.-Direct Marketing; Paul W. Briggs, V.P.-Operations; A. Daniel Franzman, VP; Jonathan Burpee, Secretary; Pasquale C. DePalma, Comptroller.

TYPE OF MARKETER
Mail order, wholesale.

BUSINESS
Burpee markets vegetable and flower seeds, bulbs, nursery stock, and garden supplies. Seeds account for about 63% of sales; plants 19%; trees 8%; shrubs, 1%. Research and hybridization are carried out at Burpee's Fordhook Farms. Company owns growing farms in PA, CA and Mexico. Heavy emphasis on flower seeds; secondary emphasis on vegetable seed marketing. Major season Feb.-May for seeds, and Sep.-Nov. for bulbs. Company markets products worldwide; employs 500-1,000 people.

COMPANY HISTORY
The company was founded in 1876 at Fordhook Farm by W. Atlee Burpee. First products were flower and vegetable seeds marketed primarily by mail to farmers. The company developed its first tomatoe and cucumber hybrids in 1945. Each year Burpee introduces new varieties of seeds--Sweet'n Early Cantaloupes, Long-Keeping Tomatoes, etc. In 1970, the business was purchased by General Foods. In 1979 it was acquired by ITT.

MARKETS
H.Q., Warminster, PA; research and hybridization, PA; mail order operations, midwest and CA.

FACILITIES
Customers 50% male/50% female; do-it-yourself vegetable growers and gardeners.

PRODUCTS, BRAND NAMES, PRICE RANGE
Burpee markets full range of seeds, bulbs, and
starters for flowering and decorative plants, vege-
tables, fruit and decorative trees and vines. Accessory lines include garden tools and equipment,
vegetable preparation accessories, indoor setups.

FINANCIAL INFORMATION

	SALES	NET INCOME	PROFIT MARGIN
1980	$42,000,000*	$1,050,000*	2.5%*

TYPE OF ADVERTISING, PROMOTION
Space advertising in newspapers and product-related
magazines. Catalogs mailed Feb./March and April/
May. Two basic catalogs: (1) main annual Burpee
Seed catalog--6-½ x 9, 180+ pages; (2) testing new
catalog for less experienced gardeners.

LIST INFORMATION
QUANTITY MAILED: 20,000,000*
AVERAGE ORDER: $17*
ACTIVE BUYERS: 990,000*
TOTAL LIST: 1,980,000
LIST SOURCE: Direct mail, space.

COMMENTS
Of Burpee's estimated $42 million in 1980 revenues,
approximately 60% or $25,200,000 came from consumer
mail order sales. The remaining 40% or $16,800,000
came from wholesale marketing to farmers, seed and
hardware stores, and institutions. Burpee's main
catalog is tailored to the needs of the experienced to
expert gardener. The main promotional emphasis is
on both the quantity and quality of the yield from
Burpee Seeds--"high yield" of "extremely large
produce." Burpee recently tested a new catalog
aimed at the market with less gardening experience
or limited space for planting. The catalog contains
20 pages with a limited offering of seeds, bulbs,
plants and gardening aids, and contains an eight
page section on garden planning. Special items
include the Patio Tower, which enables the gardener
to grow "dozens of plants in a 2' x 2' area;" the
Strawberrybush, a layered design which can accom-
modate up to 50 strawberry plants in a small area.

BUSINESS & INSTITUTIONAL FURNITURE

ADDRESS, PHONE
Business & Institutional Furniture, 611 N. Broadway, Milwaukee, WI 53202. Telephone: (414) 272-6080.

OWNERSHIP
Privately held; 100% of capital stock is owned by undisclosed private individuals.

MANAGEMENT
Greg Larson, President; Lawrence Clancy, Sec., Treas.; William Glassner, Jr., VP; George Mueller, Operations and List Manager; Randall Farah, Director of Marketing.

TYPE OF MARKETER
Mail order.

BUSINESS
B & I is one of the leading U.S. mail order marketers of office furnishings. Sales are to businesses, churches, hospitals, schools and institutions. B & I reportedly has 75,000 accounts throughout the U.S.; no international marketing. The company sells merchandise supplied by a variety of outside concerns; does no manufacturing.

COMPANY HISTORY
The business was founded as a mail order marketing operation in Wisconsin in the 1950s. It was incorporated as Business and Institutional Furniture in Wisconsin on February 12, 1960. Authorized capital consists of 200 shares of common stock with a $100 par value. Current unnamed owners purchased 100% of outstanding stock in 1975. B & I reports that sales are non-seasonal, and that the company employed 28 people in 1981.

MARKETS
Business, institutional, church and school buyers throughout the U.S.

FACILITIES

B & I leases 10,000 sq. ft. for headquarters, warehousing and fulfillment.

PRODUCTS, BRAND NAMES, PRICE RANGE

Desks, bookcases, filing cabinets, desk and folding chairs, work and conference tables, electronic and computer equipment, Accuride, Casio, Unitrex, Paymaster, 3M, Panasonic.

FINANCIAL INFORMATION

	SALES	NET INCOME	PROFIT MARGIN
1981	$8,500,000*	N.A.	--

TYPE OF ADVERTISING, PROMOTION

B & I relies solely on direct mail for their promotion and advertising. The main emphasis is on catalogs with several editions published annually. The company makes limited use of solo brochures.

LIST INFORMATION

QUANTITY MAILED:	4,500,000*
AVERAGE ORDER:	$275+
ACTIVE BUYERS:	40,000
TOTAL LIST:	200,000
LIST SOURCE:	Direct mail.

COMMENTS

Business and Institutional Furniture's total mail order sales for 1981 are estimated to be $8,500,000. Management reports that this is down from a 1979 peak of $11,000,000. Between 1979 and when current management assumed control in 1981, sales were depressed. Company officials report that they currently have some 75,000 total accounts. Their buyer file reportedly contains a sizeable percentage of annual repeat and multiple buyers and sales are steady throughout the year. The company publishes several editions of its catalog annually. The National Edition is 8-1/4 x 10-1/4, 64 pages, and offers 1,200 to 1,500 different items. The price position of this merchandise is mid to upscale with a high concentration of items between $70 and $150. In the most recent edition 40 of the 64 total pages are full-color.

CABELA'S

ADDRESS, PHONE
Cabela's, Inc., 812 13th Ave., Sidney, NE 69162.
Telephone: (308) 254-5505.

OWNERSHIP
Privately held; 100% of outstanding capital stock is owned by James and Richard Cabela.

MANAGEMENT
James W. Cabela, President; Richard N. Cabela, Vice President, Secretary, and Treasurer; Emil Assad, Controller.

TYPE OF MARKETER
Mail order, retail.

BUSINESS
Cabela's is a marketer of fishing tackle and supplies, sporting goods, and related outdoor and sporting apparel. Merchandise is sold by mail through catalogs, and through the company's one retail store. In addition to consumer sales, Cabela's sells wholesale to approximately one hundred commercial accounts. The company's sales are reportedly heaviest in early spring and fall. Cabela's reported 140 employees in 1981.

COMPANY HISTORY
The business was started in Chappell, Nebraska in 1962 to market fishing tackle by mail as a partnership between James and Richard Cabela. The company was incorporated in Nebraska on June 25, 1965. Authorized capital consists of 10,000 shares of common stock, with a $10 par value, owned equally by James and Richard Cabela. Headquarters was moved from Chappell to Sidney, Nebraska in 1968, and the retail store was opened in the same year.

MARKETS
Mail order buyers of sporting goods and apparel; sales are domestic; customers are mostly male.

FACILITIES

Leases 220,000 sq. ft. in three buildings for offices; 12,000 sq. ft. warehouse.

PRODUCTS, BRAND NAMES, PRICE RANGE

Camping equipment, archery equipment, hunting and ammunition reloading supplies, rods, reels, lures, fly-making kits, packs, jackets, rain gear. Price position is mid to low; prices range up to $110.00.

FINANCIAL INFORMATION

	SALES	NET INCOME	PROFIT MARGIN
1981	$20,000,000*	$400,000*	2%*

TYPE OF ADVERTISING, PROMOTION

The major percentage of Cabela's advertising is through catalogs which are published in the fall and spring. The company uses inquiry generating space ads in Field & Stream, Outdoor Life, Fur Fish & Game, and Sports Afield.

LIST INFORMATION

QUANTITY MAILED:	20,000,000*
AVERAGE ORDER:	$50
ACTIVE BUYERS:	396,000
TOTAL LIST:	1,200,000
LIST SOURCE:	Direct mail, space.

COMMENTS

Cabela's total sales for 1981 are estimated to be in excess of $20,000,000. This represents a 27% increase over the 1980 estimate of $15,700,000, 50% over $13,300,000 in 1979, and 122% over $9,000,000 in 1978. Management projects strong sales growth to continue over the next five years. Cabela's publishes a Spring and a Fall edition of their catalog each year. The catalogs are 8-1/4 x 10-3/4 and roughly 130 pages. They are mostly full color, with some black and white illustrations. Nearly 80% of the merchandise offered is fishing tackle and accessories. Over 50% of the items offered sell for below $10, and 75% below $20. Cabela's offers over 10,000 products, mostly private labels.

CADENCE INDUSTRIES

ADDRESS, PHONE

Cadence Industries Corp., 21 Henderson Drive, W. Caldwell, NJ 07006. Telephone: (201) 227-5100.

OWNERSHIP

Publicly held. Outstanding shares of common stock as of 12/31/80, 1,531,585. Low bid 7-5/8; high 18-1/4. No cash dividends paid.

MANAGEMENT

Sheldon Feinberg, Chairman of the Board, President; Joseph M. Walsh, Executive Vice President; Paul Hindin, Executive Vice President/Finance and Administration; Stuart J. Freedman, Vice President.

TYPE OF MARKETER

Mail order, retail, telephone sales.

BUSINESS

Cadence Industries is the holding company for over 10 subsidiaries and divisions which engage in various activities from comic book publication, to movie theater operation, to direct mail marketing of nutritional supplements, office supplies and advertising specialties. Company's two main direct mail subsidiaries are Hudson Pharmaceutical Corp. and U.S. Pencil and Stationery Co. Hudson sells vitamins and other nutritional products by mail; USCO sells pens, letter openers, stationery, and planners as ad specialties.

COMPANY HISTORY

In early 1960s, Martin Ackerman began acquiring existing companies under the United Whelan Corp. umbrella; name changed to Perfect Film & Chemical Corp. in 1967. Sheldon Feinberg took control in 1969 when declining business forced Perfect management out. Feinberg engineered massive reorganization between 1969 and 1971. By 1972, under new name Cadence Industries, operations had become profitable. Headquarters moved into new building in New Jersey in 1973.

MARKETS

Mail order sales are primarily domestic; Cadence Mail Order of Canada, Ltd., is a division of USCO.

FACILITIES
Main office in New Jersey; Canadian division (writing instruments) in Ontario. Hudson's retail nationwide.

PRODUCTS, BRAND NAMES, PRICE RANGE
Hudson manufactures Hudson, Truganic, Ecology and Spider Man children's brands; retail line is Vitamin Quota. USCO catalog contains a wide variety of promotional product offers; merchandise is manufactured and custom printed by outside concerns.

FINANCIAL INFORMATION

	SALES	**NET INCOME**	**PROFIT MARGIN**
1980	$131,340,000	$2,397,000	1.8%

TYPE OF ADVERTISING, PROMOTION
Advertising for mail order operations is done through catalogs (U.S. Pencil & Stationery), and direct mail package and inserts (Hudson). Mailings done throughout the year. Some space ads in Sunday supplements, newspapers and magazines.

LIST INFORMATION
QUANTITY MAILED: 26,500,000*
AVERAGE ORDER: $90 (USCO); $18 (Hudson)
ACTIVE BUYERS: 84,000 (USCO); N.A. (Hudson)
TOTAL LIST: 221,941 (USCO); 550,000 (Hudson)
LIST SOURCE: Direct mail.

COMMENTS
Pharmaceutical Products and Writing Instruments divisions account for a significant portion of Cadence total revenues: combined totals contributing some 37% to 40%. U.S. Pencil and Stationery and its Cadence Mail Order of Canada Division sell most of their merchandise through mail order catalogs. Division will concentrate its efforts on basic mail order operation and plans include limited product and catalog format tests. Cadence plans to expand their telemarketing operation as an adjunct to mail order, to further reduce high printing and mailing costs. Perfect Mailing Service, the mailing and fulfillment arm of USCO, has begun offering its services to businesses outside of Cadence. For Hudson Pharmaceutical, mail order was its initial form of marketing, and continues to be a strong sales contributor. Main emphasis in the consumer products segment is on aggressive advertising campaign to increase brand recognition and consumer acceptance both in mail order and retail channels.

CALHOUN'S COLLECTORS SOCIETY

ADDRESS, PHONE

Calhoun's Collectors Society, Inc., 7275 Bush Lake Road, Minneapolis, MN 55435. (612) 835-0300.

OWNERSHIP

Privately held; Stafford Calvin, Marvin Engler, and Harold Engler own 100% of capital stock.

MANAGEMENT

Stafford R. Calvin, Chairman, President; W. M. Zolchonock, Vice President of Finance; T. Lindemann, Vice President of Sales.

TYPE OF MARKETER

Mail order.

BUSINESS

Calhoun's is a 100% mail order marketer and designer of limited edition collectible items such as sculptures, stamps, plates, coins and other high-ticket items. Sales are primarily to individuals. Management reports that Calhoun's drops approximately 40,000,000 pieces of direct mail/collectible literature annually and that sales are relatively constant throughout the year. Mailing and shipping of merchandise is handled by outside services.

COMPANY HISTORY

Company was started in 1974 by Stafford Calvin and incorporated in Minnesota on May 15, 1974. The first products sold were sculptures and stamps. Although several small acquisitions have occurred, the company has grown principally through diversification into various forms of collectibles. Mail order was 100% of the original business. Company presently employs approximately 150 people.

MARKETS

Customers are 70% female. Products sold primarily in U.S. and Canada; some international sales.

FACILITIES

60,000 sq. ft. of office and warehouse space in two buildings; suburban commercial area.

PRODUCTS, BRAND NAMES, PRICE RANGE

Products include collectible items such as plates, numismatics, sculptures, museum replicas, graphics, bells. Brand name products like Royal Cornwall's, Zelda's of Apple Valley, and Calhoun's Collectors Society, Inc. Wide price range from $5 to $3,000.

FINANCIAL INFORMATION

	SALES	**NET INCOME**	**PROFIT MARGIN**
1981	$33,000,000*	N.A.	--

TYPE OF ADVERTISING, PROMOTION

Direct mail packages with limited advertising in collector and giftware publications and magazines such as Family Circle and Smithsonian; 10% of the company's advertising is spent on special catalogs, published twice a year.

LIST INFORMATION

QUANTITY MAILED:	40,000,000*
AVERAGE ORDER:	$425
ACTIVE BUYERS:	76,870*
TOTAL LIST:	600,000*
LIST SOURCE:	Direct mail.

COMMENTS

Calhoun's is a sales organization established to design, market, and broker collectible items for their society members. Most of the company's sales are continuity programs. When a customer sends in his order, he may sign up to purchase a unit every month. When an order is shipped, it contains an invoice for the duration of the program. Aside from merchandise promotion, society members receive a great deal of general product and collecting information through Calhoun's. All manufacturing and mail order fulfillment operations are contracted to outside firms. At present sales are estimated to be $33 million. Average order has increased to $425 and earnings are reportedly on an upward trend. The high ratio of pieces mailed to the number of active buyers is indicative of the quantity of collectible information mailings (aside from merchandise promotions) Calhoun's does.

CAMPING WORLD

ADDRESS, PHONE
Camping World, Inc., Beech Bend Road, Bowling Green, KY 42101. Telephone: (502) 781-2718.

OWNERSHIP
Subsidiary of Surrey Fields Corporation of Bowling Green, KY, which is privately held by David Garvin.

MANAGEMENT
David Garvin, President; Murray Coker, Vice President-Mail Order; Tad Donnelley, Vice President-Retail; William Johnson, Vice President-Finance; Steve Snodgrass, Vice President.

TYPE OF MARKETER
Mail order, retail.

BUSINESS
Camping World is a major marketer of recreational vehicle accessories and supplies. Currently the company operates five retail and service centers located in Kentucky, California, Texas, Florida, and South Carolina. Mail order operations are located near the company headquarters in Bowling Green. Camping World also manufactures and packages a limited line of its own products marketed through subsidiaries Prattco and Rite-Drain. Reported 250 employees for 1981.

COMPANY HISTORY
The company was started in 1967 by David Garvin at his father's campground and amusement park in Bowling Green. The first catalog was mailed in 1968. With initial direct mail promotions and limited retail exposure, business was almost 100% mail order. The present headquarters was built in 1973. Camping World built their west coast fulfillment facility in 1979, and moved mail order data processing into separate facility near headquarters in 1981.

MARKETS
Retail outlets located in sunbelt. Mail order operations in Bowling Green, and Valencia, CA.

FACILITIES

Mail order facility: Bowling Green, KY, Valencia, CA; Retail: KY, FL, SC, TX, and CA.

PRODUCTS, BRAND NAMES, PRICE RANGE

Air conditioners, awnings, generators, water supplies, housewares, and other RV accessories and gadgets. National brands include Coleman, Torro, Carefree. Wide price range.

FINANCIAL INFORMATION

	SALES	NET INCOME	PROFIT MARGIN
1981	$24,000,000	N.A.	--

TYPE OF ADVERTISING, PROMOTION

Two major catalogs are mailed per year, supplemented with specialized mini-catalogs and promotions. Additional advertising in specialty magazines, billboard ads, and broadcast.

LIST INFORMATION

QUANTITY MAILED:	2,000,000
AVERAGE ORDER:	$65
ACTIVE BUYERS:	250,000
TOTAL LIST:	450,000
LIST SOURCE:	Direct mail, space.

COMMENTS

The sales figure above represents Camping World's total revenues for 1981, including the sales from their retail outlets. The company's mail order sales have grown at an average annual rate of 25%. Company officials report that approximately 60% of their annual advertising budget is spent on catalog mailings and other direct mail promotions. The remainder is spent primarily on space ads in Trailer Life, Motor Home Life, Family Motor Camping, etc. The summer issue of the Camping World catalog is mailed starting in March; the winter issue dropped during the first week in September. The catalogs are 9-1/4 x 8-1/2, 96 pages, full color. Seasonal 8-page sale catalogs are mailed the day after Christmas and the day after July 4th. Flyers are mailed periodically to past buyers with coupons for mail order savings.

CARLSON MARKETING

ADDRESS, PHONE

Carlson Marketing Group, Inc., 12755 Highway 55, Minneapolis, MN 55441. Telephone: (612) 540-5000.

OWNERSHIP

Subsidiary of Carlson Companies, Inc., of Minneapolis; a diversified management company with about sixty subsidiaries.

MANAGEMENT

Curtis L. Carlson, Chairman of the Board; H. W. Greenough, Vice Chairman; E. C. Gage, President; Richard H. Adrian, Vice President and General Manager, Direct Mail Division.

TYPE OF MARKETER

Mail order, retail, syndication.

BUSINESS

Carlson Marketing Group is as diversified as its parent company with some 16 subsidiaries involved in consumer merchandising services, incentive and premium programs, and travel service. Major U.S. mail order operations include the Direct Mail Division which syndicates merchandise to banks and oil companies, and handles their fulfillment; Henniker's specialty gifts-by-mail cataloger; K-promotions, Milwaukee based in-flight magazine publisher. Carlson Marketing Group employs a total of 3,300.

COMPANY HISTORY

In 1938 Curtis L. Carlson founded the Gold Bond Stamp Co. in Minneapolis. In the early 1960's with the nationwide success of Gold Bond, Carlson initiated a broad diversification program to enter other consumer service areas. He incorporated Carlson Companies as the parent organization in 1972. Five years later he started Carlson Marketing and Motivation as a full-service consumer/business merchandising group. Name changed to Carlson Marketing Group in 1980.

MARKETS

Primarily domestic; Carlson Marketing Group, Ltd., of Toronto handles the Canadian market.

FACILITIES

Headquarters and most subsidiary operations in Minneapolis; K-Promotions in Milwaukee.

PRODUCTS, BRAND NAMES, PRICE RANGE

Direct Mail Division, Henniker's and K-Promotions all offer a wide assortment of mostly hardgoods, such as electronic items, watches, jewelry; many national brands. Limited clothing offerings. Price range generally starts around $20.

FINANCIAL INFORMATION

	SALES	NET INCOME	PROFIT MARGIN
1981	$100,000,000*	N.A.	--

TYPE OF ADVERTISING, PROMOTION

Direct Mail Division uses credit card statement inserts, catalogs, solo mailings for oil companies and banks. Also uses some space in magazines. Henniker's is a catalog operation with some space as adjunct. K-Promotions places "in-flight" catalogs.

LIST INFORMATION

QUANTITY MAILED:	50,000,000+*
AVERAGE ORDER:	$50
ACTIVE BUYERS:	12,000,000* (Direct Mail Division)
TOTAL LIST:	400,000 (Henniker's)
LIST SOURCE:	Direct Mail, space ads.

COMMENTS

Through an aggressive acquisition program initiated several years ago, Carlson Marketing has evidenced strong emphasis on direct mail for overall growth. Management reports they will seek to include more mail order operations under C.M. umbrella in coming years. Group acquired Henniker's name and lists from the Stuart McGuire Co. (Salem, VA) in the spring of '81. The first Henniker's catalog under Carlson was issued in the fall of '81 to about 1,000,000 recipients; officials are planning on four catalogs per year. K-Promotions' in-flight "shopping" magazines continue to be a strong contributor to sales with average order of $50. Management also expects some $40,000,000 in revenues from its Canadian arm, Carlson Marketing Group, Ltd. Recently acquired the Canadian catalog operations of Ambassador International. Also owns NSI Marketing, Canadian direct mail syndicator to oil companies. Carlson Marketing Group's direct mail operations are reported to figure heavily in the parent company's projected growth in sales past the $2 billion mark in 1982.

CASWELL-MASSEY

ADDRESS, PHONE
Caswell-Massey Company Ltd., 575 Lexington Ave., New York, NY 10022. Telephone: (212) 355-5775.

OWNERSHIP
The company is a wholly-owned subsidiary of privately-held Caswell-Massey Pharmacy, Inc., of New York, NY.

MANAGEMENT
Milton Taylor, President; Ralph Taylor, Vice President; Adam Taylor, Catalog/Mail Order Sales Manager; Joshua Taylor, Product Manager; Bill Padgett, VP-Sales.

TYPE OF MARKETER
Mail order, wholesale, retail.

BUSINESS
Caswell-Massey is positioned as an "apothecary" combining a wide variety of quality perfumes, colognes, toiletries, luxury soaps, and exotic accessories. They produce an extensive line of their own fragrances and products, and market a variety of other items imported from all over the world. Promotional emphasis is on high quality, luxury products. The company operates a mail order center and primary retail store described as a "functioning museum of apothecary arts," in New York City.

COMPANY HISTORY
The business was founded in 1752 in Newport, RI by Dr. William Hunter. During the Revolution Hunter's widow placed the company under the ownership of clerk Charles Feke to avoid its confiscation by the British. Ownership later passed to Rowland Hazard and Philip Caswell, and then to Caswell and William Massey. Present VP Ralph Taylor was hired to sweep the shop in 1916 when the business moved to New York. The Taylors bought the company in 1936.

MARKETS
Customers are primarily upscale, male and female, throughout U.S., Canada and overseas.

FACILITIES
Headquarters, mail order center, and laboratory in New York City; 30 retail franchises.

PRODUCTS, BRAND NAMES, PRICE RANGE
Variety of well-known fragrances marketed in various product forms including Jockey Club, Tricorn, Number Six (a favorite of George Washington's). Products of unusual character, without commercial processes and mass production techniques.

FINANCIAL INFORMATION

	SALES	NET INCOME	PROFIT MARGIN
1981	$10,000,000*	N.A.	--

TYPE OF ADVERTISING, PROMOTION
Caswell-Massey's advertising and promotional expenditures are broken down as follows: direct mail, 80%; space, 17%; radio, 2%; T.V., 1%. Space in New York Times Mag., New Yorker, GQ. Major catalog mailed mid-June, plus a Spring Compendium.

LIST INFORMATION

QUANTITY MAILED:	1,000,000+*
AVERAGE ORDER:	$38
ACTIVE BUYERS:	126,710
TOTAL LIST:	500,000*
LIST SOURCE:	Direct mail, space and inquiries.

COMMENTS
Caswell-Massey mails very unique and creative catalogs, developed in-house, utilizing turn-of-the-century motifs and engraving reproductions throughout. The company has enjoyed patronage of and designed fragrances for many celebrities in its history and uses this to enhance its positioning to serve elite or unique tastes. Mail order is major percentage of volume, though in recent years retail franchises have been sold to private owners: four new stores opened in 1981. The sales figure above is an estimate of the company's total 1981 mail order sales only. Due to their upscale position, management expects no adverse effects from spiraling postage rates. Postage and handling billed to customer at rate of 10% of order. For $1,000 pre-payment, Caswell-Massey will design a personalized scent for a customer, to be used in their products. This can be transacted completely through mail.

CHILDCRAFT EDUCATION CORPORATION

ADDRESS, PHONE

Childcraft Education Corporation, 20 Kilmer Road, Edison, NJ 08818. Telephone: (201) 572-6100.

OWNERSHIP

Publicly-held; stock traded OTC; 10% of outstanding stock held by officers.

MANAGEMENT

Lloyd Otterman, President; Stephen L. Brotman, Vice President, Secretary-Treasurer; John DiGiacomo, VP-Direct Marketing.

TYPE OF MARKETER

Mail order, retail.

BUSINESS

Childcraft markets children's educational toys and equipment to schools, day-care centers, institutions and consumers. Approximately 95% of sales are mail order, the remaining 5% from company's three retail outlets. Company manufactures some 125 products and markets over 2,000 brands--many nationally known. Products are for children of all ages, providing them with the opportunity for discovery, fun and growth. Peak sales period between June and December. Company employs 150 people.

COMPANY HISTORY

Childcraft Equipment Company was started in New York in 1945 by Benjamin Albert, and incorporated in Oct., 1952. On June 27, 1969, the name was changed to Childcraft Education Corporation. The first products manufactured were primarily play furniture and equipment, and portable storage units, which are still major sellers. Originally Childcraft operated as a wholesaler for schools; mail order was added in 1962. They have been located at present address since 1973.

MARKETS

Schools, institutions, child care centers, and consumers primarily in the U.S.

FACILITIES

Leases 140,000 sq. ft.; this space used for offices and distributing.

PRODUCTS, BRAND NAMES, PRICE RANGE

Company manufactures about 25% of the products it sells. Major percentage are national brands, including Milton Bradley. Wide variety of products include toys, furniture, playhouses, storage units, science and musical equipment. Prices: $2-500.

FINANCIAL INFORMATION

	SALES	NET INCOME	PROFIT MARGIN
1981	$16,408,933	$587,307	3.6%

TYPE OF ADVERTISING, PROMOTION

The majority of Childcraft's advertising is done through direct mail catalogs and institutional wholesaling. Catalog operations supported by limited space in magazines such as New Yorker and Parents.

LIST INFORMATION

QUANTITY MAILED: 3,000,000*
AVERAGE ORDER: $36 (consumer purchase)
ACTIVE BUYERS: 118,400
TOTAL LIST: 188,800
LIST SOURCE: Direct 80%, space 20%.

COMMENTS

Sales, earnings, net worth and net working capital have increased in each of the past three years. Sales for the fiscal year ending in 1981 increased 2.3% over 1980 sales. For the same period earnings increased 15.5%. While institutional sales decreased 3%, consumer sales increased approximately 15% as a result of higher average sale as well as some price increases. Management projects this upward trend to continue. The company's subsidiary, Childcraft Centers, Inc., has three retail branch operations, two in New York and one in Edison, New Jersey. The first opened when company started, the second in 1952, and the third, in Edison, was opened in 1973. Management reported no plans to open any new branches or to change operational procedures or facilities in the forthcoming year. Currently, the mail order division publishes two catalogs per year, mailed March and August. School catalog is published and mailed once per year. All are 8 x 11, full-color.

CLYMER'S

ADDRESS, PHONE
Clymer's of Buck's County, Inc., Pine Street, Nashua, NH 03061. Telephone: (603) 882-9500.

OWNERSHIP
Subsidiary of privately-held Direct Order Sales Corporation, 141 Canal Street, Nashua, NH 03061.

MANAGEMENT
Thomas J. Litle, President and Treasurer; Joan B. Litle, Vice President; James L. Walters, Officer.

TYPE OF MARKETER
Mail order, retail.

BUSINESS
Clymer's is a catalog marketer specializing in general, high-priced gift items. Products consist of unusual and unique gifts including collectible and handcrafted goods. Color catalogs are mailed six times per year. All Seasons Outdoor Sports Center is a mail order division of Clymer's. The division features outdoor apparel, equipment, and unique sports gifts. Sports Center catalogs are mailed four times per year. All sales are cash. The company has one retail outlet at Nashua, and employs 100 people.

COMPANY HISTORY
Business was started in September, 1937 at Point Pleasant, Buck's County, PA, by the Clymer family. In August, 1972 Clymer's moved to Nashua, NH and became a division of Doehla, Inc. On January 1, 1978 Clymer's was purchased by Thomas and Joan Litle and James Walters under the corporate name of Direct Order Sales Corporation. All Seasons Outdoor Sports Center was founded in Los Angeles in 1967 as the Sports Liquidators Catalog, and purchased by Clymer's in September, 1980 from Sportsco.

MARKETS
Clymer's sells gifts and sporting goods by mail throughout the U.S. and its territories.

FACILITIES

Warehouse, customer service, order entry offices and retail store in Nashua, NH.

PRODUCTS, BRAND NAMES, PRICE RANGE

Gift items are unique and upscale. Collectible soft sculptures, ceramics, brass, pewter, and glass. Prices range from $10 - $450. All Seasons markets hunting and fishing apparel, equipment, footwear, tools, and gifts. Prices: from $15 - $150.

FINANCIAL INFORMATION

	SALES	NET INCOME	PROFIT MARGIN
1981	$19,000,000*	N.A.	--

TYPE OF ADVERTISING, PROMOTION

Clymer's: 95% catalog mailings; space ads in House Beautiful, House & Garden, Yankee, and Better Homes & Gardens. Catalogs are mailed 6 times per year. Peak season, fall. All Seasons: 85% catalog mailings; 15% space ads.

LIST INFORMATION

QUANTITY MAILED:	9,000,000*
AVERAGE ORDER:	$35
ACTIVE BUYERS:	540,000
TOTAL LIST:	2,200,000
LIST SOURCE:	Direct mail, space.

COMMENTS

The sales figure above is an estimate of total revenues from Clymer's and All Seasons mail order operations. Mail order estimate is broken down as follows: Clymer's, $10,500,000*; All Seasons, $8,500,000*. No accurate estimate was available for the sales from company's one retail outlet. In addition, the list information combines Clymer's and All Seasons data. Clymer's catalogs are color and approximately 56 pages. All Seasons has a color catalog, 32 pages long. Promotion includes package inserts. Clymer's does not use charge card services -- all sales are cash. The 1981 postal rate increase has Clymer's reconsidering both the weight and size of their current catalog. Currently orders are processed in about a week to 10 days, peak season averages closer to 10 days.

COLLIN STREET BAKERY

ADDRESS, PHONE

Collin Street Bakery, Inc., 401 S. Seventh, Corsicana, TX 75110. Telephone: (214) 872-3951.

OWNERSHIP

Collin Street is privately held; Chairman L. W. McNutt, Jr. holds 55% of outstanding stock.

MANAGEMENT

L. W. McNutt, Jr., President and Chairman; John R. Crawford, VP; Lamar Hunt, VP; H. Maurice Pollock, VP, Secretary & Treasurer; Harry T. Cook, VP; Norman E. Shaw, VP.

TYPE OF MARKETER

Mail order.

BUSINESS

Collin Street operates bakery and distribution divisions which produce and market old-fashioned style fruitcakes and pastries. The company is a 100% mail order operation with customers in over 100 different foreign markets. A major portion of their customers are commercial accounts, churches and service groups which buy baked products in quantity as gifts. Peak sales are during the holiday seasons, and Collin Street employs up to 750 people during these times.

COMPANY HISTORY

Collin Street Bakery was founded in 1896 by Master Baker Gus Weidmann and Tom McElwee and was incorporated in Texas in September of 1908. The present controlling officers took charge in 1946. The company has been honored by Monde Selection and the New York Gourmet Society, and designated a Historical Landmark by the Texas State Historical Society.

MARKETS

Company sells products by mail throughout the U.S. and its possessions, in Canada, and overseas.

FACILITIES

The company moved into its present headquarters, baking facilities, and storage buildings in 1965.

PRODUCTS, BRAND NAMES, PRICE RANGE

Fruit cakes are 95% of company's production, marketed under DeLuxe brand name; other 5% of production is pastry. Prices range from $9 to $21 per cake, regular rate. Price list includes quantity order reductions.

FINANCIAL INFORMATION

	SALES	**NET INCOME**	**PROFIT MARGIN**
1981	$15,000,000*	N.A.	--

TYPE OF ADVERTISING, PROMOTION

Collin Street spends approximately 20% of its advertising budget on space ads in a variety of magazines and newspapers during holiday seasons. The other 80% is spent on annual mailings of direct mail packages including brochure and order form.

LIST INFORMATION

QUANTITY MAILED: 6,000,000
AVERAGE ORDER: $36
ACTIVE BUYERS: 322,000
TOTAL LIST: 900,000
LIST SOURCE: Direct mail, space.

COMMENTS

Collin Street is promotionally positioned as "A small town bakery--A world famous fruit cake." The company began its heavy involvement in mail order marketing in the early 1950's. Its main type of direct mail promotion has been a folded brochure, 8 - 1/2 x 14 - 1/2, full color. Collin Street mails to past buyers and a considerable number of prospective accounts once a year, between October and November. The peak sales season, October through early December, reflects the company's "Christmas Gift" position. Management reports that they are considering some new products to improve off-season sales, but that they will maintain primary emphasis on DeLuxe Fruit Cakes, individual attention and mailing service for customers, and Christmas sales. Collin Street's active buyer file contains a considerable number of corporate buyers, many of which are also commercial accounts which make quantity purchases. The company operates one small retail facility at headquarters for local and tourist trade.

COLONIAL PENN GROUP

ADDRESS, PHONE
Colonial Penn Group, 5 Penn Center Plaza, Philadelphia, PA 19181. Telephone: (215) 988-8000.

OWNERSHIP
Publicly held; shares traded NYSE and Midwest; 16,124,000 common shares outstanding; FY81 bids: high 24-3/8, low 13-1/2; dividend, $1.40/share.

MANAGEMENT
John J. MacWilliams, Chmn., CEO; Herbert J. Grubb, Pres.; Exec. VPs: James E. Brennan, Finance; Senior VPs: William Bennington, Corp. Affairs; Daniel Crough, Counsel and Secretary.

TYPE OF MARKETER
Mail order, direct sales.

BUSINESS
Holding company of subsidiaries engaged in mass marketing and management of insurance, group travel tours, temporary employment programs, real estate information publications, and a retirement community. Primary business is soliciting, issuing, and administering health, life, automobile, homeowners and other insurance policies. Predecessor companies of what is now Colonial Penn pioneered in mass marketing health insurance designed for older Americans.

COMPANY HISTORY
In 1955 predecessor companies of CP Group set up the first nationwide guaranteed issue group health insurance program for older persons. In 1962, offered members of National Retired Teachers Association and American Association of Retired Persons the first guaranteed issue individual life insurance policy, an exclusive arrangement which was a major factor in company growth. The company lost NRTA and AARP group health program contracts in 1981.

MARKETS
55,000,000+ Americans over 50 are potential customers. Offices: PA, HI, U.K., Norway, Italy, Spain.

FACILITIES

Hqs. with in-house ad agency, DP & direct mail ops. in Philadelphia; 6 regional offices; 5 travel offices.

PRODUCTS, BRAND NAMES, PRICE RANGE

Health (50%) is primarily indemnity-type products, service types supplement Medicare. Ordinary group and reinsurance life (10%). Property, liability, auto, homeowners, renters (30%). Tours, travel; employment service, retirement community (10%).

FINANCIAL INFORMATION

	SALES	NET INCOME	PROFIT MARGIN
1981	$1,254,498,000	$(23,368,000)	-0-

TYPE OF ADVERTISING, PROMOTION

Direct mail solicitation; direct response TV ads for auto, health, and homeowners insurance; newsletter; sponsorship of TV series Over Easy, Perspectives on Aging university lectures series; Older Worker Seminars.

LIST INFORMATION

QUANTITY MAILED:	150,000,000
AVERAGE ORDER:	Various
ACTIVE BUYERS:	'81 policyholders: 2,500,000 health
TOTAL LIST:	N.A.
LIST SOURCE:	Direct mail, space, broadcast.

COMMENTS

CP Group's Chairman, John MacWilliams, had described present situation as an era of "New Freedom" after losing endorsement of American Association of Retired Persons (AARP) and National Retired Teachers Association (NRTA) effective July 1, 1981. Increased sales efforts, more intensive product and institutional advertising on radio and TV. Write-offs in connection with the April-to-June '81 direct marketing campaign to retain group health insurance customers from AARP/ NRTA, and loss of 74% of that business despite the $18,000,000 campaign--all contributed to CP's second quarter 1981 operating loss of $3,200,000. 1981 first half operating profit plunged 97% to $999,000. In 1980, approximately 92% of direct health premiums were derived from members of AARP/NRTA. With only 26% retained, CP has launched intensive marketing activities directed toward a broader base of older Americans, and is also exploring new products. Operating expense reductions included layoffs of over 300 employees in 1980, reducing the total to 3,700 at year's end.

COLUMBIA HOUSE

ADDRESS, PHONE
Columbia House, 1211 Avenue of the Americas, New York, NY 10036. Telephone: (212) 975-8540.

OWNERSHIP
Division of publicly-held CBS, Inc., 51 West 52nd Street, New York, NY 10019.

MANAGEMENT
Benjamin Ordover, President of Columbia House Division.

TYPE OF MARKETER
Mail order.

BUSINESS
Columbia House is the world's largest mail order distributor of recorded music. Its principal business activity, the Columbia Record and Tape Club, offers members a choice of music on many recording labels. In 1980, contract was signed with First Generation Records to distribute recordings of Grand Ole Opry stars. The Canadian Record & Tape Club is promoting sales in the French-speaking consumer market. Columbia House also sells several continuity book series and craft books and kits.

COMPANY HISTORY
Columbia Record Club started in 1955 amidst great controversy in record retailing circles. At the outset, record dealers got commissions on direct sales made by Club. In the late '60s, the record club was moved from the music group into the more diversified Columbia Group and renamed Columbia House. Continuity books and craft kits added in early to mid '70s, enjoyed a few years of success, and declined. Late in '80 C.H. was transferred back into successful CBS/ Records Group.

MARKETS
Mail order record and tape buyers throughout the U.S. and Canada.

FACILITIES

H.Q., New York; main fulfillment center and manufacturing facility, Terre Haute, IN.

PRODUCTS, BRAND NAMES, PRICE RANGE

Records and tapes under many major recording labels; merchandise including phonographs, televisions, tape cassettes, and cameras; a variety of books on human behavior, the occult, warfare, automobiles, motorcycles.

FINANCIAL INFORMATION

	SALES	NET INCOME	PROFIT MARGIN
1980	$250,000,000*	N.A.	--

TYPE OF ADVERTISING, PROMOTION

Direct mail, space ads in national magazines, newspapers, Sunday supplements. Catalogs, 5" x 8", about 25 pages, are mailed 13 times a year to members. Catalog features records and tapes available through the club, which is negative option.

LIST INFORMATION

QUANTITY MAILED:	25,000,000
AVERAGE ORDER:	N.A.
ACTIVE BUYERS:	4,000,000
TOTAL LIST:	8,000,000*
LIST SOURCE:	Space, direct mail, broadcast.

COMMENTS

1980 was a disappointing year for Columbia House, which suffered a 6% dip in revenue and a 63% plunge in operating profit. In FY80 the division not only began phasing out its craft and continuity book clubs, but also signed an agreement to sell its hobby knives and miniature furniture kit operations to Hunt Manufacturing for $14.3 million in cash and notes. Intentions are to return the focus to direct marketing of audio and video entertainment. Management expects this emphasis to revitalize the Columbia Record and Tape Club, which in 1980 suffered lower than expected enrollments of new members and increased numbers of merchandise returns. CH's efforts to get in on the emerging home video market have resulted in the development of specialized musical video discs. "Mickey Mouse Disco" sold successfully in 1980, and new discs are being tested for '81 promotion.

COMBINED INTERNATIONAL

ADDRESS, PHONE
Combined International Corp., 707 Combined Centre, Northbrook, IL 60062. Telephone: (312) 564-8000.

OWNERSHIP
Publicly held; stock traded NYSE; 27,849,000 common shares outstanding; 1980 dividend: $1.45; 1980 price range: 20-3/8 to 16-1/2.

MANAGEMENT
W. Clement Stone, Chairman of the Board and Director; Ronald K. Holmberg, Executive Vice President and Treasurer.

TYPE OF MARKETER
Mail order, direct sales.

BUSINESS
Through its major subsidiary, Combined Insurance Co. of America, and that firm's subsidiaries, Combined International Corp. is a major writer of accident, health and life insurance policies. A direct sales force provides the major portion of policy sales, with mail order accounting for 7% of direct premiums. Combined International's 1981 acquisition of the Union Fidelity Corp., a major mail order insurance marketer, should boost Combined International's mail order sales considerably in coming years.

COMPANY HISTORY
W. Clement Stone, the current chairman of the board, founded the company nearly 60 years ago. The business started out with an accent on direct marketing--first of accident and later of health and life insurance products. In 1980, Combined International was created as a holding company (incorporated in Delaware) and became the parent company and sole stockholder of Combined Insurance Company of America. At that time, trading in Combined International shares began on the NYSE.

MARKETS
Sales force operates domestically and internationally; mail order is primarily domestic.

FACILITIES
Executive offices and mail order operations in North-brook, IL; Union Fidelity HQ in Trevose, PA.

PRODUCTS, BRAND NAMES, PRICE RANGE
Combined sells a variety of life and health policies including all-accident, disability, hospital, limited-accident, etc. 1980 breakdown of written premiums: accident and health 71.6%; life 16.5%; reinsurance 11.9%.

FINANCIAL INFORMATION

	SALES	NET INCOME	PROFIT MARGIN
1980	$596,201,000	$96,993,000	16.3%

TYPE OF ADVERTISING, PROMOTION
The direct sales force is the biggest source of new business; company mails to its current policyholders throughout the year to offer additional coverage. Mailings are specific offers for increased coverage and additional policies.

LIST INFORMATION

QUANTITY MAILED:	N.A.
AVERAGE ORDER:	N.A.
ACTIVE BUYERS:	N.A.
TOTAL LIST:	N.A.
LIST SOURCE:	Policyholders.

COMMENTS
Although mail order has accounted for only 7% of total direct premiums in recent years, that figure will increase as Combined International moves more aggressively into mail order. Company officials expect the acquisition of the profitable Union Fidelity Corp., a major direct mail insurance seller, to boost sales and income for 1982, and they are looking to acquire even more complementary operations. In 1980, mail order generated approximately $41,734,000 in premiums written, which represents a 5% increase over $39,728,000 the year before. This equals the 5.0% overall premium increase for Combined as a whole. Net income showed a 6.6% increase over the previous year. Management attributes their success in highly competitive insurance market to a variety of specialized programs. One example is a unique income insurance program for women.

COMMERCE CLEARING HOUSE

ADDRESS, PHONE

Commerce Clearing House, Inc., 4025 W. Peterson Avenue, Chicago, IL 60646. Phone: (312) 583-8500.

OWNERSHIP

Publicly held; stock traded OTC; FY81 shares outstanding, 9,000,001; bids: high 57-1/4, low 27; cash dividend, $1.19.

MANAGEMENT

Oakleigh B. Thorne, Chairman; Richard T. Merrill, President & CEO; Edward L. Massie, Executive VP; Bernard Elafros, VP & Treas.; John L. Randolph, VP & Secretary; Mary Ann Hynes, VP & Counsel.

TYPE OF MARKETER

Mail order, direct sales.

BUSINESS

Company is involved in publishing and updating reports on federal and state taxes, trade and labor regulations, and federal securities law. In addition it provides computer processing for income tax preparation, and other corporate services. With recent acquisitions, the company has moved into providing complete turnkey minicomputer systems, as well as on-line tax compliance services. CCH has 5,109 employees.

COMPANY HISTORY

CCH started approximately 50 years ago (incorporated in Delaware) for the purposes of keeping lawyers, accountants and corporate management abreast of an ever increasing stream of state and federal regulations. It has since expanded into new markets (Canada, Australia), and has even tested expansion into entirely different businesses such as its acquistion of Cuvaison, Inc., a California vineyard and winery operation (sold at a profit in July 1979).

MARKETS

Accountants, lawyers, tax specialists, corporations, libraries, schools, governmental agencies.

FACILITIES
Chicago headquarters. Subsidiaries in New York, Washington, D.C., Australia, England.

PRODUCTS, BRAND NAMES, PRICE RANGE
Loose-leaf reports within specific classes provide latest decisions, rules and interpretations, along with CCH explanations, on subjects such as taxes, business practices, regulations, etc. Germane booklets and casebooks complement the reports.

FINANCIAL INFORMATION

	SALES	NET INCOME	PROFIT MARGIN
1981	$312,616,775	$28,772,532	9%

TYPE OF ADVERTISING, PROMOTION
CCH uses direct mail promotions and a force of 500 sales representatives (in the U.S.) to solicit subscriptions for their publications and orders for their corporate services.

LIST INFORMATION

QUANTITY MAILED:	(Commerce Clearing House does
AVERAGE ORDER:	not release figures on their
ACTIVE BUYERS:	buyers, or make any type of
TOTAL LIST:	house list available for mar-
LIST SOURCE:	keting.)

COMMENTS
CCH is a prime example of a business-to-business direct marketer relying on both direct selling techniques and direct mail solicitations to procure orders. Company has shown steady increases in sales and earnings, with sales up 78% and net profits up 96% during the last five years. CCH has been active in acquisitions in U.S. and foreign markets: Washington Service Bureau, Inc. and Formules Municipales Ltee (the Quebec based French language publisher) in 1979; CCH Computax Systems, Inc. (subsidiary combining the acquired operations of RJ Software Systems and Professional Software Consultants, Inc.) and Multi-Tax (providing on-line tax compliance and planning services) became part of CCH operations in 1980. A promising new publication is Financial and Estate Planning, begun in 1980. At the end of 1980, orders already booked for 1981 and future years set new records for the company.

COMP-U-CARD

ADDRESS, PHONE

Comp-U-Card Of America, Inc., 777 Summer St., Stamford, CT 06901. Telephone: (203) 324-9261.

OWNERSHIP

Privately held; Walter Forbes owns majority of capital stock. Other investors own less than 25% of total capital.

MANAGEMENT

Walter Forbes, Chrmn., CEO; V. D'Agostino, Dir., Information Systems; Hsueh-wei Wang, Dir., Consumer Electronic Systems; R. Maddox, Pres., Comp-U-Claim; J. Fulmer, Pres., Marketing.

TYPE OF MARKETER

Mail order.

BUSINESS

Comp-U-Card claims to be the largest electronic shopping service in the U.S. In addition they claim to be the first toll-free shopping service, the first interactive computer shopping service and the first satellite cable TV shopping service. Operating divisions: Comp-U-Star: interactive computer shopping; Comp-U-Store: computer/video disc shopping in retail stores; Comp-U-Claim: Computer database for insurance claims adjustment; Shopping By Satellite: Cable TV shopping program.

COMPANY HISTORY

Comp-U-Card of America was started by Walter Forbes and others in 1973 with an initial investment from Management Analysis Center, Inc. of Cambridge, MA. Since that time partial interests have been sold to Merrill Lynch and Co., Federated Department Stores, Equitable Life Assurance, Reader's Digest Assoc., and most recently Jack Eckerd Corp. These investors control less than 25% of capital. Comp-U-Claim division was formed in 1979, Comp-U-Star in 1980, and Comp-U-Store in 1981.

MARKETS

Discount-minded shoppers who use their membership to get price reductions on merchandise.

FACILITIES

Headquarters and marketing operations at Stamford location; main computers in Columbus, OH.

PRODUCTS, BRAND NAMES, PRICE RANGE

Customers purchase a membership in Comp-U-Card Of America which makes services mentioned above available to them. New service provides a free VISA credit card to members. Cost of membership has risen in the past two years from $12.00 to $25.00.

FINANCIAL INFORMATION

	SALES	NET INCOME	PROFIT MARGIN
1981	$25,000,000*	N.A.	--

TYPE OF ADVERTISING, PROMOTION

Promotes general Money Saver membership through direct mail packages containing Super Value News-letter, Marketplace catalog of merchandise, discount coupons and special offers. Other divisions make heavy use of direct mail for business promotions.

LIST INFORMATION

QUANTITY MAILED:	N.A.
AVERAGE ORDER:	$25
ACTIVE BUYERS:	2,000,000
TOTAL LIST:	N.A.
LIST SOURCE:	N.A.

COMMENTS

Comp-U-Card's primary service is providing a computer database which reportedly supplies price information on over 50,000 name-brand products. Through $25 Money Saver membership, the reported 2,000,000 Comp-U-Card members receive discounts of 10% to 40% off manufacturers' suggested retail; Comp-U-Card gets a 3% to 5% commission on these sales. Income reportedly is mainly membership fees. Comp-U-Star division provides this database service to a reported 40,000 home computer owners. Comp-U-Store division plans to provide this and other product information on computer terminals and video discs in retail outlets. The company reportedly has signed with Metromedia (Seacaucus, NJ) to produce a 2-hr.-per-day cable home video shopping program (telephone ordering). In addition Comp-U-Card recently announced that through major credit card processor Banc One, they will be providing free VISA cards to qualified members.

JOAN COOK

ADDRESS, PHONE
Joan Cook, Inc., 3200 S.E. 14th Avenue, Fort Lauderdale, FL 33316. Telephone: (305) 761-1600.

OWNERSHIP
Privately held; the company is owned by a partnership between Joan and James Cook.

MANAGEMENT
James T. Cook, President; Joan Cook, Secretary and Treasurer; Stewart Haslam, Production Manager, Comptroller, and List Manager.

TYPE OF MARKETER
Mail order.

BUSINESS
Joan Cook is a 100% mail order marketer of general merchandise including novelties and gifts, household decorative and furnishing items, kitchen and bath accessories, toys, electronic devices, etc. All of the company's sales are through catalogs mailed throughout the U.S. Joan Cook does no manufacturing or international marketing, and reports that sales are fairly consistent throughout the year.

COMPANY HISTORY
The company was founded as a partnership between Joan Cook and husband James in New York City in 1955. The business moved to its present location in Fort Lauderdale in 1968. It was incorporated as Joan Cook, Inc. in Florida on September 18, 1972. Authorized capital consists of 7,000 shares of capital stock, with a $1.00 par value, which are jointly owned by James and Joan. The company reported 125 employees in 1981.

MARKETS
Mail order general merchandise buyers throughout the U.S.; no international; 91% women.

FACILITIES

Joan Cook owns a 60,000 square foot building housing headquarters and mail order operations.

PRODUCTS, BRAND NAMES, PRICE RANGE

Wide variety of general merchandise purchased from outside manufacturers. Prices range from $5.00 to $150.00 with the heaviest concentration of items between $10.00 and $30.00.

FINANCIAL INFORMATION

	SALES	NET INCOME	PROFIT MARGIN
1981	$17,000,000*	N.A.	--

TYPE OF ADVERTISING, PROMOTION

The majority of Joan Cook's promotion is through their catalogs. Catalogs are published and mailed twice annually, for a total of approximately 15,000,000 pieces. In addition the company uses space to generate catalog inquiries.

LIST INFORMATION

QUANTITY MAILED:	15,000,000*
AVERAGE ORDER:	$41
ACTIVE BUYERS:	438,000
TOTAL LIST:	997,000
LIST SOURCE:	Direct mail, space.

COMMENTS

Joan Cook is one of the leading U.S. catalog marketers of general merchandise. The company's total revenues for 1981 are estimated at between $17,000,000 and $20,000,000, and operations are reportedly profitable. Joan Cook places a major promotional emphasis on their merchandise mix being "a cut above" their general merchandise mail order competitors. Indeed their price position is significantly higher than that of competitors such as Miles Kimball. Catalogs contain a high percentage of apparel, jewelry, calculators and other electronic devices, and even a 3M Home/Office Copy machine selling for $150.00. Joan Cook's catalogs are full-color, 8-3/8 x 5-3/8, 64 to 96 pages, and contain approximately 300 items. Separate editions are published in the spring and fall each year.

COSMETIQUE BEAUTY CLUB

ADDRESS, PHONE

Cosmetique Beauty Club, Inc., 5320 N. Kedzie Ave., Chicago, IL 60625. Telephone: (312) 583-5410.

OWNERSHIP

Subsidiary of privately-held Posen Enterprises, Inc., of Chicago.

MANAGEMENT

June Posen, President; Charles Campbell, VP, General Manager; Joseph Lavin, VP; Harold Shade, VP; Carol Moriarty, Media Manager; Ed Allen, VP-Purchasing.

TYPE OF MARKETER

Mail order, continuity club.

BUSINESS

Cosmetique uses direct mail promotions and space advertising to offer membership in their beauty club. The initial $1 membership includes an introductory beauty kit reportedly worth an estimated $100. The buying program then continues as a negative-option plan. Kits are mailed to members every two months at an average selling price of $7.95 plus postage. Company also offers extensive ride-along, package insert, and statement stuffer direct mail programs.

COMPANY HISTORY

Michael and June Posen originally got involved in mail order with their Posen Enterprises vitamins-by-mail business, Golden 50 Pharmaceutical Co. In 1974, with a $5,000,000 investment drawn from the vitamin business, they started the Cosmetique Beauty Club as a subsidiary under the Posen Enterprises umbrella. The company became profitable after offering their first 12 kits in the first 2 years of operation. Cosmetique currently reports 230 employees.

MARKETS

Sells domestically; market is 100% female, age 16 and up, with median age of 26.

FACILITIES
Headquarters, telephone and computer facilities, Chicago; warehouse and fulfillment in Niles.

PRODUCTS, BRAND NAMES, PRICE RANGE
Markets kits containing such name brand cosmetics and fragrances as Schiaparelli, Lancome, Orlane, Varissa, Dionne Von Furstenberg, Jean D'Albret, Marian Bialac, Village Musk and Adrien Arpel. Introductory kit is $1; additional kits $7.95.

FINANCIAL INFORMATION

	SALES	NET INCOME	PROFIT MARGIN
1981	$26,000,000*	N.A.	--

TYPE OF ADVERTISING, PROMOTION
About 60% space ads/order cards in major women's and general interest magazines. Other 40% package inserts with other companies' deliveries. To get new names, members are offered various premiums for each friend who pays $7.95 for her first two kits.

LIST INFORMATION

QUANTITY MAILED:	10,000,000*
AVERAGE ORDER:	$10
ACTIVE BUYERS:	400,000
TOTAL LIST:	4,300,000
LIST SOURCE:	Magazines, package inserts.

COMMENTS
Through the past six years, Cosmetique's sales volume has shown steady increases, and management expects this trend to continue. Estimates indicate that from 1977 through 1978, sales doubled from $10,000,000 to $20,000,000. Management attributes success to the fact that they offer full, retail size containers of products (rather than samplers) at reduced prices. The key to profitability is volume sales, since overhead is fairly constant after a certain volume is reached. Company reports good business relationship with suppliers: Cosmetique pays for products and packaging; products are timed so members won't receive the same item in successive kits; once product is sampled in kit, customer must purchase it from retail outlet. Kits are mailed with teaser flyer about the next kit, and in some cases how-to folder. Member information such as color choices, skin tone, and skin type is computerized, and kit offerings are adjusted accordingly.

CREDIT CARD SERVICE CORP.

ADDRESS, PHONE
Credit Card Service Corp., 510 King Street, Alexandria, VA 22314. Telephone: (703) 836-8000.

OWNERSHIP
Privately held; the officers of the corporation own one hundred percent of capital stock.

MANAGEMENT
John P. Ferry, Chairman, President and Treasurer; Michael Cossel, Executive Vice President and Secretary; Walter F. Holfje, Vice President; Clifford Pendrell, Marketing Manager.

TYPE OF MARKETER
Mail order.

BUSINESS
Credit Card Service Corporation provides a central registration service for credit card holders. Under the trade style Credit Card Service Bureau of America, the company offers the following services: (1) notifies all credit card issuers involved in the event of cardholder reporting loss or theft of card; (2) notifies all issuers for the cardholder of changes of address; (3) provides interest-free emergency cash loans; (4) provides cardholder with interest-free emergency airline tickets.

COMPANY HISTORY
The company was founded in the late 1960s in Virginia by John P. Ferry and others. It was incorporated under the name Credit Card Service Corporation in Delaware on April 3, 1969. Authorized capital consists of 1,000,000 shares of common stock, with a $.10 par value, all of which is owned by Ferry and the other officers. The corporation reported 350 employees including the officers in 1981.

MARKETS
C.C.S.B. markets services by mail to lists of card holders throughout U.S. and abroad.

FACILITIES

The company leases 12,000 sq. ft. at the Alexandria, Virginia location for headquarters and all operations.

PRODUCTS, BRAND NAMES, PRICE RANGE

C.C.S.B. sells their four main services as a package program on a one or three year basis. Rates for this protection service are $12.00 annually, or $27.00 for three years. In addition, the company offers a registration service for valuable possessions.

FINANCIAL INFORMATION

	SALES	NET INCOME	PROFIT MARGIN
1981	$19,000,000*	N.A.	--

TYPE OF ADVERTISING, PROMOTION

The company markets its services by direct mail, telephone sales, and inquiry-generating space ads. They mail a series of direct mail packages to house and rented lists and place inserts in the statements of many credit card issuers.

LIST INFORMATION

QUANTITY MAILED:	N.A. (C.C.S.B. does not mar-
AVERAGE ORDER:	N.A. ket its list or make avail-
ACTIVE BUYERS:	N.A. lable any information on
TOTAL LIST:	N.A. its house buyer file.)
LIST SOURCE:	Direct mail, rentals, phone sales.

COMMENTS

Credit Card Service Corporation is one of the leading loss-notification services for credit card holders throughout the U.S. and abroad. Their chief U.S. competitor for this market is publicly-held SafeCard. C.C.S.B.'s total revenues for 1981 are estimated to be $19,000,000. Analysts estimate that this is an 80% increase over the estimated 1978 total of $10,500,000, and 228% over the 1977 estimate of $5,800,000. Operations are reportedly profitable, and sales are steady throughout the year. C.C.S.B. claims that their services are recommended to cardholders by more than 150 major banks, airlines, car rental companies, oil companies, and department stores. Aside from inserts in the statements mailed by these card issuers, and a recently-implemented and reportedly effective telephone selling operation, C.C.S.B. mails a series of direct mail packages.

CURRENT, INC.

ADDRESS, PHONE
Current, Inc., 3525 North Stone, Colorado Springs, CO 80901. Telephone: (303) 471-4910.

OWNERSHIP
Subsidiary of privately-held Looart Press, Inc.; 100% of capital stock owned by the Loo family.

MANAGEMENT
Lester B. Loo, Chairman of the Board; Gary O. Loo, President of Looart Press; Peter Polumbaum, Vice President-Marketing; Barry Nolan, President of Current, Vice President of Looart.

TYPE OF MARKETER
Mail order.

BUSINESS
Current, Inc. is the mail order catalog marketing arm of parent Looart Press which designs, publishes and markets greeting cards, specialty printed products and stationery. The company sells merchandise through a variety of unrelated retail marketing accounts and through Current catalogs. Most recently Looart has opened the first of its own retail outlets--Owl Stores, Inc.--in Phoenix, AZ. Business is seasonal, peaking around holiday seasons, and the company employs from 850 to 1,150 people.

COMPANY HISTORY
Looart Press was started in 1947 in Colorado Springs by Orin and Miriam Loo. From 1930 to 1942 when the family moved to Colorado, Orin was employed by Hallmark. The business was started in the Loo home, Orin designing greeting cards and Miriam, recipe cards and stationery. The company was incorporated in Colorado on August 1, 1950. In 1967 Looart merged with Current, Inc. New retail outlet and major addition to local production plant were started in 1981.

MARKETS
Customers are 99% female, the majority are married and employed. Mail order sales throughout U.S.

FACILITIES
Headquarters, warehousing, test kitchen, production and order fulfillment in Colorado Springs, CO.

PRODUCTS, BRAND NAMES, PRICE RANGE
High-quality, originally designed stationery and gifts--greeting cards, gift wrap, kitchen accessories, holiday decorations, calendars, children's items. Specialty items are calendars, datebooks, appointment books, etc.

FINANCIAL INFORMATION

	SALES	NET INCOME	PROFIT MARGIN
1981	$62,000,000*	N.A.	--

TYPE OF ADVERTISING, PROMOTION
Current mails catalogs four times per year, and supports them with a minimal amount of space advertising and package inserts. Catalogs are full color, 8-1/4 x 11, roughly 72 pages.

LIST INFORMATION

QUANTITY MAILED:	40,000,000*
AVERAGE ORDER:	$30
ACTIVE BUYERS:	1,172,404
TOTAL LIST:	5,000,000*
LIST SOURCE:	Direct mail.

COMMENTS
Current's estimated $62 million in sales represents an increase of some 15% over 1980. Sales increased an estimated 30% between '79 and '80, and 16% between '78 and '79. Management reported that profits were up over the past six months. Looart attributes strong sales growth to aggressive push for repeat buyers. Current reportedly processed 2.1 million orders from 1.17 million buyers in 1981, which means the average customer purchased 1.8 times. Current's customers are primarily female, aged 25-44, with some college education. These customers have expressed an interest in sewing, cooking, art, crafts and music. From Current's colorful catalogs they have purchased pattern books, cards, recipe files, and decorating items. Management reports they intend to test more "non-paper items" in the product line, and that next fall they will test a catalog with increased craft and gift lines. Long-range plans include further expansion of the manufacturing plant.

DAMART THERMAWEAR

ADDRESS, PHONE

Damart Thermawear, Inc., 1811 Woodbury Avenue, Portsmouth, NH 03801. Telephone: (603) 431-4700.

OWNERSHIP

A wholly owned subsidiary of Patrimonium, S.A., Inc., Luxembourg.

MANAGEMENT

Linda Pawloski, President; Lane Gauthier, Vice President; Mary M. Keenan, Secretary; Frank Bussone, Marketing Director; Maria Davis, Finance Director.

TYPE OF MARKETER

Mail order.

BUSINESS

Damart is a 100% mail order marketer of men's and women's quality underwear and outerwear. The company manufactures and markets a variety of thermal apparel made from their patented Thermo-lactyl (Vinyon and Acrylic) fabric. Peak sales seasons are fall and winter. Damart products are the official thermal garments of many arctic expeditions, the U.S. Bobsled Team, and many professional football teams.

COMPANY HISTORY

Damart was started in 1970 in Chicago, by Linda Pawloski as a U.S. marketer for the European manufacturing parent. The company operated for the first two years out of a one-room office. In 1970 operations were incorporated in Illinois and then moved to present location in Portsmouth, NH in 1976. Company presently employs 160 people.

MARKETS

Customers are 60% male; outdoor and winter sports enthusiasts; upscale; U.S., Canada, and Mexico.

FACILITIES
Owns 39,000 sq. ft. of office space; 215,000 sq. ft inventory and shipping facilities in Rollinsford, NH.

PRODUCTS, BRAND NAMES, PRICE RANGE
Markets top quality family thermal underwear such as pants, shirts and vests, as well as gloves, footwear, boots, coats and outerwear. All products are lightweight, and carry Damart's brand name. Prices range from $15.00 to $100.00.

FINANCIAL INFORMATION

	SALES	NET INCOME	PROFIT MARGIN
1981	$20,000,000*	N.A.	--

TYPE OF ADVERTISING, PROMOTION
Approximately 60% of Damart's promotion is through their catalog operations and other direct mail. The remaining 40% is space advertising in magazines such as Country Journal, Smithsonian, Organic Gardening, and Wall Street Journal.

LIST INFORMATION

QUANTITY MAILED:	20,000,000*
AVERAGE ORDER:	$60
ACTIVE BUYERS:	325,000
TOTAL LIST:	1,100,000
LIST SOURCE:	Direct mail, space.

COMMENTS
Pawloski started Damart selling long-sleeved top and bottom undergarments through a one-page flyer. Management reports that since initial five formative years, company's sales and profits have grown consistently. Damart reportedly spends some $2,000,000 on direct mail promotion annually. They publish several full editions of their catalog each year, plus a special "sale catalog" package with end-of-season values in February. Catalogs are 10-3/4" by 8-1/2", full-color, 16 to 44 pages long. Damart mails approximately 20,000,000 pieces of direct mail per year. Company's main promotional angle is the unequalled quality of their Thermolactyl material: very lightweight; absorbs little or no moisture; low thermal conduction coefficient (more efficient at holding heat). These factors combined make it an "ideal" material for outdoor apparel. Company has expanded product line to include sleepwear, socks, gloves and stylish outerwear in Thermolactyl.

DAY-TIMERS

ADDRESS, PHONE

Day-Timers, Inc., One Willow Lane, East Texas, PA 18046. Telephone: (215) 398-1511.

OWNERSHIP

Subsidiary of publicly-held Beatrice Foods Co. of Chicago.

MANAGEMENT

Robert C. Dorney, President and General Manager, William K. Dorney, Vice President Manufacturing; Keith Snyder, Assistant General Manager; Herb Brown, Controller.

TYPE OF MARKETER

Mail order.

BUSINESS

Day-Timers manufactures and sells business-related supplies geared toward developing time management and efficient business operations. Items printed and produced by company include calendars, planning books, compartment wallets, binders, etc. All sales are by mail. Company has over 1,000,000 customer accounts, with sales fairly steady throughout the year. Employs about 375.

COMPANY HISTORY

A Pennsylvania attorney started the business in 1951 in Allentown as a mail order seller of business diaries. Other products were added over the years. Robert Dorney had a printing company that manufactured some products for Day-Timers. His outfit eventually got involved in fulfillment and shipping, and the two operations merged in the early '60's. Beatrice Foods acquired Day-Timers in 1973 and operated it as a division until 1981, when it was incorporated as a subsidiary.

MARKETS

Market is primarily domestic with some sales in Canada and Great Britain; 90% upscale male.

FACILITIES

Headquarters in Allentown; mail order fulfillment and manufacturing, East Texas, PA.

PRODUCTS, BRAND NAMES, PRICE RANGE

Planning books (desk and wallet-size), calendars, memo pads, binders, diaries; most sold under Day-Timers brand. Also sells motivational books and cassettes, plaques, stationery and business forms, filing and storage equipment.

FINANCIAL INFORMATION

	SALES	NET INCOME	PROFIT MARGIN
1981	$38,000,000*	N.A.	--

TYPE OF ADVERTISING, PROMOTION

Mails one complete catalog for the year, around first of the year. Also offers special single products through solo mailings during the year. Catalogs contain discount coupons for special product or line of products during a specified month.

LIST INFORMATION

QUANTITY MAILED:	17,000,000*
AVERAGE ORDER:	$30
ACTIVE BUYERS:	840,640*
TOTAL LIST:	1,457,000*
LIST SOURCE:	Direct mail, space.

COMMENTS

Although company declines to divulge financial information, Day-Timers sales are estimated to have exceeded $30,000,000 in 1980 and nearly $40,000,000 in 1981. Reliable sources also indicated that profits were up during first half of FY81. Company says success is due, in part, to the nature of its business: there is a continuing need for a product that will help businessmen become more productive at work, and Day-Timers products help achieve that goal. The representative customer tends to be a businessman or professional who wants to become better organized. Even the catalog takes a sensible approach: it's printed only once a year "to keep our costs down and allow us to guarantee all prices throughout the year." Catalogs are full color, 8-1/2 by 11, approximately 114 pages. Company offers volume discount for customers who make annual purchase of $1,000 or more.

DEERSKIN TRADING POST

ADDRESS, PHONE
Deerskin Trading Post, Inc., 119 Foster Street, Peabody, MA 01960. Telephone: (617) 482-7522.

OWNERSHIP
Subsidiary of LTM, Incorporated, Peabody, MA, which is in turn 52% controlled by Initio, Inc., Carlstadt, NJ.

MANAGEMENT
Albert Brodell, Jr., President and CEO; Michael Badler, Treasurer & Secretary; Daniel DeStefano, Officer; Martin Fox, Officer; Arthur O'Farrell, Office Manager.

TYPE OF MARKETER
Mail order, retail.

BUSINESS
Company markets casual wear for men and women; limited children's apparel. Many products are made of leathers, suedes, various types of furs and animal skins. Operations consist of mail order, retail outlets, and manufacturing. Company has two subsidiaries: retail sale of shoes by Heel 'N Toe, Inc.; Deerskin Realty Trust of Framingham, MA, which owns real estate occupied by company's mail order operation and two retail stores. Other retail outlets in Danvers, Pembroke, and Lenox, MA. Employs 200.

COMPANY HISTORY
In July, 1972, company called Specialty Retailers, Inc. was organized for the express purpose of acquiring from LTM of Boston the capital stock of three subsidiaries--Deerskin Trading Post Co., T.I. Swartz & Sons, Inc., and Heel 'N Toes, Inc. LTM wanted to separate retail specialty department from manufacturing division and provide vehicle for acquiring additional retail business. In 1973, Deerskin Trading Post was merged into Specialty Retailers, Inc. Corporate name was changed to Deerskin Trading Post, Inc.

MARKETS
Customers are male and female, mid to upscale apparel and general catalog buyers; throughout U.S.

FACILITIES

Headquarters in Peabody, MA; retail and Heel 'N Toe outlets: MA, MD, VA, PA, NJ, and Wash. D.C.

PRODUCTS, BRAND NAMES, PRICE RANGE

Men's, women's and children's sportswear by mail. Heel 'N Toe sells family shoes. Manufacturing outlets sell men's suits. House brands. Price range moderate.

FINANCIAL INFORMATION

	SALES	NET INCOME	PROFIT MARGIN
1981	$18,000,000*	N.A.	--

TYPE OF ADVERTISING, PROMOTION

Direct mail promotion mainly through catalog mailings; limited solo mailings and special offers between catalogs. Heaviest mailing periods are summer and fall. Very little space advertising to support mail order operations.

LIST INFORMATION

QUANTITY MAILED:	6,500,000*
AVERAGE ORDER:	$45*
ACTIVE BUYERS:	150,000*
TOTAL LIST:	500,000*
LIST SOURCE:	Direct mail.

COMMENTS

Approximately 50% of Deerskin revenues come from mail order sales--estimated $9 million; of the remaining portion, 30% is from retail stores, and 20% is from manufacturing and manufacturers outlets. 1981 revenues were reportedly down from 1980 due to a decrease in sales and increased expenses. Though management reported "modest profits" from operations through 1979, losses in 1980 and '81 are reportedly attributable to operating loss from T.I. Schwartz & Sons subsidiary, and its disposal in November of '79. Company's current assets are reportedly $5.0 million; liabilities approximately $5.8 million. Management attributes reported decline in working capital of 17% to $(701,000), to sharp increase in prices and the Schwartz operating loss. Working capital reportedly increased to $(644,000) in '81. Plans are reportedly to focus attention on mail order and Heel 'N Toe operations; top parent Initio (mail order promtional company) could be big help although there are no reported inter-company relations.

DIRECT MARKETING CORPORATION

ADDRESS, PHONE
Direct Marketing Corp. of America, 3700 Wilshire Blvd., Los Angeles, CA 90010. (213) 381-8011.

OWNERSHIP
Subsidiary of publicly-held Beneficial Standard Corp., Los Angeles, CA.

MANAGEMENT
Henry Roth, Chairman of the Board and CEO; Cathie A. Turner, Sr. Vice President and COO; Ken Wright, Sr. Vice President, Director of Marketing; Kenneth Chao, Sr. Vice President.

TYPE OF MARKETER
Mail order.

BUSINESS
DMCA provides direct mail mass marketing for companies which market insurance and financial products. The company offers complete marketing services from creation of marketing strategies, to design of promotions, mailing, fulfillment and customer service, accounting, billing, and evaluation and reporting of performance. Appeal is to extend financial and insurance services offered to existing and new credit accounts, and to offer programs at special rates as benefits to companies' subscriber and customer bases.

COMPANY HISTORY
The initial purpose in forming DMCA in 1958 was to provide a marketing organization for insurance programs, designed to operate through credit card bases. National credit card holders responded enthusiastically to the ease of buying insurance through the mail: consumers are able to act on their own, without the irritation of selling pressure, in the privacy of their own homes. Company has grown by offering products and services from many companies, including parent's life insurance subsidiaries, as premiums or specials.

MARKETS
DMCA markets a variety of programs throughout the U.S., Europe and Australia.

FACILITIES

West Coast H.Q., L.A.; regional office, Philadelphia; in-house creative, printing and data processing.

PRODUCTS, BRAND NAMES, PRICE RANGE

Programs include supplemental life, accident and health insurance. Prices range from $5 to $15 per month, at an average of $120 per year.

FINANCIAL INFORMATION

	SALES	NET INCOME	PROFIT MARGIN
1980	$212,000,000*	$14,600,000*	6.9%*

TYPE OF ADVERTISING, PROMOTION

Company advertises through direct mail packages, inserts, space in magazines, outdoor, and broadcast.

LIST INFORMATION

QUANTITY MAILED:	43,000,000
AVERAGE ORDER:	$120 per year
ACTIVE BUYERS:	3,500,000
TOTAL LIST:	45,000,000
LIST SOURCE:	Third party clients.

COMMENTS

The above sales figures are for Beneficial National Life Company. Direct Marketing Corp. contributed 11.5% or $24.5 million in premium income. This is an 8.4% and 17.8% increase over the previous two years. Based on company figures, direct mail sales generated by DMCA mass marketing operations amounted to $420 million. While this represents an estimated 1.26% increase in overall sales since 1978, net earnings have decreased by some 7%. Management attributes this to increased price competition in the insurance-by-mail industry. In 1981 the company signed a contract to provide life, accident and health insurance mass marketing services for Puritan Life Insurance (subsidiary of G. E. Credit Corp.). DMCA Enterprises, Inc. is the company's first effort in establishing a merchandise-distribution subsidiary. The organ is PLUS Magazine and is exclusively for credit union members.

DISABLED AMERICAN VETERANS

ADDRESS, PHONE
Disabled American Veterans, 3725 Alexandria Pike, Cold Springs, KY 41076. Phone: (606) 441-7300.

OWNERSHIP
Non-profit membership organization.

MANAGEMENT
Denvel Adams, National Adjutant; Stan Pealer, National Commander; Sherman Roodzant, Sr. VP; Boniface A. Maile, National Judge; Edward Galian, 1st VP; Dennis A. Joyner, 2nd VP.

TYPE OF MARKETER
Mail order.

BUSINESS
This is a non-profit organization formed for the purpose of protecting and advancing the interest and welfare of all disabled veterans and their families. Company performs many services for its members. An important function is the organization service which acts as intermediary in establishing claims for pensions, disability, and death compensations. These services are rendered to disabled veterans without fees, since they are prohibited by law from charging a fee for this type of service. Company employs 737 people.

COMPANY HISTORY
Following WWI, a group of disabled veterans formed a national organization headquartered in Cincinnati. In 1922 the DAV began planning a Washington, D.C. office to work toward needed legislation and expedite veteran's claims. In 1935, the DAV began stationing "liaison officers" in Veterans Bureau claims offices and hospitals across the country. When WWII began, the DAV began to upgrade its facilities and training programs to meet the demands. Today DAV employs nearly 300 National Service Officers in 68 cities.

MARKETS
Disabled American Veterans and their families.

FACILITIES

Owns four interconnected buildings, comprising 150,000 sq. ft. of space on a 17 acre tract.

PRODUCTS, BRAND NAMES, PRICE RANGE

This organization provides a variety of services for the disabled American veterans including financial assistance and scholarships to dependents, disaster relief, emergency relief and health services, pensions, and rehabilitation programs.

FINANCIAL INFORMATION

	SALES	NET INCOME	PROFIT MARGIN
1980	$25,397,242	--	--

TYPE OF ADVERTISING, PROMOTION

The DAV Magazine is published and circulated monthly. Approximately nine million of these magazines are distributed annually. Magazines are 8-1/2" x 11", black and white, and contain 32 pages. Radio and television are among the other media used.

LIST INFORMATION

QUANTITY MAILED: 10,000,000*
AVERAGE ORDER: N.A.
ACTIVE BUYERS: 2,725,849
TOTAL LIST: 5,341,632
LIST SOURCE: Direct mail.

COMMENTS

The "sales" figure above represents "total support" and is broken down into (1) donations and bequests (0.6% or $145,676) and (2) contributions and revenues received from direct mail solicitations (99.4% or $25,251,566). Contributions are also received from I-Denta-Tags, which are distributed by mail to automobile owners throughout the nation. Other income is derived from a per capita tax of $3 per member, per year, for approximately 750,000 members in the U.S. Company also receives income from investments, rentals, voluntary contributions and other miscellaneous interest income. DAV is the third largest non-profit organization in the U.S. Company maintains 70 national service offices throughout the U.S. This organization is directed by a national executive committee consisting of 23 non-salaried members headed by a National Commander. The National Adjutant is a salaried position and is not a member of the commission. Company maintains an additional mail address at Box 14301, Cincinnati, OH 45214. No major projected changes in organization's operations were reported.

WALT DISNEY MUSIC COMPANY

ADDRESS, PHONE
Walt Disney Music Co., Inc., 500 S. Buena Vista, Burbank, CA 91521. (213) 840-1000.

OWNERSHIP
Walt Disney Music is a wholly-owned subsidiary of Walt Disney Productions, of Burbank, California.

MANAGEMENT
E. Cardon Walker, Chairman; Gary Krisel, President; Luther Marr, Vice President and Secretary; Donald A. Essen, Treasurer; Steven McBeth, Manager of Direct Marketing.

TYPE OF MARKETER
Mail order.

BUSINESS
Walt Disney Music Company is the direct mail marketing arm of Walt Disney Productions and sells Disney-Vista Records, Book-Records and Book-Cassettes to consumers, dealers and retail outlets throughout the U.S. Products are marketed through package insert, co-op, ride-along and syndication programs to consumers, and through direct mail packages to dealers. In addition, the company sells merchandise through the catalogs of outside major retailers.

COMPANY HISTORY
The business was originally founded as a division of Disney Productions to mass market record collections by mail. It was incorporated as a subsidiary in California on April 24, 1947, under the name Walt Disney Music Company. Authorized capital consists of 2,500 shares of common stock, $8,000 par value, of which the parent owns one hundred percent. The Music Company reported 100 employees in 1980.

MARKETS
Merchandise mix is targeted at children between the ages of two and ten years.

FACILITIES

Shares 100,000 sq. ft. with another Disney subsidiary in a studio at Burbank location.

PRODUCTS, BRAND NAMES, PRICE RANGE

A variety of record, tape and read along book collections including The Best of Disney, The Fun And Fantasy Collection, Festival of Classics, The Charlie Brown Anniversary Collection. Prices range from $9.95 to $24.95 per collection.

FINANCIAL INFORMATION

	SALES	NET INCOME	PROFIT MARGIN
1981	$10,000,000*	N.A.	--

TYPE OF ADVERTISING, PROMOTION

The music company advertises solely by direct mail. They distribute brochures through co-op and ride-along programs, syndication through other companies' mailing and fulfillment packages, and displays in major retailers' catalogs.

LIST INFORMATION

QUANTITY MAILED:	70,000,000
AVERAGE ORDER:	$30
ACTIVE BUYERS:	210,000
TOTAL LIST:	570,000
LIST SOURCE:	Package inserts.

COMMENTS

Disney is reported to be the leading U.S. producer and marketer of children's record and tape sets. The financial and list information above are for the company's insert, co-op and ride-along program sales only. Though this constitutes the bulk of their marketing and sales, the Music Company is involved in a variety of other direct mail and direct response activities. They produce their own syndication packages for large book and record clubs. They work closely with major retailers in offering their merchandise through catalog operations. They also do a limited amount of television direct response promotion, with mail order fulfillment handled by Columbia House.

DOUBLEDAY & CO.

ADDRESS, PHONE
Doubleday & Co., Inc., 245 Park Ave., New York, NY 10017. Telephone: (212) 953-4561.

OWNERSHIP
Privately held by the Nelson Doubleday family (principal owners).

MANAGEMENT
John T. Sargent, Chairman of the Board; Nelson Doubleday, President; John W. O'Donnell, Executive Vice President & Secretary; Raymond Ammarelli, Jr., Senior Vice President; James R. McLoughlin, VP.

TYPE OF MARKETER
Mail order, retail.

BUSINESS
Doubleday & Co., Inc. is a diversified corporation known primarily for its publishing operations, although its activities branch out to include retail book stores and ownership of the New York Mets. Its primary mail order operations are its general and special-interest book clubs, the largest of them being the well-known Literary Guild and the Doubleday Book Club. They also have a Science Fiction Book Club, a Mystery Guild, a Military Book Club and several other clubs serving various specialized markets.

COMPANY HISTORY
Frank Nelson Doubleday started the company in 1897 in New York as a publisher of trade books. Throughout its long existence, the company has gone by several names, including Doubleday, McClue & Co. and Doubleday & Page, but the firm has remained in the hands of the Doubleday family, with Frank Nelson Doubleday's sons and grandsons holding the operating reins. The Literary Guild, Doubleday's biggest book club, began in the 1920s around the same time as the Book of the Month Club, and the two remain steady competitors.

MARKETS
Sales are primarily domestic and Canadian, with limited international marketing.

FACILITIES
Executive H.Q., New York City; mail order, fulfillment and customer service, Garden City, NY.

PRODUCTS, BRAND NAMES, PRICE RANGE
Literary Guild selections are first offerings and are more expensive than those for the Doubleday Book clubs, which offer same books at a later time. Books are hardback. Gift merchandise is offered to club members. A Graphics Guild offers art prints by mail.

FINANCIAL INFORMATION

	SALES	NET INCOME	PROFIT MARGIN
1981	$300,000,000+*	N.A.	--

TYPE OF ADVERTISING, PROMOTION
Book club members receive monthly brochure with current book offerings. Catalogs go out in spring and for Christmas offering merchandise to members. Space ads in national magazines use special introductory offers. Some television advertising.

LIST INFORMATION
QUANTITY MAILED: 50,000,000+
AVERAGE ORDER: Varies with club.
ACTIVE BUYERS: 5,000,000+
TOTAL LIST: 9,800,000+*
LIST SOURCE: Direct mail, space.

COMMENTS
Company's total sales are estimated to be $300 million and "holding steady." Mail order contributes approximately 47% or $140,000,000. Doubleday has perhaps the largest number of book clubs in the U.S., ranging from its large, general-interest operation, The Literary Guild, to its relatively small, special-interest club, Fireside Theatre, which is advertised as America's only theatre book club, featuring scripts, anthologies and biographies of theatrical figures. The Literary Guild and Doubleday Book Club are the biggest of Doubleday's clubs, with 1,900,000 and 1,800,000 active members respectively. Both have a market that is primarily female. They attract new members through special introductory offers, found in magazines, that allow several selections for $1 with a commitment to purchase that same number of books within a year. Members who join those clubs will find offers in their monthly mailings to join Doubleday's other special-interest book clubs.

DOWNS' COLLECTORS SHOWCASE

ADDRESS, PHONE

Downs' Collectors Showcase, 2778 So. 35th St., Milwaukee, WI 53215. Telephone: (414) 643-7300.

OWNERSHIP

Division of privately-held S.C.J. Marketing, Inc. of Racine, WI (S.C.J. stands for Samuel C. Johnson of Johnson's Wax).

MANAGEMENT

William J. Spray, President; Wilfred D. Mackay, Vice President, Merchandise; Edward Waldron, Vice President-Treasurer.

TYPE OF MARKETER

Mail order, retail.

BUSINESS

Downs' Collectors Showcase is a marketer of limited-edition collector's items including plates, bells, thimbles, steins and music boxes. The company also sells a general line of gift and decorative items. Catalog sales make up more than 95% of business, with remainder generated by two retail stores in Milwaukee and Racine. About 60% of sales are made during the last six months of the year. Company employs approximately 75 people.

COMPANY HISTORY

Normal Kimball founded the company in 1948 as a catalog marketer of gifts and gadgets. After his death in 1973, his estate sold the firm to S.C.J. Marketing, which continued to operate Downs' at its original location in Evanston, IL. S.C.J. moved the operation to Milwaukee in 1978 so the firm could share computer facilities with another S.C.J. company, which was later sold. In 1975, the Downs' merchandise line was completely revamped to its current offerings of limited edition collectors items.

MARKETS

Mail order sales are domestic; market is about 95% female, median age 44, mid to upscale.

FACILITIES
HQ at above address; fulfillment center, Beloit Rd.,
Milwaukee. Retail outlets, Milwaukee, Racine, WI.

PRODUCTS, BRAND NAMES, PRICE RANGE
Primarily limited-edition collectors plates, bells and
thimbles; other collectibles and gift items. Products
manufactured specifically for company under Downs'
name. Also national brands, such as Gorham. Prices
generally range from $5 to $500.

FINANCIAL INFORMATION

	SALES	NET INCOME	PROFIT MARGIN
1981	$12,000,000*	N.A.	--

TYPE OF ADVERTISING, PROMOTION
Primarily catalogs published six times annually and
mailed throughout the year; greater emphasis on
second half of year. Catalogs are full color and
range in size from 40 to 72 pages. Some solo mailings to targeted customers; some space in magazines.

LIST INFORMATION
QUANTITY MAILED: 10,000,000*
AVERAGE ORDER: $45
ACTIVE BUYERS: 175,000*
TOTAL LIST: 750,000
LIST SOURCE: Direct mail, space.

COMMENTS
Management claims that Downs' mail order business
has increased 100% over the past five years. They
report that their customers are fairly affluent with
considerable discretionary income. The company
contends that collectibles are upscale non-essential
items, and therefore not severely affected by recessionary economy. 1981 was reported to be Downs'
best year ever, and management expects significant
sales growth in 1982. Company places equal emphasis on customers who collect for enjoyment and those
who collect for investment purposes with the intention of reselling at a profit. Downs' has an extensive buy-back program, and is emphasizing collectible lines that have a characteristic jump in value
soon after purchase. Downs' Collectors Club is an
organization offering various benefits to its members:
10% savings on purchases from Downs' catalog;
collectible newsletter; early ordering privilege to
reserve valuable collectibles at issue price; option to
buy additional merchandise not offered in catalog.
Membership is $12 annually.

WALTER DRAKE

ADDRESS, PHONE

Walter Drake & Sons, Inc., 4510 Edison, Colorado Springs, CO 80940. Telephone: (303) 596-3140.

OWNERSHIP

Privately held; 100% of capital stock owned by Walter Drake and family.

MANAGEMENT

Walter Drake, Chmn. and CEO; Alberta Drake, Pres. and Treas.; Cecil Wayman, Executive VP, Gen. Mgr.; Clovis Johnston, Mgr. of Merchandising and Marketing.

TYPE OF MARKETER

Mail order.

BUSINESS

Walter Drake is a mail order marketer of a broad line of general merchandise items. Products are lowscale gifts, kitchen and household items, novelties and some apparel. In addition, Drake operates the Walter Drake Silver Exchange, which is a pattern matching service for buying and selling pieces of sterling silver. The general merchandise operation is positioned to offer low-cost unusual gifts and novelties to middle-income customers.

COMPANY HISTORY

The company was started by Walter Drake in Colorado Springs in 1947. Drake started the business by offering personalized novelties through space advertising. With the success of this operation, he began adding general merchandise items to diversify the product mix. As the merchandise lines expanded, Drake began publishing catalogs for direct mail marketing. Management reports that the company has grown steadily over the years and currently publishes seven catalogs annually.

MARKETS

Domestic mail order market is 70% women in middle income level; no international marketing.

FACILITIES

Headquarters, order processing and retail outlet in Colorado Springs, Colorado.

PRODUCTS, BRAND NAMES, PRICE RANGE

Large assortment of labels, personalized gifts, novelty items, children's toys and gifts, stationery, records and tapes, etc. Merchandise lines are of a discretionary purchase nature. Price range for general merchandise is low end.

FINANCIAL INFORMATION

	SALES	NET INCOME	PROFIT MARGIN
1981	$40,000,000*	N.A.	--

TYPE OF ADVERTISING, PROMOTION

Approximately 85% of promotion is through catalog mailings. Catalogs are supported with space advertising in magazines such as Better Homes & Gardens, House Beautiful, and Parade.

LIST INFORMATION

QUANTITY MAILED:	22,000,000*
AVERAGE ORDER:	$9.75*
ACTIVE BUYERS:	2,100,000*
TOTAL LIST:	4,000,000*
LIST SOURCE:	Direct mail, space.

COMMENTS

Drake emphasizes the fun and convenience of gift buying through their catalogs. The catalogs are full color, 9 x 5-1/4, 96 to 104 pages long. They are published seasonally with three special gift selections per year, for a total of seven different catalogs-- about 22,000,000 copies mailed per year. Management reports that about 60% of sales are to repeat buyers. Drake Silver Exchange carries hundreds of patterns, many of which are rare or discontinued. Customers can purchase complete sets or single pieces. The Exchange buys some limited gold, silver and diamonds. Drake's estimated 1981 revenues are broken down as follows: $28 million from mail order operations and single retail outlet; $12 million from Silver Exchange operations (estimates). Management reported no major expansion or changes in merchandise lines are planned for 1982.

DRAWING BOARD

ADDRESS, PHONE

The Drawing Board, Greenwoods Industrial Park, New Hartford, CT 06057. Telephone: (203) 379-9911.

OWNERSHIP

Wholly owned subsidiary of Pitney Bowes, Inc.

MANAGEMENT

Edward Kristin, President, Steven Lett, Vice President of Marketing; Fred Madura, Vice President Planning; Carmine Adimando, Vice President of Finance.

TYPE OF MARKETER

Mail order, retail.

BUSINESS

The Drawing Board is a mail order marketer of imprinted business forms, stationery, printed labels and a large variety of general office supplies. The company buys its forms from outside manufacturers and imprints company name, etc. in house. Drawing Board has five retail outlets located in Dallas, Texas. Their catalog offers over 1,000 office products. Sales are heaviest during the months of September through December. The company employs 1,100 persons.

COMPANY HISTORY

The business was started in the mid 1950s in Dallas, Texas, by Selwyn Belofsky. Mail order was an original part of the business. The first products Belofsky marketed were phone message pads, which sold successfully, and the product line was quickly expanded to include general office supplies. Business has reportedly grown steadily over the years. On July 16, 1980, Pitney Bowes acquired the Drawing Board in exchange for 660,000 shares of its common stock.

MARKETS

Products are marketed worldwide; customers are 65% male, business buyers.

FACILITIES

Owns 80,000 sq. ft. of space for headquarters, mail order and imprinting operations.

PRODUCTS, BRAND NAMES, PRICE RANGE

Products include business forms, stationery, labels, advertising items, file systems, code-a-phone, telephone accessories, folders, greeting cards, memos, calculators. Name brands are Drawing Board and Pitney Bowes. Price ranges from $20.00 to $600.00.

FINANCIAL INFORMATION

	SALES	NET INCOME	PROFIT MARGIN
1981	$25,000,000*	N.A.	--

TYPE OF ADVERTISING, PROMOTION

Roughly 98% of the company's promotion is through their catalogs. Six full-color, 84-page catalogs and four full-color, 32-page flyers are mailed for a total of some 10,000,000 pieces annually.

LIST INFORMATION

QUANTITY MAILED:	10,000,000
AVERAGE ORDER:	$50
ACTIVE BUYERS:	274,000
TOTAL LIST:	757,000
LIST SOURCE:	Direct mail, space.

COMMENTS

The sales figure above represents an estimate of Drawing Board's 1981 mail order sales and does not include revenues from the company's five retail outlets. Pitney Bowes acquired the company for the equivalent of $22 million in P.B. stock on June 16, 1980. Subsequently Drawing Board and other P.B. mail order subsidiaries have been consolidated in the Wheeler-Group operating division. Over the past five years the Drawing Board has experienced approximately 15% annual sales growth in the mail order area. New ideas and methods are constantly being tested to improve their already successful operations. The past year has been consumed in moving headquarters to New Hartford, Ct. The company has another division called the Drawing Board Greeting Cards, which includes cards for all occasions, wrapping paper, stationery and party goods. This part of the business was not acquired by Pitney Bowes and is still privately owned.

DREYFUS CORPORATION

ADDRESS, PHONE
The Dreyfus Corporation, 767 Fifth Avenue, New York, NY 10153. Telephone: (212) 935-3000.

OWNERSHIP
Public; listed NYSE; 5,085,000 shares outstanding; market prices: high, 37-3/4; low 14-1/8; dividend: $1.13 stock split 3-for-1 on 1-28-81.

MANAGEMENT
Howard Stein, Chairman, President, CEO; Senior VPs: Julian M. Smerling, Joseph S. DiMartino; VPs: Matthew A. Baxter, Jr., Monte J. Gordon, Research, Patrick J. Nee, Daniel C. Maclean, General Counsel.

TYPE OF MARKETER
Mail order, direct sales by dealers.

BUSINESS
Dreyfus is a financial service organization which provides investment management services of two kinds: (1) as investment advisor, manager, and distributor for mutual funds; (2) as an investment advisor to individual and institutional accounts. Dreyfus Service Corporation, a wholly owned subsidiary, underwrites, distributes, and handles investment servicing for mutual funds and unit trusts; Dreyfus Management, Inc., another wholly-owned subsidiary, provides investment management for pension plans, individuals, and institutions.

COMPANY HISTORY
The company was incorporated in New York on Jan. 2, 1947. The oldest of the ten mutual funds managed by the corporation was chartered in Maryland in 1947 as Nesbett Fund, Inc., and the name was changed to Dreyfus Funds, Inc., on May 23, 1951; Dreyfus Leverage Fund--high risk investment--was formed in 1968; others followed in 1971, 1972, 1974, 1975, and 1976. The most recent addition to the company's mutual fund stable is Dreyfus Tax Exempt Money Market Fund, which began operations in 1980.

MARKETS
Investors throughout U.S.; Dreyfus Fund and Dreyfus Management International serve investors abroad.

FACILITIES

Headquarters in NYC. Office space is leased in five other cities.

PRODUCTS, BRAND NAMES, PRICE RANGE

Various funds managed by company offer investments in government securities, bank certificates of deposit, common and preferred stocks, commercial paper, municipal bonds, undervalued issues, small growth companies, fixed income obligations, and debentures.

FINANCIAL INFORMATION

	SALES	NET INCOME	PROFIT MARGIN
1981	$86,996,353	$21,469,900	24.7%

TYPE OF ADVERTISING, PROMOTION

Dreyfus has an in-house ad agency, Lois Pitts Gershon. The company has successfully used television network campaigns for image advertising (the Dreyfus lion coming out of the Wall Street station). Inquiry generating space ads appear in newspapers and magazines.

LIST INFORMATION

QUANTITY MAILED:	(Dreyfus does not make infor-
AVERAGE ORDER:	mation on its customers or any
ACTIVE BUYERS:	type of direct mail list avail-
TOTAL LIST:	able.)
LIST SOURCE:	

COMMENTS

The company's total promotional budget, including response to inquiries from direct mail, is $12 million, of which $3 million is spent in media. Howard Stein (chairman, president, and CEO) began using advertising to replace sales people in 1974 when Dreyfus Liquid Assets was introduced. Because of the competition which this money market mutual fund got from banks and similar investment funds put out by competitors, Stein decided to sell securities directly to investors as well as through the usual channel of dealers. The decision to try direct marketing was prompted by the need to eliminate the sales charge and keep the final yield as high as possible in an increasingly competitive marketplace. There are currently more than 700 registered open-end investment companies in the mutual fund industry. Of the $86.9 million total revenues earned by Dreyfus in 1980, 85% ($73,983,678) represents management fee revenue from mutual funds. 1981 was a strong performance year.

D.R.I. INDUSTRIES

ADDRESS, PHONE
D.R.I. Industries, Inc., 11100 Hampshire Ave. S.,
Bloomington, MN 55438. Telephone: (612) 944-3530.

OWNERSHIP
Privately held; Paul M. Harmon, owns 100% of
capital stock.

MANAGEMENT
Paul M. Harmon, President; Steve Zastara, Senior
Vice President, Administration; VPs: Walter Waxman,
Jim Ditzig, Mike Talbot; Bruce Brekke, V-P Pur-
chasing; Thomas Brokl, VP-Marketing.

TYPE OF MARKETER
Mail order, direct sales.

BUSINESS
D.R.I. Industries, through its two subsidiaries and
mail order operations, markets a variety of tools and
hardware "WORKSHOPS"--complete sets of various
types of hardware, organized and labelled in multibin
cabinets. Marketing Results, Inc. subsidiary syndicates merchandise for oil company and bank credit
cards. International Tools, Inc. subsidiary sells
D.R.I. products wholesale to retail outlets. Parent
company sells merchandise by mail through catalog
and direct mail packages. D.R.I. presently reports
200 employees.

COMPANY HISTORY
Paul Harmon, who worked for a large mail order
firm, was a handyman/hobbyist whose avocation led
to the creation of D.R.I. Industries. He started
offering handyman equipment and accessories by mail
in 1973; his firm beginning as a division of Direct
Response, Inc., a service company to insurers.
Harmon and Steve Zastara, who came on in 1975,
built the company up after that time, and in 1977 it
was spun off as a separate corporation under the
D.R.I. name.

MARKETS
Sells throughout the U.S.; customers are 90% male;
no manufacturing or international marketing.

FACILITIES

60,000 sq. ft. facility in Bloomington, and 20,000 sq. ft. building in Eden Prairie, MN.

PRODUCTS, BRAND NAMES, PRICE RANGE

Nail Shop, Rivet Shop, Electrical Terminal & Connector Shop, Wire Shop, and 60 other hardware and fastener "shops." Prices range from $10 to $400. D.R.I.'s top seller is the Nut & Bolt Shop, multi-bin cabinet and assorted hardware sells for about $20.

FINANCIAL INFORMATION

	SALES	NET INCOME	PROFIT MARGIN
1981	$25,000,000*	N.A.	--

TYPE OF ADVERTISING, PROMOTION

Extensive use of catalogs published quarterly. Solo mailings promoting one special product mailed periodically. Inserts with oil and bank card statements promote single products. Some magazine ads and newspaper inserts.

LIST INFORMATION

QUANTITY MAILED: 30,000,000*
AVERAGE ORDER: $30
ACTIVE BUYERS: 602,494 (home and business)
TOTAL LIST: 1,500,000*
LIST SOURCE: Direct (90%), inserts, space.

COMMENTS

D.R.I. Industries offers over 1,000 items for the handyman in each of its catalogs; apparently not enough for the company officials who feel they've "barely scratched the surface" with their offerings. Future plans call for the expansion of product lines to increase the variety of nuts, bolts and other related items. Company officials report a substantial number of multi-buyers and anticipate continued growth. The D.R.I. customer is seen as a stable, above-average earner who is a good credit risk and who enjoys making and fixing things. Management reports "demise of old-fashion hardware stores" and economic pressures are causing more people to fix up their existing home with products bought by mail. About 90% of business is generated through direct mail sales to these individuals, and company officials believe the number of weekend handymen is growing rapidly. The catalogs, which account for a substantial portion of the company's advertising, are viewed as a "hardware store in catalog form" and run about 100 pages each. Catalogs are generally black and white.

DUNHAM'S OF MAINE

ADDRESS, PHONE
Dunham's of Maine, 64 Main Street, Waterville, Maine 04901. Telephone: (207) 872-5501.

OWNERSHIP
Owned by The William Gordon Corporation whose stock is held by Robert G. Fairburn and Eileen B. Fairburn.

MANAGEMENT
Robert Fairburn, President; Eileen Fairburn, Vice President; Charles Ayotte, Vice President and General Manager.

TYPE OF MARKETER
Mail order, retail.

BUSINESS
Sells quality men's and women's apparel with well-known brand names via catalogs nationwide, and through retail stores in Waterville, Portland, and Kennebunkport, ME. Emphasis is on tradition, elegance, and exceptional tailoring. Company is known for reliance on natural fibers and classic good taste in merchandise selections. Mail order accounts for 75-80% of Dunham's total sales. Employs 35-40 people, including officers.

COMPANY HISTORY
Company started as Dolloff and Dunham in the 1880's and in the 1890's changed its name to H. R. Dunham Co. In the 1920's the company began to market Hathaway shirts and by 1950 had become "America's No. 1 Hathaway Shirt Store." With the help of suppliers, Dunham's weathered a devastating fire in the 1930's and was back in business in six months. In 1932 the first mail order effort, a postcard offering a Hathaway shirt, was mailed.

MARKETS
Upper income, affluent male (40%) and female (60%) mail order customers; nationwide.

FACILITIES
Operates warehouse, ordering center, and retail store in Waterville; stores: Portland, Kennebunkport.

PRODUCTS, BRAND NAMES, PRICE RANGE
Dunham's features items which range in price from $10 to $4,000, with major concentration at high end. Name brands include Hathaway, Malia, Southwick, Trafalgar, Hickey-Freeman, Pendleton and more; 55% women's and 45% men's clothing and furnishings.

FINANCIAL INFORMATION

	SALES	NET INCOME	PROFIT MARGIN
1981	$13,500,000*	N.A.	--

TYPE OF ADVERTISING, PROMOTION
Space advertising is approximately 95% catalog inquiry generation and 5% merchandise ads. In the past, they mailed four regular catalogs and one year-end close-out edition. Plan is to at least double the number of catalog editions published each year.

LIST INFORMATION

QUANTITY MAILED:	5,000,000
AVERAGE ORDER:	$120+
ACTIVE BUYERS:	85,000
TOTAL LIST:	200,000
LIST SOURCE:	Direct mail, space.

COMMENTS
Based on the belief that "if you stand for one thing, quality, you're not going to miss," Dunham's has shown steady, successful growth and an ever-increasing commitment to mail order. Famous personalities like Keenan Wynn, Ted Williams, Cesar Romero and others have been steady customers and vocal endorsers of the company. Management reports that 1981 sales were down slightly from the preceding year, but they don't feel that economic straits will have lasting effect due to their upscale, quality merchandise position. Mail order operations account for some 75-80% of sales or an estimated $10 million. In September, 1979, Dunham's rented 10,000 sq. ft. in the Waterville, ME post office for a new warehouse and mail order processing center. In addition to increasing mail order efficiency, the company opened a second retail outlet in Portland, ME, which is expected to generate $1,000,000 in sales in its first full year of operations. A third store was opened in Kennebunkport, ME on May 1, 1982. Their success will greatly affect possible plans for other retail outlets, possibly outside Maine.

EARLY WINTERS

ADDRESS, PHONE
Early Winters, Ltd., 110 Prefontaine Place South, Seattle, WA 98104. Telephone: (206) 622-5203.

OWNERSHIP
Privately held by William S. Nicolai and officers; 500,000 shares common stock at $1 par value; Nicolai, majority stockholder.

MANAGEMENT
William S. Nicolai, President; William H. Edwards, Vice President; Ron Zimmerman, Vice President; Steve Costie, Vice President; Lorna Walter, Controller.

TYPE OF MARKETER
Mail order, retail.

BUSINESS
Company designs and markets high quality recreational apparel and equipment. Products include tents, sleeping bags, climbing gear and more. Early Winters designs 75% and manufactures approximately 30% of products--company is known as an innovator in developing unique outdoor items. Products are sold to general public--customers are sports and outdoor enthusiasts. Mail order accounts for 90% of sales--retail outlet 10%. Company reports 150 employees.

COMPANY HISTORY
Early Winters was started in 1972 by Nicolai. Edwards, Zimmerman and Williamson--who owned and operated the successful Cheese People--joined company in 1974. Company started as manufacturer of a mountaineering expedition tent. Expanded with the introduction of Gore-tex products to backpacking market in 1976. Published first mail order catalog in winter of 1976. Incorporated in Washington, February 11, 1975. Greatly expanded product lines and mailings between 1976 and 1982.

MARKETS
Men 60%, women 40%; average age 37, average income $29,000; throughout U.S.

FACILITIES

Order processing and fulfillment, factory, warehouse, retail outlet and headquarters in Seattle, Washington.

PRODUCTS, BRAND NAMES, PRICE RANGE

Early Winters outdoor products include tents, sleeping bags, backpacks, hiking and climbing gear, apparel, cookware, camera gear, books, and first-aid supplies. Sierra Designs feature parkas, sweaters, ski equipment and more.

FINANCIAL INFORMATION

	SALES	NET INCOME	PROFIT MARGIN
1981	$10,000,000*	N.A.	--

TYPE OF ADVERTISING, PROMOTION

Advertising consists of 10 percent space and 90 percent catalog. Five catalogs annually: 1) Springs mini; 2) Summer shopping; 3) Summer mini; 4) Fall shopping; 5) Christmas gift.

LIST INFORMATION

QUANTITY MAILED:	2,500,000
AVERAGE ORDER:	$55.00
ACTIVE BUYERS:	250,000
TOTAL LIST:	600,000
LIST SOURCE:	Direct mail, space.

COMMENTS

Early Winters total sales were $10,100,000 for 1981; company sales have more than tripled in the past four years. Mail order accounts for approximately 92% of sales, or an estimated $9,290,000. The remaining sales are from E.W.'s one retail outlet. Management attributes company's success to heavy emphasis on mail order sales and high degree of specialization. E.W. is continually designing and testing new items, and manufactures some 30% of the merchandise it sells. Company recently tested a telephone ordering system and advertised toll-free number, but results were poor and the project was discontinued. Officials felt poor response was in part due to small target sample size (110,000 names). With increasing postal rates, company is planning to cut back on large catalog runs, and in turn increase publication of smaller "prospect catalogs." No plans were reported to increase retail operations; emphasis will remain on mail order for continued growth.

EASTERN MOUNTAIN SPORTS

ADDRESS, PHONE

Eastern Mountain Sports, Inc., 1 Vose Farm Road, Peterborough, NH 03458. Telephone: (603) 924-9571.

OWNERSHIP

Wholly-owned subsidiary of Franklin Mint Corp., which in turn is owned by Warner Communications.

MANAGEMENT

Thomas K. Haas, President; William Dean III, Vice President, Direct Marketing; Leo P. Smith, Controller; Robert Martin, Merchandising Manager.

TYPE OF MARKETER

Mail order, retail.

BUSINESS

Eastern Mountain Sports is a marketer of high-quality outdoor equipment and clothing, such as sleeping bags, backpacks and parkas. Company operates 20 retail stores, mostly in New England area, and approximately 80% of sales are from retail operations. Company markets the same merchandise lines by mail through their catalog division. EMS does not manufacture its products directly, but contracts outside firms to manufacture items which in many cases are designed by EMS.

COMPANY HISTORY

The company was started in 1966 by Alan McDonough in Boston as a retailer of outdoor products. In 1967, the name was changed from Mountaineering Supply Co. to Eastern Mountain Sports. Headquarters were moved to New Hampshire in 1977 after company outgrew its Boston facilities. The mail order operation was started in 1971 as an adjunct to retail and remained basically a regional concept until 1977-78, when the company began mail order marketing nationwide. Franklin Mint acquired EMS in 1979.

MARKETS

Markets throughout U.S.; 55% male, mid-to-high income, age range 18-39.

FACILITIES
Warehouse, offices and one retail store at New Hampshire address; 19 other retail stores.

PRODUCTS, BRAND NAMES, PRICE RANGE
Camping, hiking equipment and accessories, skis and accessories, outdoor clothing and footwear (parkas, vests, etc.). Sells some national brands and its own EMS brand. Products range in price from $1.95 to $400, average price $70-$80.

FINANCIAL INFORMATION

	SALES	**NET INCOME**	**PROFIT MARGIN**
1981	$29,000,000*	N.A.	--

TYPE OF ADVERTISING, PROMOTION
About 60% of EMS' advertising dollars are spent on catalogs. The remaining 40% is spent on space in newspapers and magazines, including The New Yorker, Smithsonian, Backpacker, Outside, etc. Some radio in retail areas.

LIST INFORMATION

QUANTITY MAILED:	3,500,000
AVERAGE ORDER:	$52
ACTIVE BUYERS:	112,000
TOTAL LIST:	360,000
LIST SOURCE:	Direct mail 70%, space 30%.

COMMENTS
Eastern Mountain sells products for the camper/hiker/outdoorsman, and has targeted a strong market in the college age group. Many of its retail stores are located near colleges, and a major effort is made to target direct mail promotions to this group. The company offers some 800 items through its catalogs, and up to 4,000 items through its stores. There has been a move in recent years to market more products under the private EMS label, and company finds that customers are increasingly asking for the house brand by name. Sales and profits reportedly increased through 1980: total sales are estimated to be $29 million, with mail order accounting for 20%, or about $6 million. Future plans are to greatly expand mail order operations, by offering more products through catalogs and bringing them in line with retail sales. Management expects mail order to be 50% of business within the next 5 years.

E & B MARINE

ADDRESS, PHONE
E & B Marine Supply, Inc., 150 Jackson Avenue, Edison, NJ 08818. Telephone: (201) 442-3940.

OWNERSHIP
Privately held; 100% of capital stock owned by Robert and Gerald Bench.

MANAGEMENT
Robert Bench, President and CEO; Gerald Bench, Executive Vice President and Secretary; Robert Defonte, Vice President and Treasurer; Donald Metz, Vice President.

TYPE OF MARKETER
Mail order, retail.

BUSINESS
The company sells accessories for pleasure boats through catalogs and its chain of discount centers located in Connecticut, Maryland, New Jersey, Rhode Island, and Virginia. E & B Marine identifies itself as the world's largest retailer of marine supplies serving recreation and commercial boating markets throughout the world. The company gets its products from such well-known suppliers as Aqua Meter, Danforth, Igloo, Monogram, Minolta, Powerwinch, Schaefer, etc.

COMPANY HISTORY
E & B was started in 1956 by Ernest Bench and son, Robert, as a government and industrial surplus store, on Staten Island, NY. They entered the discount pleasure boating accessory business in 1958. The company began mail order operations in 1961 when they purchased a large quantity of used astronomical timers which were being replaced by photo-electric cells to control New York street lights. E & B placed an ad in Popular Science and sold 20,000 of the timers.

MARKETS
E & B sells products by mail throughout the U.S. and abroad.

FACILITIES

Headquarters and fulfillment center in Edison, NJ. Retail stores in VA, MD, NJ, CT, and RI.

PRODUCTS, BRAND NAMES, PRICE RANGE

Company carries over 4,500 products for power and non-power boats and owners. Items include navigational and electrical equipment, hardware, safety gear, and apparel. Prices range from $1.60 to $1,795.00.

FINANCIAL INFORMATION

	SALES	NET INCOME	PROFIT MARGIN
1981	$15,000,000*	N.A.	--

TYPE OF ADVERTISING, PROMOTION

Direct mail catalogs; space ads in national sports and outdoor magazines and in Sunday supplements; customer referrals. Also promotes products through displays at the annual Newport (VA), Norwalk (CT), and Annapolis (MD) In-Water Boat Shows.

LIST INFORMATION

QUANTITY MAILED:	2,100,000
AVERAGE ORDER:	$86
ACTIVE BUYERS:	100,000
TOTAL LIST:	220,000
LIST SOURCE:	Direct mail, space.

COMMENTS

The original E & B Marine Supply corporation, formed in New York in 1959, has been dissolved, and the company has been reincorporated in CT, NJ, VA and MD. Company officials report that E & B's sales have continued to increase steadily in the past three years: 23% in 1979; 25% in 1980; 25% in 1981. E & B says that this fact is largely due to expansion in mail order marketing. In 1980 mail order was responsible for a reported $6.5 million, or 50% of total sales. In 1981 mail order contributed approximately $8 million or 53% of total revenues. The company's catalogs (8 x 11, b & w, 120 pages) have been expanded to include over 4,500 items. E & B publishes three catalogs per year and includes approximately 100 new products in each edition. The number of catalogs mailed has also been increased by 27%, from 1,650,000 in 1980, to 2,100,000 in 1981. E & B plans to continue to expand mail order operations, and to eventually provide same-day shipment for all orders.

EDMUND SCIENTIFIC

ADDRESS, PHONE

Edmund Scientific Company, 101 E. Gloucester Pike, Barrington, NJ 08007. Telephone: (609) 547-3488.

OWNERSHIP

Privately held by the New Jersey partnership of Edmund family members.

MANAGEMENT

Norman W. Edmund, Chairman of Board of Partners; Robert M. Edmund, President; Leon Parkman, VP-Marketing; Andrew Myers, VP-Finance; David McGonigle, VP-Materials.

TYPE OF MARKETER

Mail order, retail, wholesale.

BUSINESS

Edmund Scientific is a leading U.S. designer, manufacturer and marketer of optical equipment, kits, and unusual or hard-to-find science related items. Products marketed through the company's direct mail catalogs account for approximately 80% of total sales. The remaining 20% of revenues come from the company's one retail outlet (at headquarters), and from wholesale distribution to some 200 dealers in the U.S. and abroad. Edmund reported 200 employees in 1981.

COMPANY HISTORY

The business was started in 1942 by present Chairman Norman W. Edmund. As an amateur photographer, Edmund was having difficulty finding lenses in his home town. When he found a mail order ad for quantities of lenses, Edmund purchased a lot, which he in turn sold locally through a classified ad of his own. He started the company by locating and purchasing quantities of lenses, instrument parts, and war surplus, and developing his own products and kits.

MARKETS

Consumer, industrial and educational markets throughout U.S., Europe, Japan, Australia.

FACILITIES
Retail outlet, laboratories, manufacturing and mail order operations at main facility in Barrington.

PRODUCTS, BRAND NAMES, PRICE RANGE
Astroscan 2001 Telescope; Edmund RKE Eyepieces; alternate energy, biofeedback, weather monitoring and lab equipment, tele - and microscopes, tools, motors, etc. Prices range from lower dollar items to $2,000-$3,000 for larger telescopes and equipment.

FINANCIAL INFORMATION

	SALES	NET INCOME	PROFIT MARGIN
1981	$13,500,000*	N.A.	--

TYPE OF ADVERTISING, PROMOTION
Catalog is main selling tool: major mailings in September, December, and March. Primary catalog is 96 pages and 50% color. Catalog marketing supplemented with "mini" catalogs and package inserts.

LIST INFORMATION

QUANTITY MAILED:	4,000,000
AVERAGE ORDER:	Consumer,$47;Indus.& Ed.,$130
ACTIVE BUYERS:	Con, 100,000; Ind & Ed, 25,000
TOTAL LIST:	Con, 500,000; Ind & Ed,130,000
LIST SOURCE:	Space ads, rental, past buyers.

COMMENTS
Edmund reports that 80% of total revenues come from mail order sales. Of the company's estimated $11,500,000 in 1981 mail order sales, approximately 55% was to consumers, and 45% was to industrial and educational accounts. Company officials stated that over $2.5 million was spent on direct mail, promotions and space advertising in 1981. Space ads in general science periodicals, and educational and technical magazines are used to generate catalog inquiries. To combat the effects of increasing postal rates, Edmund has reduced the size of its main catalog to 92 pages. They plan to mail the full catalog less frequently, and will increase mailings of "mini-versions." Company officials believe that this will be a more cost effective strategy: increasing segmentation of lists, and tailoring the merchandise offered in smaller mailings to specific target markets. Edmund says they will continue to add 200-450 new products annually and will position to increase industrial segment sales in the 1980's.

V. W. EIMICKE

ADDRESS, PHONE
V. W. Eimicke Associates, Inc., 35 E. Grassy Sprain Road, Yonkers, NY 10710. Phone: (914) 337-1900.

OWNERSHIP
Privately held; by Victor W. Eimicke and Maxine Eimicke.

MANAGEMENT
Victor Eimicke, President; Maxine Eimicke, VP, Secretary/Treasurer; Laura Klimley, VP; Florence Forbes, Production Manager; Joel Rosenwasser, Account Manager; John Palmero, Controller.

TYPE OF MARKETER
Mail order.

BUSINESS
Eimicke publishes and markets a variety of personnel and other business forms, and general business paper products. The company sells to commercial, industrial and municipal accounts. V. W. Eimicke Ltd., located in Peterborough, Ontario, is the company's Canadian mail order operating division and was chartered in 1978. Management reports that Eimicke's sales are non-seasonal, and that the company employed 60 people in 1981.

COMPANY HISTORY
The corporation is the continuation of a business started as a proprietorship in 1946 in New York by Victor Eimicke. January 1, 1956, proprietorship was succeeded by V. W. Eimicke Associates, a partnership between Victor Eimicke and his wife, Maxine Eimicke. The company was incorporated in New York on June 6, 1958; Victor and Maxine Eimicke are the principal owners. Eimicke has been a mail order marketer since its establishment, and in recent years has entered international markets.

MARKETS
Market is international. Sells to commercial, industrial, organizational and municipal accounts.

FACILITIES
Headquarters, marketing operations, Yonkers, NY; lettershop, fulfillment, Irvington, NY.

PRODUCTS, BRAND NAMES, PRICE RANGE
Primarily markets personnel forms; also included are business forms, stationery, other office supplies, file cabinets, etc. Brand names include Eimicke Personnel and Laurel Office forms. Wide price range.

FINANCIAL INFORMATION

	SALES	NET INCOME	PROFIT MARGIN
1981	$15,000,000*	N.A.	--

TYPE OF ADVERTISING, PROMOTION
Approximately 90% of the company's advertising is conducted through direct mail and package inserts. The remaining 10% is through catalogs which Eimicke publishes twice a year.

LIST INFORMATION

QUANTITY MAILED:	5,000,000
AVERAGE ORDER:	$60
ACTIVE BUYERS:	233,000
TOTAL LIST:	N.A.
LIST SOURCE:	Direct mail.

COMMENTS
The sales figure above is an estimate of 1981 revenues for both Eimicke Associates U.S. sales, and Eimicke, Ltd.'s sales in the Canadian market. Domestic sales accounted for approximately 80% or $12,000,000 of Eimicke's estimated 1981 revenues; the remaining 20% or $3,000,000 came from Canadian operations. Management reports that Eimicke has experienced considerable growth over the past several years. Sales have increased an estimated 15% annually since 1979. Profits have also reportedly increased proportionately. Eimicke reports that expanding product lines may cause them to increase their use of catalogs for direct mail promotion in the future. Major emphasis will still be on direct mail packages and the company's extensive package insert program.

ENCYCLOPAEDIA BRITANNICA

ADDRESS, PHONE

Encyclopaedia Britannica, Inc., 425 N. Michigan Ave., Chicago, IL 60611. Phone: (312) 321-7000.

OWNERSHIP

Privately held; outstanding capital stock held in trusts set up by William Benton.

MANAGEMENT

Charles E. Swanson, President; Raymond J. Markman, Executive VP; Harold J. Silver, Director, National Advertising Services; Alan B. Boyer, Direct Mail Manager.

TYPE OF MARKETER

Mail order, direct sales.

BUSINESS

Company publishes and markets reference works and other books which are sold through direct mail and by independent direct sales contractors. E.B. has fifteen subsidiaries including F.E. Compton & Co., Publishers; Great Books of the Western World; Encyclopaedia Britannica Education Corp. (producer and distributor of educational texts); Encyclopaedia Britannica Holding Co. (holds stock of all foreign subsidiaries). Other products marketed include films, records and more.

COMPANY HISTORY

E.B. was founded in 1768 in Scotland. Operations were moved to New York by bookseller Horace Hooper in 1899. Company continued to be financially supported by London Times until 1910 when Cambridge University took over sponsorship. In 1920 Sears, Roebuck & Co. purchased company and reorganized operations under present name. After 20 years of losses, Sears gave business to the University of Chicago. In 1943, University gave two-thirds of operations to adman William Benton.

MARKETS

Markets worldwide through wholly-owned subsidiaries in U.S. and partially-owned subsidiaries overseas.

FACILITIES
Headquarters and warehouses in Chicago; branch offices in major U.S. cities.

PRODUCTS, BRAND NAMES, PRICE RANGE
"All-New Encyclopaedia Britannica" is major product--price, $395 per set. Other products: Britannica Junior Encyclopaedia, The Annals of America, Britannica Atlas, The Science Library, and more. Price range $6.00 to $600.00.

FINANCIAL INFORMATION

	SALES	NET INCOME	PROFIT MARGIN
1980	$300,000,000*	N.A.	--

TYPE OF ADVERTISING, PROMOTION
Direct mail, 50%; 50% space in TV Guide, Time, Newsweek, etc. Space used to generate leads for salesmen. Estimated 90% of advertising budget is put behind Britannica III. Brochures are 11 x 8-1/2, full-color and glossy, 12 pages.

LIST INFORMATION
QUANTITY MAILED: N.A.
AVERAGE ORDER: $15 (after encyclopedia purchase)
ACTIVE BUYERS: 407,383
TOTAL LIST: 1,000,000+
LIST SOURCE: Direct mail.

COMMENTS
In 1980 gross sales approached $300 million; an estimated $87 million of this amount was generated by the 30-volume Britannica III reference set. Company announced in July, 1979, that major expansion would double sales by 1982. Strategy includes new business ventures abroad, new marketing strategies in the U.S., new products recycled from existing offerings and perhaps an acquisition in the telecommunications field. Company has successfully developed local-language materials when new companies are started overseas. Reference works and books, as well as other merchandise, are sold door-to-door by independent sales people. To promote sales, company makes heavy use of space advertising and direct mail promotions. Typical mailing pieces place heavy emphasis on the advantages home reference material offers--"make studying more fun." Recently, company placed sales persons in 500 bookstores to sell Britannica III reference sets.

FIDELITY PRODUCTS

ADDRESS, PHONE
Fidelity Products, Inc., 5601 International Parkway, Minneapolis, MN 55440. Telephone: (612) 536-6500.

OWNERSHIP
Fidelity Products is a division of Fidelity File Box, Inc., which is a wholly-owned subsidiary of Liberty Diversified Industries of Minneapolis, MN.

MANAGEMENT
Ben Fiterman, President; Thomas Anglo, Gen. Mgr.; Michael Fiterman, Executive Vice President; Bernice Fiterman, Vice President; Peter Simon, Treasurer; David Lenzman, Secretary.

TYPE OF MARKETER
Mail order.

BUSINESS
Fidelity Products Company is the mail order marketing arm of Fidelity File Box, Inc. The company markets a wide assortment of containers, shipping supplies, packaging materials, warehouse supplies, data and word processing supplies, and general office equipment. The containers, files, and corrugated storage boxes Fidelity sells are manufactured by the parent and its four other subsidiaries. Other word processing supplies and general office equipment are purchased from outside manufacturers.

COMPANY HISTORY
Fidelity File Box, Inc. was founded as a subsidiary of Liberty Diversified to market the boxes and containers produced by the parent. It was incorporated in Minnesota on March 27, 1961. Fidelity Products Company mail order operations were started in 1962. Since that time data and word processing products and general office equipment have been added to the mail order merchandise mix. Liberty Diversified and its five subsidiaries reported 1,200 employees in 1981.

MARKETS
Fidelity sells by mail to business and industrial accounts throughout the U.S.; buyers are 74% male.

FACILITIES
Parent and subsidiary headquarters and manufacturing operations share 190,000 sq. ft.

PRODUCTS, BRAND NAMES, PRICE RANGE
Fidelity, Fideli-Pack, Kraft, Marsh, IBM, Bubble Pak, Rubbermaid, Penco, Panasonic, Unitrex, Victor; virtually everything for office and warehouse organization. Wide price range.

FINANCIAL INFORMATION

	SALES	NET INCOME	PROFIT MARGIN
1981	$20,000,000*	N.A.	--

TYPE OF ADVERTISING, PROMOTION
Fidelity Products relies entirely on direct mail for promotion. The company publishes four major catalogs each year, plus a variety of direct mail packages promoting a specific product or group of items.

LIST INFORMATION

QUANTITY MAILED:	5-9,000,000
AVERAGE ORDER:	$130
ACTIVE BUYERS:	126,000
TOTAL LIST:	353,000
LIST SOURCE:	Direct mail.

COMMENTS
Fidelity Products total mail order sales for 1981 are estimated to be $20,000,000. Fidelity started in 1961 mailing 3,000 pieces of a one-page flyer offering one product. Currently the company publishes the following annual full-color catalogs: (1) Supplies and Equipment for Office & Industry -- 8 x 9-1/4, 112 pages; (2) Catalog of Data and Word Processing Products -- 8-1/4 x 10, 48 pages; (3) Fideli-Pack -- (containers, shipping supplies, packaging materials, warehousing supplies) 8-1/4 x 10, 36 pages; (4) Gift Collection -- (gift packages of fruit, nuts, jellies, meat and candy) 8-1/2 x 10-3/4, 12 pages. In addition to catalogs, Fidelity is a heavy mailer of direct mail packages promoting single products to past buyers. A typical package contains an 11x17 folded brochure promoting the specific item or group of products, a promotional letter, and in many cases an insert offering a premium for ordering. These packages are also used to generate catalog inquiries and sell merchandise to rented lists.

HENRY FIELD

ADDRESS, PHONE
Henry Field Seed & Nursery Co., 407 Sycamore Street, Shenandoah, IA 51602. (712) 246-2110.

OWNERSHIP
Subsidiary of Amfac, Inc., Honolulu, HI; part of Amfac Mail Order Division.

MANAGEMENT
Don Kruml, President; Lee Gingery, VP-Advertising Manager; Orville Dragoo, VP-General Manager; Mike Rucker, Controller; Nick Reavis, Merchandising Manager.

TYPE OF MARKETER
Mail order, retail.

BUSINESS
Henry Field is the newest addition to Amfac's blossoming Mail Order Division, which last year reported sales in excess of $35 million. Field joined Gurney in this relatively new Amfac division. Field produces and markets seeds, bulbs, live nursery stock and gardening accessories through its catalogs. Company also has retail Garden Centers in Omaha, NE and Shenandoah, IA. Field employs an average of 120 full-time people.

COMPANY HISTORY
The company was started 90 years ago by Henry Field. The original business was selling seeds, plants and tree starts through the mail to farmers mostly in the midwestern states. Henry Field Seed & Nursery was incorporated in 1935. Operations have been greatly expanded to include increased growing fields, and the addition of gardening equipment and accessories. Field was acquired by R. J. Foster in 1959, and sold to Amfac in October, 1980.

MARKETS
Mail order customers throughout the U.S.; home and farm owners; 60% male.

FACILITIES

Offices, warehouses, growing fields in Shenandoah, IA; Garden centers in Shenandoah and Omaha, NE.

PRODUCTS, BRAND NAMES, PRICE RANGE

Seeds, trees, shrubs, bulbs, plants, gardening equipment. House brands are: "Green King" hybrid elm; "Turnbull" giant pear; "McNeilly" everbearing potato. Price range from less than $1 to more than $100.

FINANCIAL INFORMATION

	SALES	NET INCOME	PROFIT MARGIN
1981	$12,000,000*	N.A.	--

TYPE OF ADVERTISING, PROMOTION

Field mails five catalogs per year (major mailings spring and fall) including newest "late bird sale" book replacing annual sale folder. Additional advertising is space in newspapers, and shelter and garden magazines. Special promotions: free gifts and discounts.

LIST INFORMATION

QUANTITY MAILED:	9,000,000
AVERAGE ORDER:	$21
ACTIVE BUYERS:	689,000
TOTAL LIST:	1,258,000
LIST SOURCE:	Direct mail, space.

COMMENTS

Of Henry Field's estimated $12 million in sales for 1981, roughly 90% came from mail order operations. The company's two Garden Center retail outlets contributed a total of 5%, and the remaining 5% came from limited wholesale marketing. The product sales breakdown is as follows: seeds and bulbs, 53%; trees and plants, 19%; shrubs, 10%; accessories and equipment, 18%. Field's catalogs are 8-½ x 11, full color, regularly 100 pages long. Product descriptions are complete with growing instructions and projected results, and general gardening and landscaping tips. Management reports that severe economic conditions inversely affect their sales of fruit-bearing and edible plants and trees. "When food prices go up, people will plant fruit instead of shade trees." Root plants and fruit trees are selling well, and officials say that food producing plants are up a "healthy 20% to 30%." Company is working on dwarf varieties for urban consumers.

FIGI'S

ADDRESS, PHONE
Figi's, Inc., 630 South Central Avenue, Marshfield, WI 54449. Telephone: (715) 387-1771.

OWNERSHIP
Subsidiary of publicly-held American Can Company, Greenwich, Connecticut.

MANAGEMENT
John H. Figi, Jr., President; Richard Hewitt, Executive Vice President; Raymond Leg, Sr., Vice President; George Douma, Vice President-Purchasing; David Cain, Vice President-Finance.

TYPE OF MARKETER
Mail order.

BUSINESS
Company sells cheeses and other food gifts by mail to consumer and business gift markets; also sells gourmet cookware and specialty food items to consumers via its gourmet cookware catalogs. The number of employees ranges from about 400 during the summer months to about 1,750 during the peak selling months of November and December.

COMPANY HISTORY
Company was started in 1944 by John Figi, Jr., who was a federal cheese inspector at the time. Figi's was sold to W. R. Grace in 1968 and was transferred into Chemed Corp., a wholly-owned subsidiary of W. R. Grace, in 1971. Company was sold to Metromedia in 1978. In 1981, Figi's was purchased by American Can Company.

MARKETS
U. S. consumer and business gifts markets. Customers for food & cookware merchandise are 63% female.

FACILITIES
Headquarters, fulfillment, manufacturing plant, warehousing and cold storage facilities in Marshfield.

PRODUCTS, BRAND NAMES, PRICE RANGE
Aged cheese; smoked meats; nuts; cookies; jam; candies; potted bulbs; gourmet pots, pans, dishes, bowls, hard-to-find utensils; cookbooks; specialty baking items. Prices: gift foods, $5.95-$49.45; gourmet items, $3.50-$460.00.

FINANCIAL INFORMATION

	SALES	NET INCOME	PROFIT MARGIN
1980	$33,000,000*	N.A.	--

TYPE OF ADVERTISING, PROMOTION
Virtually 100% of Figi's promotion is through catalogs mailed to house list and extensive list rentals. "Gifts In Good Taste" food catalog is 6-½ x 9-½, full-color, roughly 80 pages. "Collection For Cooking" gourmet books are 8-½ x 5-½, full-color, usually 60 pages.

LIST INFORMATION

QUANTITY MAILED:	31,000,000
AVERAGE ORDER:	$41
ACTIVE BUYERS:	Food: 731,733; Gourmet: 71,162
TOTAL LIST:	1,568,000
LIST SOURCE:	100% direct mail.

COMMENTS
Figi's mails six different catalogs per year: the gourmet cookware catalog (added in 1979) each spring and fall; and gift food catalog mailings for Christmas, Valentines Day, Easter, and Mothers Day. The traditional line of gift foods accounted for 95% of total income in 1980. Figi's buys from creameries in Wisconsin and from vendors throughout the country, manufacturing only "Kave-Kure"--a cheddar cheese spread. Company owns and operates Figi's Data Center, a computerized order-processing service for its own use and for rental to clients. They have provided customized computer services to several other mail order companies. Following Figi's acquisition by American Can in July, 1981 for an unspecified amount, it is operating as a unit of Fingerhut. Fingerhut's Bill Johnson says the two marketers will operate separately with John Figi, president, reporting to him: "We are looking for synergistic opportunities between the two companies--marketing opportunities--rather than operations.

FINGERHUT

ADDRESS, PHONE

Fingerhut Corporation, 4400 Baker Road, Minnetonka, MN 55343. Telephone: (612) 932-3100.

OWNERSHIP

Subsidiary of publicly-held American Can Company, American Lane, Greenwich, CT 06830.

MANAGEMENT

Theodore Deikel, Exec. VP of American Can, Chrmn & CEO of Fingerhut; William C. Johnson, President; Steve Platt, VP Business Development; Howard Goldberg, Sr. VP Marketing & Merchandising.

TYPE OF MARKETER

Mail order.

BUSINESS

Company is a mail order marketer of general merchandise. Products include apparel, home furnishings and appliances, power and hand tools, gourmet cheeses, etc. Fingerhut is one of the largest direct mail marketers of consumer products; employs 2,710. Six Wiman Corp. facilities manufacture apparel and outerwear. Color Graphics Corp., a subsidiary in the Minnesota area, provides printing services. A second subsidiary, Imperial Plastics, manufactures plastic products for Fingerhut and other markets.

COMPANY HISTORY

Fingerhut started in 1948 manufacturing plastic seat covers. Operations were expanded in the '50s when company began marketing products from other manufacturers by mail, including tools, dishes, towels, etc. Apparel manufacturing began in 1959 with line of car coats, and by the mid '70s Fingerhut was manufacturing 50% of the merchandise it sold. Ill-conceived expansion into Europe contributed to a $7.5 million loss in 1975. Fingerhut merged into American Can in November, 1978.

MARKETS

Lower to middle income households; potential market reportedly 63% of U.S. families.

FACILITIES
Corporate H.Q., distribution and fulfillment, separate mailing and shipping plants, all in Minnesota.

PRODUCTS, BRAND NAMES, PRICE RANGE
Home furnishings and appliances, power and hand-tools, stereos, luggage, apparel, leisure and travel goods, gourmet foods and accessories. House and national brands including Sunbeam, Tappen, Cannon, Lady Pepperell, Brother, York, Royal, etc.

FINANCIAL INFORMATION

	SALES	NET INCOME	PROFIT MARGIN
1981	$310,000,000*	N.A.	--

TYPE OF ADVERTISING, PROMOTION
Advertising through solo mailings, multi-mailers, and multi-product catalogs. Uses direct mail packages of folders, brochures, and letters. Catalogs are full-color and are published and mailed seasonally.

LIST INFORMATION
QUANTITY MAILED:	250,000,000
AVERAGE ORDER:	$59
ACTIVE BUYERS:	3,500,000
TOTAL LIST:	17,000,000
LIST SOURCE:	Direct mail.

COMMENTS
In 1980 Fingerhut Corporation's sales, "exceeding $250 million," were approximately 14.5% of American Can's Consumer Products/Distribution division total revenues. Mail order merchandise sales breakdown is as follows: home furnishings, 36%; leisure and travel items, 15%; portable home appliances and tools, 14%; apparel, 33%; other, 2%. Approximately 22% of company's operating budget is spent on direct mail market research and testing, and marketing information system. In 1980, company introduced two new catalog merchandise lines: Great Impressions, a 48-page catalog of large-size women's apparel; Artisans of China, a collection of decorative handcrafted items from mainland China. In the fall of 1980, Fingerhut began researching order-taking and fulfillment via cable television; began test of in-home "shop and bank system" in San Diego in the spring of 1981. American Can's acquisition of Figi's (1981) added gift foods and gourmet cooking accessories by mail under the Fingerhut group.

FIRST COINVESTORS

ADDRESS, PHONE

First Coinvestors, Inc., 200 Willets Road, Albertson, NY 11507. Telephone: (516) 294-0040.

OWNERSHIP

Publicly held; 1,000,000 common shares outstanding; traded OTC.

MANAGEMENT

Stanley Apfelbaum, President; Don Lewis, Senior Vice President, Finance; Walter Breen, Vice President; Jack Lee, Executive Vice President; Terry Apfelbaum, Secretary.

TYPE OF MARKETER

Mail order.

BUSINESS

First Coinvestors markets rare coins and stamps by mail, through single and continuity offers. The company also acts in an advisory capacity for amateur and investment collectors. Through its subsidiary FCI Press, Inc., the company publishes books and guides on coin and stamp collecting. F.C.'s other wholly-owned subsidiary, First Stampvestors, Inc., is a mail order marketer of stamps. F.C. also has offices in Munich, Germany, and currently reports 170 employees.

COMPANY HISTORY

The company was started in 1967 by the current president Stanley Apfelbaum, an attorney by profession who was also interested in rare coins for investment purposes. F.C. was incorporated under Delaware laws on February 14, 1969. Authorized capital was 2,000,000 shares of common stock at $.10 par value; 159,000 shares issued and outstanding. On Jan. 31, 1971, A.S. Coin Co. and J.A. Scott & Company, Inc. were acquired.

MARKETS

Customers throughout the U.S.; mostly men over 30 with upscale incomes; buying their own home.

FACILITIES

Headquarters and mail order operations in Albertson, NY; foreign office, Munich.

PRODUCTS, BRAND NAMES, PRICE RANGE

Rare coins and stamps. Various publications on collection for enjoyment and investment purposes, and coin and stamp values. Advisory services for coin and stamp collecting as an investment program. Accessories for collectors.

FINANCIAL INFORMATION

	SALES	NET INCOME	PROFIT MARGIN
1980	$19,934,955	$1,216,341	6.1%

TYPE OF ADVERTISING, PROMOTION

The company publishes a monthly advisory investment newsletter and mails direct mail promotions. Uses space advertising in Barrons, Wall Street Journal, Money, Moneysworth, American Collector, and American Business.

LIST INFORMATION

QUANTITY MAILED:	2,000,000
AVERAGE ORDER:	$450
ACTIVE BUYERS:	20,000
TOTAL LIST:	88,000
LIST SOURCE:	Direct mail, space ads.

COMMENTS

First Coinvestors sales have increased substantially over the past four years: from $6.6 million in 1978, to $10.7 million in 1979, and jumping over $19 million in 1980. Net earnings have climbed from a loss in 1978 to $1.2 million in 1980. Management reports that sales for the first ten months of 1981 were up compared to the same period in 1980, and company expects profits to be up substantially for 1981. First Coinvestors attributes the increasing success of their operations to their high percentage of multibuyers. They feel that people are becoming more aware of coins and stamps as a solid and potentially high dollar investment. F.C. attempts to provide the commodities, plus accessories and current collection information, all through the convenience and ease of mail order.

FOSTER & GALLAGHER

ADDRESS, PHONE
Foster & Gallagher, Inc., 6523 N. Galena Road, Peoria, IL 61601. Telephone: (309) 691-4610.

OWNERSHIP
Privately held by Thomas S. Foster, Edward L. Miller, and Melvyn R. Regal (Galena Enterprises, Inc.).

MANAGEMENT
Thomas S. Foster, President; Edward L. Miller, Executive Vice President; Melvyn R. Regal, Executive Vice President, Secretary, Treasurer; James E. Radke, Vice President, Marketing.

TYPE OF MARKETER
Mail order.

BUSINESS
Galena Enterprises has four mail order subsidiaries under Foster & Gallagher (mail order gift house) control: American Boutique, women's cosmetics; Breck's, spring flowering bulbs; Spring Hill Nurseries, flower and vegetable seeds, horticultural accessories; Magazine Market Place, special magazine subscriptions. All subsidiaries operate out of Peoria, except Spring Hill (Tipp City, Ohio).

COMPANY HISTORY
Thomas Foster and Helen and Frank Gallagher started "F.G. Mail Order, Inc." in 1951. Sold to Stanley Home Products in 1965, but Foster, Miller and Regal bought the company back in 1975 after forming Galena Enterprises (holding company). In 1976 the name was changed from F.G. Mail Order to Foster & Gallagher, Inc., the name still used "synonymously" with Galena. In late 1970's, Galena added to Foster & Gallagher gift operation by purchasing ailing American Boutique, Breck's and Spring Hill companies.

MARKETS
Sells by mail domestically. American Boutique, Breck's and Spring Hill customers primarily women.

FACILITIES

Headquarters and fulfillment, Peoria, IL; American Boutique and Mag. Mkt. Place have NY offices.

PRODUCTS, BRAND NAMES, PRICE RANGE

American Boutique, name-brand women's cosmetics, $2.50-$50; Breck's, Dutch bulbs (tulips, daffodils, etc.), average $12; Spring Hill Nurseries, fruit, flower and vegetable seeds, shrubs, trees, etc., $2-$30. Magazine Mkt. Place, special magazine subscriptions.

FINANCIAL INFORMATION

	SALES	NET INCOME	PROFIT MARGIN
1981	$35,000,000*	N.A.	--

TYPE OF ADVERTISING, PROMOTION

100% catalog, all full-color. American Boutique, mini-catalogs issued every two months throughout the year; Breck's, spring and fall; Spring Hill Nurseries, spring; Magazine Market Place, January and July.

LIST INFORMATION

QUANTITY MAILED:	27,000,000*
AVERAGE ORDER:	$6 to $32 (Total for all
ACTIVE BUYERS:	N.A. Galena subsidiaries.)
TOTAL LIST:	13,500,000
LIST SOURCE:	Direct mail.

COMMENTS

The past year (1981) has brought about some major changes in the company that is most often associated with its Foster & Gallagher gift operations. Galena discontinued its Foster House and Helen Gallagher gift businesses in January, 1981, and was planning to sell its retail operations by the end of the year. The Foster House name will be retained, but company officials say they plan to stick with just the four mail order operations that have been acquired over the past decade. When Galena took over American Boutique, Spring Hill Nurseries, and Breck's, all were having financial trouble. Galena officials report they've been able to turn things around and have shown an increase in mail order sales of about 10% per year. Management confirms that 1980 sales were running in excess of $25,000,000, and they expected considerably higher figures for 1981. Operations are reportedly profitable. Company expects continued growth in mail order, with long-range plans to expand outside list usage.

FOX STANLEY PHOTO

ADDRESS, PHONE
Fox-Stanley Photo Products, Inc., 8570 Tesoro Dr., San Antonio, TX 78286. Telephone: (512) 828-9111.

OWNERSHIP
Publicly held; stock traded NYSE; 3,478,769 common shares outstanding; 1981 dividend: $.68; 1981 market prices: high, 13; low, 7-3/8.

MANAGEMENT
Donald W. Becker, Chairman; Carl Newton, Jr., Vice Chairman; Carl Newton III, President; William Kirkman, President - Dealer Division; Gary Greenberg, President - Retail Division.

TYPE OF MARKETER
Mail order, retail, and wholesale.

BUSINESS
Fox-Stanley is one of the nation's leading mail order, retail, and wholesale photofinishing and photo supply services. Retail Division operates 1000 retail stores and drive-up kiosks throughout U.S. Dealer Division provides photofinishing, supplies, marketing support and training for some 7,000 wholesale accounts. Special Markets Division operates nationwide mail order services. Company supports division operations with 26 photofinishing plants. Company reported over 5,000 employees in 1981.

COMPANY HISTORY
Fox Photo was founded by Carl Newton in 1905, and merged with Stanley Photo in 1961. Mail order photofinishing was main business of Fox Photo in its formation. In 1970's mail order operations were greatly expanded with the acquisition of other mail order companies, retaining their names, and benefiting from the consolidation of facilities. In fiscal '81, company opened 247 new stores and kiosks --the largest number of stores added in any one year, and financed entirely from internal cash flow.

MARKETS
The Mail Order Division serves 1.3 million customers throughout the United States.

FACILITIES

General offices are located in San Antonio, with 26 processing plants in the South and Midwest.

PRODUCTS, BRAND NAMES, PRICE RANGE

Mail Order Division offers several brands to serve both the amateur and professional photofinishing markets. Amateur Brands: Fox Photo; Ball Photo; Pic-Parade; Filmway; Owl Photo. Professional Brands: Fox Professional Color Labs; 35 Unlimited.

FINANCIAL INFORMATION

	SALES	NET INCOME	PROFIT MARGIN
1981	$153,514,000	$6,246,000	4.1%

TYPE OF ADVERTISING, PROMOTION

Consists of seasonal mailings, space advertising in newspapers, multi-page promotions in leading photography publications, outside list mailings, and package inserts. Company spent $10,558,000 on all advertising in '81; 16% over 1979.

LIST INFORMATION

QUANTITY MAILED:	750-850,000
AVERAGE ORDER:	$8-$15
ACTIVE BUYERS:	850,000
TOTAL LIST:	1,400,000
LIST SOURCE:	Direct mail, space.

COMMENTS

The Special Markets segment totalled $13,462,000 in sales for fiscal 1981; approximately 9% of company's total revenues. There was a 9.5% decrease in sales for 1980-1981, compared to a 4.5% decrease for 1979-1980. Operating profits for the division were down 35% between '80 and '81. The company attributes this drop to competitive pressure and says that they are removing themselves from the low-price portion of the market. Through "35 Unlimited" and "Fox Professional Color Labs," mail order is positioning to serve the amateur and professional 35mm format user. In addition Fox-Stanley eliminated school photography and promotional portrait division. The company discontinued many discount services, but negative effect on sales was balanced by increased profit margins. Mail order profitability improved with special promotions of photo-related merchandise included with customer prints to increase average order. Supplemental seasonal mailings offer photo albums, gift frames, etc.

FRANKLIN MINT

ADDRESS, PHONE
Franklin Mint Corporation, Franklin Center, PA 19091. Telephone: (215) 459-6000.

OWNERSHIP
Wholly owned subsidiary of Warner Communications, Inc., New York, NY.

MANAGEMENT
Charles Andes, Chmn., CEO; Brian Harrison, President & COO; Charles Wickard, VP Marketing; Martin Breisblatt, VP Marketing Services; Douglas Briggs, VP Market Planning; Walter Fish, VP Marketing.

TYPE OF MARKETER
Mail order.

BUSINESS
Company develops, manufactures and markets a wide range of collectible, luxury, jewelry, home decor and leisure products. There are three principle operating divisions--The Franklin Mint, The Franklin Library, and Franklin Mint International. Company is the largest commercial mint in the world and mints legal tender for foreign governments. Franklin markets primarily through direct mail and print media. Company is testing two retail outlets which will market products similar to those offered by mail.

COMPANY HISTORY
Joseph Siegel started the General Numismatic Corp. on July 1, 1966. Company was incorporated in Philadelphia in 1964; name changed to Franklin Mint Corp. in 1972. Company began as a minter and seller of numismatic products--medals, ingots and legal tender for foreign governments. In mid '70s company diversified into other product lines--metallic sculpture collectibles '71, crystal in '76, and collector records and heirloom furniture '77. On March 2, 1981, Franklin Mint merged with Warner Communications, Inc.

MARKETS
Franklin markets throughout the U.S. and in 17 foreign countries; customers, upscale collectors.

FACILITIES
Corporate headquarters and facilities at Franklin Center, PA, suburb of Philadelphia.

PRODUCTS, BRAND NAMES, PRICE RANGE
1) Franklin Porcelain--decorative plates, figurines, vases, bells, thimbles and tankards; 2) Jewelry; 3) Numismatic--coins, medals, and ingots; 4) Philatelic related products; 5) Fine Books, collector records, home decor, luxury and leisure products.

FINANCIAL INFORMATION

	SALES	NET INCOME	PROFIT MARGIN
1980	$360,086,000	$21,858,000	6.1%

TYPE OF ADVERTISING, PROMOTION
Direct mail to past buyers and outside lists. "The Collectors Almanac" is a monthly publication for F.M. Collectors Society members. In addition, company is a heavy user of space advertising to generate new customers.

LIST INFORMATION
QUANTITY MAILED:	25,000,000+*
AVERAGE ORDER:	N.A.
ACTIVE BUYERS:	1,200,000*
TOTAL LIST:	2,013,000
LIST SOURCE:	Space ads, direct mail.

COMMENTS
Franklin Mint has become Warner Communication's new Direct Response Marketing Division. Franklin's 1980 sales increased some 27% over 1979; after-tax earnings climbed 35%. Warner officials report that without the effect of the Franklin acquisition, Warner 1981 second quarter earnings would have increased 56% over second quarter '80. Consolidating Franklin's results, second quarter earnings were up 66% to a record $42.6 million. Warner reported $6.2 million in pre-tax operating income for Franklin in second quarter '81; "sharply ahead of last year's results." Franklin is noted for innovative promotional copy dubbed "Segelese" (after company founder). This style has been used successfully to market esoteric collectors items to non-collectors--to develop a non-specialist, not especially upscale market for higher priced collectibles. Company claims that customers have a collector's attitude rather than investment orientation; reportedly 90% of customers intend to keep purchases as family heirlooms.

FREDERICK'S OF HOLLYWOOD

ADDRESS, PHONE

Frederick's of Hollywood, 6608 Hollywood Blvd., Hollywood, CA 90028. Telephone: (213) 466-5151.

OWNERSHIP

Publicly held; stock traded ASE, FY81 average shares outstanding, 1,414,000; market prices: high 12-1/2, low 5-3/8; FY81 cash dividend, $0.39.

MANAGEMENT

Frederick N. Mellinger, President and Chairman; Robert W. Hansen, Executive VP; Joseph A. Nussbaum, VP Mail Order Division; Colleen Menerey, VP Finance; Leslie Cooper, Merchandise Director.

TYPE OF MARKETER

Mail order, retail.

BUSINESS

Frederick's sells a complete line of women's fashions, dresses, sportswear, shoes, swimwear, lingerie and foundations. The name has become a household word and is synonymous with fashions that accentuate female sensuality. In recent years the company has developed a limited line of complementary menswear. The mail order business produces roughly 1/3 of total revenues.

COMPANY HISTORY

The company was founded in New York in 1946 by Frederick Mellinger, and was moved to California approximately one year later. It became a public company in 1972. In its 36 years of operation, Frederick's has grown to a $40 million business with 138 retail stores in 33 states, and a mail order operation serving customers throughout the U.S. Company employs approximately 850 people.

MARKETS

Customers are mostly mid to upscale females; recent emphasis on men's fashions and marketing.

FACILITIES

Headquarters and mail order facilities in Hollywood, CA.

PRODUCTS, BRAND NAMES, PRICE RANGE

Women's apparel and fashion accessories, including shoes, jewelry, intimate apparel, health and beauty aids; some menswear; adult books, games, sexual aids. House brands. Moderate prices.

FINANCIAL INFORMATION

	SALES	NET INCOME	PROFIT MARGIN
1981	$39,300,000	$2,231,000	5.7%

TYPE OF ADVERTISING, PROMOTION

Six major catalogs, 5 secondary editions of those with new cover and some new merchandise, totaling 11 separate mailings yearly. Also uses package inserts and space advertising in national magazines. Aggressively promotes its toll-free telephone ordering service.

LIST INFORMATION

QUANTITY MAILED:	11,000,000 annually
AVERAGE ORDER:	$50
ACTIVE BUYERS:	488,000
TOTAL LIST:	1,200,000
LIST SOURCE:	Direct mail, space.

COMMENTS

Frederick's had record sales in 1981: up 20.5% from $32.6 million to $39.3 million. Net earnings increased 31.2%, from $1.7 million in 1980 to $2.2 million in 1981. Mellinger attributes Frederick's ability to maintain a positive trend for the past several years to their "unique specialty niche." Management sees few competitors as yet in their area of the lingerie-by-mail market. First quarter FY82 performance is as follows: sales at $9.6 million--up 9.2% over same period last year; net earnings were down 40.4% from $285,000 last year to $170,000. Management claims that increase in revenues is mostly due to price increases and the opening of new retail outlets (eight in this quarter compared with four in first quarter, 1980). First quarter is historically low-volume for company. Frederick's reportedly spends well over $1,000,000 annually on advertising. Different catalogs are mailed 11 times per year, and company makes heavy use of direct mail packages to specific target groups--particularly now in their effort to increase percentage of male buyers.

GANDER MOUNTAIN

ADDRESS, PHONE

Gander Mountain, Inc., P.O. Box 128, Hwy. W., Wilmot, WI 53192. Telephone: (414) 862-2331.

OWNERSHIP

Privately held; Vincent Shiel owns 75% of the capital stock.

MANAGEMENT

Vincent W. Shiel, Chairman & Chief Executive; Robert S. Sturgis, Jr., President; Thomas Curry, Vice President and Treasurer; Richard Chernof, Secretary.

TYPE OF MARKETER

Mail order, retail.

BUSINESS

Gander Mountain is primarily a mail order marketer of outdoor recreational equipment and sporting goods. In addition the company has one retail outlet located at headquarters. The merchandise mix includes men's and women's outdoor apparel and footwear, and sports-oriented gifts. The company does no manufacturing and no international marketing. Gander currently employs 97 people.

COMPANY HISTORY

The business was started in 1960 by Robert Sturgis, and was incorporated in June of that year. Originally the company was a mail order and retail marketer of firearms, ammunition and other hunting supplies. The corporate name was shortened from Gander Mountain Shooter & Supply, Inc. in the late 1960's. Gander Mountain, Inc. reportedly filed a petition for arrangement under Chapter 11. Plan of reorganization filed June 8, 1981, was accepted in August of 1981.

MARKETS

Products are sold domestically; customers are mostly middle-to-high income level males, 40-45 years.

FACILITIES
Headquarters, retail outlet, and mail order operations in 35,000 sq. ft. of leased space in Wilmot, WI.

PRODUCTS, BRAND NAMES, PRICE RANGE
Primary products sold are outdoor sporting goods such as camping equipment, tents, fishing rods and reels, knives, scopes, airguns, apparel, and gift items like belts, buckles, clocks, etc. Name brands include Bushnell, Weaver, Redfield.

FINANCIAL INFORMATION

	SALES	NET INCOME	PROFIT MARGIN
1981	$12,000,000*	N.A.	--

TYPE OF ADVERTISING, PROMOTION
Catalog mailings constitute approximately 90% of Gander's advertising. The company publishes four different catalogs per year and mails roughly 8,000,000 copies annually. Catalogs are supported with space in sports and outdoor magazines.

LIST INFORMATION
QUANTITY MAILED: 8,000,000
AVERAGE ORDER: $51
ACTIVE BUYERS: 181,200
TOTAL LIST: 788,000
LIST SOURCE: Direct mail (90%), space (10%).

COMMENTS
The sales figure above represents an estimate of Gander Mountain's total 1981 mail order sales only. The company's retail sales are estimated to be $1 million, making the company's total revenues for 1981 approximately $13 million. Management reports that they are projecting a minimum annual overall sales increase of 10% to 15% over the next several years. Gander's seasonal catalogs are 8 - 1/2 x 11, full color, 80 to 100 pages, and contain over 5,000 items. Black powder guns are reportedly a major seller, both assembled and in kit form. No changes in mail order strategy were reported for the coming year.

GARDEN WAY

ADDRESS, PHONE

Garden Way, Inc., 102nd St. and Ninth Avenue, Troy, NY 12180. Telephone: (518) 235-6010.

OWNERSHIP

Privately held by Richard Denholtz, Dean Leith, Jr., George Done, Carl Grimm, and employees.

MANAGEMENT

Richard Denholtz, Chairman; Dean Leith, Jr., President; Carl Grimm, Sr. VP, Treasurer; Jairo Estrada, Exec. VP Operations, Chief Financial Officer; Ed Schofield, Exec. VP, Marketing Secretary.

TYPE OF MARKETER

Mail order, retail.

BUSINESS

Company manufactures and markets garden tillers and garden carts, publishes books and buys products to be sold by mail. Garden Way sells to wholesalers, dealers and the general public--has six retail outlets across the country. Subsidiaries are Garden Way Manufacturing, Garden Way Associates (in-house ad agency), Garden Way Research, Garden Way Publishing and Garden Way Retail. Company has demonstration/service centers in 4 markets. Employs 1250.

COMPANY HISTORY

Noroton Publishing was started in 1940 by Lyman Wood and partner Wally Boren. Original operation marketed inspirational books and literature through mail order. In 1966 Noroton started an in-house ad agency, Precision Marketing Associates, with Wood, Leith, Lundberg, Denholtz and John Keane. In '67, Wood offered the seven men equal partnerships in Garden Way, as well as 62% of Watco Machine Products. Originally manufactured and marketed by mail the Troy-Bilt roto tiller.

MARKETS

Customers are 70% male; average age 47; segment do-it-yourselfers, sub-segment gardening; U.S.A.

FACILITIES

Headquarters, Troy, NY and Charlotte, VT; computer, lettershop facilities, Waterford, NY.

PRODUCTS, BRAND NAMES, PRICE RANGE

About 800 garden tools--tillers, garden carts, fruit grinders, presses, loading ramps, work benches and storage equipment. House brands: Troy-Bilt and Garden Way. National brand small appliances, yogurt makers, dehydrating equipment, etc.

FINANCIAL INFORMATION

	SALES	NET INCOME	PROFIT MARGIN
1981	$120,000,000*	N.A.	--

TYPE OF ADVERTISING, PROMOTION

Space ads, catalogs, co-op mailings, and package inserts. Catalogs: 1) Country Kitchen for utensils, food preserving items, dehydrators, grain mills; 2) G.W. Books on gardening; 3) G.W. Research markets gardening and outdoor equipment.

LIST INFORMATION

QUANTITY MAILED:	N.A.
AVERAGE ORDER:	$100*
ACTIVE BUYERS:	610,000*
TOTAL LIST:	N.A.
LIST SOURCE:	Direct mail, space.

COMMENTS

Mail order accounts for 70% of sales. Company's 1981 sales were estimated to be $120,000,000; roughly a 50% increase since 1978. Considerable amount of recent new customers and accounts represent a large after-market which is just getting started. Garden Way targets several market segments: Garden Way Cooperative Media targets consumers who respond by mail to win energy related prizes. About 90% of customers are male. Country Kitchen customers are 60% female, average age 47, median income $22,000, and 99% are married. Garden Way Research buyers are 85% male, average age 47, and median income $20,000. Currently, company advertises in about 100 magazines and newspapers. Also promotes with inserts in over 100 U.S. and Canadian seed company catalogs. Spot T.V. supports Sunday newspaper preprints. Six times a year, company mails "Troy-Bilt Owners News." Management is reportedly planning to merge Garden Way Manufacturing and Garden Way Associates into parent company.

GEICO CORPORATION

ADDRESS, PHONE
GEICO Corporation, GEICO Plaza, Washington, DC 20076. Telephone: (301) 986-3000.

OWNERSHIP
Publicly held; traded NYSE; 20,070,099 common shares outstanding; FY81 market prices; high, 29-3/8; low, 14-3/8; FY81 dividend: $.48.

MANAGEMENT
John J. Byrne, Chairman; Paul J. Hannah, Vice Chairman; William B. Snyder, President-GEICO Corp. and GEICO; Harry I. Bond, President-Criterion Insurance; John J. Krieger, President-GEFCO.

TYPE OF MARKETER
Mail order, direct sales.

BUSINESS
GEICO Corporation's principal direct response subsidiary, GEICO, writes preferred risk family automobile and homeowners insurance. Another mail order subsidiary, Criterion, writes standard and nonstandard risk policies for military, young drivers, older citizens, etc. Government Employees Financial Corp. (GEFCO), unconsolidated affiliate in Denver, CO., provides consumer finance services and insurance brokerage services to U.S. citizens living abroad.

COMPANY HISTORY
GEICO, founded in 1936, was one of the first insurance companies to solicit virtually all of its new business by direct mail. In 1960, the company formed a direct sales force as an additional means of drawing new business, but continued to rely on direct mail to renew or increase the coverage of existing policies. Criterion was organized in 1961 to write non-preferred auto policies. In a 1979 paper reorganization, GEICO Corp. was formed as the parent company. GEICO reported 3,496 full-time and 704 part-time employees.

MARKETS
GEICO: D.C. and all states except NJ; Criterion: D.C. and all states except MA, NJ & SC.

FACILITIES
H.Q. in Washington, DC; regional offices in Wash.,
DC, Macon, GA and Woodbury, NY; 11 sales offices.

PRODUCTS, BRAND NAMES, PRICE RANGE
GEICO insures preferred risk family automobiles 95%,
home and boatowners 5%; Criterion insures standard
risk family autos and motorcycles.

FINANCIAL INFORMATION

	SALES	NET INCOME	PROFIT MARGIN
1981	$727,453,000	$83,286,000	11%

TYPE OF ADVERTISING, PROMOTION
Direct mail advertising programs; space ads in
magazines and newspapers; other media advertising
including radio and television spot announcements.

LIST INFORMATION
QUANTITY MAILED:	N.A.
AVERAGE ORDER:	N.A.
ACTIVE BUYERS:	1,750,000*
TOTAL LIST:	5,000,000*
LIST SOURCE:	Direct mail, space.

COMMENTS
The sales figure above is total 1981 revenues for
GEICO Corporation. Total revenues increased 6%
over $684 million in 1980, and net earnings were up
37% over 1980 totals. The jump in earnings reflects
the sale in 1981 of 66% interest in GELICO subsidiary
to the Legal & General Group of the United Kingdom.
GEICO Corp's 1981 dividend was 12% higher than the
1980 dividend. Company officials reported some
disappointment in the growth of mail order subsidiary GEICO's automobile business. GEICO plans to
be positioned to serve the preferred-risk driver with
quality insurance at lower cost, through direct mail
and direct sales channels. Criterion complements its
service by offering insurance to standard or non-
preferred customers. GEICO's automobile premiums
written in 1981 totalled $626 million, up 5.4% from
$593 million in 1980. While claims decreased 3.2% in
1981, settlement costs rose rapidly. Management
reports increased emphasis on direct mail to the
preferred market.

GENERAL NUTRITION

ADDRESS, PHONE
General Nutrition, Inc., 921 Penn Avenue, Pittsburgh, PA 15222. Telephone: (412) 288-4600.

OWNERSHIP
Publicly held; stock listed NYSE. FY80: 8,263,933 common shares outstanding; market prices: high 26-1/8, low 13-1/4; cash dividend: $0.06.

MANAGEMENT
David Shakarian, Chmn & CEO; Bart Shakarian, Vice Chmn; Gary Daum, Pres & Secty; VP's: Kenneth Chane, Retail; Michael Graves, Operations; George McTurk, Mail Order.

TYPE OF MARKETER
Mail order, retail.

BUSINESS
GNC is a vertically integrated company that manufactures vitamins, minerals, nutritional foods, supplements, beverages and personal care products; markets them through company owned stores, by direct mail, and in fruit-and-nut kiosks in shopping malls. Company maintains test kitchens for creating new all-natural food products, and laboratories for developing personal care and nutritional supplement items. In addition, GNC markets a variety of specialized food preparation appliances.

COMPANY HISTORY
Forerunner of General Nutrition was a business founded by David B. Shakarian in 1935, with the first store opened in Pittsburgh, PA. Company's growth during the 40's and 50's was principally through mail order sales. Incorporation took place in 1955. Major expansion of retail store sales occurred in the late 60's. In 1976 came significant increases in production of food and beverage products. In 1979, with the opening of its Greenville, SC, manufacturing plant, it began producing certain of its vitamin products.

MARKETS
Mail order sales throughout U.S., Canada & U.K. Retail stores in 47 states in U.S., plus Canada.

FACILITIES
Manufacturing plants in ND, SC; packaging plant in PA; distribution centers in GA, ND, NJ, PA, TX.

PRODUCTS, BRAND NAMES, PRICE RANGE
Vitamins and minerals are sold in single and multi-forms. Nutritional supplements: protein powders and bone meal; principal food products: nuts, seeds, cereals, herb teas, juices, dried fruits; personal care products. House brand: Golden Harvest.

FINANCIAL INFORMATION

	SALES	NET INCOME	PROFIT MARGIN
1980	$241,611,000	$12,900,000	5.3%

TYPE OF ADVERTISING, PROMOTION
General Nutrition publishes a catalog containing over 3,000 health related products, and a Natural Sales catalog offering natural foods and vitamin products. Customers are primarily women. Also, direct mail packages and space in newspapers and magazines.

LIST INFORMATION

QUANTITY MAILED:	30,000,000+
AVERAGE ORDER:	GNC: $18.75; NS: $22.70
ACTIVE BUYERS:	GNC: 816,434; NS: 128,414
TOTAL LIST:	1,431,527
LIST SOURCE:	Direct mail, space.

COMMENTS
Management attributes consistent increases in net earnings to significant like-unit sales gains, expansion in the company's manufacturing capacity, growth in mail order sales, and careful management of operating costs. Increased sales volume in 1980 reflects GNC's emphasis on promotion expansion--a 28% increase (to $12.5 million) in advertising expenditures (primarily newspaper advertising) over 1979. Proportion of '80 sales among the company's product categories is as follows: vitamins, minerals, 24%; personal care and other products--9%. 1980 was GNC's first year of public ownership; company traded over-the-counter until Dec. 22, 1980, when its stock was accepted for trading on the New York Stock Exchange. In 1980 GNC acquired a business in Great Britain which sells nutritional foods and supplements to mail order customers and to independent stores. GNC reported second quarter '81 sales gain of 39.8%; net earnings up 24.6%.

GOKEYS

ADDRESS, PHONE
Gokeys, Inc., 84 S. Wabasha, St. Paul, MN 55107. Telephone: (612) 292-3933.

OWNERSHIP
Wholly-owned subsidiary of CML Group of Concord, MA.

MANAGEMENT
Thomas G. Blexrud, President; Paul Felegy, Chief Financial Officer; Ed Bennet, General Merchandising Manager; Marilyn Murlowski, VP-Retail.

TYPE OF MARKETER
Mail order, retail.

BUSINESS
Gokeys sells high-quality men's and women's casual clothing, outerwear, shoes, luggage and some unique gifts. The company manufactures shoes, boots and some luggage at their St. Paul facilities. Reportedly 70% of business is through mail order, with remaining 30% through sales at four Minnesota retail stores. Sales are heaviest around the fall months, when as many as 140 people are employed. Employment falls to about 90-100 during slower period (May-June).

COMPANY HISTORY
Noah Gokey, a French-Canadian boot and shoe maker, started the company in 1850 in Jamestown, NY. Horace Thompson purchased the company in 1926. Thompson moved the operations to St. Paul, where many Scandinavian bootmakers were without jobs, and began making one of the company's most famous products, the snake-proof "Boote Sauvage," in 1939. In 1946, the company was incorporated in Minnesota, and the CML Group acquired Gokeys in 1973.

MARKETS
Gokeys sells by mail throughout the U.S.; customers are 60% female.

FACILITIES

Offices, mail order and manufacturing operations in St. Paul; four retail stores in Minnesota.

PRODUCTS, BRAND NAMES, PRICE RANGE

Sells national-brand footwear, men's and women's casual apparel, rugged outerwear, luggage, gifts and some sports equipment. Prices range from $1.50 up to $300. About 350-400 items are offered per catalog.

FINANCIAL INFORMATION

	SALES	NET INCOME	PROFIT MARGIN
1981	$10,000,000*	N.A.	--

TYPE OF ADVERTISING, PROMOTION

Approximately 90% of Gokeys advertising is through their catalogs which are mailed eight times a year. In addition they use some limited space in newspapers and national magazines.

LIST INFORMATION

QUANTITY MAILED:	800,000*
AVERAGE ORDER:	$60
ACTIVE BUYERS:	74,000
TOTAL LIST:	200,000*
LIST SOURCE:	Direct mail, space.

COMMENTS

Of Gokeys total revenues (above) roughly $7 to $8 million are estimated to come from mail order operations. The company publishes several editions of its catalog per year which are full-color, 8 x 11, and range from 32 to 56 pages. Catalogs are mailed four times in the fall, twice in the spring, and twice in the summer. Footwear started out as the backbone of Gokeys and remains perhaps the biggest seller today, even though the combined sales of men's and women's clothing surpasses footwear sales. Mail order sales have reportedly grown significantly over the past five years, and the company has added two new retail outlets since 1979. Management reports that they will place fairly equal emphasis on mail order marketing and retail stores for future growth. Gokeys currently spends over $1,000,000 annually on advertising.

GOLDBERG'S MARINE

ADDRESS, PHONE
Goldberg's Marine Distributors, Inc., 202 Market St, Philadelphia, PA 19106. Telephone: (215) 627-3700.

OWNERSHIP
Privately owned by the Goldberg family.

MANAGEMENT
Harry Goldberg, President; Charles Goldberg, Vice President; Jacob Goldberg, Secretary & Treasurer; Richard Goldberg, Catalog Director; Larry Goldberg, Mail Order Fulfillment Division.

TYPE OF MARKETER
Mail order, retail.

BUSINESS
Company markets high quality marine and pleasure boating supplies to customers worldwide. Catalogs carry about 9,000 items including a variety of nautical clothing for men and women, ship-to-shore radios and sophisticated electronic devices, and other boating equipment and accessories. Mail order accounts for approximately 80% of the business. Sales are heaviest during the months of March through August. Company employs 70 people at peak season and 40 during September - February.

COMPANY HISTORY
The company was started in 1946 in Philadelphia by Harry, Jacob and Charles Goldberg. Initially, Goldberg's marketed WWII military surplus and unusual hardware and equipment. In an effort to develop the company in a leisure time/outdoor recreation direction, management reoriented merchandising to boating and marine supplies. Significant retail expansion in 1956; rapid expansion of mail order business between 1970 and 1978.

MARKETS
Products are marketed worldwide, primarily to up-scale, family-oriented males.

FACILITIES

Mail order and 100,000 sq. ft. warehouse at PA location; three retail outlets, Philadelphia and NY.

PRODUCTS, BRAND NAMES, PRICE RANGE

Management reports "virtually every type of product used on pleasure boats, both power and sail," every national brand sold in the U.S.; house brands include "Sea-Gee," "Four Winds," "Sail-King," "Super Sail-King," "Eagle." Price range: $0.50 to $5,000.

FINANCIAL INFORMATION

	SALES	**NET INCOME**	**PROFIT MARGIN**
1981	$19,000,000*	N.A.	--

TYPE OF ADVERTISING, PROMOTION

Approximately 80% of advertising is through the four Goldberg catalogs published per year. Catalogs are supported with space advertising in consumer magazines such as Smithsonian, New York Times and trade magazines like Boating, Sailing and Yachting.

LIST INFORMATION

QUANTITY MAILED:	2,500,000
AVERAGE ORDER:	$85
ACTIVE BUYERS:	175,000
TOTAL LIST:	300,000
LIST SOURCE:	80% direct mail, 20% space ads.

COMMENTS

Goldberg's sales for 1981 were reportedly 15% ahead of 1980, in keeping with a 15%-20% annual sales increase over the past several years which is expected to continue. The company mails four separate catalogs per year. The main or "master" catalog (8-1/2" x 11", 230 pages, mostly b&w) is mailed at the end of December. Three seasonal catalogs (8-1/4" x 10-1/2", 72 pages) are mailed in February, June and September. Goldberg's has recently expanded their marine apparel lines to include such items as jackets, skirts, slacks, shorts, footwear and ties. The new lines are expected to draw a larger potential customer base, attracting not only boating enthusiasts, but more general fashion-conscious outdoor types.

GRACO

ADDRESS, PHONE

Graco, Inc., 60 Eleventh Avenue N.E., Minneapolis, MN 55413. Telephone: (612) 378-6000.

OWNERSHIP

Publicly held; 2,291,284 common shares outstanding; stock traded OTC; 1980: dividend, $.92; market prices: high, $21; low, $16.

MANAGEMENT

David A. Koch, President and CEO; Mark G. Christopher, Vice President of Manufacturing and Distribution; Robert Hasse, Vice President; James W. Maltzold, Vice President.

TYPE OF MARKETER

Mail order, wholesale, direct sales.

BUSINESS

Graco Inc. designs, manufactures and markets fluid handling equipment and related products used to pump, transfer, mix, dispense and apply fluids and semi-solid materials. The key components in most fluid handling products are specialized pumps which Graco manufactures. Products are marketed primarily to commercial and industrial concerns, worldwide. The company currently employs 1,800 full time people. Sales are reportedly non-seasonal.

COMPANY HISTORY

The business was started in 1926 by Leil and Russel Gray. It was originally incorporated as Gray Company in South Dakota in 1926. The company was reincorporated as Graco, Inc. in Minnesota on December 18, 1947, and became publicly-held in 1969. Management reports that their steady growth over the years is mainly due to in-house technological developments in both product design and manufacturing operations.

MARKETS

Graco sells merchandise by mail and direct selling agents worldwide; commercial customers.

FACILITIES
Graco has a five-building complex in Minneapolis housing H.Q., marketing and manufacturing.

PRODUCTS, BRAND NAMES, PRICE RANGE
Commercial and industrial fluid handling equipment, specialized pumps, air, hydraulic and electric-powered spraying equipment, accessories and parts. Brand names include Hydra-Spray, Graco-Roto-Flo, and Hydro-Clean. Wide price range.

FINANCIAL INFORMATION

	SALES	**NET INCOME**	**PROFIT MARGIN**
1980	$116,892,000	$5,397,000	4.6%

TYPE OF ADVERTISING, PROMOTION
Graco mails a variety of catalogs, direct mail packages, and product brochures for inquiry generation as well as mail order sales. The company uses space advertising in industrial and trade publications to generate leads for direct sales and direct mail.

LIST INFORMATION

QUANTITY MAILED:	N.A.	(Graco removed its list
AVERAGE ORDER:	N.A.	from the market in 1979.)
ACTIVE BUYERS:	N.A.	
TOTAL LIST:	N.A.	
LIST SOURCE:	N.A.	

COMMENTS
Graco's total revenues for 1980 increased 5.9%, but earnings declined 48%. Management reported that the drop in profits was due to higher costs of products sold and additional operating expenses in marketing and distribution activities. Sales to customers in the U.S. amounted to $74,000,000 in 1980 (down 3.7%). International sales were $42,500,000 representing an increase of 28.5%. International sales have increased 52% over the past three years and now represent 36.3% of total sales. Graco now sells products in 70 foreign countries. The company makes extensive use of direct mail not only for a major percentage of both domestic and foreign sales, but also as a promotional tool for direct selling operations. Direct mail is used by the company's main distribution branches to identify prospects, reinforce sales calls, and to develop repeat purchasing by wholesale buyers. Graco has thirteen foreign subsidiaries which use direct mail promotions and mail order marketing.

W. W. GRAINGER

ADDRESS, PHONE
W. W. Grainger, Inc., 5500 W. Howard St., Skokie, IL 60077. Telephone: (312) 982-9000.

OWNERSHIP
Publicly held; stock traded NYSE, MSE; 14,205,999 common shares outstanding; 1980 dividend: $.98; 1981 market prices: high, 44-5/8; low, 33-1/4.

MANAGEMENT
David W. Grainger, Chairman, President; Jere D. Fluno, VP-Finance; Donald W. Hansen, VP-Administration; Wiley N. Caldwell, VP-Distribution; George T. Mathews, VP-Manufacturing.

TYPE OF MARKETER
Mail order, wholesale.

BUSINESS
W. W. Grainger is a nationwide distributor of a wide array of electric motors and controls, pumps, air compressors, hydraulics, heating and air conditioning equipment, power and hand tools, lawn and garden equipment. The Distribution Group sells through a branch network and by mail through their MotorBook catalogs. The Manufacturing Group produces a substantial portion of the electric motors marketed. The company presently operates 163 branches in 46 states.

COMPANY HISTORY
The company was founded in 1927 by W. W. Grainger in Skokie, Illinois. Grainger has from the start been involved in the direct marketing of motors, pumps, compressors, etc., to wholesale market. The MotorBook catalog has been published and expanded continuously since company was formed. MotorBook published in 1982 lists over 9,600 items plus extensive technical and application data. Grainger reported 5600 employees for 1980.

MARKETS
Grainger sells to distributors, dealers, contractors, and industrial and commercial maintenance markets.

FACILITIES
Corporate, Skokie, IL; Distributon Group, Niles, IL;
Manufacturing Group, Cedarburg, WI.

PRODUCTS, BRAND NAMES, PRICE RANGE
About 70% of sales are products bearing company
registered trademarks: DAYTON, DOERR, TEEL,
DEMCO, DEM-KOTE, SPEEDAIRE; other 30%, national
brands. Widely varying price range.

FINANCIAL INFORMATION

	SALES	NET INCOME	PROFIT MARGIN
1981	$859,659,000	$56,265,000	6.5%

TYPE OF ADVERTISING, PROMOTION
Grainger's main promotional tool is their MotorBook
catalog. Catalog is 1000+ pages with mono-color
highlighting of merchandise items. Company also
does some space advertising in trade publications.

LIST INFORMATION
QUANTITY MAILED:	1,650,000
AVERAGE ORDER:	$111
ACTIVE BUYERS:	716,000
TOTAL LIST:	N.A.
LIST SOURCE:	Direct mail, space.

COMMENTS
Grainger reported a 10.8% increase in sales for 1981,
from $775.7 million to $859.7 million. Earnings
increased 15.3% from $48.8 million to $56.3 million.
Grainger's 1980 sales represent approximately
7,800,000 transactions, with the average total purchase for the year at approximately $1,211. The
lines of merchandise carried in the MotorBook catalog
have been expanded at an annual rate of 5% to 10%.
The main catalogs currently contain over 10,000
items. Two editions are published annually in January and July, plus MotorBook Supplements containing offerings of new merchandise. Customers
purchase by mail or telephone in response to catalogs, and over-the-counter at branch outlets.
Regional Distribution reportedly ships 1.1 million
pounds of merchandise each business day. Grainger
currently has over 1700 vendor/suppliers and is
expanding the branch network. The company reportedly spent $41.8 million in 1980 developing the
Distribution Group.

GRAYARC

ADDRESS, PHONE

Grayarc Company, P. O. Box 2944, Hartford, CT 06104. Telephone: (203) 379-9911.

OWNERSHIP

Wholly-owned subsidiary of Pitney Bowes, Inc.

MANAGEMENT

Edward Kristin, President; Steven Lett, Vice President-Marketing; Fred Madura, Vice President-Planning; Carmine Adimando, Vice President-Finance.

TYPE OF MARKETER

Mail order.

BUSINESS

Grayarc is a manufacturer and mail order marketer of high quality, imprinted business forms and labels. Among the variety of products available is a wide selection of office supplies and equipment including stationery, envelopes, pressure sensitive labels and anti-fatigue mats. Grayarc manufactures the majority of the products offered in their catalogs. Management reports that sales are heaviest from October through December, and the company employed 500 people in 1981.

COMPANY HISTORY

The company was started in 1926 in Brooklyn, New York. It has been a mail order operation since its establishment. The first products marketed were labels and imprinted business forms. The business was later acquired by the Dictaphone Corporation. On May 11, 1979, Pitney Bowes completed acquisition of Dictaphone Corporation, thus acquiring Grayarc which is now part of Pitney Bowes' Wheeler Group operating division. Headquarters were recently moved from Brooklyn to New Hartford.

MARKETS

Primarily U.S.; products are marketed to industrial and business accounts.

FACILITIES

Newly-constructed plant, containing 150,000 sq. ft. for offices, mail order and manufacturing operations.

PRODUCTS, BRAND NAMES, PRICE RANGE

Products include imprinted business forms, labels, office supplies and equipment such as calculators, cordless telephones, labels, stationery, envelopes and copiers. Brand names include Pitney Bowes, Sharp, 3M. Prices: $10 - $600.

FINANCIAL INFORMATION

	SALES	NET INCOME	PROFIT MARGIN
1981	$16,250,000*	N.A.	--

TYPE OF ADVERTISING, PROMOTION

One hundred percent of Grayarc's advertising and promotion is through their direct mail catalogs. The catalogs are 8-1/2 x 11, full-color, 64 pages, and are published and mailed seasonally.

LIST INFORMATION

QUANTITY MAILED:	10,000,000*
AVERAGE ORDER:	$65
ACTIVE BUYERS:	240,000
TOTAL LIST:	453,000
LIST SOURCE:	Direct mail.

COMMENTS

Grayarc's estimated 1981 sales of $16.25 million represents an increase of roughly 19% over the estimated total of $13.7 million for 1980. The company has recently joined two other Pitney Bowes mail order subsidiaries, the Drawing Board and Monarch Marking Systems, in the newly-formed Wheeler Group operating division. Total mail order sales from these subsidiaries in 1980 was estimated at $69,000,000 or 5% of Pitney Bowes total revenues. Grayarc contributes an estimated 20% of the Wheeler Group mail order total. Over the past five years Grayarc has experienced a 10% to 12% annual increase in sales. Management reports that they will step-up direct mail promotions in 1982 by including biannual sales flyers in their mailing schedule. During the past year, the company moved into their new $6.6 million New Hartford facilities. Management reports that Grayarc plays a vital role in plans for the Wheeler Group to serve as a full-service business system, equipment and supply mail order source.

G-R-I CORPORATION

ADDRESS, PHONE
G-R-I Corporation, The G-R-I Building, 65 E. SouthWater, Chicago, IL 60601. (312) 977-3700.

OWNERSHIP
Publicly owned; listed AMEX; FY81 shares outstanding, 2,603,090; 1400 shareholders; 1981 market prices: high, 7; low, 3-3/8.

MANAGEMENT
Maurice H. Bronner, Chairman; Allan A. Marver, Vice Chairman, Secretary; David R. Rubin, President and CEO; Senior VPs: Anthony Brown, Anthony DeNunzio, Thomas Dulick.

TYPE OF MARKETER
Mail order.

BUSINESS
G-R-I Corp. is the parent company of The Butterfly Group, World of Beauty, S.A.V.E. (Shoppers' Association for Value and Economy), Homeward House, Beauty Buy Book, and Epicure mail order catalogs. The corporation and its subsidiaries are engaged in the sale of consumer products by direct response mail order marketing primarily through continuity club programs. The List Service division offers highly selective lists of over 15,000,000 women mail order buyers to mail order as well as retail package goods companies.

COMPANY HISTORY
Founded in 1958 by Maurice H. Bronner, G-R-I Corp. has evolved in the last two decades into a diversified mail order business. World of Beauty acquired in 1965 from R. R. Donnelley; Canadian World of Beauty, added in '71, was sold Dec. 1, 1980; S.A.V.E. developed in the mid '70s and Beauty Buy Catalog began in '78. Butterfly Group was developed and tested in '76 before being incorporated into World of Beauty. G-R-I employs 500 people.

MARKETS
Continuity club members and catalog buyers in all 50 states and Canada. Customers mostly female.

FACILITIES
Executive offices, Chicago, IL; distribution center, LaGrange, IL; buying office, New York City.

PRODUCTS, BRAND NAMES, PRICE RANGE
Four classes of products: World of Beauty - famous name cosmetics; S.A.V.E. - national brand grocery, household and toiletry items; Beauty Buy Book - costume jewelry, cosmetics, beauty related products; Homeward House -Oneida stainless flatware.

FINANCIAL INFORMATION

	SALES	**NET INCOME**	**PROFIT MARGIN**
1981	$67,600,000	$2,600,000	3.8%

TYPE OF ADVERTISING, PROMOTION
Direct response space advertising in national magazines and newspapers; direct mail catalogs, package inserts, cooperative promotions: $27.36 million advertising budget in 1980.

LIST INFORMATION
QUANTITY MAILED: 50,000,000*
AVERAGE ORDER: Varies by program.
ACTIVE BUYERS: 3,000,000
TOTAL LIST: 12,000,000
LIST SOURCE: Direct mail, space.

COMMENTS
Energies of management in 1980 were directed toward a recovery program following the 1979 major net loss of $4.5 million. Areas of examination and change included media used for advertising and promotion, market research and development, and strengthening of management itself. The Canadian operation (Canadian World of Beauty) was sold Dec. 1, 1980. All changes resulted in a decreased net loss for FY80 of $753,000. For FY80 product sales: grocery, household and toiletry items contributed 35%; cosmetic collections, 36%; stainless steel flatware, 16%; and specialty catalog sales, 11%. In first quarter '81, with sales of $16.3 million, G-R-I profits dipped once again to ($1.4 million). Slight improvement in the second quarter ('81) brought in sales of $22.5 million, but earnings loss was ($1.01 million). Finally in the third quarter of '81, with sales down nearly 40% below the same period last year, earnings rose to $560,000.

GROLIER

ADDRESS, PHONE

Grolier, Inc., Sherman Turnpike, Danbury, CT 06816. Telephone: (203) 797-3500.

OWNERSHIP

Publicly held; stock traded Philadelphia Stock Exchange; FY81 bids: high 3, low 1-3/4; preferred stock dividend: $1.20; 10,598,559 common shares.

MANAGEMENT

Robert B. Clarke, Chairman, President, CEO; Andrew J. Reinhart, Executive VP; Richard M. Clark, Senior VP, Gen. Counsel, Secretary; George F. Hunger, VP, Treasurer.

TYPE OF MARKETER

Mail order, direct sales, retail.

BUSINESS

Grolier and its 19 direct and 55 indirect wholly-owned subsidiaries publish and/or sell encyclopedias and other reference works through independent sales representatives. It also sells these publications and other merchandise including juvenile books, educational publications and large-type reading materials by mail order and telephone sales. Direct mail is handled through Grolier Enterprises and subsidiaries in Canada, Australia, South Africa and England.

COMPANY HISTORY

Company was formed in 1936 as the Grolier Society from a business originally started in 1895. Direct marketing operation (Grolier Enterprises) began with the sale of annual supplements and yearbooks to customers in the U.S. and Canada who already owned Grolier reference sets. Present name was adopted in January, 1960. Company moved headquarters from New York to Connecticut in April, 1977. Began using telephone marketing centers in 1978, primarily in the U.S. and Canada, and telephone sales were $42 million in 1981.

MARKETS

U.S., Canada, and approx. 30 foreign countries. List estimated at 8 million with 4 million actives.

FACILITIES
Company HQ in Danbury, CT; offices in NY, Canada, Mexico, Latin America, Europe.

PRODUCTS, BRAND NAMES, PRICE RANGE
Over 65 multi-volume encyclopedia and other reference sets in 5 languages. Titles include Encyclopedia Americana, The New Book of Knowledge,
Encyclopedia International, Animal Kingdom. Prices
from about $110 to $850, single book-club editions
about $4.

FINANCIAL INFORMATION

	SALES	NET INCOME	PROFIT MARGIN
1981	$344,786,000	$14,285,000	4.1%

TYPE OF ADVERTISING, PROMOTION
Company uses direct mail, package inserts, billing
inserts to installment customers; cooperative advertising and, for Grolier Enterprises' Children's Book
Club, TV spots and space advertising in magazines.

LIST INFORMATION

QUANTITY MAILED:	80,000,000/year
AVERAGE ORDER:	Varies by program
ACTIVE BUYERS:	4,000,000
TOTAL LIST:	8,000,000
LIST SOURCE:	Direct mail, space, list rental.

COMMENTS
Through re-organization of various foreign operations and elimination of unsound diversification in
the U.S., Grolier has made considerable progress in
recent years in turning around a serious loss situation. Improved operating margins primarily attributable to its direct marketing operations in the U.S.
and Canada. Revenue for 1981 was $344.8 million, up
10% over 1980. Net income for 1981 was $14,285,000,
an increase of over 50% over 1980. Average order
for direct mail programs includes low end of $2.95 on
the Children's Book Club for three-to-nine-year-
olds; $24.95 for single offer merchandise buyers;
$12.95 for annual and yearbook buyers; $150 for
multi-mail-order buyers (type of Grolier offer); and
$5.98 to $350 for continuity series mail order buyers.
Total mail order sales are estimated to be $90 million
in '78, $104 million in '79, and $116 million in '80.

GROSSET & DUNLAP

ADDRESS, PHONE

Grosset & Dunlap, Inc., 51 Madison Avenue, New York, NY 10010. Telephone: (212) 689-9200.

OWNERSHIP

Wholly-owned subsidiary of Filmways, Inc., of Los Angeles.

MANAGEMENT

Richard L. Block, Chairman; Eric Gusstavson, Vice President of Finance, Secretary; Edward L. Stein, Vice President of Marketing; M. Ostrow, Vice President, Controller & Treasurer.

TYPE OF MARKETER

Mail order, wholesale.

BUSINESS

Grosset & Dunlap is a publisher and mail order marketer of reprint and original books in both hard and soft cover. Their current domestic catalog lists some 5,000 titles including self-help, how-to, cooking and diet books, fiction and non-fiction, religious and inspirational, etc. Grosset is best known as a publisher of books for children and young adults; juvenile line includes over 1,000 titles. Paperbacks are published by the Ace and Tempo subsidiaries. The company employs approximately 500 people.

COMPANY HISTORY

The business was started in 1898 under the partnership of entrepreneurs Grosset and Dunlap. In 1968 NGC Publishing (subsidiary of National General Corp.) acquired the outstanding capital of the company, changing the name to Grosset & Dunlap, Inc. In March of 1974 National General Corp. merged with American Financial Corporation, making Grosset a jointly held subsidiary. Filmways, Inc. purchased 100% control of Grosset & Dunlap on October 16, 1974.

MARKETS

Sells internationally to book wholesalers, retailers, schools and libraries.

FACILITIES

Headquarters, marketing operations and 360,000 sq. ft. warehouse in New York.

PRODUCTS, BRAND NAMES, PRICE RANGE

Grosset has several lines of juvenile books, including "Picture Books," "Classical Series," "Library Prebind Editions," "How and Why Books," and paperback "Tempo Books." Adult lines include Berlitz language and cookbooks, "how-to" and "self-help", etc.

FINANCIAL INFORMATION

	SALES	NET INCOME	PROFIT MARGIN
1981	$35,400,000	($5,958,000)	-0-

TYPE OF ADVERTISING, PROMOTION

Grosset & Dunlap uses direct mail packages to market their continuity and single title programs to both consumer and commercial buyers. In addition they place inquiry generating space ads in trade and book review publications, and national magazines.

LIST INFORMATION

QUANTITY MAILED:	N.A.	(The company markets
AVERAGE ORDER:	N.A.	a wide variety of lists
ACTIVE BUYERS:	N.A.	for its club, collection
TOTAL LIST:	N.A.	and single-title mail
LIST SOURCE:	N.A.	order programs.)

COMMENTS

Grosset & Dunlap's 1981 revenues dropped 2%, from $36 million in 1980 to $35.4 million in 1981. This is a 36% decrease from the company's high in 1979 of $55.4 million. The 1981 deficit in operating earnings improved by 30%, from ($8,527,000) in 1980, to ($5,958,000) in 1981. Management reports that the 36% drop in overall sales, and considerable losses for the company over the past two years reflect the elimination of adult fiction trade books and juvenile hardback books from Grosset & Dunlap's merchandise mix, as well as discontinuation of their promotional gift books lines. The company is reportedly refocusing on its historically successful lines of juvenile soft cover, self-help, cooking, and how-to books. Non-fiction hardbacks the <u>Pritkin Program</u> and <u>RN: the Memoirs of Richard Nixon</u> sold extensively by mail and through wholesale distribution in '80 and '81. Grosset & Dunlap makes heavy use of direct mail for sales, as promotion to wholesale buyers and for direct selling agents.

ADDRESS, PHONE

Gump's, 250 Post Street, San Francisco, CA 94108. Telephone: (415) 982-1616

OWNERSHIP

Division of publicly-held Macmillan, Inc. of New York.

MANAGEMENT

Robert Leitstein, President; James Hegarty, Vice President, General Manager; Mary Lou Klar, Vice President-Jewelry; William Goulet, Sales Promotion and Direct Market Manager.

TYPE OF MARKETER

Mail order, retail.

BUSINESS

Gump's markets high-quality line of gift items, such as crystal, china, jade figurines and other objects d'art. Company is especially well-known for its oriental jewelry, art and other decorative items. Gump's markets by mail and through its two retail stores in San Francisco and Houston. (Ratio of mail order sales to retail sales undetermined.) Gump's designs many of the items it sells but does no manufacturing. Sales are heaviest during the Christmas season.

COMPANY HISTORY

Company was started by the Gump family in 1861 in San Francisco. It began as a retail operation selling saloon mirrors for bars and bordellos. Line was expanded to its current type of offerings around the turn of the century. The Gump's facilities were destroyed in the great earthquake, but the family kept the business going as a retail operation. The mail order operation was added around 1950. Macmillan Inc., known primarily for its publishing operations, acquired Gump's in 1969. Second store in Houston opened in 1981.

MARKETS

Mail order market is predominantly domestic, middle to upscale female, average age 35.

FACILITIES
Offices, shipping, retail in San Francisco. Second
retail store in Houston.

PRODUCTS, BRAND NAMES, PRICE RANGE
Semi-precious and fine stone jewelry, figurines and
other gift items; china, brass and crystal items; oriental gifts; fashions for women. Prices range from
$10 up to $35,000 and more, depending on current
catalog offerings.

FINANCIAL INFORMATION

	SALES	NET INCOME	PROFIT MARGIN
1980	$10,000,000*	N.A.	--

TYPE OF ADVERTISING, PROMOTION
Gump's main promotional emphasis is on its catalogs,
which are published seasonally. Space advertising,
primarily to generate mail order inquiries, is done in
newspapers and 23 national-circulation magazines.

LIST INFORMATION

QUANTITY MAILED:	2,000,000*
AVERAGE ORDER:	$80*
ACTIVE BUYERS:	60,000*
TOTAL LIST:	300,000*
LIST SOURCE:	Direct mail, space.

COMMENTS
Gump's financial operations are closely guarded, and
the company does not market its list, but its parent
firm reported that the exclusive specialty store had
record sales in 1980 with the prospects for future
growth excellent. The company mails the four
editions of its catalogs in January, March, May and
August, with a special mailing during the Christmas
season. Catalogs are 8-1/4" by 9", full color, and
range from 34 to 82 pages. Although Gump's plans
to continue expansion of its mail order operations,
there is an anticipated simultaneous expansion of the
retail area. The Houston store opened in late 1981,
and other stores in major metropolitan areas are
planned. Company attributes its long and successful
history to the development and maintenance of a
quality image along with the development of quality
merchandise at fair prices. Rumors have existed for
some time that Macmillan is interested in selling
Gump's.

GURNEY SEED AND NURSERY

ADDRESS, PHONE

Gurney Seed and Nursery Co., 2nd and Capitol, Yankton, SD 57079. Telephone: (605) 665-4451.

OWNERSHIP

Wholly-owned subsidiary of publicly-held Amfac, Inc. (NYSE); with Henry Field comprising Amfac Mail Order Division.

MANAGEMENT

Don Kruml, President; Keith Price, Vice President-Marketing; Wayne Bryant, Advertising Manager; Jim Waltrip, Merchandising Manager; Gary Idt, Controller.

TYPE OF MARKETER

Mail order.

BUSINESS

Gurney is Amfac's major horticulture mail order operation. They produce and market a wide variety of vegetable and flower seeds, and fruit and ornamental nursery stock. In addition they market a line of related gardening aids, and kitchen and canning supplies. On an average, 35% of sales are seeds, 30% plants, 16% trees, and 8% shrubs. Gurney produces about 40% of what it sells, and the rest is contracted to outside growers and manufacturers.

COMPANY HISTORY

The company was founded in 1866 by C. W. Gurney, and has been in the Yankton, South Dakota area since its establishment. In 1947 the business was consolidated into United Seeds. In 1960 it was acquired by American Garden Products. In March of 1980 the American Garden Products group of companies was acquired by Amfac, and the Amfac Garden Products division was formed. In its 115 years in business, Gurney has grown to total assets of over $33,000,000.

MARKETS

Gurney fills over 2,000,000 orders per year, serving all 48 contiguous states.

FACILITIES

The company owns 500 acres, and rents 113 acres of farmland, cold storage, and packing facilities.

PRODUCTS, BRAND NAMES, PRICE RANGE

Over 90% of the products marketed are sold under the Gurney name. Prices range from $.09 to over $50.00. Company has developed market positioning as "the vegetable seed specialist."

FINANCIAL INFORMATION

	SALES	NET INCOME	PROFIT MARGIN
1981	$28,000,000*	$1,400,000*	5.0%*

TYPE OF ADVERTISING, PROMOTION

Company has two major mailings per year: 66-page catalog featuring full range of products, which is mailed each spring; a 28-page catalog featuring fall planted items. Catalogs are 4-color and tabloid size.

LIST INFORMATION

QUANTITY MAILED:	12,000,000
AVERAGE ORDER:	$15
ACTIVE BUYERS:	1,850,000
TOTAL LIST:	4,000,000
LIST SOURCE:	Direct mail, space.

COMMENTS

Amfac claims that they are the largest wholesale ornamental horticulture company in the nation, and that Gurney is one of the three largest garden product mail order operations. Industry experts estimate that the total horticulture mail order business is about $414,000,000 annually; giving Gurney some 6.7% of the market. Gurney was basically unaffected by widespread price cutting in the industry in 1980 to reduce inventory (predominately in wholesale container-grown merchandise) and has continued to show its annual sales increase of over 20%. Their primary markets are suburban and rural consumers, 80% male. In addition to their catalogs and space ads, Gurney mails two special flyers in the spring, and uses package inserts. About 90% of sales occur in the first 6 months of the year, with a peak in April-May.

HALL'S CATALOG

ADDRESS, PHONE

Hall's Catalog, 505 Armour Road, North Kansas City, MO 64116. Telephone: (816) 274-8668.

OWNERSHIP

Subsidiary of Hallmark Cards, Inc.; part of Hall's Merchandising, Inc. division. Majority of capital stock owned by the Hall family.

MANAGEMENT

Donald J. Hall, Vice Chairman and President; David H. Hughes, Executive Vice President and CEO; Robert L. Stark, Group Vice President and Secretary; Ed Disborough, Group VP.

TYPE OF MARKETER

Mail order.

BUSINESS

Hall's Catalog is one of fifteen subsidiaries of greeting card, paper party accessory manufacturer Hallmark Cards, Inc. Hallmark's retail merchandise operations include Hall's Crown Center retail stores and mail order marketer Hall's Catalog. Hall's sells a wide range of high-quality, high-priced ladies' fashions, decorative home furnishings, giftware, jewelry and more. All marketing is by mail through the company's four annual catalogs.

COMPANY HISTORY

Hallmark was started in 1907 in Norfolk, NE, by Joyce Hall and brothers R.B. and William Hall. Original products were cards and paper products. Additional general merchandise operations were started in the 1950's. The Hall's Merchandising, Inc. division was chartered in 1980. Hall's Catalog was incorporated into the Merchandising Division as the Hallmark Cards, Inc. mail order catalog subsidiary in the same year.

MARKETS

Mail order market is throughout the U.S.; no international. Customers primarily upscale, female.

FACILITIES
H. Q. at Armour Road location; order processing
and warehousing on Pershing Road, Kansas City

PRODUCTS, BRAND NAMES, PRICE RANGE
Product mix keys on elegance in fashions, housewares and decorative home furnishings, and a
variety of quality gifts and jewelry. House brands
plus national brands including Wallace, Reed &
Barton, Lenox, etc. Price range upscale.

FINANCIAL INFORMATION

	SALES	**NET INCOME**	**PROFIT MARGIN**
1981	$11,000,000*	N.A.	--

TYPE OF ADVERTISING, PROMOTION
Major portion of Hall's Catalog advertising is through
their catalogs mailed four times per year. Catalogs
are supported by merchandise and inquiry generating space ads in New Yorker, Smithsonian, Natural
History, etc.

LIST INFORMATION
QUANTITY MAILED: 7,000,000*
AVERAGE ORDER: $65
ACTIVE BUYERS: 109,961
TOTAL LIST: 600,000*
LIST SOURCE: Direct mail, space.

COMMENTS
Hall's Catalog contributed an estimated $11 million in
revenues to Hallmark in 1981. This represents
approximately 1.0% of total revenues for the parent
company. Estimates are that Hall's has averaged a
10% to 15% increase in annual sales over the past ten
years. Hall's mails several different catalogs per
year including their special holiday gift book. The
catalogs are full-color and format varies between
8-1/2 x 11 and 8-1/2 x 5-1/2; 20 to 32 pages.
Customers are 95% affluent women with families.
Currently 40% of mail order sales are telephone
orders in response to catalog mailings. The company
is placing major emphasis on educating customers in
the use of their toll-free ordering number which
they say cuts considerable time off of order processing and fulfillment. In addition, Hall's says that
on average phone orders are approximately 25%
higher than mail orders.

THE HAMILTON GROUP

ADDRESS, PHONE
The Hamilton Group Limited, Inc., 21 W. Church St., Jacksonville, FL 32203. (904) 358-4111.

OWNERSHIP
Part of Charter Communications Division of Charter Company, Inc., Jacksonville, FL.

MANAGEMENT
John W. Graham, President; Joseph J. Calderone, Vice President; Norm Brown, Vice President.

TYPE OF MARKETER
Mail order.

BUSINESS
The Hamilton Group markets porcelain plates and figurines (80%) and silver and gold medallions (20%). The company sells these and other limited edition collector's items through two mail order operations: Joy's Limited Editions (specializing in medium-priced collectibles), and The Hamilton Collection (featuring more expensive precious metal commemoratives). Company employs approximately 80 persons, including officers.

COMPANY HISTORY
The company was started in 1971 and was incorporated in Illinois on March 23, 1972, with authorized capital consisting of 50,000 shares of common stock at $1 par value. In April, 1978, all of Hamilton's stock was sold to The Charter Company, and headquarters was moved from Arlington Heights, Illinois, to Jacksonville, Florida. In 1981 the name was changed from Hamilton Mint, Inc. to The Hamilton Group Limited, Inc., and John Graham succeeded James Smith as president.

MARKETS
65% female; mail order customers from middle to high income families in the U.S. and abroad.

FACILITIES

Headquarters in Jacksonville, Florida; shipping center in Wheeling, Illinois.

PRODUCTS, BRAND NAMES, PRICE RANGE

Commemorative plates, stained glass, medals, figurines, medallions and ingots, silver and pewter items, porcelains, bells, ornaments, thimbles. Brand names: Heinrich Porcelain Fabrik, Goebel, Haviland, Lenox, Royalerlin, Gorham.

FINANCIAL INFORMATION

	SALES	NET INCOME	PROFIT MARGIN
1981	$23,000,000*	N.A.	--

TYPE OF ADVERTISING, PROMOTION

Direct mail packages include a personalized letter, brochure, and an order card or reservation form. Products are also introduced via space advertising in magazines such as Smithsonian and National Geographic, and in Sunday supplements.

LIST INFORMATION

QUANTITY MAILED:	8,000,000*
AVERAGE ORDER:	Hamilton, $292; Joy's, $45
ACTIVE BUYERS:	H., 38,000; J., 100,000
TOTAL LIST:	H., 66,900; J., 164,000
LIST SOURCE:	Direct mail, space.

COMMENTS

Management reports that Hamilton's sales and net earnings for 1981 are up considerably compared to 1980. Total combined revenues for Hamilton and Joy's mail order for 1981 are estimated to be $23 million. Hamilton does not use catalogs for direct mail. Promotions consist mainly of direct mail packages to current and repeat buyers (80%); the remaining percentage are packages and brochures to rented lists of high-income, high-ticket mail order buyers. Through the different merchandise offered and the very different price structures of Hamilton Collection and Joy's, the Group is positioned to serve both mid and upperscale collectors and investors with high-quality merchandise. Promotions make strong statements on the potential appreciation and value customers can expect.

HANOVER HOUSE

ADDRESS, PHONE
Hanover House Industries, Inc., 224 W. 34th Street, New York, NY 10016. Telephone: (212) 971-8300.

OWNERSHIP
Company is a subsidiary of publicly-held Horn & Hardart, of New York City.

MANAGEMENT
Harold L. Schwartz, President and CEO; Burnell J. Lawrence, Executive Vice President; Holly McMunn, Vice President for New Business Ventures; Ann Miller, List Director.

TYPE OF MARKETER
Mail order.

BUSINESS
Hanover House sells a variety of merchandise through mail order catalogs under names Hanover House (gifts and novelties); Old Village Shop, New Hampton General Store, Pennsylvania Station and Adam York (all four with gifts, apparel, etc.); Lana Lobell, First Editions and Chelsea Collection (all three with women's apparel); Freestyle (sports, outdoor apparel & equipment); and Lakeland Nurseries (nursery and garden stock).

COMPANY HISTORY
Company was started as Lana Lobell, Inc., in 1940 by Boris Leavitt; name was changed to Hanover House Industries in 1948. Name became HIJ Corp. when incorporated in Pennsylvania in 1972. Was sold to Horn & Hardart (the Automat and Burger King franchise people) in January, 1973; name back to Hanover House Industries. Since then has expanded by acquisition of mail order business and start-up of new catalogs aimed at different income segments. Employs about 400.

MARKETS
Markets products throughout the U.S. and overseas; customers are low to high income buyers.

FACILITIES

Headquarters in New York; warehouse and mail order handling and fulfillment facilities in Hanover, PA.

PRODUCTS, BRAND NAMES, PRICE RANGE

Lana Lobell women's shoes and apparel, First Editions women's fashions, Old Village Shop colonial style specialties, New Hampton General Store general merchandise, Hanover House general merchandise and novelties. Price ranges from $5 to $550.

FINANCIAL INFORMATION

	SALES	NET INCOME	PROFIT MARGIN
1980	$100,000,000*	N.A.	--

TYPE OF ADVERTISING, PROMOTION

Company advertises in shelter magazines, TV Guide, newspapers, Sunday supplements. For direct mail, uses rented lists and house lists; actively exchanges lists with appropriate mail order companies.

LIST INFORMATION

QUANTITY MAILED:	75,000,000*
AVERAGE ORDER:	$14-$76
ACTIVE BUYERS:	3,000,000*
TOTAL LIST:	5,000,000*
LIST SOURCE:	Direct mail, space.

COMMENTS

Hanover House has grown rapidly in the past several years, with expanded merchandise lines and a variety of new catalogs. By continuing to add new titles to the list of Hanover catalogs, with some product overlap and targeted at similar income markets, the company is reportedly increasing the profitability of its entire operation. Chelsea Collection's target customer, for example, is the 30 to 45-year-old career woman, and new catalogs for this division have attracted considerable response for 1980 and 1981. Average orders start at $14 for Hanover House; Old Village Shop is $22; Lakeland/ Ferndale Nurseries is $23; New Hampton General Store is $25; Lana Lobell is $28; Pennsylvania Station is $42; Freestyle is estimated at $52; First Editions, $65; Chelsea Collection, $72; Adam York estimated at $76. In 1981 Hanover began a program to build credit customers for their upscale catalogs by offering a $5.00 discount on the first credit account order.

H. E. HARRIS

ADDRESS, PHONE

H. E. Harris and Co., Inc., 645 Summer Street, Boston, MA 02210. Telephone: (617) 269-5200.

OWNERSHIP

H. E. Harris is a wholly-owned subsidiary of General Mills, Inc. of Minneapolis, Minnesota.

MANAGEMENT

Robert Hatch, Executive Vice President, General Mills Specialty Retailing Division; Wesley P. Mann, Jr., President, H. E. Harris; J. J. Kelly, Sales Manager; Peter S. Shaw, Director of Retail Sales.

TYPE OF MARKETER

Mail order.

BUSINESS

H. E. Harris is part of the Collectibles Group of the General Mills Specialty Retailing Division. The company is a 100% mail order marketer of postage stamps and philatelic supplies. Approximately 50% of Harris' sales are wholesale to stamp trading agencies and shops. The other 50% of revenues come from sales to consumer collectors. The company does no manufacturing and sells merchandise throughout the world. Harris reported 280 employees in 1981.

COMPANY HISTORY

The business was founded in Massachusetts in 1916 by H. E. Harris. Originally the company was a proprietorship, trading rare stamps by mail. The company was purchased by General Mills, and incorporated as a subsidiary in Delaware on April 23, 1973. Authorized capital consists of 2,000 shares of common stock with no par value, of which the parent owns 100%. Under new ownership, Harris added a variety of stamp collecting and displaying accessories to their product mix.

MARKETS

Harris sells stamps and accessories to collectors of all ages and income levels; U.S. and abroad.

FACILITIES
The company rents 80,000 square feet for offices, mail order operations and warehousing.

PRODUCTS, BRAND NAMES, PRICE RANGE
All types of postal and commemorative stamps and plate blocks, guides and price indexes, mounting and display accessories, magnifying glasses, coins and coin collecting supplies. Brands include: Harris, Honorbilt, Masterwork, US/BNA.

FINANCIAL INFORMATION

	SALES	**NET INCOME**	**PROFIT MARGIN**
1981	$16,000,000*	N.A.	--

TYPE OF ADVERTISING, PROMOTION
Harris relies primarily on direct mail packages to consumer and commercial accounts for promotion. In addition they use space advertising in related consumer and business publications, national magazines and local newspapers.

LIST INFORMATION

QUANTITY MAILED:	N.A.	(H. E. Harris does not
AVERAGE ORDER:	N.A.	market its list or make
ACTIVE BUYERS:	N.A.	available any information
TOTAL LIST:	N.A.	on its buyer file.)
LIST SOURCE:	N.A.	

COMMENTS
H. E. Harris claims to be the leading U.S. marketer of stamps and stamp collecting supplies. Total revenues for 1981 were estimated to be $16,000,000. Mail order sales to consumers and wholesale mail order sales to commercial accounts each contribute approximately 50% of Harris' total annual revenues. The company accounted for approximately 4% of General Mills' "Specialty Retailing and Other" Group total sales of $379,000,000. While sales for the entire group increased by 6%, from $356 million in 1980 to $379 million in 1981, company officials reported that Harris suffered decreases in both sales and earnings in 1981. This was reportedly due to a generally depressed stamp/collectibles market and the outlook for 1982 was uncertain. The company had expected improved 1982 sales after significantly increasing their distribution to wholesale buyers in 1981. Harris mails direct mail packages periodically throughout the year and makes heavy use of premium offers to quantity and repeat buyers.

HARRY & DAVID

ADDRESS, PHONE

Harry & David, Inc., Box 712, 2518 S. Pacific Highway, Medford, OR 97501. Telephone: (503) 776-2121.

OWNERSHIP

Wholly-owned subsidiary of publicy-held Bear Creek Corporation of Medford, Oregon.

MANAGEMENT

David H. Holmes, Chairman of the Board; John R. H. Holmes, President; David S. Stump, Vice President; Glenn Harrison, VP; Harry E. Knight, VP & Treasurer; Robert G. Wilson, VP.

TYPE OF MARKETER

Mail order.

BUSINESS

Harry & David is a grower and marketer of a variety of fruits and berries--their specialty being pears. In addition, they process preserves, pickles, vinegars and syrups, and market cheese, meat, nuts and sweets purchased from other producers. Products are sold by mail in baskets and decorative gift packages, and in collections through company's Fruit-of-the-Month Club. H & D owns 1,764 acres of fruit orchard in Medford; other growing contracted to outside orchards.

COMPANY HISTORY

Brothers Harry and David Holmes inherited Bear Creek Orchards in southern Oregon in 1914. Their sons are presently chairman and president of parent Bear Creek Corp. Harry and David developed the hybrid, red-colored pear known as the "Royal Riviera." This pear was marketed primarily in Europe until the depression, when efforts were turned toward the domestic market. U.S. catalog operations began in 1934, and the Fruit-of-the-Month Club was started in 1940. Parent Bear Creek was formed in 1972.

MARKETS

Mail order throughout U.S. and Canada; sales to single and multi-buyers and club members.

FACILITIES

Growing fields, corporate offices, processing, manufacturing and warehouse facilities in Medford, OR.

PRODUCTS, BRAND NAMES, PRICE RANGE

Boxes and baskets of fruits, candies and baked goods, cheeses and nuts, preserves, smoked hams, turkeys, pheasants, salmon and oysters. Specialty "Fruit-of-the-Month Club." House brands. Price range $8-$175; median $21.

FINANCIAL INFORMATION

	SALES	NET INCOME	PROFIT MARGIN
1981	$40,610,000*	$1,624,400*	4%*

TYPE OF ADVERTISING, PROMOTION

Space in magazines and newspapers, inserts in invoices and order confirmations. Primary advertising through catalogs. Heavy emphasis on specialty products--"Fruit-of-the-Month Club, it's the original... one and only!" Six catalogs per year; major season October-December.

LIST INFORMATION

QUANTITY MAILED:	20,000,000*
AVERAGE ORDER:	$60.00
ACTIVE BUYERS:	415,000
TOTAL LIST:	735,000
LIST SOURCE:	Direct mail, space, referrals.

COMMENTS

In 1981 Harry and David's fruit and food products contributed an estimated $40,610,000 in sales, roughly 40% of Bear Creek Corp.'s total net revenues. Sales are mainly mail order, although fruit that does not meet gift-quality standards, excess produce not sold by direct mail, and certain varieties grown for wholesale distribution are marketed through outside commercial channels. Between 1979 and 1980, H&D's total sales increased 19%; between 1980 and 1981, about 18%. Net earnings are not reported for Bear Creek's subsidiaries, but at an overall annual margin of 4%, H&D's net earnings are estimated at $1,624,400. During 1981, Fruit-of-the-Month Club accounted for about 36% of fruit and food sales, or approximately $14,620,000. Management reports that 71% of Harry & David's sales are made in the second half of the calendar year. Catalogs are 8-1/4"x11", full color, roughly 30 pages.

HEATH COMPANY

ADDRESS, PHONE

Heath Company, P.O. Box 1288, Benton Harbor, MI 49022. Telephone: (616) 982-3200.

OWNERSHIP

Subsidiary of publicy-held Zenith Radio Corp. of Glenview, IL.

MANAGEMENT

William E. Johnson, President; David Altwies, Vice President of Direct Marketing; Terry Ravenscraft, Controller; Murray Nichols, Market Research Manager.

TYPE OF MARKETER

Mail order.

BUSINESS

Heath Company offers a wide variety of do-it-yourself electronic kits that run the gamut from digital wind computers to color television sets, shortwave equipment and furniture. The company buys parts and provides them in a kit with detailed assembly manuals. Some products are also offered pre-assembled, but the company's main business is their kits. Most all of domestic sales are via mail, but the company owns distribution offices in Europe that use both mail and retail outlets for marketing. Company employs 1,200.

COMPANY HISTORY

Edward Heath started the business in 1918 selling WWI surplus aircraft parts. When supplies ran out he switched to marketing full-size aircraft kits. When Heath was killed in a test plane accident in l933, the company temporarily went out of business. In 1935 Howard Anthony purchased the assets and moved to Benton Harbor, MI to manufacture aircraft parts. In 1947 Anthony decided to package surplus electronic equipment in kits offered by mail. Company acquired by Zenith in 1979.

MARKETS

Mail order sales are both domestic and international. Market is about 99% male, middle-to-high income.

FACILITIES

All kit packaging, assembly and mail order out of offices in Benton Harbor.

PRODUCTS, BRAND NAMES, PRICE RANGE

Wide array of do-it-yourself electronic kits ranging from marine items, audio equipment, shortwave and ham radio equipment, computers, televisions, home protection devices, automotive equipment. Most sold under the Heathkit name.

FINANCIAL INFORMATION

	SALES	NET INCOME	PROFIT MARGIN
1980	$90,000,000*	N.A.	--

TYPE OF ADVERTISING, PROMOTION

Heath's primary emphasis is on catalog promotion; Published four times a year, each is 8-1/2" by 9-1/2", mostly black and white, approximately 100 pages. Special promotions go to first-time and in-active buyers; some use of billing inserts and space.

LIST INFORMATION

QUANTITY MAILED:	8-9,000,000
AVERAGE ORDER:	Various
ACTIVE BUYERS:	1,000,000*
TOTAL LIST:	2,500,000*
LIST SOURCE:	Direct mail, space, rentals.

COMMENTS

Company officials have indicated that Heath's annual sales hover around $90,000,000 with profitable oper-ations. Sales for the first six months of 1981 were reported to be up 5% over the same period in 1980, and a profit was also reported. Company officials say there are a lot of well-educated, professional people, primarily men, who find a relaxing and rewarding outlet in the assembly of electronic kits. Although about half have some technical background, the company's promotions emphasize that detailed instructions make it easy for almost anyone to as-semble the kits. The company prides itself on its assembly manuals and allows customers to order one before ordering the actual kit. They also provide technical assistance by phone. The Heath Company has been benefitting from the recent boom in home computers and offers a varied line of both assembled and build-it-yourself computers. They are also moving into furniture kits and testing a solar water heater kit as they look toward increased involvement in solar technology.

HERRSCHNERS

ADDRESS, PHONE

Herrschners, Inc., 999 Plaza Drive, Schaumburg, IL 60195. Telephone: (312) 843-6920.

OWNERSHIP

Company is part of the Direct Mail Marketing Division of publicly-held Quaker Oats Co., Chicago, Illinois.

MANAGEMENT

Sam B. Slade, President; Joseph Pickard, Manager, Marketing Services.

TYPE OF MARKETER

Mail order.

BUSINESS

This 83-year-old firm is a 100% mail order marketer of supplies for needle and hobby crafts including hard-to-find accessories, domestic and imported yarns, needles and hooks for knitting and crochet items, kits for afghans, knitted and crocheted sweaters, embroidered skirts and apparel, baby items, toys, latch hook rugs, pillows and wall hangings. Its Christmas catalog also features a wide variety of handcrafted gift items, as well as a complete line of accessories and notions. Employs 245 persons.

COMPANY HISTORY

Herrschners claims to be the oldest needlework mail order business in the U.S. Founded in 1899 by Frederick Herrschner, it was purchased by Needlecraft Corporation of America in the 1960's. Needlecraft in turn became a subsidiary of Quaker Oats in 1972. Herrschners is now removed from Needlecraft operations and is one of three businesses in Quaker Oats' Direct Mail Marketing Division (the other two being Brookstone Company and Joseph A. Bank Clothiers). First mailing to Canadian markets in 1980.

MARKETS

Mail order customers throughout the U.S. and in Canada; customers 98% mid-scale female.

FACILITIES
Mail order operations centered in Schaumburg, IL; distribution center located in Stevens Point, WI.

PRODUCTS, BRAND NAMES, PRICE RANGE
Most yarns and threads carry Herrschners label. Product line includes Spinnerin, J&P, Lily, DMC, Bucilla, and Paterna brands. Kits range up to $49.95.

FINANCIAL INFORMATION

	SALES	**NET INCOME**	**PROFIT MARGIN**
1981	$27,400,000*	N.A.	--

TYPE OF ADVERTISING, PROMOTION
Herrschners mails approximately 25 million catalogs per year and makes heavy use of outside lists. Catalogs are supported with space in women's and crafts magazines. Approximately 95% of sales come from direct mail catalog operations.

LIST INFORMATION

QUANTITY MAILED:	25,000,000*
AVERAGE ORDER:	$21
ACTIVE BUYERS:	900,000
TOTAL LIST:	2,500,000
LIST SOURCE:	Direct mail (95%), space (5%).

COMMENTS
Herrschners appears to be benefitting from Quaker Oats' decision to move it out of the Needlecraft Division and into the Direct Mail Marketing Division. Quaker management reported sharp gains for Herrschners in 1981. In 1981 Herrschners sales were reportedly 12% ahead of 1980, though operating income had dipped slightly. Craft catalog sales were not as high as expected, in keeping with industry experts' views that the entire crafts-by-mail industry has flattened. Attempt to reach a "growing needlework market among younger consumers" with afghan, stitchery and rug kits (rather than adding new craft lines) has reportedly not met management's expectations. 1980 entrance into the Canadian market has been "a positive step" in building active buyers. Canadian catalog is not crafts-oriented but contains some 185 items of furniture and accessories.

HIGHLIGHTS FOR CHILDREN

ADDRESS, PHONE
Highlights for Children, Inc., 2300 West Fifth Avenue, Columbus, OH 43216. (614) 486-0631.

OWNERSHIP
Privately held; 100% of capital stock owned by Garry and Jack Myers and families.

MANAGEMENT
Richard H. Bell, Chairman of the Board; Jerald H. Solinger, President; Roland DeMott, Vice President; Walter B. Barbe, Editor-In-Chief; Kent Brown, Managing Editor.

TYPE OF MARKETER
Mail order, direct sales.

BUSINESS
Highlights For Children publishes a variety of educational materials, books and magazines. The company markets these products by mail to consumers, libraries, schools and other commercial accounts, and through a force of door-to-door independent direct sales representatives. Highlights' target market is families with children between the ages of two and twelve. The company is most widely known for its children's magazine, Highlights For Children. Highlights reported 249 employees in 1981.

COMPANY HISTORY
The business was started in 1946 by Doctor Garry C. Myers and Caroline Myers, who were both previously involved in children's education. The first edition of Highlights For Children magazine was published in June of 1946. Individual title publishing and marketing operations were added later, primarily as incentives to schools and teachers for Highlights subcriptions. In 1978 Essential Learning Products operations were added, offering a variety of teaching aids. Highlights was incorporated in Delaware on February 18, 1946.

MARKETS
Families, schools, libraries, supply outlets; United States, Canada, several foreign countries.

FACILITIES
Business headquarters and marketing operations, Columbus, OH editorial offices, Honesdale, PA.

PRODUCTS, BRAND NAMES, PRICE RANGE
Children's magazine, Highlights For Children; penmanship supplies and textbooks, collection of reprints of individual titles, reference books including atlases and dictionaries, and other classroom aides.

FINANCIAL INFORMATION

	SALES	NET INCOME	PROFIT MARGIN
1981	$18,000,000*	N.A.	--

TYPE OF ADVERTISING, PROMOTION
Highlights uses direct mail to promote magazine subscriptions and their other various published products, as well as space advertising in educational and teaching and library trade publications. Emphasis on "quality and educational value" of products.

LIST INFORMATION
QUANTITY MAILED:	N.A.
AVERAGE ORDER:	$15
ACTIVE BUYERS:	1,188,000*
TOTAL LIST:	2,182,000
LIST SOURCE:	Direct mail, space, referral.

COMMENTS
Highlights uses direct mail not only for sales of merchandise but as an inquiry generator and sales support for direct selling agents -- particularly in the case of schools and libraries. What started as premium/incentive program for magazine subscribers has been expanded into a major segment of Highlights business. Aside from direct mail packages advertising their books and educational materials, Highlights makes heavy use of inserts in book distributors catalogs and trade publications. The company reports that referrals generate a significant number of inquiries. Highlights produces all of its inserts and direct mail promotions in-house.

LAWSON HILL

ADDRESS, PHONE

Lawson Hill Leather & Shoe Co., Inc., 61-A Emery St., Sanford, ME 04073. Telephone: (207) 324-0161.

OWNERSHIP

Privately held; Verniez Leurent of Roubaix, France, owns 51% of capital stock.

MANAGEMENT

Robert Goldstein, President and Treasurer; Herbert Simpson, Merchandise Manager.

TYPE OF MARKETER

Mail order.

BUSINESS

Lawson Hill is a 100% mail order marketer of ladies' shoes and other leather accessories. The company sells mainly to individual customers, but does have several wholesale accounts. Consumer sales are through catalogs mailed six times per year. L.H. carries a variety of name brands but does no manufacturing. Management reports sales are heaviest between January and February, and July and August. Company employs 28 people.

COMPANY HISTORY

Lawson and Marcia Hill, whose background was in shoe manufacturing, started their firm in 1969. The company was incorporated in Massachusetts in 1976. Verniez Leurent purchased 51% of the business from the founders in 1978. The company expanded rapidly in the early 1970's, but growth has been limited in recent years. Lawson Hill headquarters was moved from Waltham, MA, to its present location in 1981.

MARKETS

Customers are low-middle to mid scale, throughout the U.S.; no international marketing.

FACILITIES
Executive offices, warehouse and mail order facilities in a 30,000 sq. ft. old mill building in Maine.

PRODUCTS, BRAND NAMES, PRICE RANGE
Mostly casual, leather name-brand ladies shoes, including Naturalizer, Red Cross, Bass, Penaljo, etc. Shoes are mid-priced.

FINANCIAL INFORMATION

	SALES	NET INCOME	PROFIT MARGIN
1981	$15,000,000*	N.A.	--

TYPE OF ADVERTISING, PROMOTION
About 95 percent of advertising is through catalogs. The remainder is space in newspapers and magazines. The 24-page, full-color catalogs are mailed in January, March, May, July, September & November.

LIST INFORMATION
QUANTITY MAILED: 6,000,000
AVERAGE ORDER: $50+
ACTIVE BUYERS: 200,000
TOTAL LIST: 750,000
LIST SOURCE: Direct mail, space.

COMMENTS
When sales grew dramatically two and three years ago, Lawson Hill management discovered that they were literally outpacing the capacity of their mail order operations. Company officials say it was a matter of growth for growth's sake, and they were unable to handle the shipping. Lawson Hill has started remedying the situation by taking a new approach: instead of trying to enlarge the number of customers, the company is working to satisfy its current customers and build up its multi-buyer base. It's a conscious braking maneuver emphasized by a cutback in mailings. Company officials say they are mailing less but more selectively. In addition, Lawson Hill phased out its line of men's shoes and is now catering strictly to women. A recent move to a new office building-warehouse in Maine was made to cut back on plant and labor costs. Lawson Hill spends roughly 25% of their sales or $3.8 million annually on space advertising and catalog operations.

HONEYBEE

ADDRESS, PHONE

Honeybee, Inc., Box 243, 502 Felix St., St. Joseph, MO 64501. Telephone: (816) 233-1333.

OWNERSHIP

Subsidiary of privately-held Einbender's, Inc., of St. Joseph, MO.

MANAGEMENT

Edwin Einbender, President & Treasurer; Lester Einbender, Vice President; Ron Einbender, Secretary.

TYPE OF MARKETER

Mail order, retail.

BUSINESS

Honeybee sells women's ready-to-wear fashions ranging from casual and sports clothes to dressy apparel and evening wear. Accessories include boots, scarves, hats, cummerbunds, ties, jewelry for party wear. All merchandise is acquired from outside manufacturers and suppliers. Business is somewhat seasonal, with highest sales in the fall (through December) and in early spring. Honeybee reported 100 employees in 1981.

COMPANY HISTORY

The parent company, Einbenders, Inc., was established in 1930 in St. Joseph, Missouri as a retail marketer of women's fashions and accessories. Honeybee was started in 1964 as a retail boutique and mail order marketer of mid to upscale, quality apparel and shoes. The company was incorporated in Missouri on December 5, 1964. Authorized capital consists of 5,000 shares of common stock at $1 par value, parent Einbender owns 100% of capital.

MARKETS

Mail order customers nationwide. Retail stores in MO, IL, KY, NY, & PA.

FACILITIES

Headquarters in St. Joseph, MO; warehouse and mail order fulfillment, Huntingdon Valley, PA.

PRODUCTS, BRAND NAMES, PRICE RANGE

Designer names include Bagatelle, Crazy Horse, Penrose, Liz Claiborne, Cecily, J. G. Hook, Fox Run, Katherine Stein, Mamselle, Calvin Klein. Prices reflect the medium to better-grade quality of merchandise offered.

FINANCIAL INFORMATION

	SALES	NET INCOME	PROFIT MARGIN
1981	$12,000,000*	N.A.	--

TYPE OF ADVERTISING, PROMOTION

Honeybee's main promotional emphasis is on their catalogs which are published four times a year. The company's catalogs are full-color, 8 x 11, 32 pages. Emphasis on upscale, "high class" styles and quality.

LIST INFORMATION

QUANTITY MAILED: 1,000,000*
AVERAGE ORDER: $75
ACTIVE BUYERS: 113,000
TOTAL LIST: 300,000*
LIST SOURCE: Direct mail.

COMMENTS

Company officials report that Honeybee serves a discriminating mid to upscale segment of the women's apparel and accessory market, and emphasizes name brand quality merchandise in their product mix. The sales figure above is an estimate of the company's 1981 mail order sales and does not include revenues generated by Honeybee's eight retail outlets. Mail order is estimated to contribute 75% of Honeybee's annual volume, making total sales for 1981 approximately $16 million. Management reports that the company's profit margin was up slightly over the 1980 level. In recent catalogs Honeybee has made attractive use of outdoor and elegant location shooting to display their quality apparel.

HORCHOW MAIL ORDER

ADDRESS, PHONE

Horchow Mail Order, Inc., 4435 Simonton Road, Dallas, TX 75231. Telephone: (214) 233-1008.

OWNERSHIP

Subsidiary of privately held Horchow Corporation. Parent company owns 100% of capital stock.

MANAGEMENT

S. Roger Horchow, Chief Executive, President; Jim Mabry, Vice President & Secretary/Treasurer; Carolyn Horchow, Officer.

TYPE OF MARKETER

Mail order.

BUSINESS

Horchow Mail Order is a subsidiary of Horchow Corp., which was formed in 1973 as a holding company. Horchow Mail Order sells a variety of gifts, collectibles, home furnishings and decorations, and apparel through four different catalog operations: Horchow Collection, Trifles, Grand Finale, and New Perspective. Company is a 100% mail order marketer. It is considered to be upscale in position and is known for the uniqueness and variety of its merchandise: many imports, artistic decorations, and Horchow exclusives.

COMPANY HISTORY

The business was originally started under the name Kenton Mail Order, Inc. in 1971, and incorporated in Delaware in February of that year. The company was having financial problems when Roger Horchow purchased it from Meshulam Riklis for a reported $1,000,000. The name was changed to Horchow Mail Order, Inc. by a charter amendment in January of 1974. Horchow Mail Order reportedly lost $1,000,000 in each of its first two years of operation, but has been enjoying an annual sales growth rate of about 23%.

MARKETS

Customers are affluent, upscale; mostly female, 30-55 years of age; average family income, $78,000.

FACILITIES

Headquarters, order processing, warehousing, customer service, Dallas, Texas.

PRODUCTS, BRAND NAMES, PRICE RANGE

Unique kitchen accessories, dinnerware, small appliances, children's gifts, apparel, jewelry, decorator items, books, kits, and more. House brands-- L'envoi by Horchow. National brands: J. Halston, Texas Instruments, etc.

FINANCIAL INFORMATION

	SALES	NET INCOME	PROFIT MARGIN
1981	$40,000,000*	N.A.	--

TYPE OF ADVERTISING, PROMOTION

Major promotional emphasis is on direct mail. Horchow mails some 40 million pieces per year. Catalogs are 8 x 10-1/2, full-color, 34 pages. New Perspective piece is 9-1/4 x 12, full-color, 32 pages. Catalogs are supported by solo mailings and limited space.

LIST INFORMATION

QUANTITY MAILED:	40,000,000
AVERAGE ORDER:	$50.00
ACTIVE BUYERS:	460,000
TOTAL LIST:	1,500,000
LIST SOURCE:	Mail order (99%).

COMMENTS

Horchow's 1980 sales are estimated at $32,000,000. 1981 sales are estimated at $40,000,000. Horchow's emphasis is on upscale, luxury merchandise ranging from the mid to high end in price. The Horchow Collection catalog carries a wide variety of merchandise under $50 but also contains the extreme upscale Horchow lines. Trifles merchandise is a mix of luxury items at "more affordable prices." Grand Finale carries high-ticket merchandise at sale prices. Horchow's latest offering, the New Perspective catalog, is a collection of gifts, preppy fashions, jewelry, accessories, etc. The merchandise mix is targeted at a younger, more equally male/female market, and the prices are more midscale.

IDEALS PUBLISHING

ADDRESS, PHONE

Ideals Publishing Corp., 11315 Watertown Plank Road, Milwaukee, WI 53226. (414) 771-2700.

OWNERSHIP

Ideals is a wholly-owned subsidiary of Canadian-based Harlequin Enterprises, Ltd., which is a division of Torstar Corporation.

MANAGEMENT

Don A. Gottschalk, President; R. Stanik, Vice President, Retail Sales; D. Woods, Vice President, Special Markets; J. Lipscomb, Vice President, Consumer Sales; J. Ruse, Vice President, Publishing.

TYPE OF MARKETER

Mail order.

BUSINESS

Ideals is a publisher and distributor of a variety of magazines and books. These publications are sold through continuity programs and subscriptions, entirely by mail, throughout the U.S. and Canada to consumers and retail outlets. The company's operations are divided into three major groups: the publication and sales of Ideals Magazine; publication and sales of books on home improvement and cooking; publication and sales of inspirational and children's books.

COMPANY HISTORY

The business was founded in Milwaukee in 1944 by Van B. Hooper to publish Ideals Magazine. The magazine was originally sold only through mail order subscriptions. The company was incorporated as Ideals Publishing, Inc. in Wisconsin on July 5, 1973. On July 7, 1977 all of Ideal's assets and capital stock were purchased by Harlequin Enterprises, which is a wholly-owned subsidiary of the Torstar Corporation of Ontario. Ideals reported 100 employees in 1981.

MARKETS

Mail order book buyers and magazine subscribers throughout U.S. and Canada; 75% women.

FACILITIES

Ideals leases 75,000 sq. ft. at Milwaukee location for publishing, distributing and headquarters.

PRODUCTS, BRAND NAMES, PRICE RANGE

The annual subscripton rate for Ideals Magazine is $15.95. In addition the company publishes and markets a variety of books through single-title and continuity programs with a wide price range.

FINANCIAL INFORMATION

	SALES	NET INCOME	PROFIT MARGIN
1981	$10,000,000*	N.A.	--

TYPE OF ADVERTISING, PROMOTION

Ideals reports that approximately 15% of their total annual sales is spent on advertising. Magazine subscriptions are promoted through inserts and space advertising; book sales through direct mail packages and mini-catalogs.

LIST INFORMATION

QUANTITY MAILED:	N.A.	(Ideals markets a variety
AVERAGE ORDER:	N.A.	of lists of magazine sub-
ACTIVE BUYERS:	N.A.	scribers segmented by
TOTAL LIST:	N.A.	country, book buyers
LIST SOURCE:	N.A.	by type of book, etc.)

COMMENTS

Ideals Publishing management reported that the company's total sales for 1981 were in excess of $10,000,000, and that operations were profitable. The company is reportedly positioning itself to become a stronger competitor with rivals Sunset, Better Homes & Gardens and Good Housekeeping. Ideals recently began marketing two new continuity clubs for cookbooks and children's books. The company recently acquired Structures Publishing Company which will greatly enhance Ideals penetration of the "how-to", home improvement book market. At present Ideals is using direct mail packages, including 16-page mini-catalogs to promote their single-title and continuity series book offerings. Management reported no changes in their direct mail marketing strategy for the coming year. Catalogs are published twice a year and mailed in February and October.

JS&A GROUP

ADDRESS, PHONE

JS&A Group, Inc., 235 Anthony Trail, Northbrook, IL 60062. Telephone: (312) 564-7035.

OWNERSHIP

Privately-held; 100% of capital stock owned by Joseph Sugarman.

MANAGEMENT

Joseph Sugarman, President & Treasurer; Wendy C. Sugarman, Vice President and Secretary; Mary Stanke, Executive Vice President.

TYPE OF MARKETER

Mail order.

BUSINESS

JS&A is a mail order marketer of unique electronic devices. In addition, roughly 10% of volume comes from advertising services provided by JS&A's in-house ad agency. The company has developed a substantial mail order business by marketing products from outside manufacturers, under creative and off-beat names, through the company's uniquely styled catalogs and space ads. JS&A does no manufacturing or international marketing, and presently employs 20 people.

COMPANY HISTORY

Joseph Sugarman started the company in 1965 as Joe Sugarman and Associates. Sugarman began marketing merchandise by mail in 1971: a Craig electronic calculator promoted to approximately 1,000,000 people reportedly grossed $500,000 in the first year. In the early days of his mail order business, Sugarman reported he was successful with 2 out of 10 items promoted. Currently JS&A claims that about 8 out of 10 items they promote sell successfully.

MARKETS

Mostly well-educated men in managerial or professional positions with high disposable incomes.

FACILITIES

Headquarters, office, and order processing housed in one building in Northbrook, Illinois.

PRODUCTS, BRAND NAMES, PRICE RANGE

Electronic devices include "Busy Buttons" (telephone dialing accessory), "Locloc" (digital watch shaped like a padlock), "TalkTalk" (headset walkie-talkie), alarm systems, air ionizers, electronic games--a variety of "Products That Think."

FINANCIAL INFORMATION

	SALES	NET INCOME	PROFIT MARGIN
1981	$15,000,000*	N.A.	--

TYPE OF ADVERTISING, PROMOTION

JS&A produces their own space ads which detail the many uses and qualities of various products. Space ads run in Scientific American, Popular Science, Playboy, in-flight magazines, etc.

LIST INFORMATION

QUANTITY MAILED:	N.A.
AVERAGE ORDER:	$92
ACTIVE BUYERS:	300,000
TOTAL LIST:	700,000
LIST SOURCE:	Space (75%), direct mail (25%).

COMMENTS

JS&A is reported to be the first company to market by mail pocket calculators, liquid crystal digital watches, and computer blood pressure systems. JS&A has greatly reduced the cost of their catalog operations by placing a major promotional emphasis on space advertising to generate catalog inquiries. Catalogs are mailed to a past or "proven buyer" file and to new inquiries. This reduces cost by decreasing "blanket" mailings and increasing response rates. Catalogs are full-color, 8 - 1/2 x 11, 48 pages, and contain 16 new items per edition. Possible Justice Department hearing is still pending in JS&A's alleged violation of FTC "30-day notification" consumer protection rule.

JACKSON & PERKINS

ADDRESS, PHONE
Jackson & Perkins Company, P. O. Box 1028, Medford, OR 97501. Telephone: (503) 776-2400.

OWNERSHIP
Subsidiary of publicy-held Bear Creek Corporation of Medford, Oregon.

MANAGEMENT
David H. Holmes, Chairman of the Board; John R. H. Holmes, President; David S. Stump, Vice President; Glenn Harrison, Vice President; Harry E. Knight, Vice President and Treasurer.

TYPE OF MARKETER
Mail order.

BUSINESS
Jackson & Perkins produces and markets a wide variety of seeds, bulbs, ornamental plants, bushes, berries and trees. Throughout its history, the company's specialty has been its award-winning hybrid roses. J&P markets exclusively by mail selling to individual customers, greenhouses, and retail nurseries and garden centers. Company-owned growing fields are located in the San Joaquin Valley near Wasco, CA. Other plants and products are produced under contractual arrangements with outside growers.

COMPANY HISTORY
The business was started in 1872 by Charles H. Perkins, who raised grapes and berries in a truck garden in Newark, NY. Specialization in roses began with the development of their first hybrid strain by E. Alvin Miller in 1908. Since that time the company's growing and testing operations have been moved to Arizona and finally to California. In 1939, requests from patrons at the World's Fair prompted J&P to begin mail order marketing. Today J&P claims to be largest U.S. private horticultural researcher.

MARKETS
Mail order throughout the U.S.; customers are 60% female, do-it-yourselfers and gardeners.

FACILITIES

H.Q., Medford, OR; 27 buildings and 2370 acres of growing land, Wasco, CA; research Tustin, CA.

PRODUCTS, BRAND NAMES, PRICE RANGE

Roses, strawberries, rhubarb, raspberries, boysenberries, grapes, asparagus, dwarf fruit trees, flowering bulbs, shade and flowering trees, shrubs and others. House brands--hybrid roses, "Proud Hand," "First Prize," "White Masterpiece," etc.

FINANCIAL INFORMATION

	SALES	NET INCOME	PROFIT MARGIN
1981	$45,567,000	1,800,000*	4%*

TYPE OF ADVERTISING, PROMOTION

Primary advertising through catalogs. Heavy emphasis on specialty products--Rose of the Year Award Roses. Catalogs are full-color, 8-1/4 x 10-3/4, 40 pages. Some space in newspapers and magazines, and package and statement inserts.

LIST INFORMATION

QUANTITY MAILED: 20,000,000*
AVERAGE ORDER: $35
ACTIVE BUYERS: 675,689
TOTAL LIST: 1,400,000*
LIST SOURCE: Direct mail, space ads, referrals.

COMMENTS

In 1980 Jackson and Perkins accounted for 49% of Bear Creek's revenues or $42,476,000; in 1981 45% or $45,567,000. Between '79 and '80 sales increased by 15%; between '80 and '81 by 7%. Though parent does not divulge earnings, based on an overall profit margin of 4%, J&P's net earnings are estimated to be $1,823,000. The company produces over 100 different varieties of roses which account for approximately 60% of J&P's net sales. Most all of the roses and lilacs marketed are grown in the company's San Joaquin fields. They are harvested in November and December and shipped to Medford, OR where they are kept dormant in cold storage until sold. J&P introduces several new varieties of hybrid flowers per year. It takes roughly 7-10 years to develop marketable quantities of a new hybrid. In 1981 J&P formed a new subsidiary, J&P Luwasa, Inc., to market plants grown in the Swiss-developed Luwasa Hydroculture System.

JENSEN TOOLS

ADDRESS, PHONE
Jensen Tools, Inc., 1230 S. Priest Drive, Tempe, AZ 85281. Telephone: (602) 968-6241.

OWNERSHIP
Wholly-owned subsidiary of Bliss & Laughlin Industries, Inc.

MANAGEMENT
Even T. Collinsworth, Jr., President; T.P. Crigler, Vice President/Treasurer; Dennis W. Sheehan, Vice President/ Secretary; Uma Nandan, Vice President; General Manager; Henry T. Burgess, Ad. Mgr.

TYPE OF MARKETER
Mail order.

BUSINESS
Jensen markets electronic tools, tool kits, and construction tools to field engineers, technicians, watchmakers, repairmen, hobbyists, and users of precision tools. Products are marketed by mail to commercial and industrial accounts worldwide. Jensen manufactures only the tool kits it sells; all other merchandise is supplied by outside manufacturers. Management reports that business is non-seasonal and the company employs 150 people.

COMPANY HISTORY
Jensen was started in 1963 in Phoenix, Arizona by Sheldon Gates and Sherman Jensen, and was incorporated as a branch of Bliss & Laughlin Industries on December 31, 1975, in Delaware. In a charter amendment on June 14, 1979, the corporate name was changed from Jensen Tools and Alloys, Inc., to its present name. Mail order was an original part of the business, and the first products sold were soldering irons and electronic tool kits. In 1979 the business moved from Phoenix to Tempe, Arizona.

MARKETS
Products are marketed worldwide; sales to commercial and industrial accounts (70%) and consumers (30%).

FACILITIES
Rents 15,000 sq. ft. for office space, warehousing and mail order fulfillment operations.

PRODUCTS, BRAND NAMES, PRICE RANGE
Products include electronic tools, tool kits, test meters, a variety of construction tools such as screwdrivers, wirecutters, wrenches, etc. Products are marketed under Jensen's brand name. Price ranges from $2 to $500.

FINANCIAL INFORMATION

	SALES	NET INCOME	PROFIT MARGIN
1981	$15,000,000*	N.A.	--

TYPE OF ADVERTISING, PROMOTION
Approximately 80% of the advertising is done through catalogs. Five full-color catalogs are published and mailed annually. Large catalogs have 144 pages; smaller editions have 64 pages. Space ads appear in many trade publications.

LIST INFORMATION

QUANTITY MAILED:	10,000,000*
AVERAGE ORDER:	$36*
ACTIVE BUYERS:	281,000
TOTAL LIST:	1,000,000*
LIST SOURCE:	90% direct mail, 10% space ads.

COMMENTS
Comparative statements on Jensen Tools indicate a growing sales volume, evidenced by increased operating assets and profitability. Jensen turned in an estimated $15 million in sales in 1981; approximately 6% of parent's total revenues. Jensen has removed its list and buyer file from the market. Bliss & Laughlin Industries, Inc., of Hinsdale, IL, operates as a manufacturer of finished steel, bars, casters, metal products and construction tools. Parent company owns 100% of capital stock, and has 50 other subsidiaries active in diversified interests worldwide. Jensen is constantly testing new products and adding new merchandise to their catalogs. The tool kits Jensen manufactures are marketed primarily to field engineers involved in computer repair. The kit is designed to appear as a quality attache case. The interior includes pallets and pockets used for tools and other repair equipment and parts. Management reported no changes will occur in mail order operations or facilities in the forthcoming year.

JEWELART, INC.

ADDRESS, PHONE
Jewelart, Inc., 16734 Stagg St., Van Nuys, CA 21409. Telephone: (213) 786-4813.

OWNERSHIP
Privately held by Edward H. Okun Management Co.

MANAGEMENT
Edward H. Okun, President; Karen Ferguson, Vice President; Howard Ferguson, Secretary-Treasurer.

TYPE OF MARKETER
Mail order.

BUSINESS
Jewelart manufactures and markets a variety of costume jewelry items and some higher-quality 14K gold jewelry. The company has one retail outlet at headquarters, but markets most all of its merchandise by mail. Jewelart manufactures about 30% of the merchandise it sells, including costume and some gold-plated pieces. The major portion is supplied by outside distributors. The company presently reports 82 employees.

COMPANY HISTORY
The business was started by Bernard Jonas in Van Nuys, California, in 1967. Jonas started Jewelart as a mail order marketer of costume jewelry. The three principals of Edward H. Okun Management Company purchased the company from Helene and Bernard Jonas (now deceased). Company has always been located at Van Nuys address.

MARKETS
Sells by mail domestically, with women making up about 98% of market. Average age range, 20-40.

FACILITIES

General office, shipping, warehouse, and light manufacturing at Van Nuys headquarters.

PRODUCTS, BRAND NAMES, PRICE RANGE

Classically-styled costume and some 14K gold jewelry, ranging in price from $1.50 to $300. Jewelry items run gamut from rings to necklaces, bracelets, etc.

FINANCIAL INFORMATION

	SALES	NET INCOME	PROFIT MARGIN
1981	$14,000,000*	N.A.	--

TYPE OF ADVERTISING, PROMOTION

Virtually 100% of Jewelart's advertising is through their catalogs. In 1981 the company used space in one Sunday supplement to support catalogs. Approximately 2,000,000 copies of four catalog editions are mailed.

LIST INFORMATION

QUANTITY MAILED:	8,000,000
AVERAGE ORDER:	$20
ACTIVE BUYERS:	467,000
TOTAL LIST:	2,000,000
LIST SOURCE:	Direct mail.

COMMENTS

Jewelart sells merchandise primarily to women who are interested in a classic jewelry look at reasonable, affordable prices. Company officials report that sales have increased steadily over the past several years. Sources indicate that Jewelart's 1981 sales are an estimated $14,000,000, and that operations are profitable. Major effort to improve machinery and efficiency of mail order fulfillment will continue through 1982. Jewelart mails four separate catalogs per year: September, December, April and June. Catalogs are full-color, 8 x 11, about 50 pages. Company experimented with a 16-page Sunday supplement last year, but reported no plans to continue this type of advertising. Jewelart at one time offered materials for making jewelry at home, but discontinued this operation several years ago claiming that it was unprofitable.

JOHNNY APPLESEED'S

ADDRESS, PHONE

Johnny Appleseed's, Inc., 50 Dodge St., Beverly, MA 01915. Telephone: (617) 922-2040.

OWNERSHIP

Privately held by members of the Seamans and Browning families.

MANAGEMENT

Peter B. Seamans, Chairman; Hollis T. French, President; Donald C. Seamans, Executive Vice President; James F. Shaughnessy, Treasurer; Russell Copeland, Vice President-Retail.

TYPE OF MARKETER

Mail order, retail.

BUSINESS

J.A.'s is a mail order and retail marketer of men's and women's apparel and accessories, quality furnishings and gifts. Approximately 92% of sales are from mail order, the remaining 8% from 5 retail stores which draw tourist trade in the northeastern Massachusetts area. Mail order marketing is through J.A.'s catalogs mailed throughout the year. The company does no manufacturing. Appleseed's reports 150 employees.

COMPANY HISTORY

J.A.'s was started in 1912 by Samuel Batchelder, and incorporated in Massachusetts on March 22, 1912. The business was originally incorporated under the name of Boston & Lockport Company. On August 16, 1973, the corporate name was changed to Johnny Appleseed's, Inc. The original business was selling gifts and ready-to-wear by mail. Management reports that business has grown steadily over the years.

MARKETS

Customers are 99% female, 40+ years of age, middle income level; throughout U.S.; no international.

FACILITIES

H.Q. and mail order, Beverly, MA; retail stores in Beverly, Concord, Marblehead, and Westwood.

PRODUCTS, BRAND NAMES, PRICE RANGE

Men's apparel, women's apparel, sports clothes, higher priced furnishings and gifts; products also include footwear, fashion accessories and home appliances. Merchandise is marketed under Johnny Appleseed's name. Price ranges from $10 to $100.

FINANCIAL INFORMATION

	SALES	**NET INCOME**	**PROFIT MARGIN**
1980	$18,500,000*	N.A.	--

TYPE OF ADVERTISING, PROMOTION

Appleseed's main promotional emphasis is on their catalogs mailed six times per year. In addition, the company promotes catalogs, some merchandise, and retail stores through a limited amount of space advertising.

LIST INFORMATION

QUANTITY MAILED: 12,000,000*
AVERAGE ORDER: $55
ACTIVE BUYERS: 225,000
TOTAL LIST: 500,000
LIST SOURCE: Direct mail, space ads.

COMMENTS

Johnny Appleseed's, Inc. has ten stockholders, no one of which owns controlling interest. The principal stockholders are the Seamans and Browning families. This present ownership has been maintained since 1965. Appleseed's total 1980 sales are estimated at $18.5 million. Of the total, approximately 92% or $17 million came from mail order catalog operations. The remaining 8% or $1.5 million came from J.A.'s retail stores. Sales reportedly increased 16% between 1979 and 1980, and 20% between 1978 and 1979. Management reports that operations are profitable and that upward trend is expected to continue. No retail expansion or changes in catalog marketing strategy are reportedly expected in the coming year. Catalogs are full color, 8-1/2 x 11, and about 44 pages long. J.A.'s issues separate catalogs in Jan., Feb., Apr., July, Sept., and Oct., and mails approximately 12,000,000 per year.

CHARLES KEATH

ADDRESS, PHONE

Charles Keath, Ltd., 4030 Pleasantdale Rd., NE, Atlanta, GA 30340. Telephone: (404) 449-3100.

OWNERSHIP

Privately held; 100% of outstanding capital stock is owned by Charles Edmondson.

MANAGEMENT

Charles Edmonson, President; Robert Brayton, VP-Gen. Mgr. and Treas.; Eleanor Edmondson, VP-Creative Dir., Sec.; Josh Deweese, Controller.

TYPE OF MARKETER

Mail order.

BUSINESS

Charles Keath, Ltd. is a 100% mail order marketer of women's apparel and accessories, jewelry, decorative home furnishings and gift merchandise. Keath buys the merchandise it markets from a variety of domestic suppliers and manufacturers, but does no manufacturing of its own. The company is mid to upscale in price position, and emphasizes the quality and luxury aspects of its apparel and gifts for women. Charles Keath's sales are reportedly non-seasonal.

COMPANY HISTORY

The business was started by Charles Edmonson in Atlanta in 1978 with a reported initial investment of $106,500. Authorized capital consists of 1,000,000 shares of common stock, with no par value, all outstanding shares owned by Mr. Edmondson. Charles Keath, Ltd. was incorporated in Georgia on February 1, 1978. Sales have reportedly grown consistently through the company's four years of operation, and management reported 120 employees in 1981.

MARKETS

Keath sells merchandise throughout the U.S.; no international marketing. Customers are 95% female.

FACILITIES
Headquarters, marketing and fulfillment operations all at Atlanta location.

PRODUCTS, BRAND NAMES, PRICE RANGE
Women's fashions: casual to evening wear, house coats, purses, belts, a variety of jewelry; home furnishings: decorative lamps and tables, knick-knacks, kitchen accessories. Prices range from $10 to $500; average mail order purchase: $60.

FINANCIAL INFORMATION

	SALES	NET INCOME	PROFIT MARGIN
1981	$16,500,000*	N.A.	--

TYPE OF ADVERTISING, PROMOTION
Charles Keath relies solely on direct mail for promotion; no space advertising. The company publishes and mails six editions of its catalog annually.

LIST INFORMATION

QUANTITY MAILED:	12,000,0000
AVERAGE ORDER:	$60
ACTIVE BUYERS:	220,000
TOTAL LIST:	400,000
LIST SOURCE:	Direct mail.

COMMENTS
Keath's estimated total 1981 sales of $16.5 million dollars represent an increase of 38% over the estimated 1980 level of $12 million. The company's sales have grown rapidly in its short history. Sales for 1981 represent a 300% increase over the estimated 1979 sales of $4 million. Management reported that earnings were up for the first six months of 1982. Analysts feel that Keath is currently very volume oriented, probably at the expense of a higher earnings ratio. The company publishes six editions of its main catalog each year -- "a new catalog every two months." The catalogs are full-color, 8-1/2 x 11, 36 pages, and offer roughly 200 items. In addition to their main catalog mailings Keath uses mini-catalogs for special direct mail offers irregularly throughout the year.

KING-SIZE COMPANY

ADDRESS, PHONE

King-Size Company, Inc., 24 Forest St., Brockton, MA 02402. Telephone: (617) 588-8600

OWNERSHIP

Privately-held by Knapp King Size Corp., of Brockton, MA. Authorized capital: 1,000 common shares; parent owns 100% of outstanding stock.

MANAGEMENT

James E. Kelly, President; Robert Grady, Treasurer; David E. Place, Clerk and Secretary.

TYPE OF MARKETER

Mail order, retail.

BUSINESS

King-Size is a manufacturer and mail order marketer of men's apparel, shoes and accessories. The company specializes in big and tall styles and sizes of merchandise for the larger than average man. About 95% of King-Size's sales are mail order, with the remaining 5% generated by the company's chain of retail stores. Sales are reportedly non-seasonal and the company does no international marketing.

COMPANY HISTORY

Knapp King Size Corporation was founded in 1953. The King-Size Co. catalog marketing operation was started and incorporated in 1967. Originally King-Size marketed only shoes by mail. Men's clothing and accessories were added to the catalog merchandise mix in the early 1970's. The company has always specialized in styles for the hard-to-fit, larger man. King-Size reported 100 employees.

MARKETS

Customers are predominately middle income males; natural base exists among hard-to-find size group.

FACILITIES
Headquarters, warehouse, order processing, retail outlet, all at central facility in Brockton, MA.

PRODUCTS, BRAND NAMES, PRICE RANGE
Men's clothing ranging from warm-ups to three-piece suits; coordinated slacks and jackets, coats, coveralls, jeans, sleepwear and robes, etc. Shoes are a specialty item: dress, casual and western footwear. Prices range from low to $75.00; median is $31.00.

FINANCIAL INFORMATION

	SALES	NET INCOME	PROFIT MARGIN
1981	$24,000,000*	N.A.	--

TYPE OF ADVERTISING, PROMOTION
Space in magazines and newspapers, package inserts, television, and catalogs. Package inserts are full-color and glossy and include full price list. Discounts and premiums offered with purchases.

LIST INFORMATION
QUANTITY MAILED: 20,000,000*
AVERAGE ORDER: $65
ACTIVE BUYERS: 300,000
TOTAL LIST: 1,000,000
LIST SOURCE: Direct mail, space.

COMMENTS
The sales figure above is an estimate of King-Size 1981 mail order sales only. The company's retail operations generated an estimated $1.5 million in sales, making King-Size total estimated revenues for 1981 $25.5 million. The company is positioned to serve the larger-than-average male and provides his size merchandise in such name brands as Wrangler, London Fog, Botany "500", Frye and Hush Puppies. The majority of items are marketed under private label. King-Size produces their own catalogs and other direct mail promotions in-house. The catalogs are full color and between 80 and 96 pages, and are mailed ten times per year. In addition to regular catalogs King-Size mails collections several times per year.

L'EGGS DIRECT MARKETING

ADDRESS, PHONE
L'eggs Direct Marketing, P. O. Box 2495, Winston-Salem, NC 27102. Telephone: (919) 725-2900.

OWNERSHIP
Part of L'eggs Products Division of Hanes Corp., which is a subsidiary of Consolidated Foods Corp. of Chicago, IL.

MANAGEMENT
P. R. Currier, President; Roy D. Asch, VP-Sales; W. F. Karnbach, VP-Marketing; Charles W. Chambers, Vice President and General Mgr, L'eggs Direct; Bob Klapprodt, Production Mgr, L'eggs Direct.

TYPE OF MARKETER
Mail order, retail.

BUSINESS
The Hanes Group consists of companies which manufacture and distribute a variety of consumer packaged goods, apparel and cosmetic products. The Group includes Hanes Hosiery, Hanes Knitwear, Hanes Printables, L'erin Cosmetics, Specialty Apparel, and L'eggs. Hanes mail order operations are carried out through the L'eggs Direct Marketing arm. L'eggs maintains a strict division between mail order and retail merchandise, thereby serving exclusive bases through each type of marketing.

COMPANY HISTORY
Hanes Corporation, acquired by Consolidated Foods in January, 1979, is the management organization for the companies that make up the Hanes Group. Hanes entered the mail order business in 1974 with L'eggs Direct Marketing. L'eggs had begun removing "regular" stockings from the market and replacing them with pantyhose. Women wrote letters asking if they could order regular stockings. In response to this, L'eggs Direct Marketing was formed, offering stockings by mail.

MARKETS
Primarily middle-income women, mail order buyers of hosiery products.

FACILITIES
Headquarters in Winston-Salem, NC; manufacturing
plants and warehouses in NC, VA, SC, and GA.

PRODUCTS, BRAND NAMES, PRICE RANGE
Hanes Group hosiery brands include L'eggs, Sheer
Energy, Hanes, Underalls, Slenderalls, Today's Girl,
Winteralls, and the newly-marketed, medium-priced
"Hanes Too!" Hanes Knitware manufactures and
markets men's and boy's underwear.

FINANCIAL INFORMATION
	SALES	**NET INCOME**	**PROFIT MARGIN**
1981	$24,000,000	N.A.	--

TYPE OF ADVERTISING, PROMOTION
Boutique displays in retail and specialty stores.
New products are promoted via national TV advertising and space ads. Hosiery and clothing handled
by L'eggs Direct Marketing are advertised in direct
mail packages and catalogs.

LIST INFORMATION
QUANTITY MAILED:	10,000,000*
AVERAGE ORDER:	$15
ACTIVE BUYERS:	743,000
TOTAL LIST:	1,245,000
LIST SOURCE:	Direct mail, space ads.

COMMENTS
Of the Hanes Group's total sales of $792 million in
1981, L'eggs sales accounted for slightly more than
one third. It is estimated that the mail order share
of L'eggs sales for 1981 was about 9% (nearly $24
million). Here is a prime example of a company that
has greatly increased its market share by developing
a direct mail approach to specific segments of its
marketing universe, in conjunction with an effective
and widespread retail distribution system. Hanes'
most successful mail order operation to date has been
the "seconds" line, which they offer as L'eggs brand
slightly imperfect Hosiery at 30% to 60% off the retail
price of the first-quality line. Thus they are able
to recover all costs, plus turn a profit, on the
approximately 3% of daily production of L'eggs products coming out with slight imperfections. L'eggs
Direct Mail developed an integrated strategy rather
than a one-shot "dumping ground" approach, and
cultivated a broad base of repeat customers.

LAND'S END

ADDRESS, PHONE
Land's End Direct Merchants, 2317 N. Elston Ave., Chicago, IL 60614. Telephone: (312) 384-4170.

OWNERSHIP
Privately-held, independent company; Gary Comer owns 100% of capital stock.

MANAGEMENT
Gary Comer, President; Dale Elliot, Vice President-Operations; Bernard Ror, Vice President - Creative Services; Paul C. Kramer, Vice President - Finance and Controller; Dan Lynch, Marketing Manager.

TYPE OF MARKETER
Mail order, retail.

BUSINESS
Land's End offers a wide variety of clothing and accessories for outdoor-oriented people. The company manufactures its own line of duffel bags and contracts with other manufacturers for many of its other products, which include luggage, casual clothing and clothing accessories. At least 90% of sales are generated through catalogs, with the remainder coming from the company's retail store in Chicago. Sales tend to be heaviest during the fall. Land's End employs 400.

COMPANY HISTORY
Gary Comer started the business in Illinois in 1963 as a retailer of yachting accessories and hardware. Mail order operations were added two years later with the first edition of the Yachtsman equipment guide. In the mid-70's management completed a major restructuring of Land's End's merchandise mix and positioning. Today the company sells outdoor and sporting apparel, carrying bags, and a line of casual apparel.

MARKETS
Sales by mail are primarily domestic with some overseas. Market is about 80% male.

FACILITIES

Executive offices and retail shop at Chicago address; warehouse and fulfillment in Dodgeville, WI.

PRODUCTS, BRAND NAMES, PRICE RANGE

Canvas and nylon duffel bags, luggage, coolers, shorts, shirts, jeans, shoes, rain gear, sport coats and other leisure/outdoor apparel and accessories. Products sold under Land's End name. Prices generally run from $6.00 to $80.00.

FINANCIAL INFORMATION

	SALES	NET INCOME	PROFIT MARGIN
1981	$22,000,000*	$660,000*	3.0%*

TYPE OF ADVERTISING, PROMOTION

Primarily catalogs, which are published and mailed four times per year. All catalogs are full-color, 8-1/2 x 11, and 75-100 pages long. Some fliers and solo offerings with orders; space in national magazines.

LIST INFORMATION

QUANTITY MAILED:	12,000,000*
AVERAGE ORDER:	$50
ACTIVE BUYERS:	358,000
TOTAL LIST:	800,000*
LIST SOURCE:	Direct mail, space.

COMMENTS

The sales and profits estimates above are for mail order operations only and do not include revenues from the company's retail outlet. Land's End sales increased an estimated 158% between 1979 and 1981. Company officials attribute the increase to an aggressive marketing effort which included larger mailings and improvement of the catalog. Overall, sales in the mail order area have grown by well over 100% in the past five years, and the outlook is for continued expansion. Sales for 1982 are expected to show an increase over 1981, and management reports that profits for the last six months are up. Last year, the company began experimenting with space ads in national magazines to promote catalog operations. Major product mix shift from boating equipment to outdoor and sporting apparel appears to have been very beneficial for Land's End.

LANE BRYANT

ADDRESS, PHONE
Lane Bryant, Inc., 11 W. 42nd Street, New York, NY 10036. Telephone: (212) 930-9200.

OWNERSHIP
Publicly held; stock traded NYSE; 4,566,095 average common shares outstanding; 1981 dividend, $1.03; sale to Limited Stores being negotiated.

MANAGEMENT
Arthur Maslin, Chairman; Steven Kaplan, President; Peter Canzone, President of Mail Order Division; Richard Deitchman, Executive Vice President, Mail Order; Philip Blanco, Senior Vice President.

TYPE OF MARKETER
Mail order, retail.

BUSINESS
Lane Bryant is a national retailer and mail order marketer of special size apparel, shoes and accessories, primarily for women and girls. The company operates 204 Lane Bryant stores and 27 Smart Size stores. Subsidiaries include the Coward Shoe chain, Farr's Family Shoes (national catalog operation), and Olof Daughters (Scandinavian and European footwear importer). Large and tall size apparel and shoes and maternity clothing are marketed through Lane Bryant and Tall Collection catalogs.

COMPANY HISTORY
Company was founded in 1901 by Lena Bryant, who started as a seamstress of maternity clothes and later branched into large women's fashions. In 1978 mail order marketing was separated from retail operations and set up as a separate division. Reorganization was completed in 1981. Lane Bryant acquired Olof Daughters of Sweden in 1979. Most recent acquisition was Farr's Shoes in 1981. Including Farr retail operations, company reported 29 new stores in 1981.

MARKETS
Customers are mostly female; Lane Bryant sells by mail throughout the U.S. and its territories.

FACILITIES

Headquarters, NY; fulfillment center & Data Management Center, Indianapolis; retail stores nationwide.

PRODUCTS, BRAND NAMES, PRICE RANGE

Women's big and tall apparel, accessories and footwear. Tall apparel brands: Levi, Fire Island, Trissi, Liz Claiborne, Jordache, and Peddie of California. Lane Bryant brands: Fire Island, Lady Devon, Trissi, and Echo. Price range to $150.

FINANCIAL INFORMATION

	SALES	NET INCOME	PROFIT MARGIN
1981	$400,404,000	$11,131,000	2.8%

TYPE OF ADVERTISING, PROMOTION

Space advertising in National Star, Parade, TV Guide, National Enquirer, and free standing inserts. Catalogs and single sheet solo mailings. Promotion is value-oriented with emphasis on style and comfort for the hard-to-fit woman.

LIST INFORMATION

QUANTITY MAILED:	40 to 50 million*
AVERAGE ORDER:	$22*
ACTIVE BUYERS:	7,000,000
TOTAL LIST:	12,000,000*
LIST SOURCE:	Direct mail, space.

COMMENTS

In 1979, Lane Bryant's mail order operation suffered from low sales and inventory problems. Aggressive merchandising, and expense and inventory control in all operations resulted in increased profits during the first quarter of 1980. Mail order sales contribute approximately 40% of total revenues. Company after-tax margin is approximately 3%. Compared to the top 25 primary ready-to-wear mail order businesses, Lane Bryant ranks number two with $160 million in mail order sales. Large inventories are a key factor in Bryant's success--30% to 50% greater than the average women's wear operation. "Nancy's Choice" is the newest catalog, which will feature up-graded merchandise lines. It is positioned to attract new consumers in expanded sizes and higher price range. Response to the first two editions of "It's Me," a new magazine for special-sized women, has reportedly been positive. Lane Bryant will reportedly be acquired by The Limited Stores in calendar 1982.

LEANIN' TREE PUBLISHING

ADDRESS, PHONE

Leanin' Tree Publishing Company, 6055 Longbow Drive, Boulder, CO 80301. (303) 530-1442.

OWNERSHIP

Privately-held by Edward P. Trumble and Patricia Trumble - each holds 50% of capital, consisting of 4,000 shares of common stock with no par value.

MANAGEMENT

Edward P. Trumble, President; Patricia Trumble, Secretary and Treasurer; T. Henry Hutchinson, Officer; T. Robert Whitthorn, VP-Finance.

TYPE OF MARKETER

Mail order, wholesale.

BUSINESS

Leanin' Tree publishes and markets greeting cards through mail order to individuals and wholesales their products by mail to approximately 15,000 retail merchants throughout the U.S. The company's peak season is Christmas and the number of employees increases from 70 to 250 during this period. The major emphasis is on western and wildlife themes. The company also operates a museum of western art displaying contemporary western art, bronze sculptures, etc.

COMPANY HISTORY

Leanin' Tree was started in 1949 by Edward and Patricia Trumble. In their first year of operation only 4 cards were offered - each with cowboys and all by artist Bob Lorenz. The business was a part-time operation until 1965. The company was incorporated in Colorado on February 9, 1975. Wildlife cards were first published in 1951 - early locomotive scenes by Howard Fogg in 1961 and ski cards in 1968. The product line currently offers 191 cards in 6 principal categories.

MARKETS

Individuals 60%; business 40%; wholesale to retail outlets in U.S.A. -- 15,000 dealers.

FACILITIES

Headquarters, publishing, warehousing, order processing and fulfillment, Boulder, CO.

PRODUCTS, BRAND NAMES, PRICE RANGE

Primary product line cards: western themes-cowboys, Indians, horses, ranches; wildlife themes-animals, birds, mountains, etc; ski themes-Santa skiing, etc. Also posters, stationery, and calendars. Prices are mid-scale.

FINANCIAL INFORMATION

	SALES	**NET INCOME**	**PROFIT MARGIN**
1981	$11,000,000*	$550,000*	5.0%*

TYPE OF ADVERTISING, PROMOTION

Consists of 80% direct mail and 20% space. Space ads placed in Field & Stream, Outdoor Life, Ski, Western Horseman, Skiing, and more. Peak season Christmas. Catalog is full-color, 8-1/2" by 5-1/2", about 31 pages.

LIST INFORMATION

QUANTITY MAILED:	8,000,000*
AVERAGE ORDER:	$20
ACTIVE BUYERS:	200,000
TOTAL LIST:	533,000
LIST SOURCE:	Direct mail 80%, space 20%.

COMMENTS

Leanin' Tree's combined consumer and wholesale mail order sales for 1981 are estimated to be $11 million. Of this total, reportedly 45% or an estimated $5 million was generated by sales to consumers and businesses for personal use. The remaining 55% of estimated sales were by mail to retailers. While Leanin' Tree's sales have climbed an estimated 42% over 1980, and 92% over 1979 levels, their after-tax margin is reportedly dropping. This fact may indicate that the company is currently trying to build volume at the expense of earnings. Leanin' Tree's marketing strategy targets a customer who looks for unique and personally-styled products. Their customers are mostly upscale in education and income. New product lines in 1981 included a collection of Norman Rockwell reproductions and new Thanksgiving cards. Personalized envelopes have also been added to the merchandise mix.

LEEWARDS

ADDRESS, PHONE

LeeWards Creative Crafts, Inc., 1200 St. Charles Road, Elgin, IL 60120. Telephone: (312) 888-5800.

OWNERSHIP

Subsidiary of publicly-held General Mills, Inc., Minneapolis, Minnesota.

MANAGEMENT

Larry Kunz, President; VPs: John Flatley, Finance; Max Fratto, Store Operations; Tom Hawn, Employee Relations; Craig Stokely, Marketing; Chic Sheehan, Direct Marketing; Wally Dail, Distribution.

TYPE OF MARKETER

Mail order, retail.

BUSINESS

LeeWards is a part of General Mills Specialty Retailing Group, and sells hobbycraft items and needlecraft kits and materials. Approximately 65% of the company's sales come from its 33 retail outlets. The remainder of sales are from LeeWards catalog operations. The company is positioned to serve as "America's Homecraft Center." Most recent marketing strategy is to offer smaller, upscale craft units in multiple markets. Tests have been positive and management plans to increase implementation.

COMPANY HISTORY

The business was started in 1945 by Ralph Fried and Sidney Fink, and named after the LeeWard Islands. Originally Fried and Fink wholesaled surplus Army parachute thread to stores. In 1950 the company added yarn products, opened a retail store in Elgin, and began marketing their products by mail. In the 1950's, LeeWards began manufacturing and marketing craft kits. Gross annual sales were reportedly $10,000,000 when the company was acquired by General Mills in 1969.

MARKETS

U.S. middle and upper income women; 90% married; 61% have children.

FACILITIES
Company headquarters in Elgin, Illinois; 33 retail stores throughout the U.S.

PRODUCTS, BRAND NAMES, PRICE RANGE
Yarn, rug-making and felt supplies, macrame, needlepoint and crewel supplies and kits, embroidery and quilting supplies and kits, art supplies, and seasonal decorations. Brand names: Beautysilk, Storm King, Bucilla, Deft, Formby's, house brands.

FINANCIAL INFORMATION

	SALES	NET INCOME	PROFIT MARGIN
1981	$100,000,000*	N.A	--

TYPE OF ADVERTISING, PROMOTION
Company advertises heavily for inquiries in women's magazines such as Family Circle, McCall's, and Woman's Day; uses newspaper and television advertising within each geographic location; extensive catalog operations.

LIST INFORMATION

QUANTITY MAILED:	20,000,000
AVERAGE ORDER:	$26
ACTIVE BUYERS:	900,000
TOTAL LIST:	10,000,000*
LIST SOURCE:	Customer orders, ad inquiries.

COMMENTS
Mail order contributed an estimated $35.1 million of LeeWards total sales. LeeWards sales are estimated to be 2.5% of General Mills total revenues. G.M. management reports that overall performance for the Specialty Retailing division was unsatisfactory in 1981: sales grew only 6.4% and operating earnings were 50% below the previous year at $13.2 million. Poor performance was attributed to weak collectible operations. LeeWards sales volume was reportedly up 15% and profits increased over last year. LeeWards management stated that they are changing the thrust of their mail order operations by shifting the product mix away from craft materials and components to complete craft kits. Ten years ago LeeWards merchandise mix was about 50% components. At present it is roughly 90% kits. The kits reportedly reduce overhead and labor expenses. Company is seeking to reduce catalog costs, which have risen dramatically in the past year.

LEICHTUNG, INC.

ADDRESS, PHONE
Leichtung, Inc., 4944 Commerce Parkway, Cleveland, OH 44128. Telephone: (216) 831-6191.

OWNERSHIP
Privately held; Ric and Penelope Leichtung own 100% of capital stock.

MANAGEMENT
Ric Leichtung, President; Joshua Leichtung II, Vice President; Penelope Leichtung, Corporate Secretary.

TYPE OF MARKETER
Mail order.

BUSINESS
Leichtung, Inc. markets a wide variety of woodworking equipment, general power and hand tools, home and automotive specialties, and craft implements. The company sells both to individuals and distributors. Leichtung is positioned to serve upper bracket individuals with large discretionary income and considerable leisure time. Major promotional emphasis is on the upscale home workshop: "The Workbench People." Leichtung reported 55 employees in 1982.

COMPANY HISTORY
The business was established in 1966 as a partnership between Arnold Galmitz and Ric Leichtung called Leichtung & Galmitz Sales. The company was incorporated in Ohio on February 12, 1969. In 1974 Galmitz retired and the name was changed to Leichtung, Inc. In that same year Penelope Leichtung became active as Secretary. Joshua Leichtung became a Vice President in 1980. Authorized capital consists of 200 shares of common stock with no par value.

MARKETS
Mostly male, age 25-60, upper-income; primarily throughout U.S.

FACILITIES

Owns 42,500 sq. ft. building for office space and fulfillment operations.

PRODUCTS, BRAND NAMES, PRICE RANGE

Uncle Henry, Buck, Dreizack and Rapala knives and cutting tools; Bausch & Lomb glasses and magnifiers; Lervad workbenches; craft kits; tool sets. Wide range of prices: $10-$1,000. Two of the company's more popular items sell for $600 and $1,000.

FINANCIAL INFORMATION

	SALES	NET INCOME	PROFIT MARGIN
1981	$11,000,000*	N.A.	--

TYPE OF ADVERTISING, PROMOTION

Leichtung mails catalogs 7 to 10 times per year and is constantly updating the merchandise offered. Products from one given catalog to the next may change as much as 50%. Limited space advertising in woodworking magazines.

LIST INFORMATION

QUANTITY MAILED:	10,000,000
AVERAGE ORDER:	$70
ACTIVE BUYERS:	235,000
TOTAL LIST:	260,000
LIST SOURCE:	Direct mail, space, referrals.

COMMENTS

Management reported that Leichtung's total sales increased by over 85% in 1981. The company's total revenues for 1981 are estimated to be $11,000,000, compared to 1980 estimate of $5,900,000. Peak sales are reportedly November through January, with a sharp drop off in the summer attributed to the seasonality of the use of home workshop products. Leichtung reported that spiraling postal rates and the recessionary economy have not affected the company's sales. Management reports that their upscale buyer has not been affected, nor are they concerned with increasing general mail order competition for the upscale market. The plan is to continue to improve merchandise offered, with an emphasis on good presentation of products in attractive catalogs and ads. Leichtung currently publishes two editions of their catalog each year. The catalogs are full-color, 8-1/4 x 5-3/8, 120 pages, and offer approximately 400 different items. Leichtung does no manufacturing.

FRANK LEWIS FRUIT

ADDRESS, PHONE
Frank Lewis Fruit Co., 100 N. Tower Road, Alamo, TX 78516. Telephone: (512) 787-9971.

OWNERSHIP
Wholly-owned subsidiary of Standex International Corp., Salem, New Hampshire.

MANAGEMENT
Frank Schultz, President; Harry D. Goodwin, Vice President & Controller; Robert E. Masotta, Secretary & Treasurer.

TYPE OF MARKETER
Mail order.

BUSINESS
Frank Lewis is actually the mail order gift foods arm of Standex mail order subsidiary, Crest Fruit Co., Inc. Company's main operation is packing and marketing Royal Ruby Red Grapefruit. Emphasis is on club memberships for regular shipments of food gift packs including grapefruit, smoked meats, dried fruit, nuts, pastries and avocados. Main product is grapefruit gift pack for holiday giving during peak Christmas season. Company has added canned grapefruit juice and slices to round out usually slack summer months.

COMPANY HISTORY
Crest Fruit was formed by Frank Schultz and Fred Petch in Alamo, Texas, in 1966. The company originally marketed Royal Ruby Red Grapefruit (developed by Frank Lewis in 1929) by mail. Crest was incorporated in Texas on Oct. 19, 1970. In 1973, the company was acquired by Standex International. At that time grapefruit sales totalled approximately $5 million annually. Since then it has reportedly grown to over $15 million in annual sales, and employs 245 people during the peak season.

MARKETS
Products are sold internationally, but primarily in the U.S., to all income levels.

FACILITIES

Owns two-story building (60,000 sq. ft.) for head-quarters and mail order operations in Alamo, TX.

PRODUCTS, BRAND NAMES, PRICE RANGE

The primary product marketed is the Royal Ruby Red Grapefruit. In addition, company offers an assortment of mixed food gift packages to club membership and commercial accounts. Brand names include "Frank Lewis," "Shield," and "Crest."

FINANCIAL INFORMATION

	SALES	NET INCOME	PROFIT MARGIN
1981	$15,000,000+*	N.A.	--

TYPE OF ADVERTISING, PROMOTION

Four major catalog mailings a year: a September Grapefruit Club mailing, gift catalogs in fall and spring, and canned juice and sections promotion in summer months. Direct mail pieces promote club memberships by offering a free first shipment.

LIST INFORMATION

QUANTITY MAILED:	5,000,000
AVERAGE ORDER:	$45 (club members)
ACTIVE BUYERS:	101,000
TOTAL LIST:	173,000
LIST SOURCE:	Direct mail, list rental.

COMMENTS

Frank Lewis sales have reportedly grown about 7% to an estimated $15 million in 1981. This is an increase of approximately 300% since its acquisition by Standex. Net earnings are reportedly on an upward trend. Company's main promotional emphasis is on repeat sales to club members from which come about 80% of their revenues. Other 20% of sales are to some 50 standing commercial accounts. Direct mail promotions include four editions of catalog per year: 5" x 7", 12-16 pages, full color, containing about 30 items at an average unit cost of $26.94; direct mail packages to existing and potential members offering bonuses for joining club. Company mails roughly 4,000,000 catalogs per year. Sales are heaviest in November and December. "Crest" is the company's commercial line of produce, sold to commissaries and grocers.

LILLIAN VERNON

ADDRESS, PHONE
Lillian Vernon Corporation, 510 South Fulton Ave., Mount Vernon, NY 10550. Telephone: (914) 699-4131.

OWNERSHIP
Privately held; 100% of capital stock owned by Lillian M. Katz and family.

MANAGEMENT
Lillian Katz, President; Fred Hochberg, Vice President-Marketing; Ray Slypter, Vice President-Lists and Purchasing; Joel Rudich, Vice President, Operations.

TYPE OF MARKETER
Mail order, retail, wholesale.

BUSINESS
Lillian Vernon is a mail order marketer of gifts, housewares and furnishings, games, and gourmet and stationery items. The company has an in-house ad agency, Gramatan Advertising, which handles all catalogs, space ads and mailing pieces. Other operating divisions include: Provender, which wholesales L.V. exclusives and imports through mail order and showrooms; The New Company, manufacturer of Christmas ornaments, jewelry and premium products; Lillian Vernon Italia, European buying office.

COMPANY HISTORY
Vernon Specialties Co. was started by Lillian Katz in 1951 with a space ad for mail order purses and belts. An investment of $495 in Seventeen magazine ad in September 1951, drew $16,000 in sales in six weeks. Company developed a multi-magazine ad program and later began publishing catalogs. The company name was changed to Vernon Products with the addition of manufacturing operations. In 1965, Lillian Vernon Corporation was formed as an exclusively mail order marketer.

MARKETS
Mail order sales throughout the U.S.; no international. Customers are mostly female.

FACILITIES
Headquarters, Mount Vernon; warehouse, Portchester and Elmsford; fulfillment, New Rochelle.

PRODUCTS, BRAND NAMES, PRICE RANGE
Figurines, brass items, tableware, gourmet accessories, toys, leather goods, sewing notions, health and beauty aids. Personalized Lillikins tree ornaments. House and national brands--Caverswall, Old Foley of Staffordshire, Goebel, etc.

FINANCIAL INFORMATION

	SALES	NET INCOME	PROFIT MARGIN
1981	$40,000,000*	N.A.	--

TYPE OF ADVERTISING, PROMOTION
Advertising in trade and shelter publications, and promotional packets. Catalogs are 8-1/2 by 5-1/2, full-color and glossy, 136 pages. "Free" gift with every $10 of merchandise purchased.

LIST INFORMATION

QUANTITY MAILED:	35,000,000
AVERAGE ORDER:	$30
ACTIVE BUYERS:	1,500,000
TOTAL LIST:	3,000,000
LIST SOURCE:	Direct mail, space.

COMMENTS
In 1981 Lillian Vernon celebrated its 30th year in the mail order business, with a reported annual sales growth rate of 30%. About 85% of sales are mail order to individual customers. The remaining 15% come from manufacturing and wholesaling operations. Of the 3,000 different products sold by the company, about 75% of them are imported. The company's manufacturing operations produce 12% of the merchandise sold, including 150 items of copyrighted design. Newest catalog venture is Lillian Vernon At Home collection. The catalog is full color, 9 x 11, 32 pages, and contains a line of unique, high quality home furnishings and decorations; some imports. Management reports that Provender wholesale operation continues to receive a healthy response to gourmet cookware, bath and soap items. Lillian Vernon mail order operation has grown from $1.5 million in 1970 to an estimated $40 million in 1981.

LORD & BURNHAM

ADDRESS, PHONE
Lord & Burnham, 2 Main Street, Irvington, NY 10533. Telephone: (914) 591-8800.

OWNERSHIP
Division of publicly-held Burnham Corporation of Irvington, NY.

MANAGEMENT
Burnham Bowden, Chairman; John W. Murray, President; Vice Presidents: Charles G. Dill, Charles E. Moeser, Richard E. Olson; Peter F. Sherwood, Vice President, Treasurer; Michael B. Killeen, Controller.

TYPE OF MARKETER
Mail order, direct sales.

BUSINESS
Lord & Burnham manufactures and sells upper-priced greenhouses, solaria and related equipment for private, commercial and industrial use. Mail order accounts for about 30 percent of sales, with the bulk of sales being handled directly through agents. A Canadian subsidiary, Lord & Burnham Co., Ltd., of St. Catherines, Ontario, sells the same products directly through agents for the Canadian market only. The Lord & Burnham Division employs about 1,110 people.

COMPANY HISTORY
Mr. Lord and his son-in-law, Mr. Burnham, went into business together in Buffalo, NY, around 1856, primarily building conservatories for the wealthy. They moved to Rochester, NY, and finally to Irvington in 1911, and became known for their commercial greenhouses. The business thrived and facilities tripled around World War II. The company began mail order operations just before the war. In 1954, Lord & Burnham switched from wooden to aluminum greenhouses.

MARKETS
Individuals, 60%; commercial growers, 20%; industrial growers and others, 20%. Market is domestic.

FACILITIES
Manufacturing, sales and executive offices in Irvington; four regional direct sales offices.

PRODUCTS, BRAND NAMES, PRICE RANGE
L&B manufactures and sells Orlyte hobby and Blue Ribbon commercial greenhouses. The Orlyte is 7' high, 6' x 22', and costs $1,000 and up. Blue Ribbon is 30' high, 40' x 200', and costs $30/sq. ft. Also manufactures and sells related equipment.

FINANCIAL INFORMATION

	SALES	**NET INCOME**	**PROFIT MARGIN**
1980	$83,000,000	$4,000,000	4.8%

TYPE OF ADVERTISING, PROMOTION
About 90% of the company's advertising is through space ads in general gardening magazines and professional gardening publications. About 10% of advertising budget is allocated to catalogs, which are mailed on request only.

LIST INFORMATION
QUANTITY MAILED: 85,000
AVERAGE ORDER: $2,200
ACTIVE BUYERS: 92,000 (consumer only)
TOTAL LIST: 280,000
LIST SOURCE: Inquiry-generating space ads.

COMMENTS
Direct mail for Lord & Burnham serves not only as an inquiry generator and customer service support for direct sales forces, but also contributed a substantial $24.9 million in merchandise sales in 1980. Company officials report that hobby greenhouses have met with excellent response in the marketplace, and that consumer sales are outstripping commercial. L&B actively sought consulting to improve their mail order operations in 1980 and is reportedly implementing programs to increase their consumer market penetration. Management says that new mail order push will target upscale women. Consumer sales effort may prompt increased direct mailings and perhaps direct mail which is not in response to space inquiries. Sales reportedly up for all Burnham divisions in 1981. Total sales for the nine months ended Sept. 30, 1981, were $57 million with net earnings of $3.1 million. This compares to $49 million in sales and $2.1 million in earnings for the same period in 1980. Of the 1981 partial revenues, an estimated $17 million were mail order sales.

MACMILLAN BOOK CLUBS

ADDRESS, PHONE

Macmillan Book Clubs, Inc., 866 Third Avenue, New York, NY 10022. Telephone: (212) 935-2000.

OWNERSHIP

A division of publicly-held Macmillan, Inc., New York, NY; listed NYSE, Midwest, Pacific; 1980 prices: high 17-3/8, low 10-5/8; dividend, $.74.

MANAGEMENT

Edward Evans, Chairman; David J. Culbertson, President; Jeffrey R. Minot, Secretary; James P. Kressler, Vice President-Finance; Gordon H. DeWerth, Treasurer.

TYPE OF MARKETER

Mail order.

BUSINESS

Macmillan, Inc.'s operations are classified into four industry segments: Publishing, Instruction, Printing, and Distribution (which includes Macmillan Book Clubs). Macmillan Book Clubs, Inc. provides distribution of various publishers' titles through the operations of its professional and special interest book clubs. Currently there are 19 clubs in operation. Macmillan, Inc. employs a total of about 10,000 persons, 30% employed outside the U.S. Macmillan Book Clubs employs 130 persons.

COMPANY HISTORY

Macmillan, Inc. was founded in 1906 as The Crowell Publishing Co., and incorporated in Delaware in 1920. The name was changed to Macmillan, Inc. on Jan. 1, 1973. Macmillan Book Clubs was incorporated in New York on Jan. 2, 1973, and was formed as a result of the merger of Crowell Collier Book Services, Inc. (originally chartered in 1966 as a subsidiary of P.F. Collier, Inc.), and Professional & Technical Programs, Inc. (originally chartered in 1945 as Basic Books, Inc.).

MARKETS

Sells to professional and special interest mail order book club subscribers throughout the U.S.

FACILITIES

Headquarters in New York; warehouse and distribution center in Riverside, NJ.

PRODUCTS, BRAND NAMES, PRICE RANGE

Books marketed by Macmillan Book Clubs are selected to serve the interests of such professionals as scientists, teachers, nurses, business executives, computer specialists, and architects. Also appeal to special interest groups such as nature lovers.

FINANCIAL INFORMATION

	SALES	NET INCOME	PROFIT MARGIN
1980	$36,000,000*	N.A.	--

TYPE OF ADVERTISING, PROMOTION

Book Clubs promotion depends heavily on space advertising (about 70%) in magazines and Sunday supplements. Direct mail promotion is responsible for the remaining 30%.

LIST INFORMATION

QUANTITY MAILED:	10,000,000+
AVERAGE ORDER:	$60 (book club unit sale)
ACTIVE BUYERS:	509,000
TOTAL LIST:	650,000
LIST SOURCE:	Direct mail, space.

COMMENTS

Among the top ten publishers in the U.S., Macmillan, Inc. suffered its second consecutive year of net losses in 1980. While sales increased to $566 million, net losses were registered at nearly $9.3 million. Publishing remains the heart of the business, accounting for the largest percentage of the company's total revenues. The Distribution segment--which includes Gumps, Macmillan Electronic Media, and Macmillan Book Clubs--had 1980 sales of $132.5 million, or 23.4% of Macmillan's total sales. This represents a growth of 5.9%, attributable to mail order operations, as retail sales in the segment were down over 1979 levels. In May, 1981, Macmillan began negotiating the sale of Brentano's stores, saying they don't fit into the parent's plans. With 19 active clubs, Macmillan Book Clubs is the largest special interest book club operation in the U.S. It is estimated that Book Club sales account for approximately 6% of Macmillan, Inc.'s total sales.

LEW MAGRAM

ADDRESS, PHONE

Lew Magram, Fashions to the Stars, Ltd., 830 Seventh Ave., NY, NY 10019. (212) 586-4828.

OWNERSHIP

Privately held; Lew and Evelyn Magram own 100% of capital (200 shares of common stock, no par value).

MANAGEMENT

Lew Magram, President; Evelyn Magram, Secretary & Treasurer; Erv Magram, Vice President; Melanie Magram, Merchandising Manager; Bernard Krasnoff, Operations Manager.

TYPE OF MARKETER

Mail order, retail.

BUSINESS

Lew Magram sells high-quality designer and house label fashions, loungewear, and lingerie for men and women. The company also sells some jewelry and unique gift items through their catalogs. Mail order operations account for approximately 90 percent of sales, with the remainder coming from one retail store in Manhattan. Sales are heaviest from September to December and again from March to June. Lew Magram reported 35 employees in 1981.

COMPANY HISTORY

Lew Magram started the business in 1949 as a custom shirt maker. The mail order operation grew out of the retail operation as the company compiled its own list of custom shirt buyers. They also generated requests via space ads in men's magazines, and the mail order business was in full swing by the late 1960s. That area was enhanced during the 1970s when Magram began renting outside lists. The company added a line of women's fashions in 1980.

MARKETS

Sells by mail domestically. Market is about 50% male, 50% female; median age 40, middle to upscale.

FACILITIES

Retail store at Seventh Ave. address. Offices and shipping at 250 W. 54th St., New York.

PRODUCTS, BRAND NAMES, PRICE RANGE

Men's and women's casual and dress apparel, lounge-wear and some undergarments, accessories, and unique gift items. Designer names include Givenchy, Blass, Beene, Jordache, Cassini, de la Renta and Cardin. Prices from $12 to $225.

FINANCIAL INFORMATION

	SALES	NET INCOME	PROFIT MARGIN
1981	$10,000,000*	N.A.	--

TYPE OF ADVERTISING, PROMOTION

Approximately 90% of Lew Magram's advertising is through their catalogs mailed four times a year. In addition they have used space in New York Times, Smithsonian, Esquire and the Wall Street Journal.

LIST INFORMATION

QUANTITY MAILED:	4,000,000*
AVERAGE ORDER:	$100
ACTIVE BUYERS:	150,000
TOTAL LIST:	300,000
LIST SOURCE:	Direct mail.

COMMENTS

The sales figure above is an estimate of Magram's mail order sales for 1981 and does not include revenues generated by the company's one retail outlet in New York. Company officials reported that they expected sales to continue to increase and that operations were profitable. Due to their position as a marketer of mid to upscale apparel the company has reportedly not been severely affected by recent economic trends. They describe their typical customer as an affluent, well-educated suburbanite who takes great interest in personal appearance. Catalog models portray an elite, stylish, "career-oriented" look. Magram mails four catalogs a year including their holiday edition. Catalogs are full-color, digest size and either 32 or 64 pages. The company has reportedly reduced its use of space advertising, and is concentrating almost exclusively on catalogs for promotion.

MANHATTAN MARINE

ADDRESS, PHONE
Manhattan Marine and Electric, 116 Chambers, New York, NY 10007. Telephone: (212) 267-8756.

OWNERSHIP
Privately held; 100% of capital (200 shares of common stock, no par value) owned by Rose Hurwitz and family.

MANAGEMENT
Rose Hurwitz, President; David Hurwitz, Secretary.

TYPE OF MARKETER
Mail order, retail, wholesale.

BUSINESS
Manhattan Marine & Electric markets a complete line of accessories and equipment for yachtsmen, ship-yards and naval architects. In their 400+ page catalog Manhattan offers thousands of items ranging from the smallest boating hardware to full-size life rafts. Mail order is estimated to account for roughly 80% of revenues, with the remainder coming from in-store sales at headquarters outlet. Manhattan does some importing and international sales, and limited manufacturing.

COMPANY HISTORY
The business was founded in 1923 by Bernard Hurwitz. It was incorporated in New York on October 8, 1923 as Manhattan Marine & Electric Company, Inc., with authorized capital of $50,000 in common stock. Rose Hurwitz succeeded her husband as president upon his death in 1978. David Hurwitz was also elected as an officer in that year.

MARKETS
Sells by mail both domestically and overseas. Market is about 70% male, middle to high income.

FACILITIES

All operations out of four Manhattan buildings, 116-120 Chambers St., New York.

PRODUCTS, BRAND NAMES, PRICE RANGE

Thousands of boating-related items, including small hardware, navigational lights, floatation devices, life rafts, motors, furniture, marine electronic equipment. Products manufactured by and for company sold under registered "Seatest" trademark.

FINANCIAL INFORMATION

	SALES	NET INCOME	PROFIT MARGIN
1981	$20,000,000*	N.A.	--

TYPE OF ADVERTISING, PROMOTION

Manhattan's main promotional emphasis is on their catalogs which are published annually. In recent years the company has started mailing two smaller supplements each year to support the main catalog. Some space advertising in boating magazines.

LIST INFORMATION

QUANTITY MAILED:
AVERAGE ORDER:
ACTIVE BUYERS:
TOTAL LIST:
LIST SOURCE:

(Manhattan does not market its list or make available any information on its buyer file.)

COMMENTS

The above sales figure is an estimate of Manhattan Marine's total mail order sales and does not include in-store sales from the company's one outlet. At present Manhattan Marine is undergoing a major reorganization in management. The company's plans for the immediate future include the addition of a direct sales force to marketing operations in 1982. They are also in the process of increasing their product mix and are focusing efforts on specialized areas of the marine industry such as sailing. Manhattan Marine and Electric is considered to be an institution in the marine industry, and the catalog offers nearly everything related to boating. Catalogs often include a discount insert, and company began testing two 16-page annual supplements in 1981. The main catalog contains over 400 b&w pages and over 80,000 products.

MARKLINE

ADDRESS, PHONE

Markline Company, Inc., 411 Waverly Oaks Road, Waltham, MA 02154. Telephone: (617) 891-6800.

OWNERSHIP

Privately held; 100% of capital stock owned by Herbert D. Kline.

MANAGEMENT

Herbert D. Kline, President; Charles R. Hefford, Executive Vice President; Michael W. Ferguson, Vice President; David L. Keane, Controller.

TYPE OF MARKETER

Mail order, retail.

BUSINESS

Markline specializes in selling a wide variety of electronic equipment for home and office including calculators, computers, games, watches and clocks, radios, health and beauty aids, security devices, dictating equipment, phone answering units, accessories and related miscellaneous electronic items. In addition to mail order sales, Markline operates three retail units for commercial sales to business accounts and a major outlet for repairs of electronic equipment.

COMPANY HISTORY

The company was started in 1973 by Herbert Kline as a retail marketer of electronics goods. In 1977, Markline greatly expanded their operations and began offering selections of their retail merchandise mix by mail through seasonal catalogs. The company has kept pace with advances in time piece, calculator, tape recording and home video technology in the type of merchandise it offers. Markline currently employs 100 people.

MARKETS

Mail order customers throughout the U.S., 77% male. Many have a professional interest in electronics.

FACILITIES
Headquarters, warehouse, mail order operations, Waltham, MA; stores in Boston, Waltham, Atlanta.

PRODUCTS, BRAND NAMES, PRICE RANGE
Catalog covers a variety of electronic items priced from $5.95 for educational toys to $3,250 for a personal computer designed for office or home. Many national brands.

FINANCIAL INFORMATION

	SALES	NET INCOME	PROFIT MARGIN
1980	$15,000,000*	N.A.	--

TYPE OF ADVERTISING, PROMOTION
Markline's main promotional emphasis is on their catalogs which are mailed seasonally. They are full-color and the format varies between 7 x 11, 32 pages, and 8-1/4 x 11, 32 pages. Company uses minimal space advertising in some national magazines.

LIST INFORMATION

QUANTITY MAILED:	8,000,000*
AVERAGE ORDER:	$79
ACTIVE BUYERS:	112,473
TOTAL LIST:	400,000
LIST SOURCE:	Direct mail.

COMMENTS
Of Markline's estimated $15 million in total revenues for 1980, approximately 60% or $8,885,000 came from mail order sales. The balance came from the company's three retail outlets and from direct sales to commercial accounts. Although mail order sales to personal buyers via the company's two major catalogs is healthy and moving upwards, firm appears to be gearing up for heaviest growth in the commercial sales area. A company spokesperson noted that computers are gaining strength in catalog sales; however, the catalog tends to be heavy in calculators--both pocket sized and table models for home and office. Firm stresses "variety" in catalog sales, with some items in the "unusual" category (such as a language translator) part of the product mix but not heavy in buyer response. Electronic games (chess sets can run as high as $349.95) receive substantial exposure in the catalog. The burgeoning market for consumer electronics is expected to continue to bolster catalog sales.

MARY MAXIM

ADDRESS, PHONE

Mary Maxim, Inc., 2001 Holland Avenue, Port Huron, MI 48060. Telephone: (313) 987-2000.

OWNERSHIP

Privately-held; 100% of capital stock owned by Willard M. McPhedrain and family.

MANAGEMENT

Willard M. McPhedrain, President; VPs: Robert L. McManaman, Merchandising; Robert L. Smith, Jr., Mail Order; Frances L. McPhedrain; Leone White, Secretary; Richard F. Ward, Treasurer.

TYPE OF MARKETER

Mail order, retail, wholesale.

BUSINESS

Mary Maxim is a mail order and retail marketer of kits and supplies for needlecraft and rug making. In addition the company does some limited wholesaling of yarn and related needlecrafting supplies. Management reports that the company's sales are fairly consistent throughout the year. The number of company employees varies between 80 and 100 due to fluctuations in mail order business.

COMPANY HISTORY

The business was started by William M. McPhedrain (father of the current president) in Port Huron, Michigan in the early 1950's. It was incorporated in Michigan on January 1, 1956, and the present officers assumed control in 1965. The company has two subsidiary concerns related through officers and financial interest: Miss Mary Maxim of Paris, Ltd. (located in Ontario; chartered 1953); Holland Advertising, Inc. (Port Huron; chartered 1976).

MARKETS

Sells merchandise throughout the U.S. and Canada; customers are 100% craft-oriented women.

FACILITIES
Headquarters, warehousing and marketing operations located in Port Huron, Michigan.

PRODUCTS, BRAND NAMES, PRICE RANGE
Yarns, hobbycrafts, knitting patterns, stitchery accessories, craft kits, fabrics, tools and designs for rugs, sweaters, afghans, pillows, wall hangings. Price range is low to medium.

FINANCIAL INFORMATION

	SALES	NET INCOME	PROFIT MARGIN
1981	$10,000,000*	N.A.	--

TYPE OF ADVERTISING, PROMOTION
Approximately 80% of Mary Maxim's advertising is through direct mail mini-catalogs and packages. The remaining 20% is through space advertising in women's home and craft magazines.

LIST INFORMATION
QUANTITY MAILED:	5,000,000*
AVERAGE ORDER:	$29
ACTIVE BUYERS:	200,000
TOTAL LIST:	500,000
LIST SOURCE:	Direct mail, space.

COMMENTS
Of Mary Maxim's total estimated 1981 revenues of $10,000,000, approximately 90% came from mail order sales to consumers in the U.S. and Canada. The remaining 10% of revenues reportedly came from wholesale sales. This total does not include sales from the company's Ontario subsidiary (only inter-company relations are merchandise transactions). Management reports that sales have increased over the past three years, despite overall flatness of the national crafts-by-mail market. They added that profitability has improved over the same period. The company's Holland Advertising subsidiary designs, mails and places all of Mary Maxim's direct mail and space advertising. This is handled as a service and administrative transaction between the two companies. Maxim officials report that they are increasing direct mail promotion of kits of merchandise and special offers to combat the slumping crafts market.

EARL MAY

ADDRESS, PHONE
Earl May Seed & Nursery Co., P. O. Box 500, Shenandoah, IA 51603. Telephone: (712) 246-1020.

OWNERSHIP
Privately held; 100% of capital stock held by members of the May family.

MANAGEMENT
Edward W. May, President; J. D. Rankin, Jr., Executive Vice President; James B. Shaun, Vice President; Frances M. Rankin, Treasurer.

TYPE OF MARKETER
Mail order, retail.

BUSINESS
Earl May markets seeds, bulbs, trees, shrubs, roses and gardening accessories via mail and through its 54 retail outlets scattered throughout the midwest. Although the company got its start as a mail order business, the retail operations now account for about 75% of sales. Sales are heaviest in January, February and March, and the company averages about 500 employees. The retail stores offer more items than catalogs, such as pet supplies, but catalog offerings are still extensive.

COMPANY HISTORY
Earl May, father of the current president, started the business in Iowa in 1919, as a mail order marketer of seeds and nursery stock. The company opened its first retail outlet in the 1920's and since that time, May retail operations have expanded to include 54 stores in the midwestern states. Both retail and mail order operations have reportedly grown steadily in the past five years.

MARKETS
Mail order sales are nationwide; retail sales in Midwest. Market is 50% male; middle-to-high income.

FACILITIES

Headquarters, warehousing/shipping, laboratories, hybridization plant, all at Shenandoah location.

PRODUCTS, BRAND NAMES, PRICE RANGE

Seeds, bulbs, trees, shrubs, roses; seeders, sprayers, cultivators and related accessories. Company sells such national brands as Ortho and Scotts as well as its own Earl May insecticides and fertilizer. Prices start at $.65.

FINANCIAL INFORMATION

	SALES	NET INCOME	PROFIT MARGIN
1981	$21,000,000*	N.A.	--

TYPE OF ADVERTISING, PROMOTION

May mails two editions of its catalog per year; main book in January, and fall supplement during September. The company also uses inquiry-generating space ads in gardening, home and farm magazines.

LIST INFORMATION

QUANTITY MAILED: 2,250,000
AVERAGE ORDER: $18
ACTIVE BUYERS: 150,000
TOTAL LIST: 600,000
LIST SOURCE: Direct mail, space.

COMMENTS

While some nursery marketers stress one specialized area such as seeds, Earl May Seed & Nursery places equal emphasis on all its merchandise lines including farm seeds, garden seeds, nursery stock, fertilizer and accessories. The company reported that in 1981 business was "much better than last year; good in the whole gamut of live plants, flower seeds, and gardening merchandise." Mail order sales account for an estimated 25% of May's total revenues--some $5.4 million. An estimated $16.2 million came from the Earl May Nursery & Garden Store chain. Including the main spring edition of the catalog (50% color, 88 pages) and the fall supplement (six pages), May mailed over 2,000,000 pieces in 1980. In 1981 the company mailed 1,400,000 copies of the spring book and plans are for increased fall flyer mailing.

McGRAW-HILL

ADDRESS, PHONE

McGraw-Hill, Inc., 1221 Avenue of the Americas, New York, NY 10020. Telephone: (212) 997-1221.

OWNERSHIP

Publicly held; stock traded NYSE; 24,964,000 shares outstanding; cash dividend: $1.68; market prices: high, 56; low, 39-3/8.

MANAGEMENT

Harold W. McGraw, Jr., Chairman and CEO; Joseph L. Dionne, President and COO; Theodore S. Weber, Jr., Executive VP-Administration and Staff Services; John B. Cave, Executive VP-Finance.

TYPE OF MARKETER

Mail order, retail, wholesale, direct sales.

BUSINESS

McGraw-Hill is a diversified group of publishing and marketing operations, divided into the following segments: Books and Education Services; Publications; Information Systems (computer software); Financial Services; Broadcasting (four television stations); Economic Information Services (on-line economic data bases). While all of these divisions use direct mail for inquiry generation and marketing purposes, it is of greatest significance in the book and book club division.

COMPANY HISTORY

James A. McGraw began publishing activities in 1888 and the McGraw Publishing Company was incorporated in 1899. John A. Hill incorporated the Hill Publishing Company in 1902. Both specialized in publishing business and professional journals. The two cooperated on book publishing operations beginning in 1909. In 1917 the two firms merged to form the McGraw-Hill Publishing Company, Inc.

MARKETS

U.S. and international; business executives and professionals, technical people, general consumers.

FACILITIES

Headquarters New York; regional sales and service offices in 315 locations worldwide.

PRODUCTS, BRAND NAMES, PRICE RANGE

Mc.-H. produces and markets a variety of books, guides, films and study programs under the following division titles: Gregg, College, CTB, Sheppards, CRM/McGraw-Hill Films, Schaum, Webster, EDL and Instructo.

FINANCIAL INFORMATION

	SALES	NET INCOME	PROFIT MARGIN
1981	$1,110,125,000	$98,117,000	8.8%

TYPE OF ADVERTISING, PROMOTION

Direct mail, newspaper inserts, magazines, radio and TV--all types of advertising. Book company makes heavy use of direct mail packages to businesses, school book services, various educational programs, retail outlets.

LIST INFORMATION

QUANTITY MAILED:	N.A.
AVERAGE ORDER:	$25
ACTIVE BUYERS:	237,000 (books); 252,000 (clubs)
TOTAL LIST:	N.A.
LIST SOURCE:	Direct mail (100%).

COMMENTS

McGraw-Hill Book Company reported $355 million in revenues for 1980, representing a $20.1 million (6%) increase over 1979. Subject category sales breakdown is as follows: higher education, 34%; professional and training, 33%; home study, 10%; trade publishing, 3%. The General Books division includes single title sales and the following seven book clubs: Chemical, Civil, Electronic and Mechanical Engineering, Architecture, Computer and Business Management, and Accounting. Mail order sales contributed 100% of General Books/Clubs sales--an estimated $18 million--which was roughly 5% of total Book Company sales. Virtually all of the other Book Company divisions use direct mail for inquiry generation, direct sales support, or merchandise sales. About 16% of McGraw-Hill total revenues come from direct mail. McGraw-Hill currently markets 40 different lists. Management reports that the Book Company achieved outstanding results despite being hampered by funding restraints in several school markets.

STUART McGUIRE

ADDRESS, PHONE
Stuart McGuire Co., Inc., 115 Brand Road, Salem, VA 24153. Telephone: (703) 389-8121.

OWNERSHIP
Publicly held; stock traded OTC; 958,851 common shares outstanding; 1980: low bid, 3/4; high bid, 1-1/2; no dividends paid in the last five years.

MANAGEMENT
E. Cabell Brand, Chairman of Board, CEO; Charles P. Gallopo, President; W. Douglas Johnstone, Executive VP; Robert Brady, VP-Finance; Rene Partleton, VP-Merchandising; Jimmy J. Tickle, VP-Operations.

TYPE OF MARKETER
Mail order, direct sales.

BUSINESS
McGuire is involved in the direct marketing of men's and women's footwear, clothing, jewelry and watches. Mail order segment distributes products (primarily footwear) directly to the customer by mail. Direct selling segment receives its orders from sales solicitors who maintain their own inventory or function as independent contractors. Until recently, company had an advertising services segment, Brand-Edmonds Advertising Agency (full service ad. agency). Company reported 300 employees for 1980.

COMPANY HISTORY
The business was started as "Ortho-Vent Shoe Company" in 1904 by W. Lee Brand. The present name was adopted in 1968, and the company went public in 1970. It was originally a direct selling company and expanded into mail order operations in 1975. In early 1981 company disposed of three subsidiaries acquired in 1979: Hennikers (mail order gifts); the Association of Informed Travellers (mail order travel advisory); and Gem Finders Society, Inc.

MARKETS
Continental U.S., Puerto Rico and U.S. possessions; primary marketing emphasis on low-priced footwear.

FACILITIES
Principal location, Salem, VA; independent contractors throughout the U.S.

PRODUCTS, BRAND NAMES, PRICE RANGE
Stuart McGuire Shoes and Clothing; Ortho-Vent Shoes and Clothing, Leathercrest Shoes, Leathercrest Values and Jewelry, Lady-Soft Step, Marshmellows, and others. Lines of specialty gifts and semi-precious gems have been eliminated.

FINANCIAL INFORMATION

	SALES	**NET INCOME**	**PROFIT MARGIN**
1980	$52,500,000	($1,764,000)	-0-

TYPE OF ADVERTISING, PROMOTION
Direct Selling Div. promotes its products through 150,000 sales solicitors using a full color catalog which is published twice a year. The Mail Order Div. publishes catalogs distributed directly to the customer. Promotional costs were $2,061,000.

LIST INFORMATION
QUANTITY MAILED:	17,600,000
AVERAGE ORDER:	$35
ACTIVE BUYERS:	494,000
TOTAL LIST:	2,368,000
LIST SOURCE:	Direct mail, space.

COMMENTS
Mail order division primarily sells footwear by mail. Company is actively pursuing growth in mail order business, and is reporting increased sales in spite of declining retail demand for footwear. Efforts to diversify in 1979 resulted in undesireable sales mix and heavy write-offs due to unusually high inventories. Problems in managing the three non-footwear subsidiaries acquired in 1979 resulted in their sale in the fall of 1981. Excluding the impact of these subsidiaries, total sales increased 9% in 1980 (mail order up 40%). In 1980 mail order sales were an estimated $25.9 million; roughly 49% of total revenues. Company has experienced problems in past with high cost of unclaimed C.O.D. packages through direct selling operation. In future, C.O.D. sales will be restricted to sales rep.'s with high sales and low unclaimed quotas. Repositioning towards solely footwear and apparel, and cost control, resulted in $18,000,000 in sales in first 6 months of 1981: $2,000,000 over projected levels.

MEREDITH CORPORATION

ADDRESS, PHONE
Meredith Corporation, Locust at 17th, Des Moines, Iowa, 50336. Telephone: (515) 284-3000.

OWNERSHIP
Publicly held; listed NYSE; FY81: 3,172,300 common shares outstanding; dividend $1.46.

MANAGEMENT
E. T. Meredith III, Chmn.; Robert A. Burnett, Pres. & CEO; Group Presidents: James Conley, Broadcasting; John Gregg, Printing; Wayne A. Miller, Publishing; James A. Riggs, Real Estate.

TYPE OF MARKETER
Mail order, retail.

BUSINESS
Company conducts its operations through four divisions: Publishing Group publishes Better Homes & Gardens and other special interest magazines and books; includes Family Shopping Service and B.H.&G. Crafts Club mail order operations. Printing Group provides printing services for in-house publications and for outside customers on a contract basis. Broadcasting Group operates radio & T.V. stations. Allied Products & Services provides marketing services for real estate firms and is testing direct mail insurance sales.

COMPANY HISTORY
The company was founded in Des Moines, Iowa, in 1902 as the publisher of Successful Farming magazine, was incorporated in Iowa on August 8, 1905. In 1922, company created its second publication, Better Homes & Gardens magazine. In October 1925, charter was amended, changing the name from Successful Farming Publishing Co. to Meredith Publishing Co. Name was changed to Meredith Corporation on October 17, 1967. Forty-seven percent of the stock is owned by E. T. Meredith; the remaining is owned by public.

MARKETS
U.S.; Australian edition of Better Homes & Gardens magazine.

FACILITIES

HQ, publishing center: Des Moines; direct mail & shipping: Clarion, IA; publishing: NY & Boston.

PRODUCTS, BRAND NAMES, PRICE RANGE

Family Shopping Service sells kits and materials for needlework, holiday decorations, glass etchings, caligraphy, quilting, soft toys, etc. B.H.&G. Crafts Club sells books and guides for crafts, home improvement, refinishing and do-it-yourself home repair.

FINANCIAL INFORMATION

	SALES	**NET INCOME**	**PROFIT MARGIN**
1981	$403,425,000	$23,595,000	5.9%

TYPE OF ADVERTISING, PROMOTION

Direct mail; space advertising in magazines (particularly special interest magazines published by the company) and in Sunday supplements; testing of direct mail sales of insurance to house list of magazine subscribers.

LIST INFORMATION

QUANTITY MAILED: 22,000,000
AVERAGE ORDER: Varies by product.
ACTIVE BUYERS: 9.5 million: magazines, books, kits
TOTAL LIST: 11,000,000
LIST SOURCE: Direct mail, space ads.

COMMENTS

Family Shopping has reportedly experienced a decline in performance due to reduced consumer response to their direct mail operations. Management attributes poor operating results to severe economic conditions which have negatively affected entire crafts-by-mail industry. Problems in book mail order started in summer of '78 and continued through '79, when operating profits for book publishing dropped more than 80%. In 1980 Meredith cut back quantity of direct mail pieces mailed and focused attention on house list. Total mail order volume decreased, but operating profits rose. Experimental "B.H.&G. Craft Creations" home party plan was dropped. With increased emphasis on mail order, Crafts Club sales improved: sales for craft books jumped from estimated $8.4 million in FY80 to approximately $14 million in FY81. Mail order operations produced the largest increase in revenues for Meredith in '81. Family Book Service and Crafts Club presently have over 70 titles on the market. Meredith is continuing its three year test of direct mail insurance services.

METROPOLITAN MUSEUM OF ART

ADDRESS, PHONE

Metropolitan Museum of Art, Fifth Avenue and 82nd Street, New York, NY 10028. (212) 879-5500.

OWNERSHIP

Non-profit, civic organization.

MANAGEMENT

Paul M. Jones, Mail Order Manager; Merwyn Worthman, Associate Manager; Helen Golden, Associate Manager; Herman Felton, Fulfillment Supervisor; Mary Medford, Catalog Sales Supervisor.

TYPE OF MARKETER

Mail order, retail.

BUSINESS

Museum shops and mail order operations market reproduction prints and oils, imported glassware, replicas, postcards, Christmas cards and more. Emphasis is on a quality line of merchandise. Sales from shops and mail order help support museum acquisitions, exhibit programs, etc. Mail order accounts for 64% of total merchandise revenues.

COMPANY HISTORY

The Museum began offering merchandise by mail through a catalog in 1920. Initially the offerings were mostly art reproductions on Christmas cards. In the '40s and '50s Director Francis Henry Taylor popularized the mail order operation by expanding the merchandise lines. The Museum's seventh director, Thomas Hoving, is credited with increasing shop space within the Museum and greatly expanding the catalog operation. Between 1967 and 1979, total merchandise sales increased 35% per year.

MARKETS

Customers are mid to upper scale; the Museum sells merchandise by mail throughout U.S. and abroad.

FACILITIES
Headquarters, order processing and fulfillment, customer service, retail outlets, New York, NY.

PRODUCTS, BRAND NAMES, PRICE RANGE
Books, prints, records, audio-visual material, posters, miniatures, porcelain plates and figurines, silver candlesticks, glass and crystal copies, cards, oils, etc. Specialty items are reproductions from exhibitions. Price range upscale.

FINANCIAL INFORMATION

	SALES	**NET INCOME**	**PROFIT MARGIN**
1981	$19,000,000*	N.A.	--

TYPE OF ADVERTISING, PROMOTION
Space in upscale magazines and newspapers. Catalogs are mailed on request and given to museum visitors--books are 8-1/2 by 5-1/2, full-color and glossy. Seasonal catalogs as well as single mailings promoting publications, special items, etc.

LIST INFORMATION
QUANTITY MAILED: N.A.
AVERAGE ORDER: $42
ACTIVE BUYERS: 300,000
TOTAL LIST: 1,000,000
LIST SOURCE: Direct, space, museum visitors.

COMMENTS
The above figure represents total mail order sales. Reported percentage breakdown of sales is mail order, 64% and retail, 36%. Total retail sales are estimated to be $10.7 million, and total merchandise sales, approximately $29.7 million. At this rate, merchandise sales contributed approximately 4.2% of the Museum's $700 million in gross sales and receipts for 1981. The museum has developed a successful operation by not only mailing their catalogs directly to customers, but by circulating them to museum visitors. The mail order operation reportedly softened in 1978, but has experienced continuous growth rate of 15% per year since 1979. Aside from collections of perennial items in the product mix such as reproductions of more famous art works and the museum's line of Christmas cards, the Met uses special catalog editions to market reproductions from major exhibits. The Met's special catalog for the King Tut exhibition grossed $2.3 million in the first six months.

MICHIGAN BULB

ADDRESS, PHONE

Michigan Bulb Company, Inc., 1950 Waldorf N.W., Grand Rapids, MI 49504. Telephone: (616) 453-5401.

OWNERSHIP

Privately held; 100% of capital is owned by the officers.

MANAGEMENT

Ronald Laub, President; John Littleton, Executive Vice President; Thomas Stumb, Vice President-Finance, Secretary and Treasurer; Daniel Holbert, Vice President-Operations, Assistant Secretary.

TYPE OF MARKETER

Mail order.

BUSINESS

The Michigan Bulb Company is a mail order marketer of horticultural products and accessories including bulbs, seeds, flowers, shrubbery and garden tools. Products are sold through direct mail and space advertising. The company's subsidiaries include: (1) Flower of the Month, Inc. -- mail order marketer of flower seeds and bulbs; (2) Littleton Advertising, Inc. -- Michigan-based advertising agency; (3) Vitaleaf, Inc. -- Indiana-based horticultural labs.

COMPANY HISTORY

The original Michigan Bulb Company was founded by Forest Laub, and incorporated in Michigan on December 2, 1946. On January 1, 1969, Pacific American Industries of Los Angeles purchased all outstanding capital. In 1975, the company was sold to Rockwood Gardens, operated as a subsidiary for a year, and finally merged with the parent to form the new Michigan Bulb Company. Authorized capital consists of 50,000 shares of common stock, no par value, all of which is owned by the officers.

MARKETS

Mail order sales throughout the U.S.; no international. Customers are mostly homeowners.

FACILITIES

Company owns 75,000 sq. ft. building for head-quarters and operations.

PRODUCTS, BRAND NAMES, PRICE RANGE

Wide assortment of flowering plants, vines, hedges, fruit trees, and fruit and vegetable seeds. Prices range from $1.50 to $12.00, with discounts for assortment offers and quantity purchases.

FINANCIAL INFORMATION

	SALES	**NET INCOME**	**PROFIT MARGIN**
1981	$20,000,000*	N.A.	--

TYPE OF ADVERTISING, PROMOTION

The major percentage of Michigan Bulb's promotion and advertising is through direct mail packages containing brochures, sweepstakes offers and price listings. In addition, they are a major user of space advertising in consumer publications.

LIST INFORMATION

QUANTITY MAILED:	12,000,000*
AVERAGE ORDER:	$10
ACTIVE BUYERS:	1,400,000
TOTAL LIST:	2,850,000
LIST SOURCE:	Direct mail, space.

COMMENTS

The sales figure above is an estimate of parent company Michigan Bulb's mail order sales, and does not include revenues from the company's subsidiary operations. Flower of the Month is reportedly a substantial mail order marketer of hybrid garden - variety flowers. Vitaleaf, Inc., started in 1980, is involved in hybridization and development of plant and vegetable seeds. Littleton Advertising is a full-service ad agency which handles all promotions for Michigan Bulb and other accounts. The parent's direct mail packages include a full-color, 9-1/2 x 11, four-page brochure. These are published several times per year, with main editions in the spring and fall. In addition Michigan Bulb conducts a $100,000 sweepstakes offering cash and merchandise prizes as special incentives. The brochure also offers a variety of free merchandise and discounts as pre-miums for quantity purchases and multiple orders.

MILES KIMBALL

ADDRESS, PHONE
Miles Kimball Co., Inc., 41 W. 8th Avenue, Oshkosh, WI 54903. Telephone: (414) 231-3800.

OWNERSHIP
Wholly-owned subsidiary of Harlequin Holding, Inc. of Ontario, Canada.

MANAGEMENT
Alberta S. Kimball, Chairman; Edward Leyhe, President; Thomas Drummond, Vice President Operations; Clair Martin, Vice President Finance.

TYPE OF MARKETER
Mail order, wholesale.

BUSINESS
Miles Kimball is a mail order marketer of a wide assortment of housewares, kitchen utensils, jewelry, hardware, toys, decorative items, novelties and Christmas cards. Sales are heaviest during the Christmas season, which is reflected by the number of employees (ranging from 250 to 1,500). Miles Kimball products are sold directly to consumers, and wholesale to retail stores.

COMPANY HISTORY
Miles Kimball started the company in 1934 in Wisconsin, selling printed products by mail. The company was incorporated in that year as Direct Mail Associates. The name was changed to Miles Kimball in 1940. The merchandise mix has been gradually modified with the addition of lines mentioned above. In 1980 Harlequin Holding, Inc. acquired Miles Kimball, but no changes were made in staff, merchandise selection, or marketing operations.

MARKETS
Kimball sells by mail throughout the U.S.; market is mostly female and crosses age and income lines.

FACILITIES
Headquarters, warehouse/fulfillment and greeting card printing operations in Oshkosh.

PRODUCTS, BRAND NAMES, PRICE RANGE
Over 2,000 items ranging from the useful to the fanciful. One-page sampling includes an electric footwarmer, a sinus mask, scented drawer liner paper, bentwood coat/ hat racks, personalized luggage tags. Prices are generally well under $25.00.

FINANCIAL INFORMATION

	SALES	NET INCOME	PROFIT MARGIN
1981	$40,000,000*	N.A.	--

TYPE OF ADVERTISING, PROMOTION
Virtually all of Miles Kimball's promotion is through catalog mailings with very limited use of space in newspapers and magazines. Main catalogs are full color, 8-1/4 x 10-1/2, 64 or 196 pages. Supplements (5 x 8-1/2) are sent out periodically.

LIST INFORMATION
QUANTITY MAILED: 40,000,000*
AVERAGE ORDER: $18
ACTIVE BUYERS: 1,480,000
TOTAL LIST: 3,065,000
LIST SOURCE: Direct mail, space.

COMMENTS
Miles Kimball's 1981 revenues were estimated to be over $40,000,000 from sales to individual customers. Company officials reported that 1981 was a very strong year with total revenues for the first eight months showing a 20% increase over the same period in 1980. Earnings are reportedly on a steady increase. Kimball's operations are broken down as follows: consumer mail order sales, 60%; mail order wholesaling to retail customers, 25%; design and printing of Christmas cards, 15%. The company sold merchandise to some 1.5 million individuals and 3,000 hardware, drug and gift shop dealer accounts. Many of Kimball's 2,000 items per catalog would be difficult to find in retail stores. Often the items are not in common demand, but their presence in Kimball's "novelty/gift catalogs helps them to sell themselves". Aside from greeting cards, all other merchandise is purchased from outside manufacturers.

MOA CORPORATION

ADDRESS, PHONE
MOA Corporation, 4795 Fulton Industrial Blvd., Atlanta, GA 30336. Telephone: (404) 601-7311.

OWNERSHIP
Privately held; T.J. Munchak owns 100% of capital stock.

MANAGEMENT
Don L. Chapman, Chairman of the Board; Carl W. Hopper, President; Joel L. Jones, Secretary-Treasurer.

TYPE OF MARKETER
Mail order, retail.

BUSINESS
MOA Corporation is the parent of two mail order operations geared toward the upscale, fashion-conscious woman. Peachtree Report, the older of the two, markets women's apparel, jewelry, accessories and some gift items. The newer operation, Regalia, just got underway in late 1981 and will sell only ready-to-wear women's clothing and lounge apparel. Both offer higher-priced, quality women's clothing, but Regalia's items will be a little less expensive than Peachtree Report's. Company employs 61.

COMPANY HISTORY
MOA Corporation was formed in December, 1978, and the first Peachtree catalog was mailed in April, 1979. The firm started by purchasing the mailing list from the bankrupt Kaleidoscope operation and was heavily into gift items at first. The product mix was changed around 1980 to place a greater emphasis on fashion. In late 1981, company started competing sister operation, Regalia, with the first catalog mailed in December, 1981.

MARKETS
Market is about 95% female, upscale, 30 years old and up. No international marketing.

FACILITIES
Offices and fulfillment center in 30,000 sq. ft. building in Atlanta. Also has two retail outlets in area.

PRODUCTS, BRAND NAMES, PRICE RANGE
Primarily ladies' ready-to-wear, loungewear, access-
ories, jewelry. Peachtree Report also sells some gift
and houseware items. Major brands include Pierre
Cardin, Casi, Bill Tice, Bill Blass, Maggy London,
Christian Dior, Eve Stillman.

FINANCIAL INFORMATION

	SALES	**NET INCOME**	**PROFIT MARGIN**
1981	$10,000,000*	N.A.	--

TYPE OF ADVERTISING, PROMOTION
Catalogs, 98%. Six catalogs are issued a year for
Peachtree Report, including two specials that feature
only Pierre Cardin dresses under "Cardin for Peach-
tree" logo. Four catalogs are planned for Regalia.
Space in Southern Living, Glamour, Vogue.

LIST INFORMATION
QUANTITY MAILED:	10,000,000
AVERAGE ORDER:	$75+
ACTIVE BUYERS:	110,000*
TOTAL LIST:	500,000
LIST SOURCE:	Direct mail, rentals.

COMMENTS
In its brief history, MOA Corporation has managed
to increase sales each year. Corporate officials
anticipate extended growth for calendar year '82 with
addition of the Regalia operation--projected '82 sales
estimated at $12 to $15 million. Management attributes $25 jump in average order ('80 to '81) mainly to
re-orientation of product mix from gifts to women's
fashions. MOA continues to rely on large average
orders rather than high response rate to mailings.
For Peachtree and Regalia combined, company mails
some 900,000 catalogs and supplements per month.
MOA anticipates increasing this to 12,000,000 pieces
annually to achieve sales increase above. Marketing
strategy emphasizes heavy rental of "proven upscale
buyers" lists to generate higher average order and
increase upscale apparel position.

MUSICAL HERITAGE SOCIETY

ADDRESS, PHONE
Musical Heritage Society, Inc., 14 Park Road, Trinton Falls, NJ 07724. (201) 544-8446.

OWNERSHIP
Privately owned; 100% of capital stock owned by Albert Nissim.

MANAGEMENT
Albert Nissim, President; Dorothy Nissim, Secretary-Treasurer; Robert Nissim, General Manager; Jeffrey Nissim, Director of Artists & Repertoire; Ken Musiakiewicz, Comptroller.

TYPE OF MARKETER
Mail order.

BUSINESS
Musical Heritage Society is primarily a mail order classical record club, marketing records, cassettes, books, stereo equipment, video cassettes, and other related products. MHS markets records and blank cassettes under the company name, but all other merchandise is provided by outside suppliers. The majority of sales are on a continuity basis to society members, but single-purchase offers are made to non-members. Main focus is on classical series, but some American contemporary selections are available.

COMPANY HISTORY
The Society was founded in the early 1960's in Manhattan by Dr. Michael Niada (founder of Westminster Records). The company was purchased and incorporated in New York by Albert Nissim in June of 1976. Management reports continuous expansion of the merchandise offered and the catalog operations. The Society's most current catalog offers over 3,000 different record and tape titles, making it one of the largest record clubs of its type in the world today.

MARKETS
Customers are 60% male, upscale; primary market is U.S.; also Canada, France and England.

FACILITIES
Headquarters in Trinton Falls, NJ, contain offices, warehouse, and mail order operations.

PRODUCTS, BRAND NAMES, PRICE RANGE
Products include Musical Heritage Society records and cassettes: $4.95 for members, $7.75 for non-members. Other merchandise, such as stereo equipment and accessories, video cassettes and other related products from $2.00 to $2,000.

FINANCIAL INFORMATION
	SALES	**NET INCOME**	**PROFIT MARGIN**
1981	$10,000,000*	N.A.	--

TYPE OF ADVERTISING, PROMOTION
Aside from catalogs published twice a year, MHS members receive an informational "magazine" published 18 times a year. A major portion of the company's inquiries and new members are respondents to space advertising in magazines.

LIST INFORMATION
QUANTITY MAILED:	2,000,000*
AVERAGE ORDER:	$18
ACTIVE BUYERS:	N.A.
TOTAL LIST:	N.A.
LIST SOURCE:	Direct mail, space.

COMMENTS
Through its continuity program and sales of related merchandise, MHS' total revenues for 1981 were an estimated $10,000,000. Management reports that approximately 80% of their initial inquiries are from space ads in upscale and music-related magazines. Catalogs containing the full line of merchandise offered are published in September and March and mailed several times throughout the year. The MHS magazine is 64 pages and is mailed every three weeks to Society members. Company officials report that currently 90% of sales are domestic; 10% to the countries mentioned above. Plans are to increase mailings to potential foreign markets. MHS has installed a Hewlett-Packard Series 33 computer system with twenty terminals for order processing, inventory and customer service. The Society is reportedly planning a major expansion of mail order facilities in the near future.

MYRON MANUFACTURING

ADDRESS, PHONE
Myron Manufacturing Corp., 61 West Hunter Avenue, Maywood, NJ 07607. Telephone: (201) 843-6464.

OWNERSHIP
Privately-held; Myron and Elaine Adler each own 50% of capital stock.

MANAGEMENT
Myron Adler, President; Frank Growney, Vice President; Elaine Adler, Secretary; Richard Lindner, Treasurer; Beverly Yellen, Vice President-Marketing.

TYPE OF MARKETER
Mail order.

BUSINESS
Myron manufactures and markets a full line of calendars, business planners, and pocket diaries. In addition, it sells a variety of items such as key chains, stationery seals and portfolios. Merchandise may be imprinted with company names for use as advertising and premium items. All sales are through direct mail, including the Myron catalogs published twice a year. Peak sales are in the fall. The company employs 400 people.

COMPANY HISTORY
The company was started by Myron and Elaine Adler in 1949. The original business was marketing imprinted calendars and pocket planners to business executives. As the product line diversified the company began marketing through catalogs. In 1981 Myron broke ground for a new office and manufacturing complex in Maywood.

MARKETS
Mail order sales to executives of business concerns throughout the U.S. and Canada.

FACILITIES

Headquarters, manufacturing, and fulfillment located in Maywood, New Jersey and Toronto, Can.

PRODUCTS, BRAND NAMES, PRICE RANGE

Products include desk diaries, planners, calendars, pocket diaries, portfolios, ring binders, report covers, business card caddies, notebooks, presentation folders. Prices range up to $105 for single item purchases.

FINANCIAL INFORMATION

	SALES	NET INCOME	PROFIT MARGIN
1981	$22,500,000*	N.A.	--

TYPE OF ADVERTISING, PROMOTION

Myron mails two different catalogs per year and supports these mailings with direct mail packages to past buyers. The company has recently started a telemarketing program and is a moderate user of rented lists.

LIST INFORMATION

QUANTITY MAILED: 6,000,000*
AVERAGE ORDER: $150
ACTIVE BUYERS: 125,000
TOTAL LIST: 385,000
LIST SOURCE: Direct mail (100%).

COMMENTS

Myron Manufacturing has been a steadily-growing mail order company for over 30 years. Management attributes their relatively consistent sales growth to the development of a strong repeat-buying trend within their active buyer file. Myron is solely a business-to-business marketer and has an active file of some 125,000 accounts, which represents an increase of 18% over 1980. Myron's total revenues for 1981 are estimated at $22.5 million. Management reports that in the near future, they will be working to reduce internal costs, and that they will continue to increase the merchandise offered in their Spring and Fall catalogs. Myron's chief competitors in this mail order market are Baldwin-Cooke and Day-Timers.

NATIONAL LIBERTY

ADDRESS, PHONE

National Liberty Corp., Liberty Park, Malvern, PA 19355. Telephone: (215) 648-5000.

OWNERSHIP

Subsidiary of publicly-held Capitol Holding Corporation, Louisville, Kentucky.

MANAGEMENT

J. Dever Gregg, Chairman; Robert Rakich, President; James A. Blue, Executive VP & Treasurer; John W. Keller, Sr. VP; Gerald F. Beavan, VP; Donald D. Kennedy, Jr., VP.

TYPE OF MARKETER

Mail order, direct sales.

BUSINESS

National Liberty markets and services life, accident and health insurance policies, and annuities. The company's principal mail order and direct selling operation is National Liberty Marketing, Inc. which uses direct mail and an agent selling force to market the above products. Other subsidiaries include National Home Life Assurance, National Independent Life Insurance, National Liberty Life Insurance, National Liberty International, and National Information Systems, which supplies data-processing services to outside companies.

COMPANY HISTORY

National Liberty, organized in 1967 for insurance and marketing subsidiaries, was an out-growth of a company formed by Arthur S. DeMoss in 1959. Originally DeMoss sold health insurance by direct mail to the specialized market of non-drinkers. An agency selling division was added to direct response operations in 1974. Capitol purchased National Liberty in 1980 for a reported $358.7 million in cash and debentures. Direct marketing arm National Liberty Marketing employs 175 people.

MARKETS

Moderate-income individuals; specialized groups include veterans, women, the elderly, non-drinkers.

FACILITIES
National Liberty Marketing headquarters and direct
mail marketing operations in Valley Forge, PA.

PRODUCTS, BRAND NAMES, PRICE RANGE
N.L. Marketing offers life, health and accident
insurance, and annuities. Plan names include A & H
and Gold Star. Policies are priced to appeal to
people of limited to moderate means.

FINANCIAL INFORMATION

	SALES	NET INCOME	PROFIT MARGIN
1980	$274,000,000*	N.A.	--

TYPE OF ADVERTISING, PROMOTION
N.L. Marketing uses direct mail, inserts, space ads,
and television spots. The company mails over
100,000,000 direct mail packages annually (not including inserts). N.L. recently instituted a telemarketing operation to renew lapsed policies.

LIST INFORMATION
QUANTITY MAILED: 100,000,000 pcs; 125,000,000 inserts
AVERAGE ORDER: N.A.
ACTIVE BUYERS: 2,400,000
TOTAL LIST: 3,400,000
LIST SOURCE: Direct mail, space, broadcast.

COMMENTS
After National Liberty eliminated group and casualty
insurance (not profitable parts of its operation) and
increased emphasis on marketing its more profitable
products, yearly net income began to increase
steadily: $10,941,000 in 1976; $13,277,000 in 1977;
$19,415,000 in 1978; $24,697,000 in 1979; and
$20,408,000 through the third quarter of 1980 (after
which time the company was sold to Capitol Holding
Corporation). While direct response life insurance
historically produces better profit margins, this
company's carefully selected policyholders have
produced equal, and in some years better, profit
margins for direct response accident and health
insurance. Direct response revenues nearly doubled
between '74 and '79. In the same period direct
response pre-tax earnings jumped from $9,900,000 to
$28,000,000. Direct marketing operations accounted
for an estimated 84% of National Liberty's total
revenues.

NATIONAL WHOLESALE

ADDRESS, PHONE

National Wholesale Co., 400 National Boulevard, Lexington, NC 27292. Telephone: (704) 246-5904.

OWNERSHIP

Privately held; Edward Smith owns 100% of capital stock.

MANAGEMENT

Edward C. Smith, Sr., President; Joe Athay, Executive Vice President; Edward C. Smith, Jr., Vice President.

TYPE OF MARKETER

Mail order, wholesale.

BUSINESS

National markets a variety of hosiery, pantyhose, and men's and women's underwear. The company does no manufacturing, but designs products and has them produced to specification by three outside mills. National has one retail outlet, but the majority of sales to both individual consumers and commercial accounts are by mail. Promotional emphasis is on selling quantities of discounted basics to low-budget consumers and low-end marketers.

COMPANY HISTORY

National Wholesale was started in the late 1940's by Edward and Sarah Smith. Originally the company sold quantities of hosiery by mail to retail stores. In 1952 National began sending direct mail offers to individual consumers. Early mailings were direct mail packages, and the company did not start publishing catalogs until the mid 1970's. National presently employs 60 people.

MARKETS

Customers are mostly female, low-budget housewives throughout the U.S.; no international marketing.

FACILITIES

Offices, warehousing, wholesale and consumer mail order operations, Lexington, NC.

PRODUCTS, BRAND NAMES, PRICE RANGE

Variety of hosiery--knee-hi's, queen-size, cotton-soled, ultra-sheer, mesh, stretch, and more. Apparel--dresses, slack suits, hand bags, sleepwear, slippers and underwear. Some men's apparel and thermal underwear. House and national brands.

FINANCIAL INFORMATION

	SALES	**NET INCOME**	**PROFIT MARGIN**
1981	$11,000,000*	N.A.	--

TYPE OF ADVERTISING, PROMOTION

All of National Wholesale's advertising is through their direct mail packages containing single-sheet bonus offers and catalogs. The company regularly offers premiums such as free merchandise and quantity purchase discounts.

LIST INFORMATION

QUANTITY MAILED:	10,000,000*
AVERAGE ORDER:	$20*
ACTIVE BUYERS:	359,000
TOTAL LIST:	1,101,000
LIST SOURCE:	Direct mail.

COMMENTS

National Wholesale's 1981 revenues from consumer mail order sales were estimated to be $11,000,000. No accurate information was availabe on revenues generated by sales to commercial accounts. National processes approximately 500,000 consumer catalog orders per year, from eight catalog and direct mail package mailings throughout the year. Main catalogs are 8-1/2 x 5-1/2, full-color, 40 pages, and emphasize discount and low-priced merchandise. Supplemental packages are used for special offers and holiday sales.

NATIONAL WILDLIFE FEDERATION

ADDRESS, PHONE

National Wildlife Federation, 1412 Sixteenth St., NW, Washington, D.C. 20036. Telephone: (202) 797-6800.

OWNERSHIP

Publicly-supported, non-profit, non-governmental, educational and scientific organization.

MANAGEMENT

C. Clifton Young, President; Dr. Jay D. Hair, Executive VP; Senior VPs: J. A. Brownridge, James Davis, Gomer Jones.

TYPE OF MARKETER

Direct mail, fund raising & membership solicitation.

BUSINESS

NWF is the largest non-profit, non-government, conservational education organization in the nation, with over 4.2 million members and supporters. Publishes four magazines, sponsors outdoor educational programs, and litigates environmental disputes of national importance. Approximately 26% of total revenue comes from direct mail sale of nature educational materials; fund raising and membership solicitation by mail account for about 12% and 57% of revenue, respectively.

COMPANY HISTORY

NWF was organized in 1936 following a wildlife conference called by Franklin D. Roosevelt. Its first important legislative victory was passage of the Pittman-Robertson Act of 1937--still a major source of funding for U.S. wildlife conservation. Today it has independent affiliates in all 50 states and three U.S. territories. At end of '80, NWF had 1,183,033 Affiliate Members; 818,101 Associate Members; 813,651 Ranger Rick Nature Club Members; 1,702,578 Contributors.

MARKETS

The Federation draws funding and members from throughout the U.S. and its territories.

FACILITIES

Headquarters in Washington, D.C.; Laurel Ridge Conservation Education Center in VA.

PRODUCTS, BRAND NAMES, PRICE RANGE

Magazines: National Wildlife, International Wildlife, Ranger Rick's Nature Magazine, Your Big Backyard; assortment of conservation pamphlets; nature educational materials include Christmas cards, books, calendars, stamp albums, birdfeeders.

FINANCIAL INFORMATION

	SALES	**NET INCOME**	**PROFIT MARGIN**
1980	$30,429,936	-0-	-0-

TYPE OF ADVERTISING, PROMOTION

Direct mail and in-house promotions of nature educational material; direct mail membership and donation drives; promotes materials designed for use in elementary and secondary classrooms; sponsors outdoor education seminars and summer camps.

LIST INFORMATION

QUANTITY MAILED: (The Federation does not market its list or make available information on its buyer file.)
AVERAGE ORDER:
ACTIVE BUYERS:
TOTAL LIST:
LIST SOURCE:

COMMENTS

The figures above represent gross receipts and sales for this non-profit organization. In 1980, NWF spent more than $22 million on education, legislation, and litigation which helped to secure the following results: passage of Alaska Lands Bill, creation of a $1.6 billion Superfund to deal with toxic wastes, legal and legislative victories against ocean dumping, organization of the International Wildlife Federation. NWF raises 57% of its money by offering memberships in various clubs and programs. The publications group produces magazines for club and program subscribers, free pamphlets on conservation, and books for sale to house list made up of club subscribers and contributors. The wildlife book Living Wild: The Secrets of Animal Survival sold 41,000 copies by direct mail in three months. A recently updated series of 12 nature publications, Your Big Backyard, is aimed at three-to-five-year-olds, over 90,000 of whom are receiving monthly installments.

NEIMAN-MARCUS

ADDRESS, PHONE
Neiman-Marcus, 1624 Main St., Dallas, TX 75201.
Telephone: (214) 741-6911.

OWNERSHIP
Subsidiary of publicly-held Carter Hawley Hale Stores, Inc., of Los Angeles.

MANAGEMENT
Richard Marcus, Chrmn.; Phillip Miller, President; Ron Foppen, Exec. VP; John Gailys, Exec. VP-Finance; Tom Alexander, Exec. VP-Media/PR; John Giesecke, Sr. VP, Dir. of Mail Order.

TYPE OF MARKETER
Mail order, retail.

BUSINESS
Neiman-Marcus is one of Carter Hawley Hale's "high fashion specialty stores," and is best known for its unique offerings of clothing, home furnishings, epicure items and unusual gifts. A major percentage of the company's sales are by mail, the remaining portion generated by the company's sixteen retail stores. N-M is able to maintain a high degree of exclusivity in its product offerings by privately contracting with outside manufacturers and suppliers for merchandise.

COMPANY HISTORY
The business was started in 1907 by two Dallas families, the Neimans and Marcuses, who opened the first high-fashion retail store in Dallas. There was some experimentation with direct mail promotion in the 1930's and 40's when the company sent brochures to its retail customers, but mail order was not in place as a major marketing operation until the 1950s. Carter Hawley Hale acquired Neiman-Marcus in 1969 at a time when it had four stores in Texas.

MARKETS
Mail order sales throughout the U.S. and 41 foreign countries. Customers are primarily upscale.

FACILITIES
Headquarters and separate mail order warehousing and fulfillment center in Dallas, TX.

PRODUCTS, BRAND NAMES, PRICE RANGE
About 80% of line is apparel and includes shoes, accessories and loungewear. Emphasis on high-fashion and quality. Labels include Neiman-Marcus and designer names. Other merchandise: home furnishings, gifts, toiletries, gourmet foods.

FINANCIAL INFORMATION

	SALES	NET INCOME	PROFIT MARGIN
1980	$270,000,000*	N.A.	--

TYPE OF ADVERTISING, PROMOTION
Mail order operation primarily promoted via catalogs, which are published 18 times a year. Apparel catalogs are seasonal; other catalogs are specialized in areas like home furnishings and menswear. Some experimentation with solo mailings.

LIST INFORMATION

QUANTITY MAILED:	25,000,000*
AVERAGE ORDER:	$70*
ACTIVE BUYERS:	260,000*
TOTAL LIST:	N.A.
LIST SOURCE:	Direct mail.

COMMENTS
The sales figure above is an estimate for N-M's total operations. Mail order contributed an estimated 10% or $27,000,000 in revenues in 1981. Christmas '81 mail order sales were "substantially" ahead of 1980's, according to executives, and the reason seems to be linked to the offering of more exclusive items. Lower-priced items were removed from the Christmas '81 catalog and placed in the October mailings, which produced "dramatically" better results than the October '80 effort. There is an increase in competition from other high-fashion specialty marketers, but Neiman-Marcus plans to remain one of the leaders by expanding its line of exclusive items, improving its research of customer profiles, revamping its mailings to include more specialized catalogs. In the coming months, customers can expect a home furnishings catalog, an epicure catalog and other specialty mailings. Company will continue its unique Christmas catalog with its renowned "his-and-her" gift (a robot was the 1981 offering).

NEW ENGLAND BUSINESS SERVICE

ADDRESS, PHONE

New England Business Service, Inc., 500 Main Street, Groton, MA 01450. (617) 448-6111.

OWNERSHIP

Publicly held; stock traded OTC; 4,125,847 average common shares outstanding; FY81 bids: high 28, low 18; dividend: $.62; 3-for-2 split April, 81.

MANAGEMENT

Jay R. Rhoads, Jr., Chairman; Richard H. Rhoads, President; VPs: George Burnham, Robert Findlay, Richard Mack, Charles McLatchy, Dean Smith.

TYPE OF MARKETER

Mail order.

BUSINESS

NEBS Business Forms, company's flagship division, designs, produces, and markets (exclusively by mail) a line of standardized business forms and other printed products as well as several kinds of forms, holders and dispensers. Company sells principally to small businesses located throughout the U.S. and Canada. Forms and systems produced by NEBS are designed to assist basic business activities such as promotion, sales, service, billing, contract agreements.

COMPANY HISTORY

Albert E. Anderson started the business in the back of a barbershop in Townsend, MA, in 1952, and the company was incorporated in MA in 1955. In 1975 the company initiated a toll-free IN-WATS phone sales program, which accounted for 40% of total order placement in fiscal 1981. NEBS Business Forms Ltd., a Canadian subsidiary located in Midland, Ontario was started in 1978. NEBS sales and profits have grown at an average annual rate of 25% over the past ten years.

MARKETS

Most of NEBS customers are very small businesses (20 employees or fewer) in U.S. and Canada.

FACILITIES
H.Q. in Groton, MA; production plants in Townsend, MA, Petersborough, NH, and Maryhill, MO.

PRODUCTS, BRAND NAMES, PRICE RANGE
Typical products are work orders, repair tags, ledgers, statements, pricing and mailing labels. Specialized forms include invoices for stores, fuel meter tickets, pest control agreements, jewelry appraisal forms. Product line has over 400 items.

FINANCIAL INFORMATION

	SALES	**NET INCOME**	**PROFIT MARGIN**
1981	$78,982,000	$6,683,000	8.5%

TYPE OF ADVERTISING, PROMOTION
Direct mail of catalogs and flyers created by the company's advertising department. Solicits responses from prospect lists compiled from a library of over 4,000 current telephone directories.

LIST INFORMATION

QUANTITY MAILED:	36,000,000+
AVERAGE ORDER:	$32
ACTIVE BUYERS:	700,000 small businesses
TOTAL LIST:	1,500,000
LIST SOURCE:	Direct mail, telephone directories.

COMMENTS
1981 sales increased 24% over 1980 levels, and net income increased 16%. NEBS received and shipped approximately 2.5 million orders, 90.2% within six working days and 99.2% within ten working days of the order placement. Strategy for future growth is focused on the newly formed and very active Corporate Development Group, which is responsible for new products. Company introduced over 40 new products in 1981 which--together with products added in 1980--accounted for 40% of total 1981 sales growth. Corporate Development Group is also positioning NEBS to meet expected future demands for desk-top computer forms and supplies. Company emphasizes customer service, and 70% of yearly sales volume is repeat business. In order to serve its Far West customers more efficiently, NEBS plans to build a production plant on recently purchased site in Flagstaff, AZ.

NEW PROCESS COMPANY

ADDRESS, PHONE

New Process Company, 220 Hickory Street, Warren, PA 16366. Telephone: (814) 723-3600.

OWNERSHIP

Public; listed AMEX; FY81: 9,511,828 common shares outstanding; market prices: high 11-5/8, low 5-3/8; cash dividend, $.73 per share.

MANAGEMENT

John L. Blair, President; Alan J. Blair, Executive Vice President; Robert W. Blair, Vice President and Secretary; Giles W. Schutte, Vice President and Treasurer; John J. Smith, Vice President, Planning.

TYPE OF MARKETER

Mail order.

BUSINESS

New Process sells men's and women's apparel and accessories, as well as home furnishings, by direct mail. None of the products are designed or manufactured by the company. All merchandise is procured from a number of independent suppliers and sold under several trademarked brand names. Competition for sales is with other direct mail apparel businesses, retail department stores, specialty shops and discount store chains.

COMPANY HISTORY

The business was started in Pennsylvania in 1910 by John L. Blair, Sr. (father of the current president). Throughout its history, New Process has been a mail order marketer of men's and women's apparel designed and manufactured by outside concerns. The addition of home furnishings and expansion of the accessory line have been the only major changes in the merchandise mix. The business has grown relatively consistently and presently employs over 1,600 people.

MARKETS

New Process serves over 12,000,000 customers located in all 48 contiguous states.

FACILITIES
General offices are located in Warren, PA, with Distribution Center located in nearby Irvine, PA.

PRODUCTS, BRAND NAMES, PRICE RANGE
Women's dresses, sportswear, pantsuits, coordinated separates, etc.; men's suits, sport coats, slacks, shirts, shoes, etc.; home furnishings such as appliances, blankets, bedspreads, etc. Merchandise is low to medium in price position.

FINANCIAL INFORMATION

	SALES	NET INCOME	PROFIT MARGIN
1981	$231,342,871	$10,955,785	4.7%

TYPE OF ADVERTISING, PROMOTION
New Process mails direct mail packages which include promotional letters and full-color brochures featuring apparel and furnishing items. Mailings often include samples of fabrics being offered.

LIST INFORMATION

QUANTITY MAILED:	208,000,000
AVERAGE ORDER:	$40
ACTIVE BUYERS:	12,000,000
TOTAL LIST:	25,000,000*
LIST SOURCE:	Direct mail.

COMMENTS
Sales volume increased slightly in 1981 for this industry leader, but income declined significantly. Cost of goods sold increased because of higher shipping costs and slightly lower margins. Selling, general and administrative expenses were up primarily due to higher wages and printing and paper costs. Sales increased 16.6% in the first quarter of 1981 over 1980, but decreased 9.14% in the second quarter from 1980 figures. After-tax profits for the first half of 1981 were 108% higher than profits for the first half of 1980 ($6.06 million against $2.92 million), and probably reflect meaningful cost reductions including results from newly developed computerized capabilities that allow the company to concentrate mailing efforts to those customers most likely to respond to advertising. Sales were up .4% and net earnings were up 90% for fiscal '81 over '80, bringing the margin back in line at 4.7% compared to 2.5% for 1980.

OLD PUEBLO TRADERS

ADDRESS, PHONE
Old Pueblo Traders, 600 South Country Club, Tucson, AZ 85716. Telephone: (602) 795-0777.

OWNERSHIP
Subsidiary of privately-held Arizona Mail Order Company of Tucson, Arizona.

MANAGEMENT
Paul Baker, President; Gary Geisler, Vice President.

TYPE OF MARKETER
Mail order.

BUSINESS
Old Pueblo is a 100% mail order marketer of moderately-priced women's apparel and shoes. The company's merchandise lines include coordinates, dresses, jewelry, coats and more. Old Pueblo mails two major catalogs annually, and management reports that sales are relatively consistent throughout the year. The company sells products throughout the U.S., but does no international marketing. In 1980 Old Pueblo reported 70 employees.

COMPANY HISTORY
The Steinberg family started the business in Arizona in 1946. The first merchandise sold was gift items marketed through a catalog. Women's apparel and shoes were not added until later. Ownership changed hands several times before the company was acquired by the Arizona Mail Order Company in 1975. Old Pueblo reportedly had a history of profitable operations at the time of this acquisition.

MARKETS
Old Pueblo's customers are 100% female; mail order buyers of popular fashions and accessories.

FACILITIES

Headquarters, mail order operations, and warehousing in Tucson, AZ.

PRODUCTS, BRAND NAMES, PRICE RANGE

Dresses, coordinated jackets, skirts and slacks, caftan robes, hose, coats and sweaters, sleep wear and more. National brands include Ayers Unlimited, Herman Geist, Paul of California, Butte Knit, Sakri, Servin and Flair. Price: up to $300; median $42.00.

FINANCIAL INFORMATION

	SALES	NET INCOME	PROFIT MARGIN
1981	$12,000,000*	N.A.	--

TYPE OF ADVERTISING, PROMOTION

Direct mail 98%; space in Better Homes & Gardens, House Beautiful, Ladies Home Journal and others. Main direct mail promotion is through full-color catalogs mailed several times throughout the year.

LIST INFORMATION

QUANTITY MAILED:	10,000,000*
AVERAGE ORDER:	$55
ACTIVE BUYERS:	220,000*
TOTAL LIST:	590,000*
LIST SOURCE:	Direct mail, space.

COMMENTS

Old Pueblo is positioned to market "sunbelt popular fashions" -- apparel offerings are primarily lightweight, summer fashions. The product mix, initially gift items, is almost completely apparel and shoes; the only "gifts" offered are jewelry. Old Pueblo's sales have been increasing at an estimated rate of 15% per year; after-tax income is reportedly on an upward trend. Catalogs are usually 48 pages, 8-1/2 x 11, full color. Roughly half of the items displayed are drawings; the other half are displayed in photographs. Old Pueblo's major catalog mailings are in February and August. Sales are roughly consistent throughout the year.

OLSON ELECTRONICS

ADDRESS, PHONE

Olson Electronics Corporation, 2850 Gilchrist Road, Akron, OH 44305. Telephone: (216) 798-1000.

OWNERSHIP

Wholly-owned subsidiary of Teledyne, Inc., of Los Angeles, CA.

MANAGEMENT

Sidney L. Olson, Chairman; Willis Wolf, President; Robert Lawrence, Treasurer & Comptroller; Henry M. Pelusi, Mail Order Manager.

TYPE OF MARKETER

Mail order, retail.

BUSINESS

The company is one of the leading mail order marketers of name brand hi-fidelity and audio equipment. The products include complete music systems, recording equipment, CB radios, AM/FM radios, cassettes, radar detectors, intercoms, etc., and all the parts to build and service them. Olson does no manufacturing, but markets components and equipment produced by leading national manufacturers. In addition to mail order, Olson operates eleven retail stores.

COMPANY HISTORY

The company was started in 1933 in Akron, OH by Irving J. Olson, and was soon succeeded by a partnership between Olson and Sidney Phillip. The original business was mail order marketing of electronics parts. The company was incorporated in Ohio in 1946. In 1968, Teledyne, Inc. purchased 100% of Olson's capital stock. It was reincorporated in California in January of 1968 as Olson Electronics Corporation, and presently employs 200 people, 50 at headquarters.

MARKETS

Olson sells to consumers and commercial and industrial accounts throughout the U.S; 95% male.

FACILITIES

H.Q. in Akron houses offices and mail order operations; eleven retail outlets in Illinois and Ohio.

PRODUCTS, BRAND NAMES, PRICE RANGE

Products include stereos and stereo equipment, a
wide variety of radio and television replacement
parts, intercoms, amplifiers, antennae, microphones,
telephones, security systems, etc. Company markets
all major name brand merchandise.

FINANCIAL INFORMATION

	SALES	**NET INCOME**	**PROFIT MARGIN**
1981	$15,000,000*	N.A.	--

TYPE OF ADVERTISING, PROMOTION

Business is solicited through national advertising and
trade magazines, direct mail promotions and catalogs.
Catalogs are 20-48 pages, partial color.

LIST INFORMATION

QUANTITY MAILED:	5,000,000*
AVERAGE ORDER:	$10-$2,500
ACTIVE BUYERS:	430,000
TOTAL LIST:	1,000,000*
LIST SOURCE:	Direct mail, space.

COMMENTS

Olson originally had 24 branch retail stores in the
U.S. During a major reorganization in March of 1971,
eleven of the branches were left under Olson Electronics Corp. control, some became branches of
another Teledyne subsidiary, Teledyne Mid-America
Corp., and the remaining stores became part of
Teledyne, Inc.'s retail division. Olson markets its
products to repair shops, amateur radio operators,
retail dealers, industrial concerns, and individual
consumers. Approximately 75% or $11,300,000 of
Olson's estimated $15,000,000 total sales for 1981
came from mail order sales to consumers and commercial accounts. The remaining 25% or $3,700,000
came from Olson's retail operations. Teledyne, Inc.
reported $2.9 billion in sales in 1980, and profits of
$343 million. Olson contributed an estimated .5%.

OMAHA STEAKS

ADDRESS, PHONE
Omaha Steaks International, 4400 South 96th Street, Omaha, NE 68127. Telephone: (402) 397-9310.

OWNERSHIP
Privately held by the Simon family. Frederick, Alan, and Stephen Simon hold 100% of capital stock.

MANAGEMENT
Alan Simon, President and Chairman of the Board; Frederick J. Simon, Executive Vice President; Stephen Simon, Vice President of the Food Service Division.

TYPE OF MARKETER
Mail order, wholesale.

BUSINESS
Omaha Steaks is a mail order marketer of high-quality meats including porterhouse steaks, veal, pork, lamb, hams, and more. In addition they sell a limited line of desserts, seafood and prepared dishes. Approximately 80% of mail order sales are wholesale to hotels, restaurants, institutions and railroads. Some special products are produced by the company: corned beef cured and prepared from an "old family recipe." Packaged products are tested in in-house kitchens.

COMPANY HISTORY
The business was started in 1850 by Mr. Simon in Riga, Latvia. Operations consisted of a packing house and meat market. In 1898 his son and grandson, J. J. and B.A. Simon, emigrated to the U.S. They started Table Supply Meat Co. in Omaha in 1917, supplying meats to restaurants. B. A.'s son, Lester Simon, joined company in 1929 and in 1952 he originated idea of selling steaks by mail. Company name was changed to Omaha Steaks in 1966.

MARKETS
Customers are 70% male; sells to individuals and commercial concerns throughout U.S. and Canada.

FACILITIES
Headquarters, order processing and fulfillment, packaging plant and 3 test kitchens in Omaha, NE.

PRODUCTS, BRAND NAMES, PRICE RANGE
Meats: sirloin, ham steaks, veal slices and cutlets, loin chops, pork chops, chicken, fish, cornish hens, lobster, shrimp, crabs and salmon. Prepared dishes: eggrolls, crepes, hors d'oeuvres, quiche, casseroles, cheesecakes, mousse pies, chocolates.

FINANCIAL INFORMATION

	SALES	NET INCOME	PROFIT MARGIN
1981	$25,000,000*	N.A.	--

TYPE OF ADVERTISING, PROMOTION
Roughly 90% of promotion is direct mail to house and rented lists; 10% space in national magazines. Catalogs are mailed four times a year and interspersed with direct mail packages. Premiums include gourmet cookbook by gourmet chef James Beard.

LIST INFORMATION
QUANTITY MAILED: 4,000,000*
AVERAGE ORDER: $50
ACTIVE BUYERS: 85,000
TOTAL LIST: 200,000*
LIST SOURCE: Direct mail, space.

COMMENTS
Mail order to consumers accounts for about 20% of company's revenues--$5,000,000 in 1981. Company began by marketing quality meats wholesale, later adding specialty products and consumer catalogs. Today catalog reads like a restaurant menu--i.e., boneless leg of spring lamb, flounder del rey, chicken kiev, crepes, hors d'oeuvres, cheesecakes, etc. With every order customers receive a 24-page, full-color Omaha Steaks Cookbook written by James Beard. Frozen food orders arrive in packaging that is sturdy enough to be reused as a picnic cooler. Company targets an upscale male who demands quality as well as a unique and interesting product. Catalogs are full-color, glossy, and about 30 pages. Products are presented in a "tantalizing fashion"-- meats on platter surrounded by vegetables, etc. New products include snacks and treats--"Giant Chocolate Chip Cookies" and "Super Popcorn" in a giant, reuseable tin.

ORVIS COMPANY

ADDRESS, PHONE
The Orvis Company, Inc., Manchester, VT 05254. Telephone: (802) 362-3622.

OWNERSHIP
Privately held; Leigh H. Perkins and family own 95% of capital stock.

MANAGEMENT
Leigh H. Perkins, President; Clayton E. Shappy, Executive Vice President; Howard Steere, Vice President-Manufacturing; Anne K. Secor, Vice President-Mail Order; Thomas S. Vaccaro, Treasurer.

TYPE OF MARKETER
Mail order, retail, wholesale.

BUSINESS
The Orvis Company manufactures and sells high-quality fishing rods. In addition they market other fishing equipment, shotguns, hunting apparel, women's and men's sporting and casual apparel and sportmen's gifts produced by outside manufacturers. About 74% of Orvis sales are from mail order operations; 9% from the company's three retail stores; 17% are wholesale to tackle stores. Company employs 225 people and peak volume is during the Christmas season.

COMPANY HISTORY
The Orvis Company, one of the oldest mail order companies in the country, celebrated its 125th anniversary in 1981. Charles F. Orvis started the business in 1856 as a manufacturer and mail order marketer of fishing rods. The business was expanded with the addition of fishing tackle and other sporting goods to the merchandise mix. Ownership transferred to D. C. Corkoran in 1939, and to Leigh Perkins in 1965. The company was incorporated under the present name in Vermont in 1965.

MARKETS
Orvis sells products throughout the U.S., and in Europe, Japan and Australia; customers, 80% male.

FACILITIES

Main offices and manufacturing in Manchester, VT; stores in Manchester, Houston, San Francisco.

PRODUCTS, BRAND NAMES, PRICE RANGE

About 80-85 percent of the products are sold under the Orvis name. Upper price range for fishing, hunting equipment and apparel; middle price range for country clothing and sportsmen's gifts. Some 3,500 fishing, hunting and related products offered.

FINANCIAL INFORMATION

	SALES	NET INCOME	PROFIT MARGIN
1981	$22,000,000*	N.A.	--

TYPE OF ADVERTISING, PROMOTION

Roughly 90% of Orvis' promotion is through catalog mailings. In addition they place some space ads in related magazines. The company uses package inserts and publishes a monthly newsletter, Orvis Record Catch Club News.

LIST INFORMATION

QUANTITY MAILED:	8,100,000
AVERAGE ORDER:	$80*
ACTIVE BUYERS:	200,000*
TOTAL LIST:	1,000,000
LIST SOURCE:	Direct mail, space.

COMMENTS

Orvis total revenues for 1981 are estimated to be $22 million. Of this total, 74% or approximately $16 million are from mail order sales, and 9% or $2 million from the company's retail stores. The remaining $4 million is estimated to be generated by wholesale marketing to tackle and sport shops. Since 1978 Orvis has enjoyed an average annual sales growth rate of roughly 18%, with sales increasing an estimated 15% between 1980 and 1981. Management reports that mail order sales have doubled over the past four years. Orvis says that they are interested in increasing their percentage of retail trade and are planning to open more stores in the coming years. Mail order will continue to be their main focus. While fishing rods and tackle have been the backbone of the Orvis product mix, apparel lines added in 1960 have reportedly been very successful. Orvis hopes to increase their percentage of female buyers with outdoor apparel. Japan has been a steady wholesale buyer; company publishes a catalog in Japanese.

PARAMOUNT COIN

ADDRESS, PHONE

Paramount Coin Corporation, One Paramount Plaza, Englewood, OH 45322. Telephone: (513) 863-8641.

OWNERSHIP

The company is a wholly-owned subsidiary of Paramount International Coin Corporation, Freeport, Bahamas.

MANAGEMENT

Max J. Humbert, Chairman; David W. Akers, President; J. Kevin Gregg, Vice President; John Stickle, Controller; Raymond Graham, Manager of Marketing.

TYPE OF MARKETER

Mail order.

BUSINESS

Paramount Coin is the U.S. mail order marketing arm of its foreign-based parent. The company markets coins, commemorative medals, and numismatic and philatelic accessories and supplies. All sales are through the company's mini-catalogs, brochures and direct mail packages. Paramount sells primarily to individual coin collectors and investors, as well as distributors and trading agencies throughout the U.S. and abroad.

COMPANY HISTORY

The company was founded as a mail order marketer of coins, medallions and collecting supplies in the early 1960s. It was incorporated in Ohio on October 14, 1963. Authorized capital consists of 250,000 shares of common stock with no par value. The company remained a publicly-held corporation until November of 1980. At that time all outstanding capital was purchased by Paramount International which was formed as a holding company and incorporated in Panama.

MARKETS

Collectors, investors and distributors and trading agencies throughout the U.S. and abroad.

FACILITIES
The company owns a 46,000 sq. ft. building housing headquarters and mail order operations.

PRODUCTS, BRAND NAMES, PRICE RANGE
Sets of commemorative coins and medallions, rare and collectible coins, special mint editions of foreign coins, stamp collectibles including channel strips, first day covers, single stamps; collecting and displaying accessories; guides and pricing catalogs.

FINANCIAL INFORMATION

	SALES	NET INCOME	PROFIT MARGIN
1981	$28,000,000*	N.A.	--

TYPE OF ADVERTISING, PROMOTION
Paramount relies solely on direct mail for promotion. The company publishes a wide variety of direct mail packages, brochures and syndication packages, offering collectible sets, continuity coin offerings, individual commemorative offerings, etc.

LIST INFORMATION

QUANTITY MAILED: N.A.　(Paramount does not market
AVERAGE ORDER: N.A.　its list or make available
ACTIVE BUYERS: N.A.　any information on its
TOTAL LIST: N.A.　buyer file.)
LIST SOURCE: Direct mail.

COMMENTS
Paramount Coin Corporation's total mail order sales for 1981 are estimated to be $28,000,000. This is roughly a 10% increase over the company's reported sales of $25,600,000 in 1980 (their last year as a public company). In 1980 the company reported net earnings of $887,000, resulting in a margin of 3.4%. This represents a substantial increase in earnings compared to margins of 0.6% in 1979 and 0.4% in 1978. The company mails promotional packages to collectors and distributors throughout the world. In addition they publish packages for syndication through companies such as American Express. Recent promotional mailings include: a full-color, 8-1/2 x 10-7/8, 16 page mini-catalog offering the Kings of England Collection of gold and silver proof coins; eight-page, 5-1/2 x 8-1/4 pieces on The Royal Wedding Commemorative stamps and coins; 8-1/2 x 11, eight-page catalog presenting the American Express Canada "Year of the Child" gold and silver coin collection.

GEORGE PARK SEED

ADDRESS, PHONE

George W. Park Seed Co., Inc., P. O. Box 31, Greenwood, SC 29647. Telephone: (803) 374-3341.

OWNERSHIP

Privately owned by the Park family.

MANAGEMENT

William J. Park, President; Klaus W. Neubner, Sr. Vice President; Leonard Richey, Operations Vice President; Viola Parrott, Advertising Vice President; Bruce Churchill, Comptroller.

TYPE OF MARKETER

Mail order.

BUSINESS

Park Seed sells seeds, bulbs, plants, and garden aids by mail to home gardeners, and wholesales to nurserymen and growers. Company claims to sell more flower seeds by mail than any other company. Park purchased Wayside Gardens Co. of Ohio in 1975 (relocated to South Carolina), which offers perennial and nursery stock. George Park Seed Co. employs 300 people year-round, and the number more than doubles with the addition of part-time employees during the peak season, January 1 - April 15.

COMPANY HISTORY

George Park started his company in 1868 at age 15, in Fannettsburg, PA. He began mailing seeds from his mother's garden to a list of friends and neighbors. When he retired in 1918, he had 600,000 names on catalog mailing list, and 850,000 subscribers to Floral Magazine--horticultural digest he started in 1871. He reopened the company in 1924; family took control after his death in 1935. The company is credited with manufacturing the first foil seed packet in 1962.

MARKETS

Nationwide, some Canadian sales. Average customer is married woman, 40-50 years old.

FACILITIES

Offices, mail order operations, nine large greenhouses and research facilities in Greenwood, SC.

PRODUCTS, BRAND NAMES, PRICE RANGE

Seeds, bulbs, plants, garden aids and accessories, ranging from about $.55 to $10 for seeds and $1 to $80 for equipment. Company engages in limited manufacturing, such as Park's Sow & Grow Mix and an illuminated growing tray.

FINANCIAL INFORMATION

	SALES	NET INCOME	PROFIT MARGIN
1981	$17,000,000*	N.A.	--

TYPE OF ADVERTISING, PROMOTION

Five full-color catalogs, including a Christmas gift catalog. Two other catalogs for Wayside Gardens go out for the spring and fall. Company also uses space ads in newspapers and gardening magazines, inserts and fliers.

LIST INFORMATION

QUANTITY MAILED:	(Park) 8,000,000*; (Wayside) N A
AVERAGE ORDER:	(P) $14; (W) $38
ACTIVE BUYERS:	(P) 620,000; (W) 70,185
TOTAL LIST:	(P) 1,139,000; (W) 194,000
LIST SOURCE:	Direct mail, space.

COMMENTS

While flower seeds have traditionally been the backbone of Park's business, company officials note that vegetable seeds will soon outrun flower seeds in sales. Park offers about 3,000 varieties of seeds, many of them exclusive strains developed by or for the company. Park contracts with growers who are specialists in given areas of horticulture (e.g., African Violets, green peppers), and buys a portion of their crop to increase the selections they have for testing and hybridization. Company has actively sought position as marketer of hard-to-find seed varieties and horticultural accessories--"products of the highest quality, frequently rare and often unique to mail order or Park Seed Co." Park was an early leader in offering dwarf, patio and container seed varieties. Aside from direct mail and space advertising, Park has been featured on NBC's Today Show, ABC's Good Morning America, CBS's Morning News, and Crockett's Victory Garden.

J.C. PENNEY

ADDRESS, PHONE

J.C. Penney Company, 1301 Avenue of the Americas, New York, NY 10019. Telephone (212) 957-4321.

OWNERSHIP

Publicly held; listed NYSE, Brussels & Antwerp stock exchanges; FY80: 70,000,000 common shares outstanding; price: high-26; low-20; dividend: $.46.

MANAGEMENT

Donald V. Seibert, Chairman; Walter J. Neppl, President; Senior VP's: Kenneth Axelson, Director, Finance, Public Affairs; William Howell, Director, Merchandise, Marketing & Catalog.

TYPE OF MARKETER

Mail order, retail.

BUSINESS

Penney is the second largest marketer of catalog general merchandise in the U.S. The company operates full line stores generally located in regional shopping centers and offering traditional department store merchandise lines. Soft line stores sell apparel and household textiles. Company operates catalog sales centers and insurance centers, some located within stores. Belgian stores operate under the name "Sarma" and sell apparel, general merchandise, and food.

COMPANY HISTORY

The company was founded by James Cash Penney on the merchandising slogan "Always First Quality." This led to the development of company's merchandise testing facilities--among the largest in the world. Penney began catalog operations in 1962. By 1969 Penney had one distribution center and 944 catalog centers. The number of catalog centers increased by 2,187 by 1973, necessitating another distribution facility in 1974. Two more centers were added in 1977 and 1978.

MARKETS

Middle income households in the U.S. and Belgium.

FACILITIES
Stores: 552 full line, 1,130 soft line, 76 Belgian, 361 drug, 2,187 catalog sales centers.

PRODUCTS, BRAND NAMES, PRICE RANGE
Apparel, home and automotive products; drug store merchandise; insurance. Prices moderate. Penney labels and some major brands. Continuing to develop "fashion" image with "quality apparel at popular prices."

FINANCIAL INFORMATION

	SALES	NET INCOME	PROFIT MARGIN
1980	$11,400,000,000	$233,000,000	2.04%

TYPE OF ADVERTISING, PROMOTION
Advertising expense for newspapers, television, radio, and other media, excluding catalog preparation and distribution costs, was $270 million in '80, compared with $261 million in '79 and $268 million in '78.

LIST INFORMATION

QUANTITY MAILED:	52,000,000*
AVERAGE ORDER:	$26
ACTIVE BUYERS:	14,800,000*
TOTAL LIST:	N.A.
LIST SOURCE:	Direct mail, credit customers.

COMMENTS
While earnings dropped sharply in the first half of 1980, tighter management of inventories and expenses helped slow the decline in 3rd quarter. Management claims a profitable 4th quarter based on results that exclude The Treasury discount operation, which is being discontinued. However, 1980 net income, which includes Treasury's operating losses and a provision for costs expected to be incurred in closing these stores, is down $11 million from 1979 results. JC Penney stores and catalog sales continue to be the chief contributors to earnings and showed substantial increases in 4th quarter to recover losses incurred in 1st and 2nd quarters. JC Penney Store sales were up $82 million in 1980 over 1979, and catalog sales increased $20 million in 1980 over 1979 results. Insurance operations had net '80 income of $28 million, up from $26 million in 1979. Sales in Belgian stores were up $50 million over 1979, but 1980 profits were lower.

POSTAL FINANCIAL CORPORATION

ADDRESS, PHONE

Postal Financial Corporation, 520 Pierce St., Sioux City, IA 51104. Telephone: (712) 258-0624.

OWNERSHIP

Wholly-owned subsidiary of St. Paul Companies, Inc., of St. Paul, Minnesota.

MANAGEMENT

Dean Meine, President; Senior VPs: L. Dewey Sample, Jr., Wendel H. Hefner, C. Edward Wilson, James A. Tieferbach; Michael J. Sexton, Secretary; John R. Rodehorst, Treasurer.

TYPE OF MARKETER

Mail order, direct sales.

BUSINESS

Postal Financial Corp. is a holding company for four subsidiary operations which market consumer finance and insurance programs by mail and through direct sales forms. The company's operating subsidiaries include Postal Thrift Loans, Inc., Postal Financial Corporation, Postal Finance Company, and Postal Executive Financial Services. In addition to direct mail the company conducts seminars throughout the country to promote their services. Postal Financial reported 753 employees in 1981.

COMPANY HISTORY

The company was founded in 1905 in Sioux City, Iowa, by Joseph Levitt. The first services marketed were small consumer loans. Mail order operations were introduced in 1931 to greatly increase the company's potential market. In 1969 the St. Paul Companies, Inc. acquired the business, which at the time maintained 76 offices in 13 states. Postal Financial was incorporated Nov. 7, 1978 in Iowa. At present the company has offices in 14 states, primarily in the midwest.

MARKETS

Mostly male, age 23-60, middle to upper income levels; company's sales are nationwide.

FACILITIES
Owns 50,000 sq. ft. at Sioux City location for central headquarters and mail order operations.

PRODUCTS, BRAND NAMES, PRICE RANGE
Consumer loans, including second mortgage loans, investments, and credit insurance on loans. The amount of loans vary according to the consumer credit score and the type of loan in application.

FINANCIAL INFORMATION

	SALES	NET INCOME	PROFIT MARGIN
1980	$100,600,000	$2,600,000	2.6%

TYPE OF ADVERTISING, PROMOTION
Offices use direct mail and a considerable amount of newspaper space to generate new and repeat service clients. Approximately 15% of the company's total advertising is space in Forbes, Money, Fortune, etc.

LIST INFORMATION
QUANTITY MAILED: 10,000,000
AVERAGE ORDER: $3,000 (average loan)
ACTIVE BUYERS: 100,000 (loans)
TOTAL LIST: N.A.
LIST SOURCE: Direct mail, space, referrals.

COMMENTS
While Postal Financial's sales for 1980 were up some 38% from $72.8 million reported in 1979 to $100.6 reported in 1980, net earnings fell by more than 42%, from $4.5 million to $2.6 million. Company officials reported that the most significant contributing factor in the loss in profitability was the extremely high cost of borrowings. The average cost of borrowing in 1980 was 12%, compared to 10% in 1979, and this increase amounted to a reported $7 million in additional interest cost. In recent years Postal Financial has increased its emphasis on long-term borrowings through promotion of their five year loans and sales of Series B Senior Notes. In the coming year they will reportedly concentrate on their currently profitable areas which are real estate loans, investments and second mortgage loans, and will decrease emphasis on small loan operations. Recent company wide direct mail promotions emphasize the larger, secured loans available.

PRENTICE-HALL

ADDRESS, PHONE

Prentice-Hall, Inc., Route 9 West, Englewood Cliffs, New Jersey 07632. Telephone: (201) 592-2000.

OWNERSHIP

Publicly-held; FY80: 9,911,788 common shares outstanding; cash dividend, $1.50 per share.

MANAGEMENT

Frank J. Dunnigan, Chairman and CEO; Howard M. Warrington, Vice Chairman; Donald A. Schaefer, President & Chief Operating Officer; G. L. Costello, Exec. VP; R. D. Hess, VP, Treasurer.

TYPE OF MARKETER

Mail order, direct sales, retail.

BUSINESS

Company is one of the leading publishers in the nation, producing textbooks and materials for every level of education. Academic markets include all areas of the college and university curriculum, as well as elementary, secondary, and vocational schools. The company also develops materials for world-wide markets in computer technology, and materials for business, legal, and financial markets as well as books for general readers. Prentice-Hall employs 5,800 people in the U.S. and abroad.

COMPANY HISTORY

Prentice-Hall was originally organized as a New York corporation in 1913. The present company was incorporated in 1929 in Delaware, and retained the corporate name. Since then the company has purchased an extensive list of subsidiary companies (primarily involved in publishing and in business and educational research) including Pipeline Research, Arco Publishing, and Deltak, Inc.

MARKETS

The company's divisions and subsidiaries sell throughout the U.S., and internationally.

FACILITIES

Company's main facilities are located in New Jersey, New York, and Idaho.

PRODUCTS, BRAND NAMES, PRICE RANGE

Hardcover and paperback books are sold through bookstores and mail order book clubs. Other products include test preparation reviews, training materials, text and reference books, periodicals, audiovisual aids, loose-leaf reports and updates.

FINANCIAL INFORMATION

	SALES	NET INCOME	PROFIT MARGIN
1981	$390,570,000	$33,800,000	8.7%

TYPE OF ADVERTISING, PROMOTION

Prentice-Hall uses direct mail to promote individual title and book club sales, and to promote book club membership to consumer and educational markets. Direct mail packages are supported by space advertising for book clubs in national magazines.

LIST INFORMATION

QUANTITY MAILED:	90,000,000
AVERAGE ORDER:	$40*
ACTIVE BUYERS:	6,000,000*
TOTAL LIST:	12,000,000*
LIST SOURCE:	Space and direct mail.

COMMENTS

Direct mail is responsible for an estimated 60% of Prentice-Hall's annual sales. P-H management recognizes the significance of direct mail markets, particularly for continuing growth in sales of business and professional books. Many of the divisions have their own mail order operations and substantial in-house lists. Outside lists are used to identify target groups for particular publications or services. Direct mail provides valuable reinforcement for sales calls and subscription renewals. In 1980 sales and earnings reached record highs for the company, although the profit margin was cut somewhat by interest expense on funds borrowed to acquire Deltak, Inc., in December, 1979. Deltak improves the company's position in computer technology markets in the U.S. and abroad.

PRIESTER'S PECANS

ADDRESS, PHONE
Priester's Pecans, 227 Old Fort Drive, Fort Deposit, AL 36032. Telephone: (205) 227-4301.

OWNERSHIP
Privately held; 100% of capital stock owned by Ned T. Ellis and John Ellis.

MANAGEMENT
Ned Ellis, President: Jack Capps, Director of Marketing; Charles Cook, Director of Purchasing; Rose K. Perdue, Office Manager.

TYPE OF MARKETER
Mail order, retail, wholesale.

BUSINESS
Priester's is a producer, manufacturer and marketer of pecans and a variety of food items containing pecans including cakes, candies and nut mixtures. In addition, the company markets products from outside producers and suppliers such as meats, fudge and peanut brittle. The company has a manufacturing facility where pecans are graded and packaged, a candy factory, and a retail outlet. Priester's also offers quantities of pecans wholesale by mail.

COMPANY HISTORY
The company was started in 1940 by L. C. Priester as a wholesale operation to market the pecans he produced. Mail order marketing to consumers was added in the 1950's. In 1979 the business was purchased by Ned, John and May Ellis, and was incorporated as Priester's Pecans in Alabama on January 1, 1978. The company employs up to 160 people during its peak Christmas and spring selling seasons.

MARKETS
Priester's sells by mail to individuals and businesses throughout the U.S.

FACILITIES

Mail order facility and packaging in Fort Deposit, AL; candy factory and retail outlet nearby.

PRODUCTS, BRAND NAMES, PRICE RANGE

Various selections of pecans -- mammoth size halves roasted and salted, shelled pecans, pecans covered with cane sugar, natural pecan halves; candies --pecan logs, pralines, fudge, divinity; chocolates, fruit cake, and meats. House brands.

FINANCIAL INFORMATION

	SALES	NET INCOME	PROFIT MARGIN
1981	$10,000,000*	N.A.	--

TYPE OF ADVERTISING, PROMOTION

Virtually 100% of Priester's advertising is by direct mail, through the company's two annual catalogs and holiday brochures. Promotions and photographs emphasize "personal touches that result in a high quality product."

LIST INFORMATION

QUANTITY MAILED:	2,500,000
AVERAGE ORDER:	$52
ACTIVE BUYERS:	63,000
TOTAL LIST:	150,000
LIST SOURCE:	Direct Mail.

COMMENTS

Of the estimate above for Priester's total 1981 revenues, roughly 50% came from mail order sales to consumers. The other 50% were reportedly generated by sales to wholesale accounts, and sales from the company's retail outlet. Consumer mail order and direct mail wholesaling operations are said to complement each other seasonally. Priester's maintains a "down home" emphasis in their promotions, and use a variety of packaging and product assortments to suit different tastes: mixtures of nuts and other food items, packaged in gift boxes, decorative tins, baskets, etc. Their primary emphasis is on old-fashioned "Southern Pecan Treats," including roasted pecan halves, pecan brittle, pecan rolls, bark and glace. Priester's mails two catalogs each year which are 6 x 11, full-color. The main catalog is 32 pages and the Christmas edition is 16. They have eliminated fresh fruit and cut back on meat offerings in the past year, and are reportedly considering franchising as a means of expansion.

PUBLISHERS CLEARING HOUSE

ADDRESS, PHONE

Publishers Clearing House, 382 Channel Drive, Port Washington, NY 11050. (516) 883-5432.

OWNERSHIP

Privately-held; 100% of capital owned by New York limited partnership between Harold E. and Lu Esther Mertz.

MANAGEMENT

William J. Rennert, Chairman; Robin Smith, President; Steven Stark, Vice President of Marketing; Martin Gitow, Vice President of Products Division.

TYPE OF MARKETER

Mail order.

BUSINESS

Publishers Clearing House is a promotional company which uses direct mail programs to generate magazine subscriptions. The subscriptions are then forwarded to the publishing client which fulfills and renews them through its own programs. All of Publishers promotional work is done by mail, supported by space and broadcast advertising. Subsidiary Campus Subscriptions uses displays and flyers with purchases in college bookstores, in addition to direct mail, to promote subscriptions in the college market.

COMPANY HISTORY

Lu Esther and Harold E. Mertz started Publishers Clearing House in 1953 as a direct mail promotional subscription agency. Before the mid 1960's the company relied solely on typical mailings (promotional packets) to generate subscriptions. During the mid to late 60's, the company began developing and testing one of its trademarks -- the Publishers Clearing House Sweepstakes -- in its mailings, and that remains its main promotional tool to this day. The company reported 450 employees for 1981.

MARKETS

Publishers Clearing House mails direct promotion to individuals and businesses in U.S. and Canada.

FACILITIES

Headquarters and mail order operations at separate locations in Port Washington, New York.

PRODUCTS, BRAND NAMES, PRICE RANGE

Company solicits subscriptions for more than 200 major magazines, from such general publications as TV Guide to more specialized hobby, sporting and business magazines. Prices vary with subscription.

FINANCIAL INFORMATION

	SALES	NET INCOME	PROFIT MARGIN
1981	$120,000,000*	N.A.	--

TYPE OF ADVERTISING, PROMOTION

PCH uses direct mail packages which include entry blanks for their various sweepstakes offers, ordering devices for the special magazine subscription offers, and other special premiums for individual magazines.

LIST INFORMATION

QUANTITY MAILED:	70,000,000*
AVERAGE ORDER:	$18*
ACTIVE BUYERS:	4,500,000*
TOTAL LIST:	10,000,000*
LIST SOURCE:	Direct mail.

COMMENTS

Publishers Clearing House has developed a major mail order business out of using sweepstakes and other premium and discount offers to generate new subscribers for a wide variety of national magazines. The company's revenues are derived from the special subscription rates of the new subscribers and promotional fees paid by the various magazine publishers. The real benefit to the publishers is a continuous influx of new subscribers with high repeat-subscription potential. While PCH does not market its house list, analysts estimate that based on approximately 70 million promotional packages mailed per year, the company's return rate is about 6.5%. Roughly 4,500,000 people make an average order (the cost of the special subscription) of $18.00. No purchase is necessary to enter the many sweepstakes contests offered by PCH and no estimate of the number of non-subscribing entrants was available. Promotional packages are mailed throughout the year, and different sweepstakes offers run consecutively.

QUILL CORPORATION

ADDRESS, PHONE
Quill Corporation, 100 S. Schelter Rd., Prairie View, IL 60069. Telephone: (312) 634-4850.

OWNERSHIP
Privately held; 100% of capital, consisting of 1 million shares of common stock at $10 par value, is owned by brothers Jack, Harvey and Arnold Miller.

MANAGEMENT
Jack Miller, President; Harvey L. Miller, Secretary; Arnold Miller, Treasurer.

TYPE OF MARKETER
Mail order.

BUSINESS
Quill Corporation is a mail order marketer of a full range of office supplies and equipment including paper products, business machines, furniture, and data and word processing supplies. The company buys its merchandise wholesale from a number of manufacturers and suppliers, but does no manufacturing of its own. Sales are reportedly non-seasonal, and Quill reported 325 employees in 1981.

COMPANY HISTORY
Jack Miller started the business as a direct sales supplier in 1956. Direct mail operations began that same year and the business gradually evolved into a 100% mail order operation. In 1957, Harvey Miller was admitted to a partnership interest, and the partnership continued until it was succeeded by an Illinois corporation in 1962. Corporate headquarters were moved from Northbrook, IL to present location in 1980.

MARKETS
Sells nationally to all types of businesses, professionals and institutions.

FACILITIES

Has 120,000 sq. ft. warehouse in one building, connected to a 64,000 sq. ft. office building.

PRODUCTS, BRAND NAMES, PRICE RANGE

Full range of office supplies, equipment and furniture. Sells such national brands as Scotch Tape and Pendaflex folders as well as many products under private Quill label. Prices vary according to product.

FINANCIAL INFORMATION

	SALES	NET INCOME	PROFIT MARGIN
1980	$30,000,000*	N.A.	--

TYPE OF ADVERTISING, PROMOTION

One hundred percent of Quill's promotion is through their direct mail catalogs and flyers. The company mails six major catalogs annually and drops sales flyers on an irregular basis throughout the year.

LIST INFORMATION

QUANTITY MAILED:	12,000,000*
AVERAGE ORDER:	$100
ACTIVE BUYERS:	300,000
TOTAL LIST:	N.A.
LIST SOURCE:	Direct mail.

COMMENTS

Management reported that Quill Corporation's revenues for 1980 topped $30,000,000 and that sales for 1981 showed a substantial improvement. No specific figures were available, but company officials reported that operations were profitable and that earnings were improving annually. The above list information was reported as estimates by Quill, though the company does not make its list available for rental. The company is continuing to improve its position as a full service mail order supplier of all types of business equipment and supplies. Catalog strategy will reportedly remain the same in the coming year though management is seeking to improve their customer base by increasing the number of pieces mailed to rented lists of commercial and industrial concerns. Quill officials attribute their success to developing a strong annual repeat-buying base.

RCA MUSIC SERVICE

ADDRESS, PHONE

RCA Music Service, 30 Rockefeller Plaza, New York, NY 10020. Telephone: (212) 621-6000.

OWNERSHIP

Music Service is a subsidiary of RCA Direct Marketing, Inc., owned by publicly-held RCA Corp.

MANAGEMENT

Robert Gordon, President, RCA Direct Marketing; T. P. Finn, Vice President of Operations, RCA Direct Marketing, Inc.; Tom Egold, Manager of Inventory and Production Control.

TYPE OF MARKETER

Mail order.

BUSINESS

RCA Music Service operates a record and tape club which markets classical, country/western, popular, soul and other musical forms on record, cassette and eight-track tape. Consumers are usually able to sign up through a special offer of several selections for a penny, with a commitment to purchase a specified number of additional selections over a certain time period. Company presses many of its own records sold through the club and contracts with other record companies to sell their products.

COMPANY HISTORY

RCA's record club was started during the late 1950s, a few years after CBS had gotten into the business with its Columbia Record Club. The RCA venture, apparently hampered in part by the competition's early start, drifted along as a rather lackluster operation until the early '70s. At that time, new management turned the RCA record club operations around. They apparently established a successful system for acquiring new members and helped bring the club's volume closer to Columbia's.

MARKETS

Market is domestic; about 55% male.

FACILITIES
Offices, warehouse, shipping, record manufacturing in Indianapolis; corporate headquarters in New York.

PRODUCTS, BRAND NAMES, PRICE RANGE
Records, cassettes and eight-track tapes of all types of music under various labels; record prices range from $7.98-$14.98, tapes $8.98 to $15.98. Also record racks, tape holders and related merchandise.

FINANCIAL INFORMATION

	SALES	NET INCOME	PROFIT MARGIN
1980	$87,000,000*	N.A.	--

TYPE OF ADVERTISING, PROMOTION
Approximately 90% of advertising is through direct mail packages; 10% space ads in magazines and newspapers offering negative-option record club.

LIST INFORMATION

QUANTITY MAILED: N.A.
AVERAGE ORDER: $38
ACTIVE BUYERS: 1,550,000
TOTAL LIST: N.A.
LIST SOURCE: Direct mail, inserts, space.

COMMENTS
Although 1980 was a good year for the RCA Records Division as a whole, it did not prove as successful for direct marketing arm of RCA Music Service. Both sales and net earnings for the record and tape club declined in 1980, due in part to an increase in prices and overall reduced demand in the record industry. One RCA source pointed out decreased consumer interest in records (a luxury item) in difficult economic periods. Company reported an upward trend in 1981. Music Service was "pulling out of the slump of a year ago"--management citing overall gains in mail order industry and "re-interest" in records by mail. The main selling point for the mail order record club is the premium introductory offer of several records for a penny, and including special collections in the offerings to complete the negative-option buying requirement.

READER'S DIGEST ASSOCIATION

ADDRESS, PHONE

Reader's Digest Association, Inc., Pleasantville, NY 10570. Telephone: (914) 769-7000.

OWNERSHIP

Privately held; 100% of outstanding stock owned by Lila Acheson Wallace.

MANAGEMENT

John A. O'Hara, President, CEO; Edward T. Thompson, Editor-In-Chief; James F. Adams, VP, Operations Planning; Thomas R. Esencourt, VP; Coleman W. Hoyt, VP.

TYPE OF MARKETER

Mail order, retail.

BUSINESS

Reader's Digest publishes a variety of magazines and books including the Reader's Digest magazine, published in sixteen different languages, and their collections of condensed books. In addition they market educational materials and records. Management reports that roughly 90% of their business -- subscription solicitation, books, records and materials sales -- is through mail order marketing. The company does some limited retailing of their publications. The Association employs 10,000 people.

COMPANY HISTORY

DeWitt Wallace and his wife Lila started Reader's Digest in New York in 1922 with a $5,000 investment. They began by publishing Reader's Digest magazine which they marketed by mail. In the late 1920's, RD was first placed on newsstands, but direct mail continued, as it does today, to account for the majority of sales. Condensed Books were added to the product mix in 1952, and records and how-to-books were added four years later. International markets account for 50% of sales.

MARKETS

It is estimated that Reader's Digest Association products are sold in 163 countries.

FACILITIES

Headquarters in Pleasantville, NY; branch offices scattered throughout the U.S. and other countries.

PRODUCTS, BRAND NAMES, PRICE RANGE

Reader's Digest magazine, Families magazine; Reader's Digest Condensed Books, general "how-to" books, dictionaries, records, educational products. All items are family-oriented, informational, self-help, or entertainment related.

FINANCIAL INFORMATION

	SALES	NET INCOME	PROFIT MARGIN
1981	$1,000,000,000*	N.A.	--

TYPE OF ADVERTISING, PROMOTION

Heavy use of direct mailings with sweepstakes entry form and optional order forms for variety of Reader's Digest products. Some newspaper and television ads. Recently started testing catalogs for book and record sales.

LIST INFORMATION

QUANTITY MAILED: 100,000,000+
AVERAGE ORDER: Various
ACTIVE BUYERS: 20,000,000+ (domestic)
TOTAL LIST: N.A.
LIST SOURCE: Direct mail, heavy list rental.

COMMENTS

In all Reader's Digest has nine domestic and twenty-four foreign subsidiaries. Original Print Collectors subsidiary is a mail order marketer of art lithographics and prints. In 1980 the company acquired majority interest in The Source computer-based information service. Families, the company's newest monthly magazine, proved successful during its testing phase and had its first general printing in October of 1981. Both condensed and general interest books, and records groups reported increased sales and profits for 1981. While the company does not market its house list, management reported that they mail over 100,000,000 pieces of direct mail promotion annually and have over 10,000,000 subscribers/merchandise buyers in the U.S. alone. Company officials stated that Reader's Digest Association's total sales for 1981 were in excess of $1 billion.

RECREATIONAL EQUIPMENT

ADDRESS, PHONE

Recreational Equipment, Inc., P.O. Box C-88126, Seattle, WA 98188. Telephone: (206) 575-4480.

OWNERSHIP

Recreational Equipment is a member-owned, consumer cooperative.

MANAGEMENT

Jerry Horn, President and CEO; Ken Blaker, Exec. VP; Byron Ives, Director, Merchandising; Carsten Lien, Admn.; Dennis Madsen, Director of Marketing.

TYPE OF MARKETER

Mail order, retail.

BUSINESS

REI operates as a cooperative for the purpose of manufacturing, purchasing, and selling outdoor equipment and sporting goods via mail order and through seven retail stores. Subsidiary, THAW Corporation, is a manufacturer of sporting goods. REI is owned by its members who pay a five dollar annual fee. Though they hold no stock, they have a vote at corporate meetings, and roughly 85% of the company's pre-tax earnings are paid to the membership as patronage dividends.

COMPANY HISTORY

REI began as a club for mountain climbers in the early thirties, organized as a cooperative for importing and retailing high quality outdoor equipment and clothing. Incorporated in 1956 in Washington state, REI has become one of the largest consumer cooperatives in the United States with over 1,000,000 memberships sold. Currently the co-op has 380,000 active members. The company has grown by increasing membership and mail order activities.

MARKETS

Mail order customers throughout the U.S.; seven retail stores.

FACILITIES
Headquarters, including distribution and mail order operations, in Seattle, WA.

PRODUCTS, BRAND NAMES, PRICE RANGE
A wide variety of outdoor clothing and equipment focused on but not limited to mountaineering, camping, skiing, bicycling, fishing, canoeing, backpacking. National and house brands. Prices moderate.

FINANCIAL INFORMATION

	SALES	**NET INCOME**	**PROFIT MARGIN**
1981	$55,400,000	N.A.	--

TYPE OF ADVERTISING, PROMOTION
For mail order, REI uses space advertising in national outdoor magazines. Also mails catalogs five times per year. Typical catalog is 96 pages, full color. Local advertising for retail outlets also promotes membership and mail order catalogs.

LIST INFORMATION

QUANTITY MAILED:	3,000,000
AVERAGE ORDER:	$50
ACTIVE BUYERS:	352,000
TOTAL LIST:	1,100,000
LIST SOURCE:	Active and past members.

COMMENTS
REI's profit margin is deceptively low due to the company's cooperative structure and the payment of patronage dividends. Management has provided the following figures on pre-dividend and pre-tax earnings: 1979, $1,899,000; 1980, $3,911,000; 1981, $6,782,000. Sales have increased steadily and rapidly during the past three decades. In 1961 sales were $498,750, an increase of 868% over 1951 sales of $51,514. The 1960's saw the greatest percentage increase in sales --up 1,875% to $9,840,000 in 1971. 1981 sales represent a 459% increase over 1971. REI is planning to increase the use of direct mail pieces promoting its mail order operations, and in 1982 will mail five different catalogs rather than four. About 25% of the merchandise now sold is manufactured by REI and their THAW manufacturing subsidiary.

CARROLL REED

ADDRESS, PHONE

Carroll Reed, Inc., Box 100 Main Street, North Conway, NH 03860. Telephone: (603) 356-3121.

OWNERSHIP

Subsidiary of publicly-held CML Group of Concord, MA.

MANAGEMENT

Frederick Leighton, President; Charles Farley, VP of Merchandising; David Taylor, VP of Marketing; Robert Murphy, VP of Distribution; Thomas Walsh, VP of Finance.

TYPE OF MARKETER

Mail order, retailer.

BUSINESS

Carroll Reed markets fashion sportswear and outer-wear, sells and rents ski equipment. Sales are primarily generated through seasonal catalogs with remaining volume coming from retail sales and rentals. Reed is positioned to offer classical, high-quality sportswear to the upscale female. Peak sales period is fall/winter. Company does no manufacturing. Presently employs 295 people. Operates five full-line retail outlets and nine ski shops.

COMPANY HISTORY

Carroll and Kay Reed formed "Carroll Reed Ski Shops, Inc." in 1935. Moved to North Conway location in 1936. Began offering merchandise by mail in 1939. Mr. Reed considered to be a pioneer in marketing high-quality specialty ski apparel in the U.S. Today the company has expanded product mix to market clothing to other sporting segments. In 1969 company was purchased by the CML Group; name was subsequently shortened to Carroll Reed, Inc.

MARKETS

Customers are upscale; 90% female. Sells throughout the U.S.; no international marketing.

FACILITIES

Headquarters and 30,000 sq. ft. warehouse located in North Conway, NH.

PRODUCTS, BRAND NAMES, PRICE RANGE

Products are sportswear, outerwear and ski equipment. Brand names include Evan-Picone, Stephan Casuals, Lacoste, and Etienne Aigner. Prices are mid to upper range.

FINANCIAL INFORMATION

	SALES	NET INCOME	PROFIT MARGIN
1980	$25,000,000*	N.A.	--

TYPE OF ADVERTISING, PROMOTION

Carroll Reed mails full-color catalogs five times per year. Space in women's and home furnishing magazines--Glamour, House & Garden, House Beautiful, Yankee. Limited use of package inserts and discount coupons.

LIST INFORMATION

QUANTITY MAILED:	10,000,000*
AVERAGE ORDER:	$95
ACTIVE BUYERS:	130,000
TOTAL LIST:	400,000*
LIST SOURCE:	Direct mail, space.

COMMENTS

Total sales for 1980 were approximately $25 million; 60% or $15 million was generated through mail order. Retail sales and rentals are estimated to account for the remaining 40%. Sales breakdown estimated as follows: 75% sportswear and outerwear, 15% ski equipment, and 10% ski rentals. In 1980 the company claimed the highest average order size of all mail order apparel companies, $95.00. CML management reported that both sales and profits were on the rise. Working capital is supplied for the company by CML. Carroll Reed's apparently successful marketing strategy provides the customer with classical, tweedy, New England look counted on for quality. In 1981 CML acquired The Outdoorsman retail chain which will be part of Carroll Reed. Annual sales for The Outdoorsman are reportedly $11,000,000+.

ROAMAN'S MAIL ORDER

ADDRESS, PHONE

Roaman's Mail Order, Inc., 463 Seventh Ave., New York, NY 10018. Telephone: (212) 679-8600.

OWNERSHIP

Subsidiary of privately-held Roaman's, Inc.; 100% of capital owned by the Roaman family.

MANAGEMENT

Martin Roaman, President; Egon Henner, Executive Vice President and General Manager; Evelyn Roaman, Secretary; Marvin Schwarzber, Circulation Manager; Louis Rich, Vice President.

TYPE OF MARKETER

Mail order.

BUSINESS

Roaman's Mail Order markets a full line of women's apparel, including foundations and shoes, in larger sizes. Items are low to moderately priced and sold primarily under the Roaman's label. Company also offers a line of higher-priced name-brand clothing to selected customers through the "Evelyn Roaman Collection" catalog. Heaviest sales coincide with issuance of spring and fall catalogs. Credit sales are handled through sister company Roaman's Credit Corp. Roaman's reported 400 employees.

COMPANY HISTORY

Harry Roaman, a tailor, made custom clothing in the early 1930s and found that many of his clients were larger-size women. In 1931, he created Roaman's Stores, Inc., as a retailer of large-size women's wear and accessories. Roaman's Mail Order company was founded in 1946 by Harry's son, David Roaman, and Evelyn Roaman as an outgrowth of the retail operation. In 1977, Roaman's, Inc. was created as a holding company to reorganize the Roaman's operations.

MARKETS

Sells by mail nationally. Customers are 100% women, lower to middle income, who wear larger sizes.

FACILITIES

Corporate, sales, and marketing offices in New York City; fulfillment in Saddle Brook, NJ.

PRODUCTS, BRAND NAMES, PRICE RANGE

Clothing, shoes, stockings, foundations, uniforms and other apparel for larger-sized women -- sizes 14-1/2 to 60. Roaman's Mail Order items sold under Roaman's name; items offered through the Evelyn Roaman Collection are name-brand.

FINANCIAL INFORMATION

	SALES	NET INCOME	PROFIT MARGIN
1981	$36,000,000*	N.A.	--

TYPE OF ADVERTISING, PROMOTION

Roaman's catalogs are mailed four times a year, with spring and fall mailings being the largest. Catalogs are full color and vary in size. Evelyn Roaman Collection catalogs are mailed for Christmas; first spring catalog issued in 1981.

LIST INFORMATION

QUANTITY MAILED:	10,000,000
AVERAGE ORDER:	$47.50
ACTIVE BUYERS:	500,000
TOTAL LIST:	1,700,000
LIST SOURCE:	Direct mail, space.

COMMENTS

Roaman's has been one of the most successful mail order marketers to target the larger-size woman's apparel specialty market. Management attributes their success in part to their low to mid scale price positioning. The Evelyn Roaman Collection catalog introduced in 1979 represents an experiment within the large-size market by offering a line of higher-priced apparel and accessories. The catalog was tested during the 1979 Christmas season and was reportedly successful. Roaman's now mails a fall and spring edition. The Evelyn Roaman catalog is targeted at upscale credit customers, and only about 100,000 people received the 1981 fall edition. Company officials report that they will continue to explore marketing opportunities within the large-size apparel specialty segment.

RODALE PRESS

ADDRESS, PHONE
Rodale Press, Inc., Emmaus, PA 18049. Telephone: (215) 967-5171.

OWNERSHIP
Privately held by Rodale family and others: Robert Rodale (49%); Anna Rodale (40%); M. Ackerman (2%); D. Widenmyer (2%); and other officers (7%).

MANAGEMENT
Robert Rodale, Chairman of the Board; Robert Teufel, President; David Widenmyer, Treasurer; Anna Rodale, Secretary; Marshall Ackerman, Executive Vice President.

TYPE OF MARKETER
Mail order.

BUSINESS
Rodale publishes and markets a variety of books and magazines dealing with gardening, food, health, energy and survival. The company publishes approximately 30 books a year which are sold as single title by direct mail, in continuity programs through company-operated book clubs, and to a limited degree through trade channels. Approximately 95% of the magazines Rodale publishes are sold by mail order subscription; the remaining 5% from newsstands.

COMPANY HISTORY
The business was started in 1930 by Jerome I. Rodale, and was acquired by Rodale Manufacturing in 1933. Rodale Publishing subsidiary managed business activities between 1935 and 1940, when the corporation was reorganized as a partnership between Jerome and Joseph Rodale. A series of intrafamily controlling arrangements followed, resulting in the November 4, 1953 incorporation of Rodale Press, Inc. The company's first publications were Organic Gardening, Farming, and Prevention Magazine.

MARKETS
Magazines and books are sold to a variety of consumer markets throughout the U.S. and Canada.

FACILITIES

Book distribution and headquarters Emmaus, PA; experimental farm, Allentown, PA.

PRODUCTS, BRAND NAMES, PRICE RANGE

Magazines are: Bicycling, New Farm, Organic Gardening, Prevention, Theatre Crafts, etc. Books are: Complete Book of Vitamins, Encyclopedia of Natural Health, The Synonym Finder, etc. Newsletter-- Executive Fitness.

FINANCIAL INFORMATION

	SALES	NET INCOME	PROFIT MARGIN
1981	$70,000,000*	N.A.	--

TYPE OF ADVERTISING, PROMOTION

Rodale uses direct mail packages and brochures to generate magazine subscriptions and to promote single title and book club sales. Space and broadcast advertising are used to support direct mail promotions.

LIST INFORMATION

QUANTITY MAILED:	65,000,000
AVERAGE ORDER:	$10 to $30
ACTIVE BUYERS:	5,200,000
TOTAL LIST:	8,000,000
LIST SOURCE:	Direct mail.

COMMENTS

Roughly 80% of Rodale's estimated $70,000,000 in 1981 revenues came from magazine publishing operations. The remaining 20% came from book sales. Some 2 million volumes on food, health, energy and gardening were sold in 1980 to both book club members and one-time buyers. Management reports that total sales have risen by 24% in 1979 and 17% in 1980; the increases attributed to improved subscriber bases and small increases in prices. Rodale has positioned itself to publish information on healthful, natural living. The company operates test facilities to do research in food and gardening, general health, and alternate energy sources. Prevention Magazine has grown to become the largest health-oriented publication in the world with nearly 2.5 million active subscribers. Organic Gardening subscribers are 57% male--looking for products and information that will make their lives more rewarding and productive.

SAFECARD SERVICES

ADDRESS, PHONE
SafeCard Services, Inc., 2995 North Dixie Highway, Fort Lauderdale, FL 33334. (305) 565-2131.

OWNERSHIP
Publicly held; stock traded OTC; 5,295,601 common shares outstanding; 1981 earnings per share: $.85; market prices: high, 35-2/1 low, 8-3/4.

MANAGEMENT
Peter A. Halmos, Chairman and Secty.; Steven J. Halmos, President; Vince W. Harmann, Senior VP, Marketing; Joanne J. Seehousen and John B. McKinney, Executive VPs, Marketing.

TYPE OF MARKETER
Mail order.

BUSINESS
Under contract with major companies, SafeCard offers credit card registrations and a 24-hour hotline loss notification service for card holders. Since late '79, the company has offered other continuity programs including: Date Reminder Service programs with the Almanac Appointment Book and DateMinder Calendar, and the Reference Service which includes current editions of the Guinness Book of World Records and the World Almanac. All of the company's services and products are marketed by mail.

COMPANY HISTORY
SafeCard was founded by Peter and Steven Halmos, currently Chairman of the Board and President, and was incorporated in Delaware in December, 1969. In February, 1970 it merged with a New York concern of the same name. Initially, SafeCard offered one service: lost credit card notification. In 1979 it piggybacked on its customer base and its access to mailing lists of credit card users by offering several continuity program services.

MARKETS
Market is presently limited to the availability of third party endorsements to existing credit card base.

FACILITIES

All operations at headquarters location in Fort Lauderdale, Florida.

PRODUCTS, BRAND NAMES, PRICE RANGE

Continuity consumer service programs include hotline notification of lost credit cards as well as changes of address, date reminders, and up-to-date informational services available via toll-free telephone lines.

FINANCIAL INFORMATION

	SALES	**NET INCOME**	**PROFIT MARGIN**
1981	$25,823,000	$4,524,000	17.5%

TYPE OF ADVERTISING, PROMOTION

Currently SafeCard uses only direct mail packages and inserts, and telephone marketing to solicit credit card holders. Other avenues such as national magazine space and broadcast are being considered for future efforts.

LIST INFORMATION

QUANTITY MAILED:	100,000,000
AVERAGE ORDER:	$12
ACTIVE BUYERS:	3,600,000
TOTAL LIST:	75,000,000
LIST SOURCE:	Direct mail.

COMMENTS

SafeCard's net revenues climbed 60% to $25.8 million in 1981. Net earnings rose 48% to $4.5 million for the same period. This represents a whopping $24.6 million increase over 1976 revenues of $1.2 million. SafeCard's Hotline Service, sold by direct mail, now accounts for some 70% of the company's revenues and covers the credit cards issued by 12 oil companies, 45 banks and 20 department stores. Management reports that they serve 3.6 million of the estimated 80 million card holders, and have a service renewal rate of 80%. The remaining 30% of SafeCard's revenues are generated by various spin-off direct mail operations started in the past three years. In 1979 they initiated the Date Reminder Service which currently reports 1.4 million subscribers. In 1981 they began selling the Guinness Book of World Records and the World Almanac, and previously a 24-hour reference update service. SafeCard was cleared by the SEC of allegations against its accounting principles in 1981.

SAKOWITZ

ADDRESS, PHONE
Sakowitz, Inc., 1111 Main St., Houston, TX 77001.
Telephone: (713) 759-1111.

OWNERSHIP
Privately held; principal owner, Robert T. Sakowitz.

MANAGEMENT
Robert T. Sakowitz, President-Chairman of Board; Irving J. Weiner, Exec. VP; Harry Berkowitz, Sr. VP; Floyd Wright, Sr. VP; Leonard Abrams, Sr. VP; Carol Waldrop, Director of Mail Order.

TYPE OF MARKETER
Retail, mail order.

BUSINESS
Sakowitz offers high-quality apparel, accessories, jewelry, housewares and gift items through its 16 retail stores and mail order operation. The retail stores, varying in size from department to boutique, are located primarily in Texas and account for most of the company's sales. The mail order operation is considered a store in and of itself, and although it accounts for only a small percentage of overall sales, it contributes a significant amount of dollars to the company.

COMPANY HISTORY
Sakowitz was started in 1902 in Galveston, TX by brothers Simon and Tobias Sakowitz, following in the footsteps of their merchant father. They opened Sakowitz Brothers with $2,000 in savings and six years later, in 1908, opened a second store in Houston. That second store was expanded in 1917, and that same year the Galveston store was closed. Sakowitz opened several retail stores throughout the Houston area. Other retail stores were opened throughout Texas during the 60s and 70s, and more are planned for the 80s.

MARKETS
Mail order sales primarily domestic with some overseas. Market is upscale; major percentage women.

FACILITIES

Headquarters (offices, mail order, fulfillment) in Houston; retail stores in Texas and Arizona.

PRODUCTS, BRAND NAMES, PRICE RANGE

High quality men's, women's, children's apparel; shoes; jewelry; accessories; unique gift items; kitchenware; linens; gourmet foods. Labels include Sakowitz and other quality brands. Wide range of prices.

FINANCIAL INFORMATION

	SALES	NET INCOME	PROFIT MARGIN
1981	$10,000,000*	N.A.	--

TYPE OF ADVERTISING, PROMOTION

Space ads and catalogs. Several editions of catalog published annually--8" x 10", full color, 36 to 48 pages--mailed 6 to 8 times per year. Christmas catalog increased to 75 pages.

LIST INFORMATION

QUANTITY MAILED:	N.A.
AVERAGE ORDER:	$65
ACTIVE BUYERS:	71,000
TOTAL LIST:	232,000
LIST SOURCE:	Direct mail, space.

COMMENTS

Although major percentage of Sakowitz' business is generated through its retail stores, the company's mail order operation has been successful enough to warrant doubling of operating space for 1982. Management reports that mail order operation has experienced "very significant" growth in sales over the past five years. 1981 was highlighted by Sakowitz' 30th annual Christmas catalog. Following a 13 year tradition, it included "Ultimate Gift" selections. In keeping with this year's theme, "American Know How." the section featured such eccentricities as a day with F. Lee Bailey ($15,000), an offer to star in a Janet Dailey romantic novel ($115,000), five days with American vintner Robert Mondavi ($10,000), and a $1,000,000 personal fireworks display emceed by George Plimpton. On more practical level, Sakowitz vies with Neiman-Marcus, Saks 5th Ave., etc., for the affluent, high-ticket catalog market.

SAKS FIFTH AVENUE

ADDRESS, PHONE

Saks Fifth Avenue, Inc., 450 W. 15th St., New York, NY 10014. Telephone: (212) 940-5333.

OWNERSHIP

Saks Fifth Avenue is a subsidiary operation of BATUS, Inc., which is the American operating arm of B-A-T Industries of London.

MANAGEMENT

Arnold H. Aronson, Chairman and Chief Executive Officer; Burton M. Tansky, President; Paul Leblang, Senior Vice President and Director of Marketing; David Leibowitz, Direct Marketing Manager.

TYPE OF MARKETER

Mail order, retail.

BUSINESS

Aside from its world-famous retail operation with 33 stores across the country, Saks operates Folio Collections, Inc. -- mail order marketer of Saks "haute couture" merchandise. Folio offers designer and house label apparel for men, women, and children, accessories, gifts, jewelry, and some upscale household items. Many items in the Folio Collections are manufactured exclusively for Saks, but the company does no manufacturing of its own.

COMPANY HISTORY

Horace Saks started the business in 1924 in New York with a retail store aimed at the elite, upper-crust customer. The retail operations grew substantially, and now Saks has 33 stores with more on the way. The mail order operation got its start with the publication of a Christmas catalog in 1972. That was the beginning of Folio Collections and the operation has expanded to become a significant part of Saks operations in its 10 years of existence.

MARKETS

Mail order sales are domestic. Market is primarily female, middle-high to upscale.

FACILITIES
Corporate offices and main retail store at 611 Fifth
Ave.; Folio operations at 15th St. address.

PRODUCTS, BRAND NAMES, PRICE RANGE
High-quality apparel for men, women, children;
lingerie; accessories; jewelry; high-ticket gift items;
linens; domestics. Includes designer names, Saks
house label, other national brands. Price range is
various.

FINANCIAL INFORMATION

	SALES	NET INCOME	PROFIT MARGIN
1980	$600,000,000*	N.A.	--

TYPE OF ADVERTISING, PROMOTION
Primarily catalogs, but Folio uses many direct mail
avenues (solo mailings, 16-page bill inserts, re-
mittance envelope ads). Publishes 30 catalogs a year
that vary in dimensions, number of pages, and
merchandise composition.

LIST INFORMATION
QUANTITY MAILED:	15,000,000*
AVERAGE ORDER:	$75*
ACTIVE BUYERS:	500,000*
TOTAL LIST:	1,500,000*
LIST SOURCE:	Direct mail, charge buyers.

COMMENTS
The sales figure above is an estimate of Saks total
1980 revenues. Company officials will not say how
much Folio Collections contributes to overall sales,
but report that the mail order arm is highly successful and profitable. Mail order sales over the past
two years are termed "exceptional," and contribute
from $60 million to $100 million in sales annually. In
less than 10 years, the number of catalogs published
a year has jumped from one to thirty, and distribution varies from 100,000 to over 1,000,000 per mailing. Company prides itself on its sharp, stylishly-
photographed catalogs and does not stick with one
size or design. The 1981 Christmas catalog was
divided into two parts: one, a three-booklet "his/
hers/them" attractively packaged in a red box; the
other, a catalog offering cruisewear and related
items. Company officials report that the 1981
Christmas mail order sales ran 25% ahead of 1980.
Other catalogs range from a general merchandise mix
to specialized merchandise areas.

SEARS, ROEBUCK & CO.

ADDRESS, PHONE
Sears, Roebuck & Co., Sears Tower, Chicago, IL 60684. Telephone: (312) 875-2500.

OWNERSHIP
Publicly held; stock traded NYSE, PSE, MSE; 315,600,000 common shares outstanding; 1981 dividend: $1.36.

MANAGEMENT
E. R. Telling, Chmn, Pres & CEO; Merchandise Group Officers: E.A. Brennan, Chmn & CEO; J. T. Moran, Jr., Senior Exec. VP, Merchandising; H.D. Sunderland, Senior VP, Admin. & Planning.

TYPE OF MARKETER
Mail order, retail.

BUSINESS
Sears' Merchandise Group is the largest U.S. retailer of general merchandise, selling by mail and through a nationwide chain of 854 retail stores, and 2,778 sales offices and other facilities in the U.S. Sales facilities include 14 catalog merchandise distribution centers and 107 owned and 297 leased warehouses. The Group also provides credit services to customers, having about 25,000,000 active customer credit accounts which provided 52.1% of total merchandising sales in 1980.

COMPANY HISTORY
The business was started by Richard W. Sears in 1886 as R. W. Sears Watch Co. in Minneapolis. Sears moved his business to Chicago in 1887, advertised for a watchmaker, and hired Alvah C. Roebuck from Hammond, IN. They formed a partnership, Sears, Roebuck & Co., selling watches by mail. By 1895, the 532-page catalog contained many additional items, and sales exceeded $750,000. The company went public in 1906. General Robert E. Wood opened the first retail store in 1925.

MARKETS
U.S., Canada, Brazil, Columbia, Mexico, Peru, Venezuela, and Spain.

FACILITIES
General office, Chicago; territorial offices in Atlanta, Chicago, L.A., Philadelphia.

PRODUCTS, BRAND NAMES, PRICE RANGE
Carries general merchandise categorized in over 865 product groups. Brands include Sears, Kenmore, Open Hearth Collection, Settlers Trail Collection, Renfrew Hall Collection. Prices moderate.

FINANCIAL INFORMATION

	SALES	NET INCOME	PROFIT MARGIN
1981	$8,033,500,000	$333,100,000	4.1%

TYPE OF ADVERTISING, PROMOTION
Sears mails two major seasonal catalogs; Fall and Spring, and smaller catalogs for Christmas, winter and summer. In addition they mail a variety of specialty tabloid-size catalogs for an estimated total of 450 million pieces annually.

LIST INFORMATION
QUANTITY MAILED:	N.A.	(Sears does not market
AVERAGE ORDER:	N.A.	its list or make avail-
ACTIVE BUYERS:	N.A.	able its active buyer
TOTAL LIST:	N.A.	file.)
LIST SOURCE:	Direct mail, space, charge cards.	

COMMENTS
The financial information above was reported by Sears as their total revenues and earnings for 1981. The following information was supplied for the Merchandise Group which includes Sears' mail order operations: revenues rose 8.2% in 1981 to $20.2 billion, compared to $18.7 billion in 1980; net earnings increased 24.5% from $228.9 million in 1980, to $285.0 million in 1981. Of the total Merchandising Group sales for 1981 the following percentage breakdown applies: (1) 20% of sales or $4 billion came from catalogs; (2) 51% of catalog sales or $2.04 billion came from orders placed in catalog stores; (3) the remaining 49% or $1.96 billion came from entirely non-store operations; (4) of total non-store sales, 10% or $196 million came from orders placed by mail; (5) 90% of non-store sales or $1.76 billion came from orders placed over the telephone. Sears and other "Top-Five" major general merchandisers have experienced strong competition in mail order from the proliferation of smaller specialty merchandisers.

SENTRY INSURANCE

ADDRESS, PHONE

Sentry Insurance, 1800 North Point Drive, Stevens Point, WI 54481. Telephone: (715) 346-6000.

OWNERSHIP

Sentry is a mutual insurance company, and as such is "publicly" held by the policyholders, employees, officers and directors.

MANAGEMENT

John W. Joanis, Chrmn. and CEO; William R. Schwantes, Pres.; Paul D. Durant II, VP and Treas.; Thomas J. Maney, Sec.; VPs: P. Clifford, C. McKellney, G. Brooks, and D. Llewellyn.

TYPE OF MARKETER

Mail order, direct sales.

BUSINESS

Through its 85 operating subsidiaries throughout the U.S. and abroad Sentry offers the full range of types of insurance coverage for both individuals and commercial concerns. The company has developed a variety of coverage plans which it sells by mail and through direct sales agency forces. Sentry has been an active mail order marketer in the U.S. since 1972 and internationally for the past four years. The company employs 7,000 people in the U.S.

COMPANY HISTORY

The original business, Hardware Mutual Casualty Insurance, was started in 1903 in Wisconsin. A life insurance division was established and incorporated in Wisconsin in October of 1958. Also during this time the "sentry man" logo was adopted. In 1963 the corporate name was changed to Sentry Insurance in response to popular association of the company with its logo. Mail order marketing operations were added in late 1972, and the first premiums were written by mail in 1973.

MARKETS

U.S., Australia, Bermuda, Hong Kong, Iran, Lebanon, Morocco, Netherlands, South Africa, U.K.

FACILITIES

World headquarters in newly-constructed, 500,000 sq. ft., multi-story brick building.

PRODUCTS, BRAND NAMES, PRICE RANGE

Sentry provides insurance for all areas of coverage such as casualty and property from Sentry Indemnity and Middlesex Ins., life, health, accident, disability from Sentry Life Ins., automobile and motorcycle from Dairyland Ins.

FINANCIAL INFORMATION

	SALES	**NET INCOME**	**PROFIT MARGIN**
1980	$1,122,251,000	$37,323,000	3.3%

TYPE OF ADVERTISING, PROMOTION

The domestic and international "mailing kits" contain brochures describing the product, applications for coverage and a return envelope. Advertisements also appear in magazines, newspapers, fliers, and on T.V. and radio.

LIST INFORMATION

QUANTITY MAILED:	N.A.	(Sentry does not market
AVERAGE ORDER:	N.A.	its list or make available
ACTIVE BUYERS:	N.A.	any information on its
TOTAL LIST:	N.A.	various buyer files.)
LIST SOURCE:	N.A.	

COMMENTS

Sentry's total revenues for 1980 (above) represent an increase of 7.5% over $1.8 billion in 1979. Net income climbed 228% from $11.4 million in 1979 to $37.3 million in 1980. Management reported that no accurate percentage of revenues attributable to mail order was available, but that direct mail sales, and promotions to support direct sales efforts contribute significantly to virtually all of Sentry's domestic and foreign operations. Foreign direct mail marketing has reportedly been most successful in operating divisions in Australia and the United Kingdom. Management reports that in order to decentralize activities, more of the individual subsidiaries will be setting up their own mail order marketing operations in-house. Sentry is involved in several non-insurance operations including Midstate Airlines, six radio stations, and 50% ownership of a cable television company.

SHARPER IMAGE

ADDRESS, PHONE
Sharper Image, 755 Davis St., San Francisco, CA 94111. Telephone: (415) 788-4747.

OWNERSHIP
Privately held; 100% capital owned by founder Richard Thalheimer.

MANAGEMENT
Richard J. Thalheimer, President; Alan Thalheimer, Vice President; Christine Sinnott, Secretary and Treasurer.

TYPE OF MARKETER
Mail order.

BUSINESS
The Sharper Image is a mail order marketer of high-quality electronic devices, limited apparel, gifts and luxury items, aimed primarily at the upscale professional and executive. The product mix is predominately tape and telephone equipment, watches and clocks, calculators, and electronic health monitoring devices. All of the merchandise is purchased from outside manufacturers and suppliers, with a high percentage of import items. Sharper Image's peak sales season is Christmas.

COMPANY HISTORY
The business was started by attorney Richard Thalheimer in January of 1977. Thalheimer, who is an avid runner, placed a small space ad in Runners World magazine to sell $29 electronic digital hand stop-watches. The ad produced $400 in sales. Six months later the company published its first catalog containing a variety of electronic health monitoring devices which grossed $500,000 in sales in the first year. The business has expanded rapidly in its five years of operation, and employs 120 people.

MARKETS
Domestic; upper income; 80% male, managerial, executive, professional types, 25 to 35 age range.

FACILITIES

H.Q., mail order operations, 10,000 sq. ft. warehouse at separate locations in San Francisco.

PRODUCTS, BRAND NAMES, PRICE RANGE

High-technology consumer items, such as the
Marsona Sound Conditioner, cordless telephones,
electronic watches, and men's upscale gifts and
accessories like the Recaro Chair ($900), or a suit of
armor ($2,450). Prices: from $50 to $2,500.

FINANCIAL INFORMATION

	SALES	NET INCOME	PROFIT MARGIN
1981	$33,000,000*	N.A.	--

TYPE OF ADVERTISING, PROMOTION

The company reportedly spends $6,000,000 per year
on advertising. Roughly 70% of promotion is through
seasonal catalogs, the remaining 30% through space
ads in Omni, Science Technology, business magazines, etc.

LIST INFORMATION

QUANTITY MAILED:	20,000,000
AVERAGE ORDER:	$165
ACTIVE BUYERS:	300,000
TOTAL LIST:	400,000*
LIST SOURCE:	Direct mail, space.

COMMENTS

In 1981, after only five years of operation, Sharper
Image's sales are estimated to have topped the $33
million mark. The company's catalogs are 8-1/2 x
10-3/4, full color, 56 pages, and contain roughly 170
items. The catalogs have been described as "men's
wish books," for anyone with "a love of electronic
gadgetry and the wherewithal to indulge it." The
merchandise is primarily upscale luxury items.
Popular items include the Marsona Sound conditioner
(soft rain, wave sound generator); Webcor Cordless
Telephone. Upcoming additions include loose cut and
mounted gems, bullet proof vests, and an audio-
activated light. Management reported they are
currently producing a ½-hour cable television "catalog" program, including demonstrations of products,
telephone ordering and "a lively talk show format."
The series premiered on satellite program network in
March of 1982, and will be expanded to other cable
networks in the next twelve months.

SHEPLERS

ADDRESS, PHONE
Sheplers, Inc., 6501 W. Kellog, Wichita, KS 67209. Telephone: (316) 943-2151.

OWNERSHIP
Wholly-owned subsidiary of publicly-held W.R. Grace & Co., New York.

MANAGEMENT
John Wilson, Chrmn, CEO; S.P. Braud, Sr. Vice President-Operations; John Mosley, Sr. Vice President-Finance; J. Rathke, VP; B. Voorhees, VP; C. E. Anderson, Dir. of Catalog Sales.

TYPE OF MARKETER
Mail order, retail.

BUSINESS
Sheplers sells a wide range of family outdoor wear, specializing in western wear and sports apparel for men and women of all ages, and a line of riding tack and accessories. Sales are by mail through Sheplers' catalog operations and through its eight retail stores in Texas, Colorado, Oklahoma, Kansas and Nebraska. Sales are reportedly non-seasonal. Sheplers employed a total of 2,000 people in 1981.

COMPANY HISTORY
Harry Shepler started the business in the late 1940s as a retailer of outdoor and western wear. Mail order operations did not start until a few years after the Dry family purchased Sheplers in 1967. The company was incorporated in Kansas in January, 1971, and its name was changed from Shepler's of Wichita, Inc., to the current name in 1972. The business was sold to W.R. Grace & Co. in April of 1976 through an exchange of stock.

MARKETS
Primarily domestic, some overseas; customers are roughly 75% male.

FACILITIES
Headquarters and mail order operations in Wichita; retail stores in five mid/southwest states.

PRODUCTS, BRAND NAMES, PRICE RANGE
Western style apparel and riding gear for all age groups. Prices moderate. Sells some national name brands as well as following house brands: Sheplers, Pardners, Cross Country, American Original, Plainsmen.

FINANCIAL INFORMATION

	SALES	NET INCOME	PROFIT MARGIN
1981	$50,000,000*	N.A.	--

TYPE OF ADVERTISING, PROMOTION
Sheplers produces four main catalogs which go out in six major mailings per year, and usually one special sale edition. Space ads in outdoor and recreational magazines are used to generate catalog inquiries.

LIST INFORMATION

QUANTITY MAILED:	7,000,000
AVERAGE ORDER:	$88
ACTIVE BUYERS:	164,053
TOTAL LIST:	370,000
LIST SOURCE:	Direct mail.

COMMENTS
Between 1976, when W.R. Grace & Co. acquired Sheplers, and 1978, sales reportedly jumped 70%. The ensuing years have apparently seen a continued growth in sales, especially in 1980 with the birth of the "Urban Cowboy" craze. Sheplers got its start as a retail operation, and its eight stores in the mid and southwest continue to provide the bulk of the business. Although the company declined to break sales into retail and mail order, retail accounted for an estimated 64 percent of total sales. It is estimated that mail order operations generated approximately $18 million or about 36% of Sheplers estimated total 1981 sales of $50 million. Management reported no major changes in catalog strategy for the coming year. At present Shepler's catalogs are 8-1/2 x 11, full-color. The sale book averages sixteen pages.

SHOPPING INTERNATIONAL

ADDRESS, PHONE

Shopping International, Inc., Shopping International Bldg., Norwich, VT 05055. Phone: (802) 649-1333.

OWNERSHIP

Wholly-owned subsidiary of publicly-held Bear Creek Corporation, of Medford, Oregon.

MANAGEMENT

John R. H. Holmes, Chairman of the Board, Thomas M. Butler, President; Glen Harrison, Vice President & Secretary; Gil Nysse, Treasurer; Roy Raven, VP; Melvin Simon, VP.

TYPE OF MARKETER

Mail order, wholesale.

BUSINESS

Shopping International markets a wide variety of imported crafts, jewelry, art objects, wearing apparel and other specialty merchandise purchased through agents and from suppliers around the world. Products are marketed primarily by means of direct mail catalog promotions. The company's mail order sales account for approximately 80% of the business, an estimated 20% is wholesale to gift shops and boutiques. Peak sales are reportedly from August through September, and the company employs 100 people.

COMPANY HISTORY

The business was started in Vermont in 1954 by Clinton C. Gardner. On February 20, 1974, Bear Creek subsidiary Harry & David, Inc. purchased the company. Shopping International was incorporated in Delaware on February 20, 1974. The company's sales have reportedly grown consistently through its years of operations.

MARKETS

Shopping International sells merchandise throughout the U.S.; customers are 86% female, upscale.

FACILITIES

Headquarters, mail order operations and import warehousing in 20,000 sq. ft. at Norwich, VT.

PRODUCTS, BRAND NAMES, PRICE RANGE

Imported gift items from around the world, including art objects, jewelry, music boxes, apparel and accessories, primarily for women, and specialty merchandise. General price ranges from $12.00 to $200.00.

FINANCIAL INFORMATION

	SALES	NET INCOME	PROFIT MARGIN
1981	$10,000,000*	N.A.	--

TYPE OF ADVERTISING, PROMOTION

Company publishes four major catalogs a year, which are mailed seasonally. Catalogs measure 8-1/2" x 11", full color, and contain 48 pages. Occasionally a supplemental sale catalog is mailed to customers. Advertisements appear in many major magazines.

LIST INFORMATION

QUANTITY MAILED:	7,500,000*
AVERAGE ORDER:	$50
ACTIVE BUYERS:	134,000
TOTAL LIST:	500,000*
LIST SOURCE:	Direct mail.

COMMENTS

At present Shopping International comprises Bear Creek Corp.'s Specialty Merchandise Group. However in 1980 and '81 the parent tested the following operations for possible future inclusion: a catalog of children's gifts entitled Bear Creek Collection; a line of designer jewelry marketed through direct mail brochures under the name J. R. H. Holmes & Co., Ltd.; circulars offering outdoor furniture under the name Design Options, Inc. The selections of apparel and accessories, and the size and number of Shopping International catalogs have all been increased. The Fall, 1981 edition featured individual sections of imports from 79 different lands, and offered 330 different items. Promotional emphasis is on the exotic quality of imported gifts, as well as the craftsmanship, beauty and artistic quality of their merchandise, much of which is hand-made. In April of 1982, Bear Creek announced that all Shopping International operations would be moved in the summer of 1982 to parent headquarters.

SHOPSMITH

ADDRESS, PHONE

Shopsmith, Inc., 750 Center Drive, Vandalia, OH 45377. Telephone: (513) 898-6070.

OWNERSHIP

Publicly-held; stock traded OTC; 1,362,292, common shares outstanding; 1981 market prices: high, 12; low, 6-1/4; 1981 dividend: $.06.

MANAGEMENT

John R. Folkerth, President and Chief Executive Officer; Larry A. Blank, Senior Vice President of Sales; Peter M. Jacob, Senior Vice President of Manufacturing.

TYPE OF MARKETER

Mail order, direct sales.

BUSINESS

Shopsmith is engaged in the manufacture and marketing of power and non-power woodworking tools, designed primarily for use in the home. In addition they offer a full line of accessories to their power tool line, along with other woodworking tools and accessories. Through BenchMark they offer the ShopCraft line of bench-top power tools. The company reported 1,190 employees in 1981.

COMPANY HISTORY

The original Shopsmith tool line and trademark date back to 1946. In 1972, John Folkerth purchased the tooling, machinery and remaining inventory of the Shopsmith line from Magna America for $250,000. Magna acquired Shopsmith in 1958, but had ceased production of the basic Shopsmith unit: the Mark V. After the initial start-up period, Shopsmith had reached $5 million in sales by 1977. By 1979, sales stood at $16 million, and by 1981 had passed the $60 million mark.

MARKETS

The company sells throughout the U.S. and Canada; limited sales to other foreign countries.

FACILITIES

Administrative and manufacturing facilities in Dayton, OH, Vandalia, OH, Jefferson City, MO.

PRODUCTS, BRAND NAMES, PRICE RANGE

The Shopsmith Mark V (principal multi-purpose tool) with its standard line of accessories, sells for $1,145.00. They also market ShopCraft bench-top power tools, and the Shopmate line of accessories.

FINANCIAL INFORMATION

	SALES	NET INCOME	PROFIT MARGIN
1981	$62,496,000	$2,258,000	3.6%

TYPE OF ADVERTISING, PROMOTION

Company publishes full-color catalogs and brochures on the Mark V and its accessories; the Better Woodworking catalog on other lines of woodworking tools; Hands On, The Home Woodworking Magazine. Extensive shopping mall promotions.

LIST INFORMATION

QUANTITY MAILED: 14,000,000
AVERAGE ORDER: N.A.
ACTIVE BUYERS: 75,000
TOTAL LIST: 1,000,000
LIST SOURCE: Direct mail, space.

COMMENTS

Mail order sales, which account for some 60% of Shopsmith's total revenues, were up 102.1% for 1980-1981. In the past year the company has doubled its in-house mailing list through inquiry-generating ads in national magazines and tests of outside lists. Their direct mail expense to sales ratio is well below the industry average (probably due to their high average orders). Plans are to place increasing emphasis on catalog promotion: catalogs combine interesting and useful information for home woodworkers, with advertising and offerings of Shopsmith's variety of products. Company is researching ways to improve their low quota season (summer months) with special mailings and offers. Also pushing to fully process each incoming order within 24 hours. Shopsmith was honored as #29 of Inc. Magazine's leading 100 public/independent companies. Management deserves credit for taking a moribund product, through direct mail, from $5 million to $62 million in sales in just four years.

SMITHSONIAN INSTITUTION

ADDRESS, PHONE

Smithsonian Institution Mail Order, P.O. Box 2456, Washington, D.C. 20013. Telephone: (202) 287-3566.

OWNERSHIP

Division of the non-profit government/trust Smithsonian Institution.

MANAGEMENT

Donald Press, Director of Mail Order; Josephine Rowan, Marketing Manager; Michael Cassidy, Purchasing Manager; Elton Morehouse, Operations Manager.

TYPE OF MARKETER

BUSINESS

The Smithsonian Catalogue is the selling tool of the Smithsonian Institution's Mail Order Division. The catalog offers a wide array of furniture, porcelain, silver, books, records and unusual gift items that represent the collection of the Smithsonian's thirteen museums and National Zoo. Smithsonian marketing executives keep an eye out for interesting and marketable museum pieces and go to craftsmen and manufacturers who produce items especially for catalog sales.

COMPANY HISTORY

The Smithsonian Institution was created by an act of Congress in 1846 to "increase and diffuse knowledge among men." It is an organization of research, exploration and reference for history, science, culture and the arts, and its museums and activities reflect that heritage. The Smithsonian's museum shop was started in the early 60s. The first catalog was issued in 1975 as an outgrowth of the museum shop, and the mail order operation became a separate division in 1978.

MARKETS

Mail order sales are primarily domestic, with limited foreign marketing; customers mostly female.

FACILITIES
Mail Order Division headquarters in Washington, D.C.; fulfillment operations in Springfield, VA.

PRODUCTS, BRAND NAMES, PRICE RANGE
A variety of reproductions, primarily of Americana, from museum collections including art pieces, books, furniture and decorations, models and craft kits, children's gifts, jewelry, musical instruments, etc. Prices range from $4.50 to $2,500.

FINANCIAL INFORMATION

	SALES	NET INCOME	PROFIT MARGIN
1981	$10,000,000	-0-	-0-

TYPE OF ADVERTISING, PROMOTION
The Mail Order Division publishes three catalogs per year, mailed in the spring, summer and fall. In addition to merchandise, the catalogs offer membership in Smithsonian Associates. Primary lists are Smithsonian Associates and active buyers.

LIST INFORMATION

QUANTITY MAILED:	9,000,000
AVERAGE ORDER:	$35
ACTIVE BUYERS:	300,000
TOTAL LIST:	3,000,000
LIST SOURCE:	Direct mail, rentals.

COMMENTS
In its relatively short history the Smithsonian Mail Order Division has grown rapidly, with sales reportedly tripling over the past five years. Mail order operations were initiated with one catalog, before the separate Mail Order Division was created. Presently the Division publishes three catalogs annually, with the newest being a summer edition. The summer version has been mailed to only a portion of the house list in the past two years; full roll-out is scheduled for 1982. The fall edition, mailed for Christmas sales, receives the greatest response and is mailed to roughly 3,000,000 people. The Fall, 1981 catalog was full color, 9 x 7, sixty pages, offered 200 items, and grossed more in sales than any other Smithsonian catalog to date. Though the Division does not market its list, it does seek to build its in-house file by trading lists with other non-profit and educational institutions. About 66% of their current list is Smithsonian Associates members who receive a 10% discount on catalog purchases.

SPENCER GIFTS

ADDRESS, PHONE
Spencer Gifts, 1050 Black Horse Pike, Atlantic City, NJ 08411. Telephone: (609) 645-3300.

OWNERSHIP
Spencer is a wholly-owned subsidiary of MCA, Inc., of Universal City, California.

MANAGEMENT
J. Eugene Brog, President; John L. Doyle, Executive VP; Charles Danenberg, VP, Treasurer; Gary Stern, VP-Mail Order Merchandising; George Zilling, VP-Mail Order Marketing.

TYPE OF MARKETER
Mail order, retail.

BUSINESS
Spencer is a mail order marketer of gift merchandise, and operates a chain of retail novelty shops. Retail stores are located throughout the U.S., and mail order markets include the U.S. and western Europe. Spencer sells a wide variety of low-cost specialty merchandise including gifts, novelties and products for home, office and personal use. Spencer purchases merchandise from domestic and foreign suppliers, but does no manufacturing of its own.

COMPANY HISTORY
Spencer Gifts was founded as a private company in 1947. At the time it was acquired by MCA in 1968, it had twenty retail shops in operation. At the end of 1980, Spencer had 414 stores operating in major shopping centers in 46 states. The company was involved in mail order marketing since its founding and has expanded into foreign markets in the past ten years. Spencer reported 4,500 employees in 1980.

MARKETS
Throughout the United States and Europe. Products appeal primarily to 15-25 year old age group.

FACILITIES

Offices in Atlantic City, NJ and West Germany; retail shops throughout the U.S.

PRODUCTS, BRAND NAMES, PRICE RANGE

Wide variety of gifts, gags, novelties, items for household use and decoration, auto accessories, etc. Items are generally under $20.00, concentrated in the $10.00 to $15.00 range.

FINANCIAL INFORMATION

	SALES	NET INCOME	PROFIT MARGIN
1980	$211,000,000	$8,800,000	4.8%

TYPE OF ADVERTISING, PROMOTION

Spencer mainly uses direct mail, package inserts, and some limited space advertising. The company is a frequent user of sweepstake promotional offers and dutch door inserts offering 88¢ items in newspaper supplements.

LIST INFORMATION

QUANTITY MAILED:	50,000,000+*
AVERAGE ORDER:	$13
ACTIVE BUYERS:	4,400,000
TOTAL LIST:	6,400,000
LIST SOURCE:	Direct mail (100%).

COMMENTS

Spencer Gifts, the main interest of MCA's Retail and Mail Order Division, was purchased by MCA in April of 1968 for the equivalent in traded shares of stock of $17,000,000. At the time of the acquisition, Spencer sales volume was $22 million. In 1980 Spencer was responsible for $211 million of MCA's total revenues, about 32% or $67.5 million directly attributable to mail order. While this is a substantial increase ($17,000,000) over '79 totals, operating income dropped 52.2% between '79 and '80. Management attributes this to greatly increased operating and mailing costs, and a slow down in the rate of sales. Industry experts attribute the profit decline more to inefficiencies in retail operations and poor quality of new customer intake generated by sweepstakes and 88¢ merchandise promotion.

ADDRESS, PHONE
Spiegel, Inc., 1515 W. 22nd Street, Oak Brook, IL 60521. Telephone: (312) 986-8800.

OWNERSHIP
Spiegel is a wholly-owned subsidiary of Otto Versand Corporation of West Germany.

MANAGEMENT
Henry A. Johnson, Pres., CEO; Vice Presidents: E. Spiegel, A. Paul, J. Shea, W. Killough, J. Erickson, W. Giuntoli, A. Withers, J. Stubits, P. Stinneford, R. Hirshberg, H. Funnen.

TYPE OF MARKETER
Mail order.

BUSINESS
Spiegel is estimated to be the fourth largest mail order general merchandiser in the U.S. The company primarily sells apparel, footwear and accessories for men and women of all ages. In addition they offer lines of sporting goods, home furnishings, cameras, office supplies, jewelry, children's toys and more. In addition to selling by mail, Spiegel's reports a considerable response to their telephone sales/ordering operations.

COMPANY HISTORY
The company was founded as a catalog retailing operation in Chicago in 1865 by the Spiegel family. One hundred percent of the company's capital was acquired by Beneficial Corporation in 1965. Company headquarters were moved from inner-city Chicago to suburban Oak Brook, Il. Early in 1978, Spiegel closed 230 of its catalog ordering stores. Spiegel was acquired by the second leading mail order house in Germany, Otto Versand, in the fourth quarter, 1981.

MARKETS
Spiegel's customer base consists of 3 million middle to upper income families averaging $31,600 per year.

FACILITIES
Headquarters are in Oak Brook, IL; warehouse/ distribution in Chicago, IL.

PRODUCTS, BRAND NAMES, PRICE RANGE
Company sells fashion apparel, home furnishings and accessories. Brand names include: Evan-Picone, Gloria Vanderbilt, Aigner, Mademoiselle (furs), Marisa Christini and Eva Gabor. Prices are mid to upper range.

FINANCIAL INFORMATION

	SALES	NET INCOME	PROFIT MARGIN
1981	$423,449,000	$1,681,000	.4%

TYPE OF ADVERTISING, PROMOTION
Aside from its main general merchandise catalogs Spiegel mails ten million Discover Spiegel catalogs twice a year to generate new customers. Space customer-generation campaigns appear in Vogue, Town & Country and House Beautiful.

LIST INFORMATION
QUANTITY MAILED: 46,000,000
AVERAGE ORDER: $85
ACTIVE BUYERS: 1,820,000
TOTAL LIST: 3,000,000
LIST SOURCE: Direct mail, space advertising.

COMMENTS
In the low growth, recessionary economy of 1980, Spiegel after-tax earnings dropped 90%. Between the first and second quarter of 1981 this downward trend in earnings was reversed. Net earnings for the second quarter of 1981 were $250,000, compared to a $2.9 million loss for the same period in 1980. Financial results for the third quarter of 1981 were as follows: total revenues were $97.7 million compared to $89.8 million in 1980; net earnings were $933,000 compared to $918,000 in 1980. The company was acquired by Otto Versand in the fourth quarter. In 1980 during its last full year as a Beneficial subsidiary, Spiegel sales were broken down as follows: 100% of merchandise sales were through catalogs; 60% of catalog sales were from mail orders; 40% of catalog sales were from orders placed by phone. By emphasizing designer labels in apparel and quality brands in their other merchandise Spiegel has attempted to promote more upscale image then its major general merchandise competitors.

SPORTPAGES

ADDRESS, PHONE
Sportpages Corporation, 3373 Towerwood Drive, Dallas, TX 75234. (214) 247-3101 or 484-8900.

OWNERSHIP
Privately held; principal owner, Jerry Baldridge; 100% of capital stock owned by Baldridge and officers.

MANAGEMENT
Jerry Baldridge, President and Chief Executive Officer; Emy Lou Baldridge, Vice President of Merchandising; Carl Landon, Vice President of Finance.

TYPE OF MARKETER
Mail order, retail.

BUSINESS
Sportpages is a mail order and retail marketer of men's and women's apparel ranging from warm-up suits, to quality casual apparel, to elegant evening wear. In addition the company markets sporting goods and equipment, and a line of sports-related gift items. Approximately 95% of revenues come from mail order sales, the remaining 5% from the company's Final Edition retail store. Management reports that sales are non-seasonal, and Sportpages reported 150 employees in 1981.

COMPANY HISTORY
The business was started as a joint venture in 1975 with Horchow Collections, and the first catalog was issued in 1975 under the Horchow name. In 1976 Sportpages became a subsidiary of General Recreation, Inc. When General Recreation's Board decided to discontinue the operation, Jerry Baldridge (then President of General Recreation), was allowed to purchase Sportpages in a private transaction. He severed connections with General Recreation, Inc. and acquired all Sportpages stock in July, 1977.

MARKETS
Sales are primarily domestic; customers are 80% female, 30-45, upper income.

FACILITIES

Leases 21,000 sq. ft. of office and warehouse space in Dallas, TX. Retail outlet nearby.

PRODUCTS, BRAND NAMES, PRICE RANGE

Products include top quality men's and women's fashion and sports apparel, specialty gifts, jewelry, footwear and home decorative accessories. Brand name products include Halston, Bill Blass, Von Furstenberg and many others.

FINANCIAL INFORMATION

	SALES	NET INCOME	PROFIT MARGIN
1981	$17,000,000*	N.A.	--

TYPE OF ADVERTISING, PROMOTION

Catalogs are published and mailed ten times a year; 15 million mailed annually. Catalogs are 30-64 color pages, 8½" x 11"; largest is the Christmas edition. Space ads appear in magazines such as Glamour, Mademoiselle, Harper's Bazaar.

LIST INFORMATION

QUANTITY MAILED:	15,000,000
AVERAGE ORDER:	$60
ACTIVE BUYERS:	200,000
TOTAL LIST:	400,000
LIST SOURCE:	Direct mail.

COMMENTS

Management reports that Sportpages' sales have grown rapidly over the past several years. Total sales of $17 million reported in 1981 represent a 39% increase over 1980 sales of $12.2 million, 158% over 1979 sales of $6.6 million, and 233% over 1978 sales of $5.1 million. Considerable increases in sales are reportedly due in part to the company's aggressive expansion of catalog mailings. They have grown from three to ten annual editions and more catalogs are planned. Company officials also report a significant increase in demand for women's fashions by mail. Sportpages will reportedly publish a catalog exclusively for women's fashions, and will publish a general catalog each month in 1982. The company is planning to move to larger facilities in the Dallas area and to expand their Dallas "Final Edition" retail store.

STANDEX INTERNATIONAL

ADDRESS, PHONE

Standex International Corporation, Manor Parkway, Salem, NH 03079. Telephone: (603) 893-9701.

OWNERSHIP

Publicly held; stock traded NYSE; 6,712,510 common shares outstanding; 1981 market prices: high, 20-3/8; low, 13-7/8; 1981 dividend: $.89.

MANAGEMENT

Daniel E. Hogan, Chmn & CEO; Warren S. Cooper, Pres & COO; Thomas L. King, Senior VP & Treas; Sol Sackel, Senior VP; Samuel S. Dennis III, VP; Robert E. Masotta, VP Secty & Counsel.

TYPE OF MARKETER

Mail order, retail, wholesale.

BUSINESS

Standex International is a diversified manufacturing corporation which produces and markets products for a wide variety of industries. The company has fifteen operating divisions. The Consumer Products Group has four operating divisions all of which use mail order marketing to generate a substantial portion of their sales. Aside from Crest (Frank Lewis) Fruit and Yield House Furniture (reported separately), the Division includes Club Aluminum and Dresher Brass Beds.

COMPANY HISTORY

Standex was started in 1955 and became publicly owned in 1964. Between 1975 and 1980 sales doubled and earnings tripled. Standex management credits balanced diversification for much of the Company's success. Confidence in mail order as an important part of overall marketing is best demonstrated by the achievements of the Consumer Products Group. Standex presently operates 86 plants located in 14 countries, and its products are sold throughout the world.

MARKETS

Catalog and party plan sales for Consumer Products throughout U.S.A., Great Britain and Germany.

FACILITIES

Corporate headquarters in Salem, NY; Dresher and Club manufacturing facilities in Chicago.

PRODUCTS, BRAND NAMES, PRICE RANGE

Club Aluminum markets a full line of moderately-priced cookware under the Silverstone label and their newest line LeGray Cookware. Dresher manufactures and markets high-quality, upscale genuine brass beds under the Dresher brand name.

FINANCIAL INFORMATION

	SALES	NET INCOME	PROFIT MARGIN
1981	$88,800,000	$8,200,000	9.2%

TYPE OF ADVERTISING, PROMOTION

Club Aluminum uses direct mail promotions for wholesale and consumer sales. Dresher uses small catalogs and brochures to sell to other mail order houses and furniture and department stores.

LIST INFORMATION

QUANTITY MAILED:	N.A.	(See separate reports
AVERAGE ORDER:	N.A.	for detailed informa-
ACTIVE BUYERS:	N.A.	tion on Crest and
TOTAL LIST:	N.A.	Yield House.)
LIST SOURCE:	N.A.	

COMMENTS

In 1981 the Consumer Products Group contributed $88.8 million or 24% of Standex total sales of $369.9 million and contributed 31% of corporate operating income. The figures above represent a 9% increase in sales from 1980 to 1981, but a 23% drop in earnings overall for the Consumer Products Group. Club and Dresher combined sales contributed approximately $30,000,000 or 33% of Consumer Products total revenues. Company officials reported that Club's mail order cookware sales were affected by an overall softness in the market and increased competitive pressures. They anticipate that the new LeGray line of aluminum cookware will be a strong seller in 1982. Dresher reportedly increased production in the face of growing demand for their unique brass beds. However some quality problems caused them to lose several major retail accounts early in 1981. A new management team was installed and the company has reportedly regained several of the accounts and added new ones.

STARCREST OF CALIFORNIA

ADDRESS, PHONE

StarCrest Products of California, Inc., 3159 Red Hill Ave., Costa Mesa, CA 92626. (714) 540-9172.

OWNERSHIP

Privately held; capital consists of 10,000 shares of common stock, with $1 par value.

MANAGEMENT

Timothy M. Calandra, President; Michael Donnelly, Vice President of Marketing and Advertising; Harold Clark, Vice President of Operations.

TYPE OF MARKETER

Mail order.

BUSINESS

StarCrest is a 100% mail order marketer of housewares, gift items, general merchandise, women's lingerie, hosiery and accessories. The company is positioned to serve the female bargain buyer. StarCrest does no manufacturing of its own and no international marketing of its products.

COMPANY HISTORY

Anthony B. Calandra started the company in 1971 as Hosiery Club of America. That same year, the charter was amended to change the corporate name to StarCrest Products of California. In 1976 Timothy Calandra became president of StarCrest, and the company opened a new division under the Signatures tradestyle. StarCrest currently reports 300 employees.

MARKETS

Customers are 93% women, middle income; described as low-budget, discount-minded housewives.

FACILITIES
Headquarters and fulfillment operations at Costa Mesa
location; warehouse in Irvine, CA.

PRODUCTS, BRAND NAMES, PRICE RANGE
StarCrest markets a wide variety of general mer-
chandise for home and personal use. Brand names
include Diana Marsh, Intermatic, Border-Line, Lady's
Pride, Travel King, Ecko, Exquisite Form, Micro-1,
Cardinale, Gemsonic, Hagerty.

FINANCIAL INFORMATION

	SALES	NET INCOME	PROFIT MARGIN
1981	$30,000,000*	N.A.	--

TYPE OF ADVERTISING, PROMOTION
StarCrest relies solely on direct mail packages and
inserts in magazines, newspapers and national cooperative mailings. StarCrest is a heavy user of
outside lists.

LIST INFORMATION
QUANTITY MAILED:	30,000,000*
AVERAGE ORDER:	$21 to $40
ACTIVE BUYERS:	2,083,286
TOTAL LIST:	4,753,959
LIST SOURCE:	Direct mail.

COMMENTS
Management reports that they are currently experiencing considerable growth in their active buyer
file. The company averaged 150,000 monthly hotline
buyers, and 575,000 annual multibuyers, in 1981.
In May StarCrest announced a list of 690,064 past
three months hotline buyers. Management reports
that StarCrest's sales have grown considerably in
the past several years, particularly due to the high
degree of repeat buying and their unusually high
average order despite the lowscale price position of
the product mix. The company's main direct mail
promotions contain roughly 36 separated, 5 x 8,
full-color sheets, printed front and back with merchandise offers. Management reports that the insert
program they offer for other marketers to include
promotional sheets in StarCrest mailings is a very
successful operation.

STARK BROTHERS

ADDRESS, PHONE

Stark Brothers Nurseries and Orchard Company, U.S. 54, Louisiana, MO 63353. (314) 754-5511.

OWNERSHIP

Privately held.

MANAGEMENT

John Logan, Chairman and President; Clay Logan, Assistant to President; David Schroeder, General Sales Manager; Bonnie Foster, Mail Order Sales Manager.

TYPE OF MARKETER

Mail order, wholesale.

BUSINESS

Stark Bros., one of the oldest and largest nurseries in the world, grows and markets quality fruit trees throughout U.S. The company also markets other green goods and related growing items. Marketing organization of company is broken into three sales departments: Mail Order targets the home and backyard grower and produces the greatest per-centage of revenues; the Fruit Tree Center markets fruit trees through authorized dealers nationally; Commercial Sales services commercial orchards worldwide.

COMPANY HISTORY

The business was started in 1816 by James Hart Stark who migrated from Kentucky to Missouri. Mr. Stark brought a bundle of apple scions which were grafted to native crab apple seedlings. Fruit trees were originally grown only for local trade -- later expanded into the nursery business. Stark Brothers developed the Stark Red Delicious Apple in 1893 and the Stark Golden Delicious Apple in 1914. Currently Stark owns the patents or exclusive propagation rights to more than 50 varieties of fruit.

MARKETS

Sales are primarily to Central South Atlantic and Southern states; limited international sales.

FACILITIES

1700 growing acres, HQ, test orchards, home nurseries, MO; nurseries in IL, MO, OK, AK.

PRODUCTS, BRAND NAMES, PRICE RANGE

Stark's most famous apples are the Red Delicious and Golden Delicious varieties. Many of the other fruit trees marketed are exclusive, patented varieties. Stark sells nut trees, berry bushes, ornamental shrubs, garden flowers, accessories.

FINANCIAL INFORMATION

	SALES	NET INCOME	PROFIT MARGIN
1981	$17,000,000*	N.A.	--

TYPE OF ADVERTISING, PROMOTION

Stark mails approximately 4,000,000 pieces of direct mail annually: approximately 3,000,000 catalogs and 1,000,000 solo mailings. Roughly 60% of the catalogs are mailed in the spring, and 40% in the fall.

LIST INFORMATION

QUANTITY MAILED:	4,000,000
AVERAGE ORDER:	$40
ACTIVE BUYERS:	200,000
TOTAL LIST:	1,000,000
LIST SOURCE:	Direct mail, space, rentals.

COMMENTS

Stark Brothers' total revenues for 1981 are estimated to be $17,000,000. Of this total an estimated 60% or $10,000,000 came from consumer mail order sales. Sales to wholesale buyers and other commercial accounts contributed the remaining estimated 40% or $7,000,000. Consumer mail order sales are broken down into the following product categories: fruit and nut trees, 70%; decorative and garden plants and shrubs, 20%; gardening accessories, sprays and fertilizers, 10%. Stark Brothers targets the male do-it-your-selfer who owns his own home, and usually three to five acres of land, in a rural or suburban area. Their customers are characteristically less mobile than the norm and are upscale in education and income. In 1980 Stark began testing telephone marketing using a phone staff to promote unadvertised sales and accessory lines and to propose substitute products for out-of-stock items. The test was reportedly successful and telephone marketing is now in place as a promotional operation.

STEREO EQUIPMENT SALES

ADDRESS, PHONE

Stereo Equipment Sales, Inc., 6730-A Santa Barbara Court, Baltimore, MD 21227. (301) 796-3980.

OWNERSHIP

Privately held; 75% of stock divided between Raymond Smith & Vincent Stransky; John Stern owns 25%.

MANAGEMENT

Raymond L. Smith, President; Vincent Stransky, Executive VP & Sec.; John Stern, VP & Treas.; Bruce W. Prince, VP; H. George Schweitzer, Ass't. Sec. & Gen. Counsel.

TYPE OF MARKETER

Mail order, retail, wholesale.

BUSINESS

Stereo Equipment Sales mail order operation is the Stereo Discounters catalog division. The company sells electronic components including radios, television and video cassette players, stereos, tape recorders, tapes and headphones by mail throughout the U.S. In addition to mail order the company wholesales and retails components in Maryland, Delaware, New Jersey and Pennsylvania. RCR, Inc. subsidiary retails components. Two Bee, Inc. is a commercial real estate agency.

COMPANY HISTORY

The business was started in Baltimore in 1971 by Benjamin Shumate. The Stereo Discounters mail order operation was started to increase the company's potential customer base by offering retail merchandise lines at a discount by mail. The company was incorporated in Maryland on January 25, 1971. In 1981 Shumate sold his 90% interest in the parent to the present owners. Stereo Equipment reported 200 employees in 1981.

MARKETS

Mail order buyers throughout U.S.; equally male/female, 20-40 years old.

FACILITIES
Headquarters and fulfillment center in Baltimore. Twenty-four retail stores in four states.

PRODUCTS, BRAND NAMES, PRICE RANGE
Stereo Discounters offers a full line of stereo, recording and video equipment and accessories. National brands include Sony, Kenwood, Sansui, Technics, Dual, TEAC, Pioneer, Panasonic, Audio-Techinca, etc.

FINANCIAL INFORMATION

	SALES	NET INCOME	PROFIT MARGIN
1981	$35,000,000*	$1,400,000*	4%*

TYPE OF ADVERTISING, PROMOTION
Stereo Discounters publishes three editions of their main catalog annually. In addition they produce several smaller special discount catalogs, including the Holiday Gift Buying Guide. Emphasis is on quality equipment at specially reduced prices.

LIST INFORMATION

QUANTITY MAILED:	4,500,000*
AVERAGE ORDER:	$70*
ACTIVE BUYERS:	150,000
TOTAL LIST:	312,000
LIST SOURCE:	Direct mail.

COMMENTS
Management reported that Stereo Equipment Sales' total revenues for 1981 were $35,000,000. This represents a 13% increase over total revenues of $31,000,000 in 1980, and 16% over $22,500,000 in 1979. Company officials report that mail order operations contributed an average of 50% of annual revenues: $10,500,000 in 1981; $9,300,000 in 1980; $6,800,000 in 1979. The remaining 70% of the parent's total revenues are generated by wholesale and retail store sales. Stereo Discounters' catalogs are 7-3/4 x 10-3/4, b&w with color cover, roughly 100 pages, and offer a $7 million inventory of merchandise. Special holiday mini-catalogs are 16 pages and offer special reductions on specific products. As an additional promotional service, Stereo Discounters publishes an IN-WATS number where "14 Professional Audio/Video Consultants" are available to take orders or answer technical questions.

STITCHERY INTERNATIONAL

ADDRESS, PHONE
Stitchery International, Inc., 204 Worcester St., Wellesley, MA 02181. Telephone: (617) 237-1744.

OWNERSHIP
Privately held; 100% of capital, consisting of 1,000 common shares with no par value, is owned by Susanne and William Knowles.

MANAGEMENT
Susanne Knowles, President; William B. Knowles, Treasurer; Daniel D. Levenson, Clerk.

TYPE OF MARKETER
Mail order, retail.

BUSINESS
Stitchery's main business is the direct mail marketing of needlecraft kits and supplies through "The Stitchery" catalog, to individual consumers and business and industrial accounts. Through a second catalog, "Pot-pour-ri," they sell a line of gifts and accessories for cooking, decorating and entertaining. In addition, the company operates one retail store in Wellesley, MA. Seasonal volume peaks are pre-Christmas and around the other holidays.

COMPANY HISTORY
Susanne and William Knowles started the business as a partnership in 1963. First-year sales were about $200,000. Since that time the company has enjoyed 19 years of continuous growth. The Stitchery is considered to be the fifth largest grossing mail order crafts company in the U.S. To offset the effects of a softening crafts market over the past five years, the company has been expanding its line of gifts. Stitchery reported 100 employees for 1981.

MARKETS
Mostly women buyers throughout the U.S. who are interested in needlecrafting and home decorating.

FACILITIES

Headquarters, mail order operations, and one retail store, all located in Wellesley, MA.

PRODUCTS, BRAND NAMES, PRICE RANGE

Needlecraft products include kits for making sweaters, skirts and jackets, samplers, afghans, tablecloths, and dollhouse furnishings. Prices range from $10 to $90 for The Stitchery kits; gifts and accessories are $10 and up.

FINANCIAL INFORMATION

	SALES	NET INCOME	PROFIT MARGIN
1981	$18,600,000*	N.A.	--

TYPE OF ADVERTISING, PROMOTION

Advertising expenses average about 20%-30% of sales. The company mails about 15,000,000 catalogs a year. The Stitchery uses magazine space advertising to promote the catalogs, for which respondents pay $1.

LIST INFORMATION

QUANTITY MAILED:	15,000,000
AVERAGE ORDER:	Stitchery-$34; Pot-pour-ri-$44
ACTIVE BUYERS:	S. - 250,000; P. - 145,000
TOTAL LIST:	1,060,000
LIST SOURCE:	Direct mail.

COMMENTS

While the top four mail order crafts companies are experiencing difficulty in profitably expanding operations, privately-held Stitchery International, ranked fifth in gross volume (crafts by mail), at its peak generated an estimated pre-tax net of 15%-20%. The company has an estimated gross margin of 55%-60%. In all Stitchery is estimated to control some 3% of the crafts-by-mail industry. Management attributes their success to four major factors: owners product knowledge and market sensitivity enable them to offer designs before the competition; good supplier relations permit high degree of exclusivity; good customer relations making for strong repeat base; low catalog production costs and light-handed promotion.

STURBRIDGE YANKEE WORKSHOP

ADDRESS, PHONE
Sturbridge Yankee Workshop, Inc., Blueberry Road, Portland, ME 04112. Telephone: (207) 754-9045.

OWNERSHIP
Wholly owned subsidiary of CML Group, Inc., of Concord, MA.

MANAGEMENT
John Riddle, President; Avis Whittaker, Vice President; Charles Leighton, Chairman of CML, officer of Sturbridge; Robert Todd, President of CML, officer of Sturbridge.

TYPE OF MARKETER
Mail order, retail.

BUSINESS
CML Group is a holding company and manufacturer of wooden hobby and craft products, boats, and sporting goods. Sturbridge is a mail order/retail subsidiary which markets early American reproductions of furniture, hardware, china and glass items, and gifts. Mail order marketing is through a series of catalogs and generates roughly 80% of Sturbridge's total annual sales. The remaining 20% of sales come from the company's four retail outlets.

COMPANY HISTORY
CML was started in 1969 and presently holds eight subsidiaries. Sturbridge was originally incorporated in Massachusetts on April 10, 1973, as New SYW Corporation. The name was changed to Sturbridge Yankee Workshop, Inc. on May 2, 1973. The company was re-incorporated in Maine on April 30, 1981 with authorized capital of 1,000 common shares at $1 par value. CML owns 100%. Sturbridge reported 80 employees in 1981.

MARKETS
Mostly female; homeowners with families -- interest in traditional and antique reproductions.

FACILITIES

H.Q., retail outlet, Portland, ME; stores in Sturbridge, MA, Mystic, CT, and Bedford, NH.

PRODUCTS, BRAND NAMES, PRICE RANGE

Unique early American and country style furniture; gifts; antique reproductions; bath and kitchen accessories; house and national brands -- price range: high end.

FINANCIAL INFORMATION

	SALES	NET INCOME	PROFIT MARGIN
1981	$12,200,000*	N.A.	--

TYPE OF ADVERTISING, PROMOTION

Approximately 10% of Sturbridge's advertising budget is allocated for ads in home and women's magazines. Main promotional emphasis is on catalog mailings and extensive use of package inserts.

LIST INFORMATION

QUANTITY MAILED: 3,500,000*
AVERAGE ORDER: $65
ACTIVE BUYERS: 100,000
TOTAL LIST: 400,000
LIST SOURCE: Direct mail (90%); space 10%.

COMMENTS

Sturbridge's total revenues for 1981 are estimated to be $12,200,000. Of the total, roughly 80% or $9.8 million are estimated to have come from mail order sales; the remaining 20% or $2.4 million is an estimate of the volume done by the company's four retail stores. Merchandise sales are broken down as follows: furniture reproductions (55%); hardware and accessories (15%); china and glass (15%); gifts (15%). The company's catalogs are 8-1/2 x 11, full color, and 45-50 pages; mailed seasonally. Customers are 75% female. Management reports that roughly 50% of the company's active buyer file are repeat buyers, due to the variety of items available for decorating themes. The quality of the merchandise and the upscale position of the company keep the average order high. Sturbridge claims to have found their niche in providing affordable "antiques" which are otherwise unavailable to the majority of consumers.

SUNNYLAND FARMS

ADDRESS, PHONE
Sunnyland Farms, Inc., P.O. Box 549, Albany, GA 31703. Telephone: (912) 436-5654.

OWNERSHIP
Privately held; W. Harry Willson and Jane S. Willson each own 50% of capital stock.

MANAGEMENT
W. Harry Willson, President and Treasurer; Calvin A. Tucker, Vice President; Jane S. Willson, Vice President, Secretary.

TYPE OF MARKETER
Mail order, wholesale.

BUSINESS
Sunnyland Farms is a producer and marketer of pecans, cashews, macadamia nuts, walnuts, pistachios and almonds. The company markets pecans in bulk quantities wholesale to distributors and retail outlets, and in gift and assortment packs to consumers. They produce their own pecans on over 1,000 acres of growing land. The producing affiliate is Willson Pecan Farm in Albany, GA. Other varieties of nuts are purchased from outside suppliers.

COMPANY HISTORY
The business was founded by Harry and Jane Willson as a pecan wholesaling operation in 1951. Willson had been farming pecans since 1941. The company was incorporated in September of 1972 in Georgia as Sunnyland Farms. Authorized capital consists of 1,000,000 shares of common stock at $1.00 par value. Sunnyland capital is owned equally by Jane and Harry Willson. The company reported 67 year-round and 83 seasonal employees in 1981.

MARKETS
Mail order sales throughout the U.S.: no international marketing. Customers are 65% female.

FACILITIES

Company leases 10,000 sq. ft. in two buildings for offices, warehouse and shelling plant in Albany, GA.

PRODUCTS, BRAND NAMES, PRICE RANGE

Stuart Pecans, Schley Pecans, Pecans-In-The-Shell, Mammoth Halves, Natural Halves, Toasted & Salted Pecans; individual and mixed gift assortments. Prices range from $8.50 to $160.00.

FINANCIAL INFORMATION

	SALES	NET INCOME	PROFIT MARGIN
1981	$10,000,000*	N.A.	--

TYPE OF ADVERTISING, PROMOTION

Approximately 90% of Sunnyland's advertising is by direct mail. The company publishes one main catalog annually, which is supplemented with small gift flyers during the year. The remaining 10% of advertising is space in national magazines.

LIST INFORMATION

QUANTITY MAILED:	4,000,000*
AVERAGE ORDER:	$44
ACTIVE BUYERS:	145,000*
TOTAL LIST:	370,070
LIST SOURCE:	Direct mail, space.

COMMENTS

Sunnyland Farms total revenues for 1981 are estimated to be over $10,000,000. Of this total approximately $8,000,000 are estimated to be mail order sales to consumers. The remaining $2,000,000 is estimated bulk sales of pecans to wholesale accounts. Sunnyland has reportedly developed a significant number of annual repeat buyers in its active buyer file, who buy assortment packs each year both for personal consumption and for use as gifts. Sunnyland's main catalog, "Pecans: plain & fancy," is published each year. The catalogs are full-color, 6 x 8-1/4, 40 pages, offering an assortment of nuts and fruits, pecan candies and cakes. Special gift flyers are eight-page selection and ordering device combinations. The company offers 24-hour shipping or a pre-ordering program allowing customer to specify dates for order delivery. Major promotional emphasis is being placed on quality gift assortments, not available in retail stores.

SWISS COLONY

ADDRESS, PHONE

The Swiss Colony, 1112 7th Avenue, Monroe, WI 53566. Telephone: (608) 328-8812.

OWNERSHIP

Privately held; 95% of capital stock owned by Raymond Kubly & family; 5% owned by Robert Ableman.

MANAGEMENT

Raymond Kubly, President; Robert Ableman, Executive Vice President; Kurt Schwager, Vice President, Sales.

TYPE OF MARKETER

Mail order, retail.

BUSINESS

Swiss Colony markets cheese packages, meats, gift food packages, desserts, candies, cookies and cakes. The company processes its own cold-packed cheeses and makes its own chocolates and pastries. Meats and fruits are purchased from outside manufacturers. Swiss Colony sells its products wholesale to other mail order houses, through its catalogs to consumers and through a chain of retail stores. The company employs 400 to 2,400 people depending on the season.

COMPANY HISTORY

The business was started in 1926 by Raymond Kubly, Sr. While attending the University of Wisconsin, Mr. Kubly began marketing cheeses by mail. Upon graduation he formed The Swiss Colony mail order company. During the next 55 years the mail order business was expanded, a retail franchise system was developed, and the company began producing some of its own food items.

MARKETS

Customers throughout the U.S. are middle-income, 70% female. Some corporate gift business.

FACILITIES
Headquarters, baking and processing facilities, and mail order operation all at Monroe location.

PRODUCTS, BRAND NAMES, PRICE RANGE
Swiss Colony catalogs contain an average of over 600 items, with the cost of an average item at approximately $12.00. The figures below are for total mail order sales, and do not include revenues from retail operations.

FINANCIAL INFORMATION

	SALES	NET INCOME	PROFIT MARGIN
1981	$50,000,000*	N.A.	--

TYPE OF ADVERTISING, PROMOTION
The company mails several catalog editions per year. They also mail computerized letters to past buyers and a special reminder to gift-giving buyers. Some space advertising in shelter and women's magazines.

LIST INFORMATION
QUANTITY MAILED:	20,000,000*
AVERAGE ORDER:	$40
ACTIVE BUYERS:	1,034,000
TOTAL LIST:	2,080,000
LIST SOURCE:	Direct mail.

COMMENTS
Swiss Colony's mail order operations contributed over $50 million in sales in 1981. No accurate figure was available for the company's chain of 150 retail outlets. Swiss Colony uses an IBM 370-140 and one IBM 4341 mail order processing computer for maintaining its buyer file and processing over 1,000,000 orders annually. The system tracks individual orders, provides daily statistics, and is programmed to send letters each year to major buyers reminding them what they bought and for whom in the previous year. Swiss Colony mailed approximately 20 million catalogs in 1981 with an overall estimated response rate of 5.2%. Management reports that 80% of sales are made between November 1 and December 15.

THE TALBOTS

ADDRESS, PHONE

The Talbots, 175 Beal St., Hingham, MA 02043. Telephone: (617) 749-7600.

OWNERSHIP

Unit of publicly-held General Mills' Specialty Retailing Group.

MANAGEMENT

William DeJonge, President; Barry Marchessialt, Vice President of Merchandising and Marketing; Polly Paxton, List Manager; Randolph Talbot, Chairman.

TYPE OF MARKETER

Mail order, retail.

BUSINESS

Talbots is a marketer of classic apparel for women through its mail order operations and 30 retail stores. The company is positioned to offer a full wardrobe to the middle to upper scale woman. Products range from sportswear, dresses and coats, to accessories and sleepwear. Products are primarily exclusive designs and designer brands. The Talbots does offer some men's sportswear in their catalog. Clothing accounts for 90% of their sales, while remaining 10% is gift items.

COMPANY HISTORY

Rudolph and Nancy Talbot started the company in 1947 and sold it to General Mills in 1973. In fiscal 1976, after initially poor years under General Mills, sales increased by 46%. In the past eight years The Talbots has proven itself to be the most autonomous subsidiary of General Mills, and probably its most successful mail order venture. William DeJonge was brought into the company by Rudolph Talbot, and succeeded him as president in 1978.

MARKETS

Primarily U.S. market; middle to upper scale females. Peak sales are in the fall.

FACILITIES
Company headquarters and mail order operations are in Hingham, MA; retail stores in northeastern U.S.

PRODUCTS, BRAND NAMES, PRICE RANGE
Designer brands of clothing include David Brooks, Sero, Gant, Herman Geist, Diva, Gordon of Philadelphia, Jamison, Ciao, Austin Hill, and exclusive designs for the Talbots. Price range $5.00 - $200.00.

FINANCIAL INFORMATION

	SALES	NET INCOME	PROFIT MARGIN
1981	$75,000,000*	N.A.	--

TYPE OF ADVERTISING, PROMOTION
The Talbots publishes eight catalogs and mails approximately 18,000,000 each year. The catalogs are full-color, 8 x 11, 64 pages. In addition the company uses space ads in national women's and upscale magazines.

LIST INFORMATION

QUANTITY MAILED:	24,000,000
AVERAGE ORDER:	$85
ACTIVE BUYERS:	318,400
TOTAL LIST:	800,000
LIST SOURCE:	Direct mail, space.

COMMENTS
Total revenues for 1981 are estimated $75 million. Of the total, an estimated $40 million or roughly 60% of revenues came from mail order sales. The remaining 40% we estimate was generated by The Talbots chain of retail stores. The Talbots contributed an estimated 16% of total 1981 revenues to General Mills' group of retail, collectible and furniture companies. Their sales increase of 18% in 1981 was well ahead of overall group sales increase of 6.4% or $379 million. The Specialty Retailing Group--Talbots, Eddie Bauer, LeeWards, and Wall Papers To Go -- turned in an overall sales increase of 15% for 1981. The company's Shop At Home mail order division mails approximately 3,000,000 copies of each of its eight catalogs each year. Catalogs typically contain less merchandise than the average retail store; the largest selection is in the fall edition.

NORM THOMPSON

ADDRESS, PHONE
Norm Thompson Outfitters, Inc. 13700 N.W. Science Park Dr., Portland, OR 97229. Phone (503) 644-2666.

OWNERSHIP
Privately held; authorized capital consists of 500 shares of common stock, no par value; majority stockholder is John R. Emrick.

MANAGEMENT
John R. Emrick, President; Howard B. Logan, Vice President; Daniel R. Indgjerd, Vice President, Marketing; Louis D. Jaffe, Comptroller.

TYPE OF MARKETER
Mail order, retail.

BUSINESS
Norm Thompson is a mail order and retail marketer of a wide variety of men's and women's casual and outdoor apparel and accessories, decorative home furnishings, gifts and specialty food items. A major percentage of the company's merchandise mix is imported from around the world. Thompson sells merchandise through their catalogs and three retail outlets in Oregon. Sales are reportedly heaviest in the fall. The company employed 90 people in 1981.

COMPANY HISTORY
The company was started as a mail order business in Portland, OR by B.A. Alport in 1949. The original product line was rapidly expanded from fishing flies and other tackle to include quality sportswear. The first retail outlet was opened in 1950. The company has since added a store in the Portland Airport terminal, and their newest outlet in Eugene, OR. The business was purchased by Parker Pen in 1973. In 1981 it was purchased from Parker by John Emrick, Howard Logan and outside investors.

MARKETS
Thompson sells throughout the U.S., no international marketing.

FACILITIES

The company leases 57,000 sq. ft. for offices and operating and warehouse space at Portland location.

PRODUCTS, BRAND NAMES, PRICE RANGE

Products are high quality domestic and imported casual apparel and sportswear, such as shearling wool jackets, coats, dresses, sleepwear and footwear as well as outdoor accessories, knives, luggage, gift and food items. Wide price range, up to $2,500.00.

FINANCIAL INFORMATION

	SALES	NET INCOME	PROFIT MARGIN
1981	$15,000,000*	N.A.	--

TYPE OF ADVERTISING, PROMOTION

Approximately 80% of the company's advertising is done through full-color catalogs that are published seasonally. Space advertisements appear in many magazines such as Smithsonian, New Yorker, Yankee.

LIST INFORMATION

QUANTITY MAILED:	6,500,000*
AVERAGE ORDER:	$65
ACTIVE BUYERS:	180,000
TOTAL LIST:	500,000*
LIST SOURCE:	Direct mail (80%), space (20%).

COMMENTS

Norm Thompson's estimated total 1981 revenues of $15,000,000 represent a 25% increase over reported revenues of $12,000,000 for 1980. Of the 1981 total, approximately 90% or $13,500,000 is estimated to have come from mail order operations. The remaining 10% or $1,500,000 was generated by retail sales. The Thompson 1982 Winter Catalog was 24 pages and contained 125 different items. The company's specialty import position allows mail order buyers to "Shop the World" for upscale fashions and gifts. Thompson is known for their trademark "You Be The Judge" return policy, guaranteeing that products can be returned for refund or replacement at any time for the duration of the normal life of the product. Many of Thompson's unique import items are available only through their catalogs.

TIME-LIFE BOOKS

ADDRESS, PHONE
Time-Life Books Inc., 777 Duke Street, Alexandria, VA 22314. Telephone: (703) 960-5000.

OWNERSHIP
A wholly-owned subsidiary of Time, Incorporated, New York, NY 10020.

MANAGEMENT
Joan D. Manley, Chairman; Carl G. Jaeger, President; John Steven Maxwell and David J. Walsh, Vice Presidents; Nicholas Benton, Vice President - Public Relations; George Constable, Managing Editor.

TYPE OF MARKETER
Mail order.

BUSINESS
Publishes book series sold primarily by mail plus single-title reprints of contemporary fiction and non-fiction for the mail order market. In its 20-year history, TLB has published 603 different titles in 28 series, as well as 84 single titles. Also publishes Time-Life Records -- producing and marketing 166 record albums of both classical and popular music in the past 15 years. TLB is the largest entity in the Time Inc. Books Group which also includes Little, Brown and Co. and Book-of-the-Month Club.

COMPANY HISTORY
Time-Life Books was started as a division of Time Inc. in January 1961 by Jerry Hardy, who came from Doubleday. Hardy and Managing Editor Ross developed the idea of publishing and selling books in a continuity series. TLB has launched at least one new series every year. Foreign operations were added in 1971. It is now the largest book publisher in the U.S. in sales. Books are published in 30 languages and marketed throughout the world.

MARKETS
U.S., Canada, U.K., Europe, Asia, South America, New Mexico, Australia.

FACILITIES

Editing and publishing headquarters in Alexandria, VA; subscription offices in Chicago, IL.

PRODUCTS, BRAND NAMES, PRICE RANGE

Books in the current series: cooking, gardening, health, history, home repair and improvement, and photography. Records include classical, jazz, and country and western music as well as musicals. Unit price: books, $12; records, $25.

FINANCIAL INFORMATION

	SALES	NET INCOME	PROFIT MARGIN
1981	$300,000,000*	$12,000,000*	4%*

TYPE OF ADVERTISING, PROMOTION

Direct mail promotions of TLB's series, single-title and continuity book and record programs are mailed to house and rented lists. Space ads appear in magazines, newspapers and trade publications.

LIST INFORMATION

QUANTITY MAILED:	60,000,000*
AVERAGE ORDER:	$20 to $200*
ACTIVE BUYERS:	4,000,000*
TOTAL LIST:	20,000,000*
LIST SOURCE:	Direct mail, space.

COMMENTS

Time-Life Books is the leader in U.S. mail order distribution of books sold in specific series. The figure above is an estimate of TLB's total mail order sales for records and books. Of the approximately 39 million books sold by TLB in 1981, over 12 million were sold outside the U.S. and Canada. Major overseas offices are in Amsterdam, London, Tokyo; additional offices in Barcelona, Hong Kong, Mexico City, Munich, Paris, Rio de Janeiro, Singapore, and Sydney. Book publishing by TLB, Book-of-the-Month Club, and Little, Brown and Co. accounted for 16% of Time Inc.'s revenues in 1981. In addition the company sold over 1,000,000 record albums in 1981. TLB's earnings were down in the first and second quarters of 1981 reportedly due to a weakening international market and increased editorial costs. Management's hopes for an earnings increase based on the new book series "Library of Health" so far are not realized.

TOG SHOP

ADDRESS, PHONE
The Tog Shop, Lester Square, Americus, GA 31709.
Telephone: (912) 924-8801.

OWNERSHIP
Privately held; 100% of capital stock owned by the
Rylander family.

MANAGEMENT
James D. Rylander, Chairman; Richard Hewitt,
President; Sally B. Stringfellow, Executive Vice
President; James B. Yawn, Vice President; G. Carl
Tott, Vice President.

TYPE OF MARKETER
Mail order.

BUSINESS
The Tog Shop is primarily a mail order marketer of
classic branded sportswear, shoes and accessories,
and terry cloth casual apparel for women. In addition, catalogs contain limited offerings of men's
apparel, gifts, food items, and decorative home
accessories. Tog Shop has two subsidiary operations: Sea Island Manufacturing, apparel manufacturer which sells 80% of its merchandise to
parent; Gertrude Davenport Division, which handles
advertising and merchandise buying for parent.

COMPANY HISTORY
The business was started in 1952 as a terry cloth
apparel manufacturing partnership between Emory
Rylander, Jr. and Catherine Rylander. Catalog
operations were started in 1956 as an off-shoot of
the company's wholesale terry cloth sportswear
business. In 1973 focus of the catalog shifted away
from terry cloth items toward classic branded products. Currently, classic sportswear accounts for
about 80% of the mix. In 1977 Tog Shop acquired
subsidiary Gertrude Davenport.

MARKETS
Tog Shop sells by mail throughout U.S.; customers
are 95% female, mid to upscale.

FACILITIES
Headquarters, manufacturing, 90,000 sq. ft. ware-house, and wholesale outlet in Americus, GA.

PRODUCTS, BRAND NAMES, PRICE RANGE
Apparel such as robes, beachwear, loungewear and swimwear, classic coordinates, dresses, pant suits, footwear, purses, scarves, etc. House and national brands--Etienne Aigner, Vera's, Town & Country, Daniel Green, Vitality, etc.

FINANCIAL INFORMATION

	SALES	NET INCOME	PROFIT MARGIN
1981	$22,500,000*	N.A.	--

TYPE OF ADVERTISING, PROMOTION
About 98% of Tog Shop's advertising is through the company's four seasonal catalogs. The catalogs are 5-1/2 x 8-1/2, full color, about 128 pages, and roughly 10,000,000 are mailed per year. The company uses a minimal amount of space advertising.

LIST INFORMATION

QUANTITY MAILED:	10,000,000
AVERAGE ORDER:	$61
ACTIVE BUYERS:	300,000
TOTAL LIST:	1,000,000+
LIST SOURCE:	Direct mail (98%), space (2%).

COMMENTS
The Tog Shop's 1981 estimated revenues of $22.5 million represent an increase of roughly 13% over 1980. Approximately 90% or $20,000,000 of the total income comes from mail order merchandise sales. The remaining 10% came from Sea Island Manufacturing operations. Aside from the company's four main catalogs, Tog Shop added a new catalog operation entitled Lester Square in 1978 to market special lines of designer sportswear. The company's main mer-chandise lines are positioned at the affordable end of the upper scale market. Catalogs sell coordinated outfits and accessories in the $25 to $175 price range, with additional offerings of upscale coats, jewelry, etc. Lester Square catalogs are an effort to increase penetration in the upscale market.

UNICOVER CORPORATION

ADDRESS, PHONE

Unicover Corporation, 1 Unicover Center, Cheyenne, WY 82001. Telephone (307) 634-5911.

OWNERSHIP

Privately held; majority of the total 80,000 shares of common stock are owned by James A. and H. Albert Helzer.

MANAGEMENT

James A. Helzer, President; James Willms, Executive Vice President; Roger Carstens, Vice President; Robert Hahn, Vice President - Manufacturing; H. Albert Helzer, Treasurer; Perry Dray, Secretary.

TYPE OF MARKETER

Mail order.

BUSINESS

Unicover Corporation uses the tradename Fleetwood to market first-day covers, commemoratives, mint stamps, and porcelain. Marketing is exclusively by mail. Through its subsidiary The China Stamp Agency of North America, Unicover is the official representative of People's Republic of China stamps in the U.S. Company manufactures vinyl products such as stamp albums and holders for first-day covers.

COMPANY HISTORY

Unicover Corporation was founded in Cheyenne in 1968. James A. Helzer & Company, marketing first-day covers, was founded in 1962. The tradename "Fleetwood" dates back to 1936 when "Fleetwood Cover Service" was created by Milnor Peck. In 1968 James Helzer acquired the tradename "Fleetwood" from Peck, moved the inventory to Cheyenne, and incorporated Unicover. Began marketing limited edition porcelain in late 1979.

MARKETS

Mail order customers in the U.S., Canada, Europe, Asia, Australia.

FACILITIES
Corporate headquarters, mail order operations, and manufacturing are located in Cheyenne, Wyoming.

PRODUCTS, BRAND NAMES, PRICE RANGE
First-day covers are usually priced at $2-$3. Older issues range from about $3 up to collections selling for over $2,000. Prices for "The Fleetwood Collection" of limited edition porcelain range from $39 to $50 a plate. $20 for bells.

FINANCIAL INFORMATION

	SALES	NET INCOME	PROFIT MARGIN
1981	$18,000,000*	N.A.	--

TYPE OF ADVERTISING, PROMOTION
Company uses three major marketing approaches: (1) a 38-page catalog that features back issues of first-day covers; (2) direct mail advising customers of new first-day covers; (3) space ads in magazines such as National Geographic, Smithsonian.

LIST INFORMATION

QUANTITY MAILED:	9,000,000
AVERAGE ORDER:	N.A.
ACTIVE BUYERS:	178,000
TOTAL LIST:	200,000
LIST SOURCE:	Direct mail, space.

COMMENTS
Unicover reported that total 1981 sales passed $18,000,000, representing an increase of approximately 29% over 1980 revenues. Though no figures were available, the company reported that profits were up in the past six months. Unicover considers its major competitor in philatelics to be the Postal Commemorative Society. Fleetwood's largest continuity programs include U.S. First Day Cover Society, Canada First Day Cover Society, First Day Cover of the Month Society (offering first day covers of governments around the world), and Westminster Society (collectors of issues of the British Commonwealth). Unlike members of book and record continuity clubs, members of these societies take all issues available or resign their memberships. Unicover owns and operates the National First Day Cover Museum in Cheyenne its corporate collection--valued at nearly $1,000,000. Fleetwood's numbered editions of porcelain are usually limited to 5000-7500, with 9500 being the largest.

UNITED SERVICES AUTOMOBILE ASSN.

ADDRESS, PHONE

United Services Automobile Assoc., USAA Building, San Antonio, TX 78288. Phone (512) 690-2211.

OWNERSHIP

USAA is owned by the company's policyholders, officers and employees.

MANAGEMENT

Robert F. McDermott, President; Theodore J. Michel, Executive VP; George H. Ensley, Executive VP - Finance, Treasurer; William McCrae, Senior VP; Robert P. Rennie, Executive Dir. - Marketing.

TYPE OF MARKETER

Mail order.

BUSINESS

USAA offers all forms of personal property and casualty insurance, life insurance, and mutual, money market and income funds. Services are offered exclusively to active duty and reserve military personnel, the National Guard, and military cadets. The USAA parent company and subsidiary USAA Casualty Insurance Co. offer property and casualty coverage. Other subsidiaries are USAA Life Insurance Co. and USAA Investment Management Co.

COMPANY HISTORY

A small group of military officers started the company in 1922 in San Antonio when they were having difficulty finding adequate insurance programs. It began as a non-profit seller of auto insurance. Household goods coverage and investment funds were added later. The company has experienced substantial growth since the late 1960s, when current president McDermott took over.

MARKETS

Company sells to military officers domestically and at overseas bases; 95% men, average age 35.

FACILITIES

HQ, San Antonio; offices in Frankfurt, London, NY, WA, CA, FL and CO.

PRODUCTS, BRAND NAMES, PRICE RANGE

USAA markets automobile, life and property insurance, mutual, income and money market funds.

FINANCIAL INFORMATION

	SALES	NET INCOME	PROFIT MARGIN
1980	$1,000,000,000+	N.A.	--

TYPE OF ADVERTISING, PROMOTION

Space ads (50%) in military newspapers and magazines to attract new customers. Direct mail (50%) to renew or increase coverage for existing customers. Direct mail consists of folders, brochures, looseleaf ads.

LIST INFORMATION

QUANTITY MAILED:	10,000,000
AVERAGE ORDER:	$300
ACTIVE BUYERS:	1,205,000
TOTAL LIST:	N.A.
LIST SOURCE:	Direct mail, space.

COMMENTS

With over $1 billion in total annual premium income, United Services Automobile Association ranks not only as one of the largest mail order insurance companies, but as one of the largest U.S. mail order marketers in any product segment. Total premium income passed the $1 billion mark in 1980 compared to 1979 totals of $720 million for Property & Casualty Operations and $45 million for Life Insurance Operations. Company officials expected total insurance in force by the end of 1981 to reach $7 billion, with property and casualty sales passing the $1 billion mark by early 1982. Automobile insurance is the company's leading product category generating roughly 70% of total sales. USAA claims to be the ninth largest insurer in the country with 1,200,000 current policyholders. The company employs 5,000 people.

U.S. GENERAL SUPPLY

ADDRESS, PHONE

U.S. General Supply Corp. 100 Commercial St., Plainview, NY 11803. Telephone: (516) 576-9100.

OWNERSHIP

Privately held; 100% of capital stock is owned by the officers.

MANAGEMENT

Murray Harrow, Chairman of the Board; Harold Rashbaum, President; Tom Bauer, Executive Vice President; Lewis Rocco, Vice President-Finance; Beth Sterling, List Manager.

TYPE OF MARKETER

Mail order.

BUSINESS

U.S. General Supply Corp. markets an extensive line of name-brand tools, hardware and automotive supplies at discount prices. About 95 percent of sales come from the company's direct mail operations, with the remainder coming from four catalog showrooms in the New York metropolitan area. U.S. General does no manufacturing of its own but markets over 6,000 products supplied by major tool and hardware manufacturers. The company reported 200 employees in 1981.

COMPANY HISTORY

Murray Harrow and Harold Rashbaum started the company in the mid 1950s in New York City as a mail order marketer of tools and hardware. Operations moved to Jericho, NY, where they remained for 15 years. Around 1980, the company tripled its operating space by moving to new facilities in Plainview, underscoring growth in business. The first catalog showroom was started in 1973, and three more were added around 1980.

MARKETS

The company sells by mail throughout the U.S.; customers are 95% male, age 40+, income $20,000.

FACILITIES
Offices, mail order, and fulfillment in Plainview; catalog showrooms in Long Island and Paramus, NJ.

PRODUCTS, BRAND NAMES, PRICE RANGE
Wide variety of tools, hardware and automotive products, including every major hand and electric line in the U.S. Brand names include Black & Decker and Stanley, but company markets all major brands. Prices range from $2 to $1,000+.

FINANCIAL INFORMATION

	SALES	**NET INCOME**	**PROFIT MARGIN**
1981	$28,000,000*	N.A.	--

TYPE OF ADVERTISING, PROMOTION
Approximately 95% of U.S. General's advertising is through direct mail packages to generate catalog inquiries. In addition they use some inquiry-generating space ads in shelter and home improvement magazines.

LIST INFORMATION
QUANTITY MAILED:	10,000,000+*
AVERAGE ORDER:	$36
ACTIVE BUYERS:	615,000
TOTAL LIST:	3,000,000
LIST SOURCE:	Direct mail, rentals, space.

COMMENTS
U.S. General Supply's estimated total revenues from mail order and catalog showroom operations for 1981 of $28,000,000 represent a 23% increase over the estimated 1980 level of $22,700,000. The company has reportedly experienced significant growth in recent years, with one company official reporting that the increase in the past five years was comparable to total growth for the preceding twenty years. Management attributes their success to aggressive promotional campaigns and a growing national interest in do-it-yourself home repairs and improvements. U.S. General places heavy promotional emphasis on their unique position: offering quality tools and equipment at discount prices. The company's main catalogs are published in January and July, and flyers are mailed seven times a year. The catalogs are 8 x 11, black and white, 196 pages. Flyers are digest size and offer about 220 items.

U.S. SALES CORPORATION

ADDRESS, PHONE

U.S. Sales Corporation, 9351 Laurel Canyon Boulevard, Arleta, CA 91331. Telephone: (213) 875-0404.

OWNERSHIP

Privately held; Ronald Goldman and Theodore Slavin each own 50% of capital stock.

MANAGEMENT

Ronald D. Goldman, President; Theodore J. Slavin, Secretary; Steven J. Manning, Vice President of Market Development; Robert Menick, Controller; Nick Schellong, List Manager.

TYPE OF MARKETER

Mail order.

BUSINESS

U.S. Sales Corporation is a 100% mail order marketer of general merchandise including soft goods, hardware, automotive accessories, jewelry, gifts, apparel and health-related products. In addition to merchandise sold via U.S. Sales direct mail packages, the company has a catalog mail order subsidiary, Mail Marketing, Inc., which shares corporate facilities and sells a similar line of merchandise. U.S. Purchasing Exchange is the company's other mail order operating division.

COMPANY HISTORY

The business was founded in November of 1961 by Ronald Goldman, and incorporated on April 19, 1963, in California as United States Sales Corporation. Authorized capital consists of 75,000 shares of common stock with a $50 par value. Theodore Slavin purchased 50% of capital in 1963. Wholly-owned subsidiary Mail Marketing, Inc. was incorporated in California on August 4, 1969. U.S. Sales reported 400 employees in 1981.

MARKETS

Mail order sales throughout U.S., no international marketing. Customers are 65% female.

FACILITIES
All of U.S. Sales and subsidiaries' headquarters in
10,000 sq. ft. at Arleta, CA location.

PRODUCTS, BRAND NAMES, PRICE RANGE
Apparel, tools and hardware, exercise and health
products, automotive and houseware items, gifts,
jewelry, watches, etc. Prices range from $5.00 to
$50.00. All merchandise sold under outside brand
names.

FINANCIAL INFORMATION

	SALES	NET INCOME	PROFIT MARGIN
1981	$30,000,000*	N.A.	--

TYPE OF ADVERTISING, PROMOTION
U.S. Sales and its subsidiaries rely solely on direct
mail for all advertising and promotion. U.S. Purchasing Exchange uses circulars and direct mail
packages. Mail Marketing mails catalogs containing
similar lines of merchandise.

LIST INFORMATION
QUANTITY MAILED:	10-15,000,000
AVERAGE ORDER:	$15
ACTIVE BUYERS:	2,000,000
TOTAL LIST:	3,408,000
LIST SOURCE:	Direct mail.

COMMENTS
The sales figure above is an estimate of total revenues from U.S. Sales and U.S. Purchasing Exchange
mail order operations for 1981. No accurate estimate
of Mail Marketing, Inc. sales was available. This
represents an estimated increase of 43% or $9 million
over the 1978 estimate of $21 million, and manage-
ment reports that they expect increased growth and
continued profitability. U.S. Purchasing Exchange
direct mail packages combine mini-catalogs with a
variety of incentive, premium and sweepstake offers.
A typical mailing contained (1) a full-color, 8 x
5-1/4, 32-page catalog offering 125 different items;
(2) a Mystery Bingo premium offering several surprise gifts (with $15 minimum order) (3) $100,000
Giant Jackpot sweepstakes insert; (4) a free gift
bonus insert for placing an order; (5) "Shop Early"
Bonus Gift insert for purchasing within seven days;
(6) "Magic Number" insert offering a bonus gift for
99¢.

UNITY BUYING SERVICE

ADDRESS, PHONE
Unity Buying Service Co., Inc., 840 South Broadway, Hicksville, NY 11801. Phone: (516) 576-9000.

OWNERSHIP
Publicy held; traded AMSE; 68% of stock owned by Friedman family; 136,973 common shares outstanding; the company paid no 1981 dividend.

MANAGEMENT
Albert Friedman, President & Chairman; Bernard Zimmerman, Executive VP; VPs: Arnold Gottlieb, Merchandising; Robert Muzzy, Operations; Peter Muzzy, Adv.; Irwin Eyerman, Treas. & Sec.

TYPE OF MARKETER
Mail order.

BUSINESS
Unity is basically a "factory buying club," charging a membership fee of $6 for one year, $10 for two years, and $14 for three years. This catalog mail order merchandiser then offers a wide variety of consumer products to its members at discounts of up to 50% off suggested retail prices. Management reports that business is seasonal, with peak sales occuring in October through December. Unity employs from 500 to 1500 persons, according to seasonal needs.

COMPANY HISTORY
Unity's predecessor company was started by Louis Friedman in 1932 as Louis Watch Co., and was incorporated in 1971 in Delaware. Unity Buying Service Co., Inc. was established as a Delaware corporation in February of 1972, when the shareholders of five affiliated New York corporations-- Unity Buying Service, Louis Watch, Inland Wholesale Distributors, Art National Manufacturers, and Computer Profitronics--exchanged shares of their stock for shares in the newly-formed corporation.

MARKETS
Ninety-five percent married men with incomes between $15,000 and $25,000.

FACILITIES

H.Q. and warehouse in Hicksville, NY; warehouse and distribution centers in CA, IL, & GA.

PRODUCTS, BRAND NAMES, PRICE RANGE

Name brand merchandise offered at a discount includes clothing, footwear, jewelry, cosmetics, housewares, home furnishings, and general merchandise of all kinds.

FINANCIAL INFORMATION

	SALES	NET INCOME	PROFIT MARGIN
1980	$125,245,470	$(1,182,215)	-0-

TYPE OF ADVERTISING, PROMOTION

Unity publishes a large, 468-page catalog once a year, available to members for a $1 fee. They promote their club memberships, catalogs, and merchandising services extensively by mail to rented lists.

LIST INFORMATION

QUANTITY MAILED:	8,000,000+
AVERAGE ORDER:	$50
ACTIVE BUYERS:	1,244,000
TOTAL LIST:	2,169,000
LIST SOURCE:	Direct mail.

COMMENTS

Management attributes loss for the year ending January 31, 1981 to lower sales volume of the factory buying club operations, combined with added expenses incurred by new member solicitation programs. Lower sales and further losses reportedly continued for the six months ending July 31, 1981, but management anticipated that a current major reorganization plan would bring a profitable fourth quarter (the company's peak sales season), and that the full benefits of the plan would be realized for fiscal 1983. Unity's wholly-owned subsidiaries include Mail Marketing & Fulfillment Corporation (credit card direct mail marketing), Beautiful Visions, Inc. (cosmetics by mail), and the recently acquired Sunset House, Inc. (mail order marketer of a variety of specialty merchandise).

MONTGOMERY WARD

ADDRESS, PHONE

Montgomery Ward & Co., Inc., 535 West Chicago Ave., Chicago, IL 60671. Telephone: (312) 467-2000.

OWNERSHIP

Wholly-owned subsidiary of publicly-held Mobil Corporation of New York.

MANAGEMENT

Stephen L. Pistner, President and COO; Robert Harrell, Executive Vice President-Merchandising; Chett A. Eckman, Executive Vice President-Catalog Operations.

TYPE OF MARKETER

Mail order, retail.

BUSINESS

Montgomery Ward is the fifth largest marketer of general merchandise in the U.S. Reportedly 20% of the company's sales come from mail order, 196 conventional catalog stores, and 1,428 catalog sales agencies. The major portion of their sales (80%) are from the company's retail operations including Ward stores and Jefferson Ward stores. In addition, Ward operates one of the largest U.S. auto clubs, Montgomery Ward Life Insurance Co., and the Montgomery Ward Credit Corporation.

COMPANY HISTORY

Montgomery Ward founded the company in 1872. Until after WWII, all of the company's sales were generated through catalog operations. From the outset the company sold general merchandise and saw Sears and Penney's as its major competitors. The company was incorporated in Delaware in 1960. In 1976 Mobil Corporation, which already held 54% of Marcor (Montgomery Ward holding company), acquired the remaining 46%. Much of Ward's top management was replaced at this time.

MARKETS

Ward's mail order buyers are 50% female; catalog sales throughout U.S.

FACILITIES
Headquarters, Chicago; catalog stores and agencies in 49 states; retail stores in 41 states.

PRODUCTS, BRAND NAMES, PRICE RANGE
Hard lines: tools, appliances, furniture, camping gear, lawn and garden equipment, etc. Softlines: women's, men's and children's apparel, sleepwear, hosiery, etc. House brands plus some national names: DuPont, Wrangler, Hanes, Michelin.

FINANCIAL INFORMATION
	SALES	NET INCOME	PROFIT MARGIN
1981	$5,743,000,000	($160,000,000)	-0-

TYPE OF ADVERTISING, PROMOTION
Two general merchandise catalogs--fall/winter and spring/summer. Fourteen special and promotional sale catalogs total 49,000 pages per year.

LIST INFORMATION
QUANTITY MAILED:	27,000,000
AVERAGE ORDER:	N.A.
ACTIVE BUYERS:	N.A.
TOTAL LIST:	8,700,000
LIST SOURCE:	Direct mail, list rental.

COMMENTS
In 1981 Ward reported that combined catalog operations contributed 20% of their $5.7 billion in total sales, or $1.14 billion. Of this total for catalog operations, approximately 55%, or $627 million, were non-store sales. Reportedly 18% of non-store orders were placed by mail; 82% were placed via telephone ordering numbers. The $1.14 billion in catalog sales in 1981 represents a 5.8% drop from the 1980 total of $1.21 billion, and a 10% decrease from the 1979 total of $1.27 billion. Ward's considerable annual losses were slightly improved from a reported ($162 million) in 1980, to ($160 million) in 1981. Company officials reported that this figure included $30 million in write-offs due to the closing of unprofitable Ward retail stores. The company will reportedly focus on Jefferson Ward lines of lower-priced merchandise in all of the operations to improve margins.

WARSHAWSKY/WHITNEY

ADDRESS, PHONE
Warshawsky/Whitney, 1106 S. Wabash Ave., Chicago, IL 60616. Telephone: (312) 431-6000.

OWNERSHIP
Privately held; 100% of capital stock is owned by the officers. Principal owner is Roy Warshawsky.

MANAGEMENT
Roy Warshawsky, President, Seymour Gold, Secretary; Norman Schomo, Vice President; Thomas Musgrave, Controller; Wes Hacker, List Manager.

TYPE OF MARKETER
Mail order, retail.

BUSINESS
Warshawsky and Company and its wholly-owned subsidiary J.S. Whitney are mail order and retail marketers of automotive parts, tool sets and automotive equipment, parts and accessories for recreational vehicles, trucks and motorcycles, stereo equipment and auto novelties. The company sells merchandise by mail to consumers, through retail outlets in the Chicago area, and wholesale to distributors, parts stores and automotive garages.

COMPANY HISTORY
The original Warshawsky and Company was established in 1915 in Chicago, Il, by the late Israel R. Warshawsky. The company filed a reorganization plan subsequent to bankruptcy filing in 1937. It was reincorporated in Delaware in January of 1938. Present ownership succeeded to control in 1941. Subsidiary J.C. Whitney filed a petition for arrangement under Chapter XI of the National Bankruptcy Act on June 25, 1979. Warshawsky/ Whitney reported 700 employees in 1981.

MARKETS
Mail order sales throughout the U.S.; customers are 99% male; median age 35; median income: $18,500.

FACILITIES
Headquarters, retail store and mail order operations, warehousing (935,000 sq. ft.).

PRODUCTS, BRAND NAMES, PRICE RANGE
Parts and accessories for virtually all makes and years of American and foreign automobiles; painting and body working accessories; power and hand tools; testing equipment and gauges; multi-lingual repair manuals and guides. Mid to lowscale.

FINANCIAL INFORMATION

	SALES	NET INCOME	PROFIT MARGIN
1981	$91,000,000*	N.A.	--

TYPE OF ADVERTISING, PROMOTION
Warshawsky/Whitney market products through the four annual editions of their catalogs. Direct mail is also used to sell merchandise wholesale to distributors and garages. The company uses space advertising in Road & Track, Motor Trend.

LIST INFORMATION

QUANTITY MAILED:	70,000,000*
AVERAGE ORDER:	$10 - $300
ACTIVE BUYERS:	1,327,898
TOTAL LIST:	2,327,859
LIST SOURCE:	Direct mail.

COMMENTS
Warshawsky/J.C. Whitney is one of the oldest and largest marketers of auto accessories and parts. The company's total sales for 1980 were estimated to be $90,000,000. Total sales in 1981 are estimated to have reached $91,300,000 with net earnings reportedly slightly ahead of the previous year. Warshawsky/Whitney publishes their "Everything Automotive" catalogs of parts and accessories four times per year, and mails an estimated 70,000,000 pieces annually. Their list is available by a variety of segments including buyers by type of automobile, type of credit card, state, amount or purchase, etc. The Chapter XI petition filed by J.C. Whitney in 1979 showed assets of $9,123,764 and liabilities of $31,832,738. Schedules for payment under Plan of Arrangement had not yet been confirmed by the U.S. District Court in Chicago at the end of calendar 1981. The Plan was filed on December 28, 1980.

WILLIAMHOUSE-REGENCY

ADDRESS, PHONE

Williamhouse-Regency, Inc., 28 West 23rd Street, New York, NY 10010. Telephone: (212) 691-2000.

OWNERSHIP

Publicly held; stock traded AMSE: 3,908,500 common shares outstanding; 1981 dividend: $.57; 3-for-2 stock split effective in February of 1981.

MANAGEMENT

Saul Olzman, Chairman; Martin Lewis, Pres. & CEO; Ronald Hartstein, Exec VP; VPs: Edward Downs, Finance & Admin; Arthur Fugazzi, Manufacturing; David Gersman, Marketing.

TYPE OF MARKETER

Mail order, wholesale.

BUSINESS

Williamhouse-Regency has two mail order operating divisions. The Fine Paper Converting Group designs and manufactures fine quality and commodity grade papers into specialty paper products for commerical and personal use. The company purchases paper from major U.S. mills; sells products to paper merchants, specialty trade imprinters and retail outlets. The Personalizing Group personalizes products; sells to trade customers and individuals through catalogs in retail stores and by direct mail.

COMPANY HISTORY

What is now the Fine Paper Converting Group was started as a privately-owned business in 1926. The company was incorporated as The Williamhouse in 1955. The business became public and shares were first offered for trading in 1961, and stock was soon accepted for listing in the American Stock Exchange. Williamhouse-Regency initiated quarterly dividends in 1973 and has increased the paid dividend in each successive year. The company reported over 5,700 employees in 1981.

MARKETS

Commercial concerns, wholesale buyers and individual consumers in the U.S., Canada, and Europe.

FACILITIES

Headquarters in NY; 14 processing, 18 personalizing and distributing plants.

PRODUCTS, BRAND NAMES, PRICE RANGE

Invitations, announcements, stationery, greeting cards, school and office supplies. Personalized product names: Regency, Art Point, Elite, Sound, and Howard's in U.S.; Rainbow in Canada, Carcy in France.

FINANCIAL INFORMATION

	SALES	NET INCOME	PROFIT MARGIN
1981	$181,908,000	$9,684,000	5.3%

TYPE OF ADVERTISING, PROMOTION

The company uses direct mail promotion and catalogs distributed by mail and placed in retail stores to sell merchandise to individuals and retailers. They also make limited use of space ads in newspapers and magazines.

LIST INFORMATION

QUANTITY MAILED:	6,400,000
AVERAGE ORDER:	$65
ACTIVE BUYERS:	267,000
TOTAL LIST:	497,000
LIST SOURCE:	Direct mail, retail catalog.

COMMENTS

FY81 sales for Fine Paper Converting Group were $127.3 million, up 16% from FY80 sales of $109.8 million. FY81 net earnings were $16,144,000, up 39% from FY 80 profits of $12,059,000. For the Personalizing Group FY81 sales were $54,590,000, up 23% from FY80 sales of $44,239,000; FY81 net earnings of $9,031,000 represent a 7% increase over FY80 profits of $8,417,000. 1980 and '81 margins for the Personalizing Group were 16.5% and 19.0% respectively. The company sees mail order as one of their most promising growth areas and plans to expand its merchandise mix and marketing operations in FY82. In November 1980, the company acquired Web Graphics Inc., which uses a patented process to affix personalized office products such as letterheads and envelopes to computer carrier paper. This acquisition gives the Personalizing Group new growth opportunities in the office automation market.

WILLIAMS-SONOMA

ADDRESS, PHONE
Williams-Sonoma, Inc., 5750 Hollis Street, Oakland, CA 94608. Telephone: (415) 658-7431.

OWNERSHIP
Privately held; Charles Williams owns 100% of capital stock.

MANAGEMENT
Charles E. Williams, Chairman of the Board, Howard Lester, President; Donald Jacobs, Vice President, Treasurer.

TYPE OF MARKETER
Mail order, retail.

BUSINESS
Williams-Sonoma markets gourmet and professional cookware and a line of general kitchen accessories. Sales are through mail order catalogs and six retail stores in California, Texas, Minnesota, and Washington, D.C. Mail order operations contribute approximately 60% of sales. The company's catalog merchandise mix is primarily unique gourmet and professional items, retail stores carrying more basic lines. The company reports a "boom" in gourmet item sales nationwide.

COMPANY HISTORY
The business was started in 1956 by Chuck Williams in Sonoma, CA. Originally the business was solely a retail operation. The main store was moved to downtown San Francisco where it operated as a proprietorship until 1973. The company was incorporated as Williams-Sonoma in that year. Mail order operations were initiated with two brochures in 1974, followed by three catalogs in 1975. During 1979 the company launched a promotional campaign which more than doubled mail order sales.

MARKETS
U.S.A.; customers are gourmet and professional cooks, and a growing number of amateur cooks.

FACILITIES

HQ, San Francisco; distribution center Emeryville, CA; retail outlets, CA, TX, MN, and Wash., D.C.

PRODUCTS, BRAND NAMES, PRICE RANGE

Company sells a wide variety of gourmet cookware, utensils, accessories, small appliances and food items; many imported products. House and national brands including Atlas, Kitchenaid, Cuisinart, Price range: $10 to $80.

FINANCIAL INFORMATION

	SALES	NET INCOME	PROFIT MARGIN
1981	$20,000,000*	N.A.	--

TYPE OF ADVERTISING, PROMOTION

Williams-Sonoma's "Catalog for Cooks" is published four times per year and mailed in Sept., June, April and July. The catalogs are full color, 5-1/2 x 8-1/2, offer over 200 items in 50 pages, and intersperse recipes along with the merchandise.

LIST INFORMATION

QUANTITY MAILED:	12,000,000
AVERAGE ORDER:	$39
ACTIVE BUYERS:	308,000
TOTAL LIST:	419,000
LIST SOURCE:	Direct mail, list rentals.

COMMENTS

Williams-Sonoma's total revenues for 1981 are estimated to be $20 million. Of this total an estimated 60% or $12 million came from mail order sales, and 40% or $8 million came from retail operations. The company's successful marketing strategy combines retail and mail order to exploit a recent cooking craze. Customers in this segment have an interest in gourmet dining and food preparation. "Catalog for Cooks" offers an amateur cook products and utensils that professionals use. Merchandise looks "high ticket," but is not. Recently company embarked on a campaign to double mail order sales without increasing advertising cost as a percentage of sales. They switched from five to four annual catalogs, increased the size of the January issue, added more items per page, and added "cooking ideas" and recipes to catalogs. The campaign reportedly increased sales of certain items as much as 500% over the previous year.

WISCONSIN CHEESEMAN

ADDRESS, PHONE
The Wisconsin Cheeseman, P.O. Box 1, Highway 151, Madison, WI 53701. Telephone: (608) 837-5166.

OWNERSHIP
Privately held; 100% of capital stock owned by undisclosed investors.

MANAGEMENT
Garvin Cremer, Chairman; Robert Barth, President.

TYPE OF MARKETER
Mail order, wholesale.

BUSINESS
The company markets a variety of different Wisconsin natural and processed cheeses. Cheeses are packaged with canned fish, cakes and candies, nuts, and more. Products are packed in straw hampers, reusable kitchen accessories, wicker baskets, etc. Other gifts include sweets, hams and sausages, plants, stuffed animals. Operations include Mille Lacs Co. which manufactures syrup, jelly, jams, and chocolate which are sold wholesale and through the catalog.

COMPANY HISTORY
The business was started as a part time mail order operation in Wisconsin in 1943 by Garvin Cremer. The company was incorporated as The Wisconsin Cheeseman in 1956. Subsidiary Mille Lacs, manufacturer and processor of food products, was acquired in 1960. Wisconsin Cheeseman employs between 140 and 1,500 people depending on the time of the year.

MARKETS
Mail order sales throughout the U.S.; customers are 65% women.

FACILITIES

HQ, Sun Prairie, WI; candy manufacturing plant, Madison, WI; bakery, Cincinnati, OH.

PRODUCTS, BRAND NAMES, PRICE RANGE

Variety of cheeses--swiss, blue, aged cheddar, edam, brick, American; meats--hams, smoked turkey, corned beef; candies, popcorn, fruitcake and cookies. Gift packages of cheese, meats, sweets, nuts, fresh fruit and more.

FINANCIAL INFORMATION

	SALES	**NET INCOME**	**PROFIT MARGIN**
1981	$38,000,000*	N.A.	--

TYPE OF ADVERTISING, PROMOTION

One hundred percent of Wisconsin Cheeseman's promotion is through their catalogs. Catalogs are 6-1/4 x 9-1/4, full color and 96 pages. Approximately 20,000,000 pieces are mailed once a year in the fall.

LIST INFORMATION

QUANTITY MAILED: 20,000,000*
AVERAGE ORDER: $40
ACTIVE BUYERS: 661,325
TOTAL LIST: 1,555,000
LIST SOURCE: Direct mail.

COMMENTS

Of Wisconsin Cheeseman's estimated total 1981 revenues of $38,000,000, an estimated 78% or $30,000,000 came from mail order sales to consumers. The remaining 22% came from Mille Lacs wholesale marketing operations. Management reports that 90% of the company's sales are made in the fourth calendar quarter, and the number of employees increases from 140 to 1,500 during this period. Generally the company has a lower price position than competitors such as Figi's and Swiss Colony. Over 83% of the 285 items offered in most recent catalog are under $15.00. Some 59% are under $10.00. The unique "Good Cheer" basket contains petit fours, jams and several varieties of cheese, and sells for $9.95. For $14.95 customers receive an electric warming tray with an assortment of jams, jellies, cheese and honey. Wisconsin Cheeseman uses reusable items such as decanters, picnic baskets, omelet makers, and fry pans in packaging their merchandise.

WORD, INC.

ADDRESS, PHONE
Word, Inc., 4800 W. Waco Dr., Waco, Texas 76703. Telephone: (817) 772-7650.

OWNERSHIP
Wholly-owned subsidiary of publicly-held American Broadcasting company; part of ABC's Publshing Division.

MANAGEMENT
Jarrell McCracken, Pres.; William G. Gohring, Sr. VP; Thomas Stanton, Sr. VP, Operations; Francis W. Heatherly, Exec. VP; Publishing Division; Stan Moser, Exec. VP, Records and Music.

TYPE OF MARKETER
Mail order, direct sales.

BUSINESS
Word, Inc. publishes and markets religious books, records and educational products to individuals, clergy and church groups. Word Direct Marketing Services, Inc. is the direct mail arm which operates several book and record clubs and makes all Word, Inc. products available by mail. The company has two manufacturing divisions which are also involved in direct sales to retailers and wholesalers. Word reported 400 employees in 1981.

COMPANY HISTORY
Jarrell McCracken was studying religion and broadcasting at Baylor University when he became interested in recorded music. He started Word, Inc. in Waco in the early 1950s as a marketer of religious records, and added book publishing in the early '60s. The first record club was started around 1957, and more book and record clubs have been added over the years. Mail order operations were added in the late 1950's, and were greatly expanded with the acquisition of Word by ABC.

MARKETS
Mail order sales throughout the U.S. and in Canada, England, Australia, and New Zealand.

FACILITIES

HQ in Waco, TX; branches in Los Angeles and Nashville; subsidiary Word U.K. in London.

PRODUCTS, BRAND NAMES, PRICE RANGE

Records, books and educational items of a religious nature range in price from $1.95 to $100.00. Products sold under such house names as Word Records, Myrrh Records, Canaan Records, Daysprings Records, Word books and Key Word paperbacks.

FINANCIAL INFORMATION

	SALES	NET INCOME	PROFIT MARGIN
1981	$40,000,000	N.A.	--

TYPE OF ADVERTISING, PROMOTION

Space ads in magazines constitute 90% of advertising expenditures. Catalogs are for trade sales only. Direct mailings to religious lists consist of 6 x 9 packets with a letter, brochure and order card. Heaviest mailings in Jan. - Feb., and Sept.

LIST INFORMATION

QUANTITY MAILED:	5,000,000
AVERAGE ORDER:	$35
ACTIVE BUYERS:	200,000
TOTAL LIST:	750,000
LIST SOURCE:	Direct mail.

COMMENTS

Although Christian educational products have always had their own segment of the buying public, the fairly recent "Born Again" movement in the United States has increased business substantially for Word, Inc. That, coupled with ABC's acquisition in 1974, has boosted revenues sixfold in seven years, and the company expects a 10-15 percent annual growth rate in the future. Mail order operations account for about 25 percent of business and are expected to show continued growth. The company markets Billy Graham books, always a big seller, and its list of Christian entertainers includes such artists as B.J. Thomas, Tennessee Ernie Ford, George Beverly Shea and The Imperials. Word, Inc. recently started a new operation, SongVision, which is producing Christian entertainment films. Word is planning more extensive activities in the video recording and cable fields. The company's newest products which will be available soon are two commentaries on the Bible.

WORLD BOOK ENCYCLOPEDIA

ADDRESS, PHONE

World Book Encyclopedia, Inc., Merchandise Mart Plaza, Chicago, IL 60654. Telephone: (312) 245-3456.

OWNERSHIP

Division of World Book Childcraft International, Inc., a subsidiary of Scott Fetzer of Cleveland, OH.

MANAGEMENT

Michael Goodkin, President; Patsy Bogle, Vice President-Marketing; Frank Shaffer, Vice President-Advertising & Promotions; Joe Moorhead, Vice President, Gen. Mgr. of Merchandising and Syndication.

TYPE OF MARKETER

Mail order, telephone.

BUSINESS

World Book Encyclopedia, Inc. is the mail order division of World Book Childcraft International, Inc., but does not market either the World Book or Childcraft Encyclopedias. Instead, the mail order division sells educational reference books, how-to publications and encyclopedia supplements (annuals). World Book Encyclopedia, Inc. also offers a line of gift and electronic merchandise. The mail order division employs about 100 people; sales peak: Oct.-Mar.

COMPANY HISTORY

World Book's history dates back to 1914, when a firm known as Hanson-Bellows set out to produce an encyclopedia for school use. In 1917, the first 8-volume World Book Encyclopedia was issued. In 1935, the first Childcraft Encyclopedia set was started as a result of the White House Conference on the Education of Children. The Marshall Field family purchased the company in 1945 from W. F. Quarrie. In 1978 the company was sold to Scott Fetzer of Cleveland. Mail order operations began in 1950.

MARKETS

Mail order sales in U.S., Australia and Great Britain; 60% female, age 26-50, middle income.

FACILITIES
Corporate offices and mail order operations at Chicago location; Chicago-area warehouses.

PRODUCTS, BRAND NAMES, PRICE RANGE
Educational reference and how-to books, annual encyclopedia supplements sold under World Book and/or Childcraft name. Merchandise ranges from luggage to cookware to electronics. Priced from $12.95 to $450.

FINANCIAL INFORMATION

	SALES	**NET INCOME**	**PROFIT MARGIN**
1981	$90,000,000*	N.A.	--

TYPE OF ADVERTISING, PROMOTION
World Book uses direct mail packages to house and outside lists, inserts in book shipments and invoices and syndicated package inserts. They reportedly use some space advertising but do not publish any catalogs.

LIST INFORMATION
QUANTITY MAILED:	30,000,000*
AVERAGE ORDER:	N.A.
ACTIVE BUYERS:	2,000,000*
TOTAL LIST:	4,000,000*
LIST SOURCE:	Direct mail, space.

COMMENTS
While World Book Enterprises does not market World Book or Childcraft's well-known encyclopedias by mail, the parent reports that mail order division operations are growing and profitable. Mail order sales were reported to be approximately $90,000,000. In addition, the company reported that some 22% of sales or $19.8 million was spent on advertising in 1981. World Book Enterprises does not market its buyer file, but reported that they do a considerable amount of list rental and derive names from parent's encyclopedia direct sales operations. Company officials say the mail order operation has grown by 75% over the past 5 years, but there is still more to be done in that area. Executives don't feel they are penetrating the market as fully as possible, so they plan to go to more outside lists and increase mailings. They also expect to continue expansion of their offerings in the form of new titles and merchandise. Currently 40% of the mail order division's revenues come from merchandise sales.

CAROL WRIGHT

ADDRESS, PHONE
Carol Wright Sales, 1515 Summer Street, Stamford, CT 06905. Telephone: (203) 357-8712.

OWNERSHIP
Part of the Donnelley Marketing division of the Reuben H. Donnelly Corporation, which is a wholly-owned subsidiary of Dun & Bradstreet Corp.

MANAGEMENT
John A. Cleary, President, Donnelly Marketing; John C. Holt, President, Carol Wright (Exec. VP Dun & Bradstreet); M. L. Pilert, Vice President, Carol Wright; Robert Ginsberg, Vice President.

TYPE OF MARKETER
Mail order.

BUSINESS
Carol Wright Sales, including the Carol Wright Gifts catalog operation and the Carol Wright Co-op program is the mail order marketing arm of Donnelley Marketing. The company sells a wide variety of home furnishings, kitchen and auto accessories, apparel, electronic devices and novelty items. Products are sold through catalogs, space advertising and through an extensive co-op direct mail program. Wright does no manufacturing and no international marketing.

COMPANY HISTORY
What is now Carol Wright Sales, was started as a mail order marketing operation for the marketing division of the Reuben H. Donnelley Corp. It became the separate Mail Order Division in 1972. The name Carol Wright, in use by Donnelley for their extensive co-op operation since 1970, was later applied to the mail order products division. When Donnelley was acquired by Dun & Bradstreet in 1979, Carol Wright Sales became a wholly-owned subsidiary of the new parent.

MARKETS
Mail order sales throughout the U.S. Customers are 75% female, from young families with children.

FACILITIES
Headquarters and all operations at Stamford, CT location.

PRODUCTS, BRAND NAMES, PRICE RANGE
Tools, decorative lamps, tables, towel and coat racks, pots, pans, food processors, knife and scissor sets, rain gear, travel bags. T.V. remote controls, tape recorders, children's gifts, etc. Prices range from $4.95 to $39.95.

FINANCIAL INFORMATION

	SALES	NET INCOME	PROFIT MARGIN
1981	$13,000,000*	N.A.	--

TYPE OF ADVERTISING, PROMOTION
Carol Wright's advertising and promotion is by direct mail and through space advertising in newspaper supplements. The company uses catalogs to market their full line of merchandise, and direct mail packages to promote single items.

LIST INFORMATION

QUANTITY MAILED:	60,000,000
AVERAGE ORDER:	$8
ACTIVE BUYERS:	1,200,000
TOTAL LIST:	2,700,000
LIST SOURCE:	Direct mail, space.

COMMENTS
Carol Wright's total revenues from merchandise sales in 1981 are estimated to be $13,000,000. Operations and sales are reportedly growing and profitable. Management reports that in addition to their considerable house file of three million names Wright makes heavy use of rented lists. Typical buyers are described as young families with children, 66% of which are in the $10,000 to $25,000 income bracket. Past buyers are divided into the following product categories: children's gifts (4%); clothing accessories (33%); home decorative items (33%); sewing accessories (8%); houseware products (22%). Catalogs are full-color, 5-1/2 x 8-1/4, 48 pages, and contain roughly 100 different items. Typical direct mail packages contain flyers promoting single items.

WRIGHT LINE

ADDRESS, PHONE

Wright Line, Inc., 160 Gold Star Blvd., Worcester, MA 01606. Telephone: (617) 852-4300.

OWNERSHIP

Wholly-owned subsidiary of publicly-held Barry Wright Corporation of Watertown, Massachusetts (listed NYSE).

MANAGEMENT

E. W. Housh, President & CEO; D. M. Wright, Vice President, Product & Market Development; W. K. Clemens, Vice President, Marketing; Steven A. Knoebber, Marketing Services Manager.

TYPE OF MARKETER

Mail order, direct sales, telephone.

BUSINESS

Wright Line designs, manufactures and markets accessory products for data processing systems. Special filing systems for d.p. records, d.p. work stations, and other supplies and accessories are geared toward providing solutions to problems encountered in organizing, filing, accessing and protecting various types of computer information. The company sells merchandise by mail through catalogs, by telephone from 67 branch offices and by a direct sales force of 220 representatives.

COMPANY HISTORY

The company was founded in 1934 by E. Stanley Wright and merged with Barry Controls in 1954. Major expansions over the years include the acquisition and re-incorporation of foreign subsidiaries Wright Canada Ltd. in the early 1960's, and Wright Line Gmbh of Germany in the early 1970's. Barry Wright Corporation declared a 2-for-1 stock split in December of 1978, and again in August of 1980. The company reported over 2,000 employees in 1981.

MARKETS

Considers market to be any company that relies on a computer-based information system.

FACILITIES
Manufacturing plant in Worcester; HQ, warehouses, and branch offices in U.S., Can., Germany.

PRODUCTS, BRAND NAMES, PRICE RANGE
TAPE-SEAL computer tape filing system, OPTIMEDIA cabinets, DATABANK safes, DOCU-MATE paper filing systems, System 2000 terminal workstations. Price range: $1 - $5,000. Average salesperson order: $950; average mail order: $350.

FINANCIAL INFORMATION

	SALES	NET INCOME	PROFIT MARGIN
1980	$67,068,000	$5,100,000	7.6%

TYPE OF ADVERTISING, PROMOTION
Inquiry-generating space ads in data processing trade journals; approximately 30,000 leads generated in 1981; catalogs mailed annually to house list of 160,000 names, plus inquiries and direct sales buyers.

LIST INFORMATION
QUANTITY MAILED:	700,000
AVERAGE ORDER:	$350
ACTIVE BUYERS:	100,000
TOTAL LIST:	160,000
LIST SOURCE:	Direct mail, space.

COMMENTS
Barry Wright Corporation's total net sales for 1980 were $124,489,000. Of the total, Wright Line reportedly contributed 54% or $67,068,000. This represents growth in Wright Line sales of 26% over $53,284,000 in 1979, and 52% over $43,979,000 in 1978. Wright Line's reported net earnings climbed to $5,100,000 in 1980, an increase of 21% over $4,200,000 in 1979 and 73% over $2,940,000 in 1978. Of Wright Line's total 1980 revenues, an estimated 52% or $35,000,000 came from mail order operations, the remaining 48% from the company's direct selling operations. Aggressive marketing strategies in 1980 -- expanding the field sales force and increasing direct mail promotions of new products to customers and prospects -- contributed to record sales levels. During first 6 months of '81, however, shipments were lower than anticipated and earnings were below '80 levels for the same period.

XEROX CORPORATION

ADDRESS, PHONE
Xerox Corporation, P.O. Box 1600, Stamford, CT 06904. Telephone: (203) 329-8700.

OWNERSHIP
Publicly-held; stock traded NYSE; 84,270,173 common shares outstanding; 1981 market prices: high, 64; low, 37-3/8; 1981 dividend: $3.00.

MANAGEMENT
C. Peter McColough, Chairman; David T. Kearns, President, CEO; William Glavin, Exec. VP, Reprographics, Ops.; Robert Firth, Group VP, Business Systems; Robert Moore, Pres., Publishing Group.

TYPE OF MARKETER
Mail order, direct sales, retail.

BUSINESS
Xerox is a highly diversified corporation which produces and markets sophisticated office machines and electronic equipment, telecommunications products, publications and educational materials. The following operations derive a significant percentage of their revenues from mail order marketing: Xerox Business Products Div.; Xerox Publishing Group; R. R. Bowker Co., Ginn and Co., Xerox Education Publications, Xerox Learning Systems; Xerox Retail Stores.

COMPANY HISTORY
The Xerox Corporation dates back to 1906, with the creation of the Haloid Company in Rochester, NY. Chester F. Carlson was born that same year, and about 30 years later, developed the copying technique that came to be known as Xerography. The first convenient office copier was unveiled in 1959. In recent years many Xerox operations have begun using direct mail for marketing and promotional purposes.

MARKETS
Xerox sells business products and equipment, and educational publications in the U.S. and abroad.

FACILITIES

Corporate HQ, Stamford, CT; U.S. operating head-quarters in CA, NY, and CT.

PRODUCTS, BRAND NAMES, PRICE RANGE

Reprographic, word-processing and other sophisti-cated equipment marketed under the Xerox name. Retail outlets also sell Apple, Panasonic and other major brands. Education publications market Weekly Reader publications and children's book clubs.

FINANCIAL INFORMATION

	SALES	NET INCOME	PROFIT MARGIN
1981	$8,691,000,000	$598,200,000	--

TYPE OF ADVERTISING, PROMOTION

Xerox Education Publications uses a mix of direct mail, co-op, internal and television; bulk of adver-tising for Weekly Reader and Summer Weekly Reader is direct mail. Advertising for equipment via mail has been through catalogs and packages.

LIST INFORMATION

QUANTITY MAILED:	50,000,000*
AVERAGE ORDER:	Various
ACTIVE BUYERS:	7,855,000
TOTAL LIST:	22,000,000
LIST SOURCE:	Direct mail, space.

COMMENTS

The sales figure above represents Xerox total sales for 1981. The list information above is for the Education Publications Group only. Xerox reports that no percentage of total sales attributable to mail order was available. The Xerox Publishing Group has four major mail order operations: R.R. Bowker, Ginn, Educational Publications, and Learning Sys-tems. Bowker is a mail order marketer of maga-zines, data base services and reference books. Ginn and Co. markets text books and instructional ma-terials for elementary and high schools by mail. Education Publications markets the Weekly Reader, Summer Weekly Reader, Weekly Reader Children's Book Club, and continuity encyclopedia and refer-ence sets, all by direct mail. Xerox Learning Systems provides sales and management training programs through mail order cassettes and books. Most recently, through Business Products Group, Xerox began offering of business machines and office equipment by mail.

YIELD HOUSE

ADDRESS, PHONE

Yield House, Inc., Main Street, North Conway, NH 03860. Telephone: (603) 356-3141.

OWNERSHIP

Division of Standex International Corporation, Salem, New Hampshire.

MANAGEMENT

M. Joseph Dunn, President, Coy Clement, Vice President of Direct Marketing; Jill Bigelow, Advertising and Public Relations Director.

TYPE OF MARKETER

Mail order, retail.

BUSINESS

Yield House, a division of the Consumer Products Group of Standex International, sells colonial pine furniture and home furnishing accessories direct to consumers via mail order and through ten retail stores. The company has recently converted the former Pilgrim Manufacturing plant in Merrimack, NH, to the production of Yield House-type merchandise. Aside from manufacturing finished furniture, Yield House is one of the largest manufacturers and mail order marketers of kit furniture in the country.

COMPANY HISTORY

Yield House began in 1947 in North Conway, NH, as a manufacturer of small pieces of pine furniture and accessories (pipe racks, magazine racks, stools). In 1956 the company opened its first retail store and established a factory in North Conway. The second retail store was opened in 1960 in Meredith, NH. Yield House was privately owned until 1969, when it was acquired by Standex International. The company had approximately 125 employees at that time, and now employs over 700.

MARKETS

Mail order customers throughout the U.S. Approximately 80% of buyers are women.

FACILITIES
Headquarters and fulfillment center in North Conway, NH; 5 manufacturing plants; 10 retail stores.

PRODUCTS, BRAND NAMES, PRICE RANGE
Over 200 products manufactured by YH; 98% also available in kits. Catalog features wall hutches, dining tables and chairs, coffee tables, book cases, lamps, desks, dressers, shoe racks, chests, decorative accessories. Prices range from $8.

FINANCIAL INFORMATION

	SALES	NET INCOME	PROFIT MARGIN
1981	$35,000,000*	N.A.	--

TYPE OF ADVERTISING, PROMOTION
In-house ad agency, White Mountain Advertising Inc., prepares catalogs and other promotional materials. Principal catalog is 84 pages, full color. In 1981 added a new catalog, 32-page, full color, for furniture kits only. Also uses space ads.

LIST INFORMATION
QUANTITY MAILED: 15,000,000
AVERAGE ORDER: $55
ACTIVE BUYERS: 400,000
TOTAL LIST: 865,000
LIST SOURCE: Direct mail, space.

COMMENTS
The sales figure above represents an estimate of Yield House's total mail order revenues. No accurate estimate of retail store sales was available. For several years, Yield House's growth was hampered by a critical lack of manufacturing capacity. The 1979 acquisition of the Pilgrim Manufacturing plant in Merrimack, NH, was designed to remedy the situation. With the integration and retooling completed in the 1981 calendar year, management expects YH to realize improved margins in FY82. Besides allowing the company to catch up on back orders, the new plant is equipped to manufacture larger case goods such as modular wall systems. The company's faith in its mail order operation is demonstrated by the recently added NSTA-certified packaging laboratory, warehouse and shipping building. This new facility allows testing of packaging materials and techniques and means that mail order customers can expect well packaged, undamaged products.

PRODUCT CATEGORY	PAGE